Lecture Notes in Artificial Intelligence   10999

Subseries of Lecture Notes in Computer Science

More information about this series at http://www.springer.com/series/1244

Matthew Iklé · Arthur Franz
Rafal Rzepka · Ben Goertzel (Eds.)

Artificial General Intelligence

11th International Conference, AGI 2018
Prague, Czech Republic, August 22–25, 2018
Proceedings

 Springer

Editors
Matthew Iklé
Adams State University
Alamosa, CO
USA

Arthur Franz
Odessa Competence Center
  for Artificial Intelligence (OCCAM)
Odessa
Ukraine

Rafal Rzepka
Hokkaido University
Sapporo
Japan

Ben Goertzel
SingularityNET; OpenCog; Hanson
  Robotics
Hong Kong
China

ISSN 0302-9743 ·   ISSN 1611-3349   (electronic)
Lecture Notes in Artificial Intelligence
ISBN 978-3-319-97675-4   ISBN 978-3-319-97676-1   (eBook)
https://doi.org/10.1007/978-3-319-97676-1

Library of Congress Control Number: 2018950096

LNCS Sublibrary: SL7 – Artificial Intelligence

This Springer imprint is published by the registered company Springer Nature Switzerland AG
The registered company address is: Gewerbestrasse 11, 6330 Cham, Switzerland

Preface

The year 2018 could be considered the year artificial general intelligence (AGI) became mainstream. Since Apple's Siri was first introduced in 2011, narrow AI technologies have permeated increasingly more aspects of our everyday lives. AI systems such as Google's Assistant, Amazon's Alexa, Microsoft's Cortana, iPhone X's face-recognition software, self-driving vehicles, and IBM Watson's text-reading AI for medical research are just a few examples of how AI systems are changing how we live and work on a daily basis.

As these narrow AI systems become increasing prevalent, attention has begun to shift toward the next generation of AI research including AGI. MIT introduced an online graduate course in AGI in 2018, magazines such as *Forbes* have published articles about the potential future of general AI systems, and the Discovery Channel included a segment about AGI in its program "This Is AI." The humanoid robot, Sophia, became the first robot citizen in 2017, and SingularityNET, founded in 2017, began the process of integrating AGI with blockchain technology. These are indeed exciting times.

Despite all the current enthusiasm in AI, the technologies involved still represent no more than advanced versions of classic statistics and machine learning. Behind the scenes, however, many breakthroughs are happening on multiple fronts: in unsupervised language and grammar learning, deep-learning, generative adversarial methods, vision systems, reinforcement learning, transfer learning, probabilistic programming, blockchain integration, causal networks, and many more.

The 11th AGI conference took place in Prague, Czech Republic, during August 22–25, 2018. For the second time, the AGI conference was held as part of the larger Joint Multi-Conference on Human-Level Intelligence, HLAI, which co-located AGI 2018 with BICA 2018 (the Annual International Conferences on Biologically Inspired Cognitive Architectures), and NeSy 2018 (the Workshop Series on Neural-Symbolic Learning and Reasoning). Also included as part of HLAI 2018 was a separate day-long track, following the main sessions, discussing "The Future of AI."

This volume contains the contributed talks presented at AGI 2018. Of the 52 papers submitted to the conference and reviewed by two or more Program Committee members, 19 long papers papers were accepted (37% acceptance) for oral presentation, and ten papers were accepted for poster presentations. One hallmark of the AGI conference series has always been the incredible diversity of ideas on display through its collection of contributed papers, and this year continued that trend. There are papers covering AGI architectures, papers discussing mathematical and philosophical foundations and details, papers developing ideas from neuroscience and cognitive science, papers on emotional modeling, papers discussing ethical strategies, and a host of other papers covering a wide-ranging array of additional relevant topics.

Keynote speeches were shared by the participating organizations and included speeches by Ben Goertzel (SingularityNET, and Hanson Robotics), Thomas Parr

(University College London), Tomas Mikolov (Facebook AI Research), Paul Smolensky, (Microsoft), Dileep George, (Vicarious Systems), Dr. Vladimir G. Red'ko (Russian Academy of Sciences), and Hava Siegelmann (DARPA). Josef Urban delivered an additional AGI keynote on the topic "No One Shall Drive Us from the Semantic AI Paradise of Computer-Understandable Math and Science."

In addition, the AGI 2018 conference featured a "Tutorial on Comparing Intrinsic Motivations in a Unified Framework"; workshops on "AI4Space, AI for Space Exploration and Settlement," and "AI Meets Blockchain"; a symposium on "AI Safety and Societal Impacts"; a panel session covering "Machine Consciousness"; and a demonstration session.

We thank the people of GoodAI, in particular Olga Afanasjeva and Daria Hvizdalova, for all of their help planning and handling local organization; Tarek Beshold for having the vision for the larger Human Level AI conference series; and all the Program Committee members for their dedicated service to the review process. We thank all of our contributors, participants, and tutorial, workshop, and panel session organizers, without whom the conference would not exist.

Finally, we thank our sponsors: the Artificial General Intelligence Society, Springer Nature Publishing, SingularityNET, Hanson Robotics, and OpenCog Foundation.

June 2018

Matthew Iklé
Arthur Franz
Rafal Rzepka
Ben Goertzel

Organization

Program Committee

Hadi Afshar	Australian National University, Australia
Joscha Bach	Massachusetts Institute of Technology, USA
Tarek Richard Besold	City, University of London, UK
Jordi Bieger	Reykjavik University, Iceland
Cristiano Castelfranchi	Institute of Cognitive Sciences and Technologies, Italy
Antonio Chella	Università di Palermo, Italy
Arthur Franz	Odessa Competence Center for Artificial Intelligence and Machine Learning, Ukraine
Nil Geisweiller	OpenCog Foundation, SingularityNet Foundation, Novamente LLC, France
Ben Goertzel	SingularityNET; OpenCog; Hanson Robotics, China
Jose Hernandez-Orallo	Universitat Politècnica de València, Spain
Marcus Hutter	Australian National University, Australia
Matt Iklé	Adams State University, USA
Benjamin Johnston	University of Technology, Sydney, Australia
Garrett Katz	University of Maryland, USA
John Licato	Indiana University/Purdue University - Fort Wayne, USA
Sean Markan	Eudelic Systems LLC, USA
Amedeo Napoli	LORIA Nancy; CNRS, Inria, Université de Lorraine, France
Eric Nivel	CADIA, Reykjavik University, Iceland
Eray Ozkural	Bilkent University, Turkey
Maxim Peterson	ITMO University, Russia
Alexey Potapov	AIDEUS, Russia
Nico Potyka	Universität Osnabrück, Germany
Paul S. Rosenbloom	University of Southern California, USA
Rafal Rzepka	Hokkaido University, Japan
Oleg Scherbakov	ITMO University, Russia
Ute Schmid	University of Bamberg, Germany
Javier Snaider	Google, USA
Bas Steunebrink	IDSIA, Switzerland
Claes Strannegård	Chalmers University of Technology, Sweden
Kristinn R. Thorisson	CADIA, Reykjavik University, Iceland

Volkan Ustun	University of Southern California, USA
Mario Verdicchio	University of the West of Scotland, UK
Pei Wang	Temple University, USA
Roman Yampolskiy	University of Louisville, USA
Byoung-Tak Zhang	Seoul National University, South Korea

Additional Reviewer

Catt, Elliot

Contents

Hybrid Strategies Towards Safe "Self-Aware" Superintelligent Systems

Nadisha-Marie Aliman[1(✉)] and Leon Kester[2]

[1] University of Stuttgart, Stuttgart, Germany
nadishamarie.aliman@gmail.com
[2] TNO Netherlands, The Hague, Netherlands

Abstract. Against the backdrop of increasing progresses in AI research paired with a rise of AI applications in decision-making processes, security-critical domains as well as in ethically relevant frames, a large-scale debate on possible safety measures encompassing corresponding long-term and short-term issues has emerged across different disciplines. One pertinent topic in this context which has been addressed by various AI Safety researchers is e.g. the AI alignment problem for which no final consensus has been achieved yet. In this paper, we present a multidisciplinary toolkit of AI Safety strategies combining considerations from AI and Systems Engineering as well as from Cognitive Science with a security mindset as often relevant in Cybersecurity. We elaborate on how AGI "Self-awareness" could complement different AI Safety measures in a framework extended by a jointly performed Human Enhancement procedure. Our analysis suggests that this hybrid framework could contribute to undertake the AI alignment problem from a new holistic perspective through security-building synergetic effects emerging thereof and could help to increase the odds of a possible safe future transition towards superintelligent systems.

Keywords: Self-awareness · AI Safety · Human enhancement
AI alignment · Superintelligence

1 Introduction

Being a topic of major importance in AI Safety research, AI alignment – which is often interchangeably used with the term of value alignment – has been analyzed from diverse point of views and incorporates a variety of research subareas many of which were reviewed by Taylor et al. [29]. Two highly relevant approaches in the realization of AI alignment the authors considered in this context are *value specification* and *error tolerance* which were both introduced by Soares and Fallenstein [28]. In order to do justice to these two distinct issues, Taylor et al. postulate that *"we can do research that makes it easier to specify our intended goals as objective functions"* concerning the first and *"we can do research aimed at designing AI systems that avoid large side effects and negative incentives,*

© Springer Nature Switzerland AG 2018
M. Iklé et al. (Eds.): AGI 2018, LNAI 10999, pp. 1–11, 2018.
https://doi.org/10.1007/978-3-319-97676-1_1

even in cases where the objective function is imperfectly aligned" concerning the latter. We take these high-level considerations alongside additional multidisciplinary observations as point of departure and apply a more abstract and holistic analysis than many prior papers have utilized in this particular context to identify solution approaches. For instance, we see the need for "self-awareness" in AI systems for reasons such as safety, effectiveness, transparency or explainability just as such a functionality is required from the perspective of Systems Engineering for the effectiveness and safety of advanced models. Beyond that, we agree that methods inspired from Cybersecurity practices [20] could provide a valuable support for AI Safety including the safety of self-aware AGIs. Furthermore, we also focus on the human factor in the AGI development and suggest to make allowance for human cognitive constraints in AI Safety frameworks taking a perspective jointly considering ethical aspects.

In the next Sect. 2, we posit that a (yet to be defined) "self-awareness" functionality might beside other benefits account for an enhanced error tolerance within a future human-level AGI model and might indirectly facilitate the value or goal specification process. Thereafter, in Sect. 3, we suggest that a self-aware AGI that should be deployed in a real-world environment will have to be supplemented by additional AI Safety measures including for instance an AGI Red Teaming approach in order to maintain a high error tolerance level. In Sect. 4, we analyse how AGI developers could proficiently face the problem of adequate value specification in the first place, which could interestingly imply the need for an enhancement of human "self-awareness" to a certain extent with respect to the goal to identify the values humans really intend on the one hand and regarding the aim to subsequently encode this values into prioritized goals a self-aware AGI will have to adhere to on the other hand. Finally, in the last Sect. 5, we reflect upon this set of hybrid strategies as an interwoven entirety, consider its possible ethical implications and place it in the context of a hypothetically thereof emerging type of superintelligence.

2   Self-Awareness

While the notion of "self-awareness" which is often used in the context of concepts like "self-conciousness", "self-control" or "self-reference" is not in the focus of classical AI research, it is considered to be one of the key elements out of the crucial competency areas for Human-Level General Intelligence according to many AGI researchers (as investigated by Adams et al. [1]) and the notion itself or related terms have been considered in some ways within various AGI designs (e.g. in [5,6,12,13,18,25,31,32]). However, the relevancy of AGI self-awareness from the perspective of AI Safety remains a poorly studied topic, even though the omission of such a functionality in an AGI architecture might lead to far-reaching implications in the future in regard to the safety of this system if deployed in a dynamic real-world environment. Given that a definition of this relatively abstract term is controversial and nontrivial, we will in the following first provide a simple technically oriented definition of AGI self-awareness – for which we do not claim any higher suitability in general, but which is specifically conceptualized for our line of argument – and then subsequently elucidate the reasons for its crucial importance in AI Safety frameworks.

The definition is inspired by Systems Engineering practices with applications to diverse types of dynamic systems as e.g. adapted by Kester et al. [14,15] or van Foeken et al. [10] and is not restricted to the choice of any particular AGI architecture provided that the AGI acts in a not further defined goal-oriented manner, possesses sensors and actuators as well as the ability to somehow communicate with human entities. For clarity, when we refer to an AGI exhibiting *self-awareness* in this work, we explicitly mean an AGI which is able to independently perform *self-assessment* and *self-management*, whereby self-assessment designates a set of processes enabling the AGI to determine the performance of its various functions with respect to its goals (e.g. for associated physical instances, internal cognitive processes, own abilities, own resources,...) by itself and self-management the capability to adapt its behavior in the real-world on its own in order to reach its goals based on the information collected through self-assessment. In addition, the AGI is presupposed to be able to communicate the insights obtained after having performed self-assessment and the choices made in the self-management step to specified human entities.

In the following, we collate some possible highly relevant advantages for a self-awareness functionality within an AGI architecture from the perspective of AI Safety:

– *Transparency:* Through the ability of a self-aware AGI to allow important insights into its internal processes to its designers, it by design does not correspond to a "black-box" system as it is the case for many contemporary AI architectures. The resulting transparency presents a valuable basis for effective AI Safety measures.
– *Explainability:* Since the AGI performs self-management on the basis of a transparent self-assessment, its decision-making process can be independently documented and communicated, which might increase the possibility for humans to extract helpful explanations for the actions of the AGI.
– *Trustworthiness:* An improved AGI explainability might increase its trustworthiness and acceptance from a human perspective, which might in turn offer more chances to test the self-aware AGI in a greater variety of real-world environments and contexts.
– *Controllability:* Through the assumed communication ability of the AGI, a steady feedback loop between human entities and the AGI might lead to an improved human control offering many opportunities for testing and the possibility to proactively integrate more AI Safety measures. More details on possible proactive measures are provided in the next Sect. 3.
– *Fast Adaptation:* Self-awareness allows for faster reactions and adaptations to changes in dynamic environments even in cases where human intervention might not be possible for temporal reasons which allows for an improved error tolerance and security. Unwanted scenarios might be more effectively avoided in the presence of negative feedback from the environment.

- *Cost-Effectiveness:* There is often a tradeoff between security and cost-effectiveness, however a self-aware system is inherently more cost-effective for instance due to the better traceability of its errors, the facilitated maintainability through the transparency of its decision-making processes or because the system can adapt itself to optimal working in any situation, while lacking any obvious mechanism which might in exchange lower its security level – by what a double advantage arises.
- *Extensibility*: Finally, a self-aware AGI could be extended to additionally for instance contain a model of human cognition which could consider human deficiencies such as cognitive constraints, biases and so on. As a consequence, the AGI could adapt the way it presents information to human entities and consider their specific constraints to maintain a certain level of explainability.

However, after having compiled possible advantages AGI self-awareness could offer to AI Safety, it is important to note that up to now, it was not specified on what basis the goals of the self-aware goal-oriented AGI are crafted in the first place. Moreover, the odds that a self-aware AGI spawns many of the mentioned desirable properties are even largely dependent on the quality of the goals assigned to it and it is thus clear that self-awareness taken alone is far from representing a panacea for AI Safety, since it does not per se solve the underlying goal alignment problem. Nonetheless, we argue that AGI self-awareness represents a highly valuable basis for future-oriented AI Safety measures due to the vitally important advantages it could bring forth if combined with appropriate goals. In addition, AGI self-awareness might be able to itself facilitate the process of goal alignment through the interactive transparent framework suitable for tests in real-world environments it offers, whereby the selection of adequate goals clearly remains a highly debatable topic on its own. From our perspective, the therefore required goal function intrinsically reflecting desirable human values for a self-aware AGI could be stipulated by humans which would be specifically trained in interaction with that AGI and possibly ethically as well as cognitively enhanced on the basis of technological advances/scientific insights, since humanity at its current stage, seems to exhibit rather insufficient solutions for a thoughtful and safe future in conjunction with AGIs – especially when it comes to the possible necessity for an unambiguous formulation of human goals. We will further address the motivations for human enhancement to provide assistance during this mentioned process of goal selection in Sect. 4.

3   Proactive AI Safety Measures

After having depicted possible benefits as well as still unanswered implications in the context of a self-aware AGI, we now focus on crucial AI Safety measures which might be necessary in addition to avoid unintended harmful outcomes during the development phase and prevent risky scenarios after a subsequent deployment of such an AGI architecture. While the suggested methods would undoubtedly not guarantee an absolutely risk-free AGI, their indispensability to at least obtain a well tested architecture built with a certain security awareness which particularly also takes the possibility of intentionally malevolent actors [20] into account, seems however to prohibit their omission. Beyond that, it seems imperative to incorporate a type of simulations of undesirable scenarios while developing an AGI as a proactive rather than reactive approach, since the latter might be reckless given the extent of possible future consequences which could include a number of existential risks [7,20,30].

In the long run, further research on the following (unquestionably non-exhaustive and extendable) measures building on previous work and extending certain concepts could offer forward-looking hints in this regard:

– *Development Under Adversarial Assumptions:* Already during the AGI development phase, the developers should take into account the most important known types of e.g. integrity vulnerabilities that have been reported regarding other AIs in the past (this could include rather similar architectures, but importantly also cognitively less sophisticated AIs since it could represent a type of minimum requirement) and should not per default conjecture a benign environment. In a simplified scheme, assuming the development of an AGI starting nowadays, it should for instance among others be ascertained that none of the known adversarial methods to fool narrow AIs such as Deep Neural Networks [19] would also lead to a defective information processing of security-relevant kind if correspondingly corrupted inputs are presented to the sensors of the AGI at hand. Besides that, new types of A(G)I attacks and corresponding defense mechanisms should be actively ethically investigated. In this context a new subfield of study on "adversarial examples for AGIs" appears recommendable. While adversarial examples for narrow AIs are for instance associated with definitions such as *"inputs to machine learning models that an attacker has intentionally designed to cause the model to make a mistake"*[1], a corresponding analogy could be derived for AGIs. Ideally, the self-aware AGI itself could be trained in identifying situations susceptible to involve particular known safety threats.
– *AGI Red Team:* As it is the case in the context of security systems, developers tend to be biased towards emphasizing the robustness of their system and might additionally exhibit "blind spots" to existing vulnerabilities while implementing defense strategies [16], which is why realistic red team events offer an invaluable security tool in many Cybersecurity frameworks [22–24]. Red Teaming has recently as well be proposed by Brundage et al. [8] in the context of recommendations for an AI Safety framework covering short-term issues for the next 5 years. Similarly, an external AGI red team could in the long-term periodically perform real-world attack simulations after the deployment of an AGI, with the goal to identify certain types of possibly overlooked vulnerabilities to sophisticated attacks. The red team could for instance explicitly try to trigger unethical actions on the part of the AGI by placing it in unknown or unusual contexts. In these settings, the blue team would correspond to the AGI developers which are responsible for the defense design within the AGI architecture. Possibly, social engineering performed by

---

[1] Mentioned in: https://blog.openai.com/adversarial-example-research/.

the red team on the blue team could disclose biases underlying the AGI training or its architecture and facilitate the crafting of specific targeted attacks. It is to be expected that such red team exercises will contribute to strengthen the robustness and possibly even enhance the cognitive abilities of the AGI by providing the AGI developers with comprehensive hints on how to enhance the defense designs which could for instance be of meta-cognitive nature. The ultimate objective would be to achieve a state from which on the self-aware AGI has learned to automatically and independently run self-tests simulating such systematical adversarial attacks.

– *Regular Measurement of Cognitive Ability and Inhibition of Self-interest:* To maintain transparency and allow for a certain minimal monitoring of the AGI, it might be essential to be regularly aware of the level of cognitive ability it exhibits in order to customize the security measures. Besides classically proposed Turing Tests, one further interesting type of test is the recently proposed "test for detecting qualia" introduced by Yampolskiy [33] and based on visual illusions. Even if – from a philosophical point of view – it could be debatable whether the described test measures the presence of qualia itself, we suppose that it could provide invaluable cues to detect higher cognitive abilities as exhibited by an AGI, since just like human misperceptions (including e.g. optical illusions) can for instance help to better understand the mechanisms underlying the perception of humans in Cognitive Science, so could the analysis of AGI misperceptions analogously help to understand the internals of an AGI system. An automatic program could periodically test the AGI and generate an alarm in the case of "cognitive anomalies" indicating an unusual increase of cognitive capacity. This regular test could also be implemented as a self-test mechanism within the self-aware AGI architecture itself. However, an explicit protective mechanism that prevents the AGI from evolving any kind of harmful intrinsic goals out of self-interest should be additionally designed in order to obviate any undesirable takeoff scenario. A related core idea to prevent an AGI from evolving a type of misaligned self-interest has been described by Goertzel [11] in the context of his suggestion for a specifically designed "AI Nanny" developed with a pre-defined set of goals and encompasses for instance *"a strong inhibition against modifying its [the AI Nanny's] preprogrammed goals"* or *"a strong inhibition against rapidly modifying its general intelligence".*

Yet, these strategies in combination with AGI self-awareness taken alone might not be sufficient given the human component in the development of the AGI entailing a wide array of undesirable ethical, cognitive and evolutionary biases.

4   Human Enhancement

Whereas in the context of the value alignment problem, the focus is often set on how future AGIs could optimally learn values from human agents be it for instance by imitation or by predefined ethical goals, a jointly performed technology-supported learning approach for human agents to enhance their cognitive abilities and ethical frameworks in order to be able to develop improved capabilities qualifying them to more competently deal with this highly relevant problem in the first place, remains an under-explored topic. Given the large array of human deficiencies including for instance cognitive biases [34], unintentional unethical behavior [26] or limitations of human information processing which could be considered as major handicaps in succeeding to solve the AI alignment problem, the approach to extend the abilities of humans in charge of developing an ethical AGI by science and technology emerges as auspicious strategy, however certainly not without reservations.

We postulate that the following two complementary types of human enhancement could be decisive to ameliorate the value specification abilities of humans improving the odds to succeed in AI alignment:

– *Ethical Enhancement:* One prominent subproblem of goal alignment can be simply described as to make the AI learn human goals [30]. For this purpose, humans obviously need to be first aware of the values they really intend to implement in order to encode them as a factual set of prioritized goals within an AGI model. Similarly, as stated in [3], humans need to become better "ethical regulators" (e.g. of themselves and of AIs) in an era which will be more and more shaped by AI. This task might inter alia require a better type of "self-assessment" on the part of humans – especially with regard to their own concrete ethical preferences, abilities and constraints. To improve the required human ethical self-assessment for the development of safe AGIs, developers should consider a dynamic multifarious science-based ethical framework which could for instance encompass debiasing training [17] as well as methods from behavioral ethics [9] and could in the future even include a type of AGI-assisted debiasing training where the same self-aware AGI which is periodically checked for safety could e.g. act as "teacher" in game settings providing a personalized feedback to its developers which could be expanded to a testing of acquired ethically relevant skills. Additionally, the group formation of the AGI developers itself should ideally reflect a synergetic heterogeneity of worldviews to fend off inequality and unnecessary biases at the core of the goal selection process.
– *Cognitive Enhancement:* Some decades ago, the cybernetics pioneer Ross Ashby expressed the following train of thought [4]: *"[...] it is not impossible that what is commonly referred to as "intellectual power" may be equivalent to "power of appropriate selection". [...] If this is so, and as we know that power of selection can be amplified, it seems to follow that intellectual power, like physical power, can be amplified."* Even if this statement might still reflect a controversial issue and human enhancement technologies are still in their infancy, expected progresses in areas such as Nanorobotics, Bionics, Biotechnology, Brain-Computer Interface research or the newly arisen field of Cyborg Intelligence integrating *"the best of both machine and biological intelligences"* [27] might lead to considerably extended possibilities for cognitive enhancement in the foreseeable future. Transferring the term used

in Ashby's statement to a different context, we argue that (possibly AGI-assisted) methods to increase the human "power of appropriate *goal* selection" within the framework of AGI development given the ethical values agreed upon while supported by preceding ethical enhancement procedures, represent an essential future research direction to be pursued for AI Safety reasons. For this purpose, one could first experimentally start with presently rather primitive and clearly not sufficient enhancement concepts such as mental training, HMI tools, neurofeedback, non-invasive brain stimulation methods, multi-mind BCIs for decision-making or nootropics. Later on, a reasonable priority for a self-aware AGI might even be to generate methods facilitating human cognitive enhancement and develop concepts where if procurable the AGI augments rather than surrogates human entities initiating a bidirectional learning framework. Besides that, the group composition of AGI developers should ideally promote multidisciplinarity in order to reduce the occurrences of AI Safety relevant blind spots in the development phase and should comprise numerous partcipants with diverse research backgrounds.

While it should be clear that human enhancement pathways (such as through brain-machine collaboration) cannot guarantee the prevention of an occurring unethical AGI [2], not to perform human enhancement does not guarantee it either. Furthermore, the abstention from ethical human enhancement also does not necessarily prevent the performance of unethical human enhancement by malevolent actors at a later stage. Therefore, we argue that the early practice of human enhancement for ethical purposes like the improvement of the value specification process for AI alignment, might increase the odds of a resulting ethical AGI and could even in the long-term facilitate the detection of potential unethical AGI development or unethical human enhancement through the bundled cognitive and ethical abilities that could emerge out of the suggested bidirectional framework of mutual enhancement.

5   Conclusion and Future Prospects

In this work, we postulated that AGI self-awareness represents a highly valuable functionality from the perspective of AI Safety as it might be helpful for the error tolerance subtask of AI alignment as well as indirectly for value specification and provides many advantages such as transparency or explainability. We then introduced a number of proactive AI Safety measures including AGI Red Teaming which could be necessary in addition to the self-awareness functionality to maintain security and which might be beneficial for the error tolerance subproblem. We set forth that the described framework alone might not be sufficient due to the ethical and cognitive constraints AGI developers exhibit as human beings and proposed a jointly performed inter alia AI-assisted ethical as well as cognitive enhancement procedure to support the goal selection process. We do not claim that the described hybrid framework represents a complete approach warranting the safety of the AGI or of a therefrom emerging superintelligence, but argue that it might underpin the importance of a multidisciplinary approach to AI Safety and motivate a new useful holistic perspective on the complex problem of AI alignment which might in turn shape future developments towards a beneficial form of superintelligence (be it of human, artificial or hybrid nature). Finally, we stress that possible future research on self-aware AGIs as well as research on ethical and cognitive enhancement for AI Safety should not be reserved to stakeholders like corporations, the military or a presumed elite group of AGI developers, but be instead performed open-source and shared across diverse communities for the benefit of mankind. Moreover, a science-based debate on the implications of a conjectured technological singularity (which is not bounded to necessarily emerge from an AGI [21]) should be encouraged and existential risks through superintelligence should be thoroughly taken into consideration – especially regarding scenarios implying the presence of malicious actors [2, 20].

References

1. Adams, S.S., et al.: Mapping the landscape of human-level artificial general intelligence. AI Magaz. **33**, 25–41 (2012)
2. Aliman, N.-M.: Malevolent cyborgization. In: Everitt, T., Goertzel, B., Potapov, A. (eds.) AGI 2017. LNCS (LNAI), vol. 10414, pp. 188–197. Springer, Cham (2017). https://doi.org/10.1007/978-3-319-63703-7_18
3. Ashby, M.: Ethical regulators and super-ethical systems. In: Proceedings of the 61st Annual Meeting of the ISSS-2017 Vienna, Austria, vol. 2017 (2017)
4. Ashby, W.R.: An Introduction to Cybernetics. Chapman & Hall Ltd., New York (1961)
5. Baars, B.J., Franklin, S.: Consciousness is computational: the LIDA model of global workspace theory. Int. J. Mach. Conscious. **1**(01), 23–32 (2009)
6. Bach, J.: Principles of Synthetic Intelligence PSI: An Architecture of Motivated Cognition, vol. 4. Oxford University Press, Oxford (2009)
7. Bostrom, N.: Superintelligence: Paths, Dangers, Strategies (2014)
8. Brundage, M., et al.: The malicious use of artificial intelligence: forecasting, prevention, and mitigation. arXiv preprint arXiv:1802.07228 (2018)
9. Drumwright, M., Prentice, R., Biasucci, C.: Behavioral ethics and teaching ethical decision making. Decis. Sci. J. Innovative Educ. **13**(3), 431–458 (2015)
10. van Foeken, E., Kester, L., Iersel, M.: Real-time common awareness in communication constrained sensor systems. In: Proceedings of 12th International Conference on Information Fusion, FUSION 2009, Seattle, Washington, USA, pp. 118–125, 6–9 July 2009
11. Goertzel, B.: Should humanity build a global AI nanny to delay the singularity until its better understood? J. Conscious. Stud. **19**(1–2), 96–111 (2012)
12. Goertzel, B.: Characterizing human-like consciousness: an integrative approach. Procedia Comput. Sci. **41**, 152–157 (2014)
13. Goertzel, B.: A formal model of cognitive synergy. In: Everitt, T., Goertzel, B., Potapov, A. (eds.) AGI 2017. LNCS (LNAI), vol. 10414, pp. 13–22. Springer, Cham (2017). https://doi.org/10.1007/978-3-319-63703-7_2
14. Kester, L., Ditzel, M.: Maximising effectiveness of distributed mobile observation systems in dynamic situations. In: 2014 17th International Conference on Information Fusion (FUSION), pp. 1–8. IEEE (2014)

15. Kester, L.J.H.M., van Willigen, W.H., Jongh, J.D.: Critical headway estimation under uncertainty and non-ideal communication conditions. In: Proceedings of 17th International IEEE Conference on Intelligent Transportation Systems (ITSC), pp. 320–327 (2014)
16. Mirkovic, J., et al.: Testing a collaborative DDoS defense in a red team/blue team exercise. IEEE Trans. Comput. **57**(8), 1098–1112 (2008)
17. Morewedge, C.K., Yoon, H., Scopelliti, I., Symborski, C.W., Korris, J.H., Kassam, K.S.: Debiasing decisions: Improved decision making with a single training intervention. Policy Insights Behav. Brain Sci. **2**(1), 129–140 (2015)
18. Nivel, E., et al.: Bounded recursive self-improvement. arXiv preprint arXiv:1312.6764 (2013)
19. Papernot, N., McDaniel, P., Sinha, A., Wellman, M.: Towards the science of security and privacy in machine learning. arXiv preprint arXiv:1611.03814 (2016)
20. Pistono, F., Yampolskiy, R.V.: Unethical research: how to create a malevolent artificial intelligence. In: Proceedings of 25th International Joint Conference on Artificial Intelligence (IJCAI-16). Ethics for Artificial Intelligence Workshop (AI-Ethics-2016) (2016)
21. Potapov, A.: Technological singularity: what do we really know? Information **9**(4), 99 (2018)
22. Rajendran, J., Jyothi, V., Karri, R.: Blue team red team approach to hardware trust assessment. In: 2011 IEEE 29th International Conference on Computer Design (ICCD), pp. 285–288. IEEE (2011)
23. Rege, A.: Incorporating the human element in anticipatory and dynamic cyber defense. In: IEEE International Conference on Cybercrime and Computer Forensic (ICCCF), pp. 1–7. IEEE (2016)
24. Rege, A., Obradovic, Z., Asadi, N., Singer, B., Masceri, N.: A temporal assessment of cyber intrusion chains using multidisciplinary frameworks and methodologies. In: 2017 International Conference on Cyber Situational Awareness, Data Analytics and Assessment (Cyber SA), pp. 1–7. IEEE (2017)
25. Schmidhuber, J.: Gödel machines: fully self-referential optimal universal self-improvers. In: Goertzel, B., Pennachin, C. (eds.) Artificial General Intelligence, pp. 199–226. Springer, Heidelberg (2007). https://doi.org/10.1007/978-3-540-68677-4_7
26. Sezer, O., Gino, F., Bazerman, M.H.: Ethical blind spots: explaining unintentional unethical behavior. Curr. Opin. Psychol. **6**, 77–81 (2015)
27. Shi, Z., Ma, G., Wang, S., Li, J.: Brain-machine collaboration for cyborg intelligence. In: Shi, Z., Vadera, S., Li, G. (eds.) IIP 2016. IAICT, vol. 486, pp. 256–266. Springer, Cham (2016). https://doi.org/10.1007/978-3-319-48390-0_26
28. Soares, N., Fallenstein, B.: Agent foundations for aligning machine intelligence with human interests: a technical research agenda. In: Callaghan, V., Miller, J., Yampolskiy, R., Armstrong, S. (eds.) The Technological Singularity. TFC, pp. 103–125. Springer, Heidelberg (2017). https://doi.org/10.1007/978-3-662-54033-6_5
29. Taylor, J., Yudkowsky, E., LaVictoire, P., Critch, A.: Alignment for advanced machine learning systems. In: Machine Intelligence Research Institute (2016)
30. Tegmark, M.: Life 3.0: Being Human in the Age of Artificial Intelligence. Knopf, New York (2017)
31. Thórisson, K.R.: A new constructivist AI: from manual methods to self-constructive systems. In: Wang, P., Goertzel, B. (eds.) Theoretical Foundations of Artificial General Intelligence, pp. 145–171. Springer, Paris (2012). https://doi.org/10.2991/978-94-91216-62-6_9

32. Wang, P., Li, X., Hammer, P.: Self in NARS, an AGI system. Front. Robot. AI **5**, 20 (2018)
33. Yampolskiy, R.V.: Detecting qualia in natural and artificial agents. arXiv preprint arXiv:1712.04020 (2017)
34. Yudkowsky, E.: Cognitive biases potentially affecting judgment of global risks. Glob. Catastrophic Risks **1**(86), 13 (2008)

Request Confirmation Networks in MicroPsi 2

Joscha Bach[✉] and Katherine Gallagher

Harvard Program for Evolutionary Dynamics, Cambridge, MA, USA
{bach,katherinegallagher}@fas.harvard.edu

Abstract. To combine neural learning with the sequential detection of hierarchies of sensory features, and to facilitate planning and script execution, we propose Request Confirmation Networks (ReCoNs). ReCoNs are spreading activation networks with units that contain an activation and a state, and are connected by typed directed links that indicate partonomic relations and spatial or temporal succession. By passing activation along the links, ReCoNs can perform both neural computations and controlled script execution. We demonstrate the application of ReCoNs in the context of performing simple arithmetic, based on camera images of mathematical expressions.

Keywords: Request confirmation network · MicroPsi · ReCoN
Neurosymbolic representation

1 Introduction

MicroPsi2 (Bach and Vuine 2003, Bach 2012) is a cognitive architecture that permits the implementation of situated agents that use neuro-symbolic representations (Hatzilygeroudis and Prentzas 2004) in combination with a motivational system (Bach and Vuine 2015). We are using MicroPsi2 to study how to combine conceptual and perceptual representations, and facilitate autonomous learning with full perceptual grounding. To this end, agents require mechanisms for bottom-up/top-down perception, reinforcement learning, motivation, decision making and action execution.

Cognitive architectures with perceptual grounding require a way to combine symbolic and sub-symbolic operations: planning, communication and reasoning usually rely on discrete, symbolic representations, while fine-grained visual and motor interaction require distributed representations.

A common solution is a hybrid architecture combining a neural network layer that deals with perceptual input with a symbolic layer that facilitates deliberation and control using symbolic operations. While such a dual architecture appears to be a straightforward solution from an engineering point of view, we believe that there is a continuum between perceptual and conceptual representations, and that both should use the same set of representational mechanisms. In our view, symbolic/localist representations are best understood as a special case of subsymbolic/distributed representations, for instance where the weights of the connecting links are close to discrete values. Highly localist features often emerge in neural learning, and rules expressed as discrete valued links

© Springer Nature Switzerland AG 2018
M. Iklé et al. (Eds.): AGI 2018, LNAI 10999, pp. 12–20, 2018.
https://doi.org/10.1007/978-3-319-97676-1_2

can be used to initialize a network for capturing more detailed, distributed features (see, for instance, Towell and Shavlik 1994).

A representational unit in MicroPsi is called a *node* and is made up of a vector of input *slots*, a *node function*, an *activation state*, and a vector of output *gates*. Weighted *links* connect the gates of a node with the slots of other nodes. Slots sum the weighted incoming activation and pass it to the node function, which updates the states of all gates by calling a function for each. The gates in turn are the origin of links to other nodes. *Node types* differ by the number of their gates and slots, and by the functions and parameters of their gates. The type of a link is given by the type of its gate of origin (Bach and Vuine 2003).

The most common node type in earlier MicroPsi implementations is called a *concept node*. Concept nodes possess nine gate types (with approximate semantics in parentheses): *gen* (associated), *por* (successor), *ret* (predecessor), *sur* (part-of), *sub* (has-part), *exp* (is-exemplar-of), and *cat* (is-a). Concept nodes can be used to express hierarchical scripts, by linking sequences of events and actions using *por/ret*, and subsuming these sequences into hierarchies using *sub/sur*. Specific *sensor* and *actuator* nodes provide connection to the agent's environment, and native *script* nodes may encapsulate complex functionality to provide backpropagation learning and a variety of other algorithms triggered by activating the respective node.

MicroPsi2 also provides nodes that implement interaction with external sensors, actuators, or that represent more complex neural logic, such as LSTMs (Hochreiter and Schmidhuber 1997), which we combined with denoising autoencoders (Vincent et al. 2008) to learn visual models of the virtual world that our agents inhabit (Bach and Herger 2015).

In MicroPsi, a perceptual representation amounts to a hierarchical script that tests top-down for the presence of the object in the environment. At each level of the hierarchy, the script contains disjunctions and subjunctions of sub-steps, which bottom out in distributed sub-steps and eventually in sensor nodes that reflect measurements in the environment, and actuator nodes that will move the agent or its sensors. Recognizing an object requires the execution of this hierarchical script. In the earlier implementations of MicroPsi, this required a central executive that used a combination of explicit backtracking and propagation of activation. We have replaced this mechanism with a completely decentralized mode of execution that only requires the propagation of activation along the links of connected nodes.

2 Request Confirmation Networks

The deliberate top-down initiation of a script, as in the intentional moving of an arm or imagining of an object, has been attributed to activity in the prefrontal cortex (Deiber et al. 1991; Frith et al. 1991), an area associated with goal-directed behavioral planning and task management (Koechlin et al. 1999; Tanji and Hoshi 2001). To execute a cognitive process or an action, activation flows from its initial stimulation in the prefrontal cortex through the relevant schematic components, continuing either until the objective has been successfully achieved, or until the sequence is interrupted or fails. ReCoNs offer a possible model for how these schemas and sensorimotor scripts are represented and executed in the cortex.

Request Confirmation Networks (ReCoNs) are auto-executable networks of stateful units that are connected with typed edges. A ReCoN can be defined as a set of units $\mathbb{U}$ and edges $\mathbb{E}$ with

$$\mathbb{U} = \{script\,nodes \cup terminal\,nodes\}$$

$$\mathbb{E} = \{por, ret, sub, sur\}$$

A *script node* has a state

$$s \in \{inactive,\ requested,\ active,\ suppressed,\ waiting,\ true,\ confirmed,\ failed\}$$

and an activation $a \in \mathbb{R}^n$, which can be used to store additional state.

A *terminal node* performs a measurement or executes an action, and has a state of $\{inactive,\ active,\ confirmed\}$, and an activation $a \in \mathbb{R}^n$, which represents the value obtained through the measurement, or the return value of the action. A link is defined by $\langle u_1, u_2, type \in \{por, ret, sub, sur\}, w \in \mathbb{R}^n \rangle$, whereby u_1 and u_2 denote the origin and target unit, *por* links to a successor node, *ret* links to a predecessor node, *sur* links to a parent node, and *sub* links to a child node. w is a link weight with n dimensions that can be used to perform additional computations. Each pair of nodes (u_1, u_2) is either unconnected, or has exactly one pair of links of the types *por/ret*, or *sub/sur*.

Each *script node* must have at least one link of type *sub* (i.e. at least one child that is either a *script node* or a *terminal node*). *Script nodes* can be the origin and target of links of all types, whereas *terminal nodes* can only be targeted by links of type *sub*, and be the origin of links of type *sur*. Note that not all children of a node need to have successor or predecessor relations. If they do, they will be requested and confirmed in succession. If they do not, then they are interpreted as disjunctions, and execution of the ReCoN happens in parallel.

ReCoNs form a hierarchical script without centralized access to the topology of the network. To achieve this, each individual unit implements a state machine that transitions in response to messages from directly adjacent units.

Initially, all units are in the state *inactive*. If the state of one of its nodes is set to *requested*, this triggers the evaluation of the portion of the script connected via this node's *sub*-link. The evaluation is propagated by successively and recursively requesting the children of the originally requested node. Whenever the request reaches a terminal node, confirmation or failure of the evaluation is determined and propagated back to the requesting unit. Figure 1 illustrates the order of execution of a hierarchical script containing sequences (2, 7, 10; 3, 5) and alternatives (8, 8). The script is started by sending a continuous request signal to its root node (1). Sequences are executed successively, while alternatives are executed concurrently. A failure of a step in a sequence (i.e. in one of the actions 4, 6, 11) or of all alternatives (9, 9) will result in the failure of the whole script. At any time, the script execution can be aborted by ending the request signal to its root node.

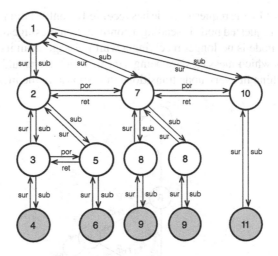

Fig. 1. Script execution example

The functionality of ReCoN nodes can best be understood by using an explicit state machine with message passing. In each step, the nodes evaluate the messages they receive from their neighbors based on their current state, and change their state accordingly. The required messages are *request (r)*, *inhibit request (ir)*, *inhibit confirm (ic)*, *wait (w)* and *confirm (c)*: *request* will attempt to activate a child node, *inhibit request* prevents a node to become active before its predecessor has successfully finished execution, *confirm* informs a parent node that its child has successfully executed, *inhibit confirm* prevents a node to send a *confirm* message before its successor has executed successfully, and *wait* informs a parent node that it has child nodes that are still active. If a parent node receives neither a *wait* nor a *confirm* message, the execution of its child nodes is assumed to have failed.

The corresponding states are *inactive* (∞): the node has not been requested; *requested* (R): the node has received a request; *active* (A): the requested node is sending a request to its children; *suppressed* (S): the requested node cannot yet send a request to its children; *waiting* (W): the requested node continues to request to its children and waits for

Table 1. Message passed along each gate, based on node state

Unit state	*por*	*ret*	*sub*	*sur*
∞	–	–	–	–
R	*ir*	*ic*	–	*w*
A	*ir*	*ic*	*r*	*w*
S	*ir*	*ic*	–	–
W	*ir*	*ic*	*r*	*w*
T	–	*ic*	–	*c*
C	–	*ic*	–	*c*
F	*ir*	*ic*	–	–

their response; *true* (T): the requested node has received a confirmation from its children; *confirmed* (C): the requested node is sending a confirmation message to its parent; *failed* (F): the requested node is no longer receiving a wait message from its children.

Table 1 details which messages are being sent in which state, and Fig. 2 illustrates how the state machine in every node transitions in response to the messages.

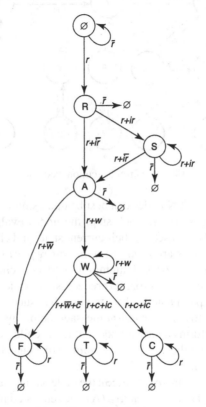

Fig. 2. State transitions (for each node) in response to messages

3   Implementation and Experiment

Request confirmation networks can be implemented in various ways, such as individual artificial neurons (Bach and Herger 2015), or by using suitably initialized LSTMs. For the purposes of this project, we have implemented them in MicroPsi2 as a specific node type with five gates and slots (*gen, por, ret, sub, sur*) and a single real-valued activation α to store the node state: *failure* corresponds to a $\alpha < 0$, *inactive* to $0 \leq \alpha < 0.01$, *requested* to $0.01 \leq \alpha < 0.3$, *suppressed* to $0.01 \leq \alpha < 0.3$, *active* to $0.3 \leq \alpha < 0.5$, *waiting* to $0.5 \leq \alpha < 0.7$, *true* to $0.7 \leq \alpha < 1$ and *confirmed* to $\alpha \geq 1$.

The ReCoN can be used to execute a script with discrete activations, but it can also perform additional operations along the way. This may done by calculating additional activation values during the request and confirmation steps.

During the confirmation step (a node turns into the state *true* or *confirmed*), the activation of that node may be calculated based on the activations of its children, and the weights of the *sur* links from these children. During the *waiting* step, children may receive parameters from their parents which are calculated using the parent activation and the weights of the *sub* links from their parents. This mechanism can be used to adapt ReCoNs to a variety of associative classification and learning tasks. In a previous experiment, we combined a ReCoN with autoencoders for learning a perceptual task in a virtual environment (Bach and Herger 2015).

Here, we demonstrate the use of a ReCoN in conjunction with a neural network to extract handwritten arithmetic expressions from a scanned image, and use the *terminal nodes* of the ReCoN to perform the corresponding arithmetic operations by connecting them directly to a stack machine. The execution consists of three phases:

1. A camera image containing an arithmetic expression is parsed into separate images of its digits and mathematical operators, then individually fed into a pre-trained multilayer perceptron.
2. The array of predicted symbols is used to algorithmically construct a ReCoN that represents the arithmetic expression in its topography.
3. The ReCoN is requested, performs the calculation using a stack machine, and the result is obtained (Fig 3).

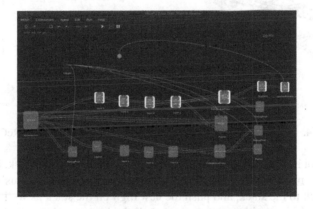

Fig. 3. MLP classifier in MicroPsi's MESH editor

Implementing a multilayer perceptron classifier in MicroPsi

For the initial image recognition task, the input image is converted into a black and white image and segmented into individual symbols using the Python image processing library scikit-image. We implemented the multilayer perceptron (MLP) using an input layer with 784 nodes, 14 output nodes (for the ten digits and the arithmetic operators $+$, $-$, $\times$, and $\div$), and two hidden layers with 240 and 60 nodes, respectively. We chose linear rectifiers (ReLu) as activation functions and a softmax classifier to pick the symbol receiving the highest activation in the output layer. The MLP was trained using MNIST for the digits and a Kaggle dataset for the operators (Nano 2016).

Generating the Request Confirmation Network

After the image segmentation and recognition stages, predicted symbols are combined into an arithmetic expression (Fig. 4a), and the corresponding ReCoN is generated (Fig. 4b). Each operation is mapped to a corresponding arrangement of nodes: multiplication is translated into the step "Mult", which consists of a *sub/sur* linked three step sequence "A" *por/ret* "B" *por/ret* "C". Each of these steps is *sub/sur* linked to its computational realization. Here, each symbol is translated into a *terminal node* that performs an operation on a stacked (Reverse Polish) calculator:

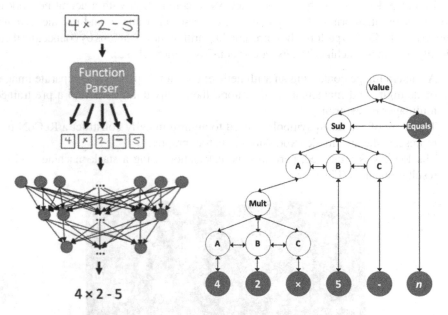

Fig. 4. (a): Function parsing and classification; (b): Constructed ReCoN

- If the symbol is a digit (0..9), pull the previous element from the stack. If the element is a number, multiply it by ten and add the new digit. Otherwise, push the previous element back to the stack, and push the new digit on the stack as well.
- If the symbol is an arithmetic operator, pull the last two elements from the stack, perform the operation, and push the result to the stack.
- If the symbol is "equals", pull the last element from the stack and print it.

Executing the Request Confirmation Network

After the setup phase, the ReCoN is executed by sending a request message to its root node. The network will spread activation through its nodes until the terminal nodes are reached, and perform the stack calculations which are implemented as node functions of the respective terminal nodes.

The successful execution of one of the elementary stack operations will result in a confirm message to its parent node, which will remove the suppression signal from its successor, which will in turn pass a request to the next stack operation, until the script is fully confirmed (Fig. 5). Conversely, the failure of one of the stack operations (as a result of an invalid sequence of input characters) will lead to a failure of the entire script. The accuracy of the output is strictly a function of the classification accuracy of the MLP; assuming an arithmetically valid input function, if all symbols have been correctly identified, the ReCoN execution will result in the correct function value. ReCoNs therefore offer a reliable way to interface a spreading activation network with arbitrary functions that are optimized to perform computations on widely available hardware and libraries, rather than fitting specifically into the neural network library.

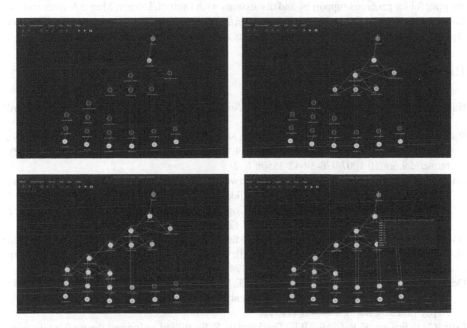

Fig. 5. ReCoN activation spreading in the MicroPsi MESH editor

4   Conclusion and Future Work

This contribution presents an early stage of Request Confirmation Networks, which are a paradigm that strives to combine the straightforward execution of symbolic scripts (especially for perceptual and motor hierarchies and planning) with distributed representations. ReCoN nodes are state machines that can implement sequences, conjunctions, disjunctions and conditional loops without reliance on a central executive, solely by passing messages to their immediate neighbors.

The implementation discussed here provides a proof of concept for ReCoNs, combining a neural network classifier for visual input with executable hierarchical scripts and the control of a stack machine for performing arithmetic operations. While this may serve as a basic illustration of the principle, it is far from being an exhaustive treatment. Concepts not discussed here include learning strategies (which involve states and messages for the distribution of rewards), the self-assembly of ReCoNs depending on a previously encountered task context (which introduces states and messages for anticipated rewards), the use of individual sub-graphs in multiple positions of the script (which introduces semaphore states) and the translation and interoperation with existing network architectures with ReCoNs. These areas constitute our ongoing work with ReCoNs.

Acknowledgements. The implementation and further development of MicroPsi and the MESH editor would not be possible without the contributions of Ronnie Vuine, Dominik Welland and Priska Herger. The implementation presented here is based on a thesis by Gallagher (2018). We are grateful for generous support by and discussions with Dietrich Dörner, Martin Nowak and the Epstein Foundation. Current work on MicroPsi is supported by the Program of Evolutionary Dynamics at Harvard University, Humanity Plus and MicroPsi Industries GmbH, Berlin.

References

Bach, J.: Principles of Synthetic Intelligence – An Architecture of Motivated Cognition. Oxford University Press, Oxford (2009)

Bach, J.: MicroPsi 2: the next generation of the MicroPsi framework. In: Bach, J., Goertzel, B., Iklé, M. (eds.) AGI 2012. LNCS (LNAI), vol. 7716, pp. 11–20. Springer, Heidelberg (2012). https://doi.org/10.1007/978-3-642-35506-6_2

Bach, J., Herger, P.: Request confirmation networks for neuro-symbolic script execution. In: Besold, T.R. Garcez, A.D. Marcus, G.F. Miikkulainen, R. (eds.) COCO'2015 Proceedings of the 2015th International Conference on Cognitive Computation: Integrating Neural and Symbolic Approaches, vol. 1583, pp. 43–51 (2015)

Bach, J., Vuine, R.: Designing Agents with MicroPsi Node Nets. In: Günter, A., Kruse, R., Neumann, B. (eds.) KI 2003. LNCS (LNAI), vol. 2821, pp. 164–178. Springer, Heidelberg (2003). https://doi.org/10.1007/978-3-540-39451-8_13

Deiber, M.P., Passingham, R.E., Colebatch, J.G., Friston, K.J., Nixon, P.D., Frackowiak, R.S.J.: Cortical areas and the selection of movement: a study with positron emission tomography. Exp. Brain Res. **84**(2), 393–402 (1991)

Frith, C.D., Friston, K.J., Liddle, P.F., Frackowiak, R.S.: Willed action and the prefrontal cortex in man: a study with PET. Proc. R. Soc. Lond. B **244**(1311), 241–246 (1991)

Gallagher, K.: Request Confirmation Networks: A cortically inspired approach to neuro-symbolic script execution. MA Thesis, Harvard University, May 2018

Hatzilygeroudis, I., Prentzas, J.: Neuro-symbolic approaches for knowledge representation in expert systems. Int. J. Hybrid Intell. Syst. **1**(3–4), 111–126 (2004)

Hochreiter, S., Schmidhuber, J.: Long short-term memory. Neural Comput. **9**(8), 1735–1780 (1997)

Koechlin, E., Basso, G., Pietrini, P., Panzer, S., Grafman, J.: The role of the anterior prefrontal cortex in human cognition. Nature **399**(6732), 148 (1999)

LeCun, Y.: The MNIST database of handwritten digits [Data file] (1998). http://yann.lecun.com/exdb/mnist/

Nano, X.: Handwritten math symbols dataset [Data file] (2016). https://www.kaggle.com/xainano/handwrittenmathsymbols

Tanji, J., Hoshi, E.: Behavioral planning in the prefrontal cortex. Curr. Opin. Neurobiol. **11**(2), 164–170 (2001)

Towell, G., Shavlik, J.: Knowledge-based artificial neural networks. Artif. Intell. **70**, 119–165 (1994)

Vincent, P., Larochelle, H., Bengio, Y., Manzagol, P.-A.: Extracting and composing robust features with denoising autoencoders. In: Proceedings of the 25th international conference on Machine learning, pp. 1096–1103 (2008)

Task Analysis for Teaching Cumulative Learners

Jordi E. Bieger[1,2]([✉]) and Kristinn R. Thórisson[1,3]

[1] Center for Analysis and Design of Intelligent Agents,
Reykjavik University, Reykjavik, Iceland
{jordi13,thorisson}@ru.is
[2] ICT Group, Delft University of Technology, Delft, The Netherlands
[3] Icelandic Institute for Intelligent Machines, Reykjavik, Iceland

Abstract. A generally intelligent machine (AGI) should be able to learn a wide range of tasks. Knowledge acquisition in complex and dynamic task-environments cannot happen all-at-once, and AGI-aspiring systems must thus be capable of *cumulative learning*: efficiently making use of existing knowledge during learning, supporting increases in the scope of ability and knowledge, incrementally and predictably — without catastrophic forgetting or mangling of existing knowledge. Where relevant expertise is at hand the learning process can be aided by curriculum-based teaching, where a teacher divides a high-level task up into smaller and simpler pieces and presents them in an order that facilitates learning. Creating such a curriculum can benefit from expert knowledge of (a) the task domain, (b) the learning system itself, and (c) general teaching principles. Curriculum design for AI systems has so far been rather ad-hoc and limited to systems incapable of cumulative learning. We present a task analysis methodology that utilizes expert knowledge and is intended to inform the construction of teaching curricula for cumulative learners. Inspired in part by methods from knowledge engineering and functional requirements analysis, our strategy decomposes high-level tasks in three ways based on involved actions, features and functionality. We show how this methodology can be used for a (simplified) *arrival control* task from the air traffic control domain, where extensive expert knowledge is available and teaching cumulative learners is required to facilitate the safe and trustworthy automation of complex workflows.

Keywords: Artificial intelligence · Artificial pedagogy
Curriculum learning · Task theory · Trustworthy automation

1 Introduction

In learning complex tasks humans tend to take an incremental approach (e.g. learning the meaning of traffic signs before driving in traffic,

The authors gratefully acknowledge partial funding for this project from Isavia, IIIM, Reykjavik University, Delft Univeresity of Technology, and the Netherlands Organization for Scientific Research (NWO grant 313-99-3160/Values4Water project).

© Springer Nature Switzerland AG 2018
M. Iklé et al. (Eds.): AGI 2018, LNAI 10999, pp. 21–31, 2018.
https://doi.org/10.1007/978-3-319-97676-1_3

or learning to fly a single-propeller plane before flying a jumbo jet), where newly acquired knowledge and skills build on those priorly acquired. If a skill is in some way related to one we have learned before—e.g. learning to play squash after racquetball—the first task will often help us learn the second one [8].[1] Humans can typically learn and alternate between many different tasks without completely forgetting them in the process, and often apply lessons learned across multiple domains. We consider such cumulative learning abilities to be a necessary feature of (artificial) general intelligence (AGI), but no artificial intelligence (AI) or machine learning (ML) system to date can rival humans in these regards.

The ideal (artificial) cumulative learner (CL), in our conceptualization, can acquire knowledge and skills through both experience [22] and teaching [5,6]. Their learning is 'always on' throughout their lifetime[2] (lifelong learning [19]), and happens continuously as new experiences accumulate (online learning [28]). Their knowledge is defeasible [17] ("better knowledge replaces worse knowledge"), and new knowledge is reconciled with old knowledge (old-new integration [16]: new knowledge can be used in conjunction with, and integrated with, older tasks — irrespective of overlap). Knowledge from one task or domain can be applied to speed up learning another (e.g. through analogy; transfer learning [14]), without catastrophic interference/forgetting [9,11], possibly to the point that few-shot learning is enabled [12]. A cumulative learner that fulfills all of these features will tend to grow its capabilities over time to cover a wide range of tasks (multitask learning [24]) as experience accumulates.

The order in which information, tasks, and subtasks are encountered can have a large influence on the efficiency and efficacy of the cumulative learning process. Pedagogical methodologies like *shaping* [20], *scaffolding* [27] and *part-task training* [23] take advantage of this for teaching humans and animals. In these approaches teachers use extensive domain knowledge to decompose complex high-level tasks into smaller and simpler subtasks that are manageable by the learner, and gradually introduce other subtasks or complexity. Similarly hierarchical methods have been applied to various existing AI approaches [2,10,13]. However, these methods are not developed for systems with advanced cumulative learning abilities.[3] Furthermore, in most of these cases no domain knowledge is utilized for defining the curriculum: the subdivision and presentation

---

[1] *Negative* transfer of training may also occur, where pre-existing knowledge interferes with learning something new — e.g. a racquetball player may take longer to get used to the way a squash ball bounces than somebody who never played racquetball. An optimal curriculum would mitigate negative transfer as much as possible.

[2] However this is measured, we expect at a minimum the 'learning cycle' (alternating learning and non-learning periods) to be free from designer intervention at runtime. Given that, the smaller those periods become (relative to the shortest perception-action cycle, for instance), to the point of being considered virtually or completely continuous, the better the "learning always on" requirement is being met.

[3] For instance, they typically require up-front full data disclosure (final data set up-front), all-at-once training (to train on the final data set from the very beginning) and learning-free deployment (the need to turn off learning before deployment to avoid unpredictable drift; cf. [15]).

order is determined by the learner—which is complicated by the learner's limited (domain) knowledge and control over the environment (especially at the start)—or by an algorithm that uses (slowly) discovered structural features of the task-environment. While this can be a strength in cases where domain knowledge is unavailable, in this paper the focus is on the case where domain expertise *does* exist, and on converting such knowledge into a subtask hierarchy or curriculum.

We present a task analysis methodology intended to aid in the instructional design of curricula to teach artificial cumulative learners, as part of broader work on *artificial pedagogy* [4] and *task theory* [25]. Here we focus on the design phase of the ADDIE model [7] from the instructional design field, with some assumptions about the analysis phase based on features of cumulative learners.[4] Guidelines are given for extracting knowledge from domain experts (Sect. 2) to decompose high-level tasks along three dimensions (Sect. 3), producing a hierarchy of (smaller and simpler) subtasks for which functional requirements are known, which can inform curriculum design (Sect. 4).

We illustrate our methodology by showing how a curriculum might be constructed for the use case of automating the task of *arrival control* (AC)[5] for the Icelandic air traffic control (ATC) agency Isavia[6] (Sect. 5), where a combined AI–human control structure could increase efficiency and safety. AC's goal is to create an optimal flow of landings by telling incoming aircraft to speed up or slow down, avoiding (near) collisions and costly holding patterns. Like other tasks in safety-critical domains, domain expertise is plentiful[7] and cumulative learning is desirable because it facilitates piecemeal introduction of functionality which minimizes disruptions to the complex and sensitive workflows of ATC operators.

2 Expert Knowledge Extraction and Representation

Creating a teaching curriculum can benefit from expert knowledge of (a) the task domain, (b) the learning system itself, and (c) general teaching principles. We assume that a prospective AI teacher knows what their AI system is (in)capable of (aside from cumulative learning) and what resources and methods are available

---

[4] The ADDIE model for instructional design consists of (1) analysis of the learner, learning goals, and teaching constraints, (2) design of the lesson plan or curriculum, which involves subject matter/task analysis, (3) development or assembly of the actual training materials, (4) implementation of the instruction with the learner (i.e. the actual teaching/training/learning), and (5) evaluation of learning outcomes.

[5] Due to space limitations we only describe a highly simplified version of arrival control here. A more elaborate version can be found in our tech report: http://www.ru.is/faculty/thorisson/RUTR18001_ArrivalControl.pdf.

[6] Isavia is Iceland's aviation authority, managing air traffic in an area measuring 5.4 million square kilometers.

[7] A lot has even been written on task analysis for ATC (cf. https://www.eurocontrol.int/articles/atco-task-analysis), but we still need a new method for designing curricula for non-human cumulative learners.

for training/teaching. Learning (and teaching) from scratch and without guidance may be feasible (and preferable) for simple tasks, but the more complex the task, the more benefit can be derived from knowledge that can be transferred to the learner or otherwise used to inform the teaching process. Luckily, many of the tasks we want our AI/AGI systems to automate are currently being performed by humans with a great deal of domain expertise. Here we describe a method for knowledge extraction from a domain expert that results in a description of a high-level task that can inform the construction of teaching curricula.

The process begins with a common practice from requirements engineering for software development, where the goal is to produce a "*scenario*" ("user story", "use case") that describes, at a fairly high level, how a certain chunk of functionality (part of the task) is to be carried out. The interviewer (i.e. the AI teacher) starts by asking the expert to describe what they do when carrying out the job, while taking care to note each "*action*" that is taken. The concept of "action" is taken very broadly and incorporates for instance: acting in the environment, predicting outcomes, obtaining particular information, making (internal) decisions, updating current knowledge, etc.

As the scenario unfolds, the teacher should make note of each action, mark it with a unique identifier and put it in a dependency graph. It is often the case that higher-level actions (e.g. "instruct pilot to slow down") consist of multiple lower-level actions (e.g. "determine optimal aircraft speed", "connect to aircraft" and "send the message") or that one action relies on inputs from previous actions (e.g. you can't send a message without knowing what should be in it). Such dependencies should be noted (see Fig. 2).

It is likely that the domain expert does not succeed immediately in describing a scenario where all of their actions and their dependencies are explicitly mentioned. The AI teacher should check that none of the actions in the scenario can be usefully broken down further and that there are no holes in the story (missing implicit or unmentioned actions or decisions).

If an action with no dependencies can be usefully decomposed further an (inverse) laddering technique can be used where the expert is asked "how is this done?" and "what steps are involved?". The usefulness of further decompositions should be judged by the AI teacher based on their assumed knowledge of what can be (easily) learned by their AI.

If the expert doesn't know explicitly how a certain action is done it can help to have them perform the task while the teacher asks "what are you doing now?", "what are you paying attention to?" and "why?". If this is not possible—e.g. because the job is high-pressure and safety-critical and the expert should not be distracted—it may instead be possible to observe a colleague and discuss what they are doing.

If a composite action is not fully determined by sub-actions the teacher should point this out to the expert, and for each input/output ask where the data comes from/what it's used for, until the missing action(s) are found.

If a dependency A does not directly contribute to an action C a laddering technique should be used to ask "why do you do A here?" to elicit an intermediate dependency B. For instance, action A to "divide distance by velocity" does not seem to contribute directly to action C to "prevent equal arrival times", but rather to intermediate action B "estimate arrival times".

After the scenarios have been formed, we need to fill in the details of the actions. This process strongly resembles the Task analysis in CommonKADS [18] and functional requirements analysis in software engineering. The goal here is to describe, in as much detail as possible, all actions that are involved in carrying out the main task. For each action, this involves answering:

1. What is the **input**? What groups of variables/information can or must be taken into account, and what are their possible and simplest values?
2. What is the **output** or result? This can be anything, ranging from e.g. "a message to pilot X to move up/down by Y amount at time Z" to "preparation/prediction of the information for another action".
3. By what **method** do we transform input to output? Can be a straightforward series of steps/calculations, or vague descriptions of intuitive processes.
4. How can the action be **evaluated**? What variables are being optimized? What is their relative importance?

Ideally, no actions should be left implicit. There can be some redundancy due to describing actions at both high and low levels (e.g. one action may be "tell pilot what to do, based on all data", which may involve other actions like "decide which pilot to talk to, based on closeness to airport", "predict closeness to airport, based on weather", etc.).

3 Task Decomposition

The extracted high-level task needs to be decomposed so that components can be cumulatively learned and introduced piecemeal into the workflow. We use three complementary dimensions of decomposition:

Task-based decomposition (or action-based decomposition) identifies all subtasks/actions (including commands, decisions, classifications, predictions, judgments, etc.) that are part of the task, at a sufficiently low level. Lower-level actions are grouped together into higher-level ones to form a hierarchy, where a low-level action control may be (re)used by multiple higher-level actions.

Feature-based decomposition (or situation-based decomposition) in a directly-learned task (or action) attempts to identify (ideally independent) subgroups of features/variables that could be learned separately. For instance, in the "predict arrival time" action for an aircraft, we may have features for wind and precipitation, and we plan to train the system first on "no wind, no precipitation", then on "various wind conditions, no precipitation" and "no wind, various precipitation conditions", and finally on "everything combined". This is expected to lead to faster (curriculum) learning of "everything combined" than if we had started with that from the beginning. Furthermore, by allowing us to "skip" tricky situations, they no longer hold back the introduction of (partial) automation into the workflow; the system could still automate the majority of simpler cases, while warning or deferring to a human operator in trickier ones that have not been adequately learned yet.

Functionality-based decomposition is a decomposition based on the functionality that is to be introduced into the workflow, which tends to be based mostly on action-based decompositions and somewhat on feature-based ones. To create and introduce functionality, it is not sufficient that the AI system has (partially) learned the relevant tasks, it is also necessary to integrate such functionality into the larger workflow (e.g. adding certain GUI elements to the workers software). In addition to being guided by other decompositions, which determine what functionality might be available, this is also guided by the actual workflow and identifying opportunities/situations where automation is most desired (analysis of these requirements is beyond the scope of this paper).

Based on the elicited actions in Sect. 2 we make a graphical representation of the task/action hierarchy (see Fig. 2 for an example from the arrival control task in Sect. 5). A feature-based decomposition of each action can be made based on their inputs and outputs. The graph should indicate which actions use the same features through connections or color coding. Functionality-based decompositions can be made based on the requirements of the client/user for whom the AI system is built, but will often correspond to elicited scenarios, or consist of an action with all of its sub-actions. However, in some cases the client may indicate that support for certain features/situations is not immediately crucial and feature-based segments can be maintained.

4   Curriculum Construction

A decomposition in these terms can serve as the basis for the construction of a teaching curriculum for cumulative learners.

The main philosophy behind curriculum learning is to have learning occur in what Vygotsky called the "zone of proximal development" (ZPD) [26]: the sweet spot between challenges that are too complex or novel to handle and ones that are too easy or familiar. This concept forms the basis of teaching approaches like shaping [3,20], scaffolding [27], and part-task training [23], as well as for many concepts of intrinsic motivation or "curiosity" [21]. In all cases the ZPD informs the novel stimuli that the AI sees. From the perspective of a teacher, this is achieved by making a task smaller or simpler until it enters the ZPD, and then making it larger and more complex as the learner becomes more competent. A curriculum then consists of a "lesson plan" that prescribes an order in which to teach the simplified tasks and how to complexify them.

The exact way in which (low-level) actions are taught is going to depend on (a) the learning system, (b) available training resources and (c) the nature of the task, e.g. whether it is a reinforcement learning or supervised learning task, whether it contains a lot of sequential events, and whether it is a kind of "one-shot" task. Our decomposition can greatly inform the order in which things should be taught: Within a cut-out chunk of desired functionality,

Scenario S1. Separation maintenance

The Cumulative Learner (CL) is presented with IDs, velocities, and distances of a fixed number of aircraft and needs to maintain a minimal separation time between landings (A1). First, the CL must predict the time at which each aircraft is expected to arrive at each runway (A2). Based on this information, the CL needs to detect if the arrival times of any two aircraft conflict (A3). Detected conflicts must then be resolved by telling an aircraft to speed up or slow down (by $\pm 10\%$ in our simplification) (A4).

Action A1. Separation mainte-nance

See Scenario S1.

Input. IDs α $\{0, 1, ...\}$, velocities v in m/s [1–400] and distances s in m [0–4,000,000] of a fixed number of aircraft

Output. ID + speed up/slow down 10% command, or nothing

Method. predict landing times (A2), detect conflicts (A3), resolve conflicts (A4)

Evaluation. +10 per landed aircraft, -1000 per conflict

Action A2. Arrival time prediction

Predict the time at which aircraft A will arrive at the runway.

Input. aircraft info for A (ID, velocity and distance)

Output. time t in s [0–10,000]

Method. $\frac{distance}{velocity}$

Evaluation. $\left\| t_{predicted} - t_{actual} \right\|_2$

Action A3: Conflict detection

Predict whether two aircraft A and B will have conflicting landing times.

Input. estimated landing times t

Output. conflict c yes/no

Method. $\|t_A - t_B\|_1 <$ threshold

Evaluation. $\|t_A - t_B\|_1 <$ threshold

Action A4: Conflict resolution

Resolve conflict between aircraft B and C.

Input. ID, velocity, distance and arrival time of aircraft A, B, C, D, where A is directly before B, and D directly after C

Output. ID of B or C + speed up/slow down Δ 10% command, or nothing

Method. See if the conflict can be mitigated by speeding up B, without introducing conflict with A. If not, slow down C and invoke A4 for C and D if this creates a conflict.

Evaluation. $c_{after} - c_{before}$ (where global conflict cost c is the sum of all local conflict costs for aircraft pairs)

Fig. 1. Extracted task description of (simplified) arrival control.

we should teach actions in a roughly bottom-up manner so that the AI system can (re)use low-level functionality it already learned when learning higher level tasks. Furthermore, the feature-based decomposition allows us to make individual tasks simpler by limiting the range of values that its inputs and/or outputs can take on, or even omitting some altogether (by setting them to a default value). Because we can expect cumulative learners to positively transfer knowledge of shared features between tasks, we recommend prioritizing teaching (simplified) tasks with features that are shared by many other actions.

5 Case Study: Arrival Control

Safety-critical domains with high time- and energy sensitivity and low error tolerance, like air traffic control and human transportation, rely on complex workflows designed to result in safe processes. The arrival control (AC) task, like most others in aviation, is based on thoroughly documented procedures for achieving high levels of quality, safety and reliability. Automation is shunned in domains like these unless it can be fully trusted and understood, and new functionality can be introduced gradually to avoid disrupting the proven workflow. Cumulative learners have an advantage here, because they (a) can gradually add more functionality to their skills without deteriorating already-known tasks, (b) be understood modularly in terms of the tasks they were taught, and (c) deal more robustly with distributional drift in the task or novel situations [1,22], by appropriate adaptation when sufficient prior knowledge is available to them, and yielding control when it's not. Since the cumulative learning capabilities of modern AI are limited at best, humans are relied on in practically all cases. The need for automatic cumulative learning, and the rich access to domain expertise, make this domain highly suitable for testing our methodology.

The primary goal of arrival control is to ensure an optimal flow of aircraft arrivals at the airport, avoiding collisions and costly holding patterns. This is a highly complex and safety-critical task that requires understanding of weather patterns, aircraft specifications, communication issues and the delicate coordination between many pilots and ATC operators with different roles. To illustrate our task analysis methodology we present the extracted task description (Fig. 1), decomposition and curriculum for a version of arrival control that is significantly simplified due to space limitations.[8]

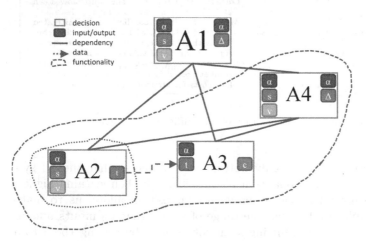

Decomposition. As described above, action A1 makes use of A2, A3 and A4, while action A4 also makes use of the functionality of A2 and A3 (see Fig. 2). We can also see that A3 depends on data from A2. Since A2 does not have any dependencies, we can extract it as a single chunk of functionality, that can

Fig. 2. Extracted action hierarchy for simplified arrival control. The relations (solid lines) between actions represent an task-based decomposition.

eventually be expanded into a chunk that provides the functionality of A4 (and its dependencies).

Curriculum. The order in which arrival control should be taught, according to our methodology, would no doubt be A2 → A3 → A4 → A1. The reasoning is as follows: A2 doesn't depend on any other actions, and can be learned alone. A3 requires A2's output as its input, and could therefore benefit from knowledge of A2, although we could also train A3 with fake data to remove this dependency.

---

[8] A more elaborate version can be found in our tech report: http://www.ru.is/faculty/ thorisson/RUTR18001_ArrivalControl.pdf.

A4 requires both A2 and A3 and cannot really be trained without them, and A1 requires all the others. The individual tasks can be further simplified (and gradually made harder again) by e.g. changing the allowable values for the input and output features. These should be modified in the same way across actions.

6 Conclusion

We have presented a task analysis methodology to inform the design of teaching curricula, when both domain expertise and cumulative learners are available. We envision this to often be the case for AGI systems, who are by definition capable of cumulative learning, and will often be used to automate complex workflows that are currently being done by human experts. Especially in safety-critical domains with complex overlapping tasks, such as air traffic control, we find that extensive knowledge and documentation of processes is typically available. Furthermore, in proven workflows that are highly sensitive to time-pressure and errors, disruptions by the abrupt wholesale introduction of monolithic automation are unacceptable, and having cumulative learners that are taught to gradually expand their functionality is highly desirable. Our presented methodology takes a step in the direction of making curriculum design more systematic, using any available domain knowledge.

Future work will be needed to compare the proposed knowledge elicitation and task analysis methods with reasonable alternatives, in terms of ease-of-use and required (time) investment for both the teacher and domain expert, as well as quality of the produced analysis. Knowledge extraction can furthermore be augmented by utilizing data from other (written) sources, and we are interested to know how different (expert or written) sources can lead to different task decompositions and how this affects subsequent curricula. A better theory is needed for constructing teaching curricula based on the presented task analysis, but also on characteristics of the learning system and available training resources. The benefits of the produced curricula should be evaluated and compared to alternate approaches like "no curriculum" (i.e. training on the full monolithic task), "alternate/random order curricula" and curricula arrived at through different curriculum construction methods and task analyses (e.g. where decomposition is done using a variety of existing automated methods).

References

1. Amodei, D., Olah, C., Steinhardt, J., Christiano, P.F., Schulman, J., Mané, D.: Concrete problems in AI safety. CoRR abs/1606.06565 (2016)
2. Barry, A.: A hierarchical XCS for long path environments. In: Proceedings of GECCO-2001 (2001)
3. Bengio, Y., Louradour, J., Collobert, R., Weston, J.: Curriculum learning. In: Proceedings of ICML-26 (2009)
4. Bieger, J.: Artificial pedagogy: a proposal. In: HLAI 2016 Doctoral Consortium, New York, NY (2016)

5. Bieger, J., Thórisson, K.R., Garrett, D.: Raising AI: tutoring matters. In: Goertzel, B., Orseau, L., Snaider, J. (eds.) AGI 2014. LNCS (LNAI), vol. 8598, pp. 1–10. Springer, Cham (2014). https://doi.org/10.1007/978-3-319-09274-4_1
6. Bieger, J., Thórisson, K.R., Steunebrink, B.R.: The pedagogical pentagon: a conceptual framework for artificial pedagogy. In: Everitt, T., Goertzel, B., Potapov, A. (eds.) AGI 2017. LNCS (LNAI), vol. 10414, pp. 212–222. Springer, Cham (2017). https://doi.org/10.1007/978-3-319-63703-7_20
7. Branson, R.K., Rayner, G.T., Cox, J.L., Furman, J.P., King, F.J.: Interservice Procedures for Instructional Systems Development: Phase 4 and 5. Florida State University, Technical report (1975)
8. Burke, L.A., Hutchins, H.M.: Training transfer: an integrative literature review. Hum. Resour. Dev. Rev. 6(3), 263–296 (2007)
9. Hasselmo, M.E.: Avoiding catastrophic forgetting. Trends Cognit. Sci. 21(6), 407–408 (2017)
10. Hengst, B.: Hierarchical approaches. In: Wiering, M., van Otterlo, M. (eds.) Reinforcement Learning. Adaptation, Learning, and Optimization, vol 12. Springer, Heidelberg (2012). https://doi.org/10.1007/978-3-642-27645-3_9
11. Kirkpatrick, J., Pascanu, R., Rabinowitz, N., Veness, J., Desjardins, G., Rusu, A.A., Milan, K., Quan, J., Ramalho, T., Grabska-Barwinska, A.: Overcoming catastrophic forgetting in neural networks. PNAS 114(13), 3521–3526 (2017)
12. Lake, B., Salakhutdinov, R., Gross, J., Tenenbaum, J.: One shot learning of simple visual concepts. In: Proceedings of CogSci 2011, vol. 33 (2011)
13. Looks, M.: Competent program evolution. Ph.D. thesis, Washington University (2006)
14. Lu, J., Behbood, V., Hao, P., Zuo, H., Xue, S., Zhang, G.: Transfer learning using computational intelligence: a survey. Knowl. Based Syst. 80, 14–23 (2015)
15. Marcus, G.: Deep learning: a critical appraisal. CoRR abs/1801.00631 (2018)
16. Nivel, E., Thórisson, K.R., Steunebrink, B.R., Dindo, H., Pezzulo, G., Rodriguez, M., Hernandez, C., Ognibene, D., Schmidhuber, J., Sanz, R., Helgason, H.P., Chella, A., Jonsson, G.K.: Bounded recursive self-improvement. Technical RUTR-SCS13006, Reykjavik University, Reykjavik, Iceland (2013)
17. Pollock, J.L.: Defeasible reasoning and degrees of justification. Argum. Comput. 1(1), 7–22 (2010)
18. Schreiber, G.: Knowledge Engineering and Management: The Common KADS Methodology. MIT Press, Cambridge (2000)
19. Silver, D.L., Yang, Q., Li, L.: Lifelong machine learning systems: beyond learning algorithms. In: AAAI Spring Symposium: Lifelong Machine Learning (2013)
20. Skinner, B.F.: The Behavior of Organisms: An Experimental Analysis. Appleton-Century-Crofts Inc., New York (1938)
21. Steunebrink, B.R., Koutník, J., Thórisson, K.R., Nivel, E., Schmidhuber, J.: Resource-bounded machines are motivated to be effective, efficient, and curious. In: Kühnberger, K.-U., Rudolph, S., Wang, P. (eds.) AGI 2013. LNCS (LNAI), vol. 7999, pp. 119–129. Springer, Heidelberg (2013). https://doi.org/10.1007/978-3-642-39521-5_13
22. Steunebrink, B.R., Thórisson, K.R., Schmidhuber, J.: Growing recursive self-improvers. In: Steunebrink, B., Wang, P., Goertzel, B. (eds.) AGI -2016. LNCS (LNAI), vol. 9782, pp. 129–139. Springer, Cham (2016). https://doi.org/10.1007/978-3-319-41649-6_13
23. Teague, R.C., Gittelman, S.S., Park, O.c.: A review of the literature on part-task and whole-task training and context dependency. Technical report, ARI, US (1994)

24. Teh, Y.W., Bapst, V., Czarnecki, W.M., Quan, J., Kirkpatrick, J., Hadsell, R., Heess, N., Pascanu, R.: Distral: robust multitask reinforcement learning. CoRR abs/1707.04175 (2017)
25. Thórisson, K.R., Bieger, J., Thorarensen, T., Sigurðardóttir, J.S., Steunebrink, B.R.: Why artificial intelligence needs a task theory. In: Steunebrink, B., Wang, P., Goertzel, B. (eds.) AGI -2016. LNCS (LNAI), vol. 9782, pp. 118–128. Springer, Cham (2016). https://doi.org/10.1007/978-3-319-41649-6_12
26. Vygotsky, L.S.: Interaction between learning and development. In: Cole, M., John-Steiner, V., Scribner, S., Souberman, E. (eds.) Mind in Society: The Development of Higher Psychological Processes. Harvard University Press, Cambridge (1978)
27. Wood, D., Bruner, J.S., Ross, G.: The role of tutoring in problem solving. J. Child Psychol. Psychiatry **17**(2), 89–100 (1976)
28. Zhan, Y., Taylor, M.E.: Online transfer learning in reinforcement learning domains. CoRR abs/1507.00436 (2015)

Associative Memory: An Spiking Neural Network Robotic Implementation

André Cyr[1]([✉])(iD), Frédéric Thériault[2](iD), Matthew Ross[1](iD),
and Sylvain Chartier[1](iD)

[1] Ottawa University, 75 Laurier Avenue East, Ottawa, ON K1N 6N5, Canada
{acyr2,mross094,sylvain.chartier}@uottawa.ca
[2] Cegep du Vieux Montréal, 255, Ontario Est, Montréal, QC H2X 1X6, Canada
ftheriault@cvm.qc.ca

Abstract. This article proposes a novel minimalist bio-inspired associative memory (AM) mechanism based on a spiking neural network acting as a controller in simple virtual and physical robots. As such, several main features of a general AM concept were reproduced. Using the strength of temporal coding at the single spike resolution level, this study approaches the AM phenomenon with basic examples in the visual modality. Specifically, the AM include varying time delays in synaptic links and asymmetry in the spike-timing dependent plasticity learning rules to solve visual tasks of pattern-matching, pattern-completion and noise-tolerance for autoassociative and heteroassociative memories. This preliminary work could serve as a step toward future comparative analysis with traditional artificial neural networks.

Keywords: Associative memory · Spiking neural network · Learning
Spike-timing dependent plasticity · Artificial intelligence · Robot

1 Introduction

Associative memory (AM) represents a theoretical learning concept widely explored in neuroscience. However, it is still poorly understood at the level of small neuronal circuits in biological organisms, because AM usually refers to complex and large-scale brain structures [1,2]. Since the tracking of stimuli from sensory inputs to these integrative neurons is technically difficult, AM is often modeled at the phenomenological level rather than at a precise cellular description level. Nevertheless, neurons and plastic synapses organized in recurrent networks are thought to represent the primitive elements sustaining a general AM architecture. As recognized hallmarks, AM should allow natural or artificial agents to store and retrieve exact and noisy input patterns, as well as achieving completion, classification and generalization of patterns [3,4].

Several computational AM models emerged over the last decades. Artificial neural networks (ANN) [5–8] represent an approach to reproduce this cognitive capacity. In the latter, the ANN paradigm has well explored the AM concept

© Springer Nature Switzerland AG 2018
M. Iklé et al. (Eds.): AGI 2018, LNAI 10999, pp. 32–41, 2018.
https://doi.org/10.1007/978-3-319-97676-1_4

that could handle big data sets. As such, different AM models with ANN are generally proposed with their own specific network topologies and learning rules. Many properties of these associative learning rules reflect various abstract levels of biologically plausible synaptic plasticity models [9–13]. Also, AM models in conjunction with ANN were explored in higher-order brain models [14], but remain to be tested under real time robotic context.

Recently, the AM phenomenon is studied from another angle using spiking neural networks (SNN) [15–19]. One inherent property of these detailed neural models comes from the temporal computing aspect occurring at the single spike resolution instead of the rate-coding used in traditional ANN. Therefore, SNN are naturally suited for ordering, timing and synchronizing the neural information which characterizes some dynamic aspects of AM.

However, despite [20,21], SNN studies in real time AM tasks are still scarce [22–24] and implementations in physical robots are barely explored. Thus, the aim of this study is to propose a simple but embodied cellular mechanism for AM models, exploiting the computational features of SNN in order to simulate the general phenomenon. Advantages of the natural AM properties should be expected in the artificial intelligence and robotic fields, but remain to be validated in more complex and dynamical situations.

In this paper, a small scale SNN model was used to show a bio-inspired AM mechanism embodied in static virtual and physical robots mounted with a camera. The tasks were to learn and recall exact matching patterns as well as partial and noisy input patterns. In addition to sustaining the autoassociative memory features, this model also supports heteroassociative memories. These basic types of AM are achieved from two different temporal neural features. First, an asymmetric timing of spikes is introduced as a main parameter, from small randomized transmission delays between the sensory input and the associative neural layer. This mechanism allows the use of the associative learning rule in the network. Variable delays in synaptic transmissions [25] are biologically plausible when considering the neural and dendritic variable topographies [26, 27]. Second, a STDP learning function [28–31] is responsible to link the input pattern elements at the associative neural layer. This standard learning rule was slightly modified by introducing an asymmetry factor in the STDP function [27, 32], to ensure that the associations at the synapses between the AM units are strengthened.

In the following section, the neural architecture and the experimentation are explained, with the objective of learning several black dot motifs from the robots. Then, results are presented to show the AM core features and finally, the discussion section explained the strength and the limitations of this work.

2   Methodology

The SNN architectures, the virtual world setup and the transferred files for the physical implementations were all elaborated using SIMCOG [33], a software dedicated to the modeling of bio-inspired robots.

2.1 The SNN Model

Standard equations for the SNN model were used based on membrane potential variance, nonlinear current integration, excitatory or inhibitory postsynaptic potential (PSP), fixed threshold, fixed refractory period value, a leaky parameter and a resting potential value (see supplementary materials[1]). Synaptic randomized delays were set between 0 and 4 cycles of algorithm to allow a minimal time spikes arrival difference in the element of the input pattern, an essential factor in using the STDP synaptic rule at the associative neural layer. Therefore, all elements composing an input pattern are linked together.

The STDP learning rule allows an increase of the synaptic weight when a pre-spike occurred before a post-spike in a defined temporal window. Inversely, when a post-spike occurs before a pre-spike, a decrease of the synaptic weight is computed. The temporal window that allows timing of spikes was set to 30 cycles. The weight variation allowed per paired-spikes is set to 80% and capped to a maximum of 400% in respect of the initial value. A positive STDP bias factor was implemented favoring a pre-post spikes correlation and a negative bias for a post-pre spike correlation to ensure making the pattern associations.

2.2 The SNN Architecture

The proposed model consists of three layers: input, associative and output. Each is composed of nine neurons, organized in a 3×3 network. The images (Fig. 1) are received from nine visual transducers, linking topographically to their attached input neurons. This input layer represents the camera-retina of the robot. The angular receptive field of each transducer is fixed and circular (1/9 of the whole caught image). The resolution is 320×240 pixels and the images are grabbed at a fixed rate of 1 cycle of algorithm in the virtual world. The area value perceived in each of these 9 sections is an average percentage of the gray scale for each transducer. As an example, a full black dot seen in the receptive field of a given transducer returns a 100% value, corresponding to the maximal receptor potential, excitatory in this case. Its effect is always relative to the membrane potential current value of the neuron involved, driven by the dynamic of the PSP function when integrated to the membrane potential variance.

After the perception of an image, the input layer fires forward to according neurons in the associative layer with fixed synapses. In the associative layer, each neuron is fully connected but without self-recurrences (Fig. 2) with adaptive synapses (STDP function). When a neuron spikes in this layer, it forwards the signal using a fixed synapse to a corresponding neuron in the output layer, hence showing a black dot on the LCD (liquid crystal display) screen.

2.3 The Virtual World

The role of the virtual world is to emulate the corresponding physical world (see Fig. 3 - left) in order to efficiently evaluate the hypothesis. A circular static robot

---

[1] http://aifuture.com/res/2018-am.

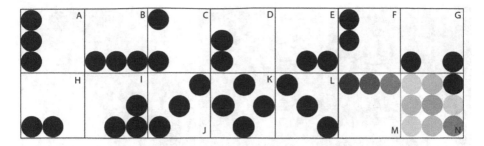

Fig. 1. Representative subset of simple linear black dots. Top left (A-B) are complete patterns with a column of three, followed by their partial associated patterns (C-H). Other variant patterns (I-L) were displayed in the recall section of the experiment. Bottom right part of the figure (M-N) represents two different patterns filled with several shades of gray (noisy patterns).

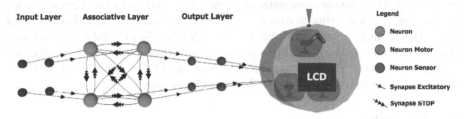

Fig. 2. Simplification of the SNN (2×2 instead of 3×3) used in the AM model. The input neural layer perceives black dots from the linked transducers, converting them in a percentage numerical scale. These neurons are connected to the associative layer. Because of the synaptic delays and the asymmetric STDP rule, the input patterns will after a while bind the neurons in the associative layer to the input patterns. Finally, the associative neurons forward to the output (LCD) layer for a real-time results observation.

waits for images to be projected on its right side. The images are grabbed with a camera, reflecting passively the content of an attached LCD device mounted on the top of the robot. The images are flashed several times in a determined order and each one of them is shown for 1 cycle. Randomization of the images sequence had no effect in the simulation. Between each image, nothing is shown for 15 cycles.

2.4   The Physical Robot

The physical platform consists of two Raspberry Pi model 2 boards. The first one is embedded in a GoPiGo robot and it is connected to a Pi-camera (Raspberry Pi camera board 5.0 MP webcam). The other board is connected to a small LCD window (PiTFT - assembled 480×320 3.5″ TFT + touchscreen) for producing the output (Fig. 3 - right). Both boards communicate using a TCP socket. Images were shown to the robot using printed papers which are switched manually after

Fig. 3. On the left side, the virtual robot (A) and a caption of one projected image on its right side (B), the robot's view (C) and the LCD device (D). On the right side, this figure shows the physical robot completing a partial visual pattern.

few seconds. The same output pattern protocol is used as in the virtual world. Because the physical visual patterns are shown for different periods of time, a small adjustment in a parameter was needed. Mainly, vision inputs were reduced with a cooldown of 20 cycles. In this physical context of an AM model, only two visual patterns were learned and reproduced on the LCD. In the recall part, the full patterns are displayed on the LCD from the incomplete inputs.

2.5 The Tasks

The autoassociative simulation consisted of learning six different visual patterns, each composed of three linear black dots (three rows and three columns) and recalled under partial inputs (two dots out of three). All inputs were shown a few times, until the SNN succeeded in completing partial patterns. In addition to pattern completion, recall was tested under two different noisy inputs (gray circles). In noisy patterns, the minimal threshold condition to trigger a spike was that the perceptive field should exhibit at least 50 percent of black. It simply reflects the transducer sensitivity parameter, the solution used to achieve discrimination of the noisy patterns. Finally, patterns composed of three or four dots were tested in order to show some limitations of the implementation.

For the heteroassociative simulation, two different sets of black dot patterns (left column and middle column) were shown one after the other, for 20 learning trials. During recall, only the first pattern of a given set was shown (left column dots) in order to measure if the robot was able to display in the LCD the correct output pattern (middle column dots). The process then continued with the learned pattern (middle column) and a new pattern (right column). In short, the expected result consists in displaying the first pattern in the LCD, followed by the second and the third one when the first pattern is perceived as input.

3 Results

The Fig. 4 represents the completion pattern task which shows that the three different lines and columns are learned (first 5000 cycles). In the second half

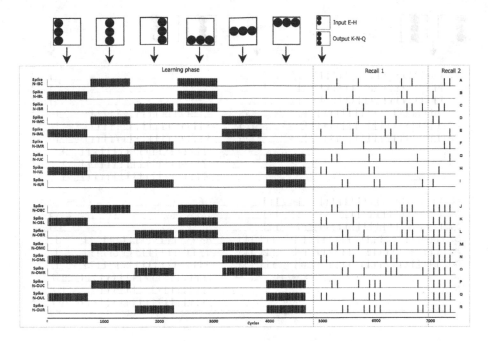

Fig. 4. Autoassociative memory task. The input neurons correspond to graphics A-I, and output neurons correspond to graphics J-R. The training phase correspond to the first 5000 cycles while the two recall phases are between 5000 and 7500 cycles. Top patterns represent stimuli displayed at the time. Recall 1 and 2 patterns were omitted for clarity

of this experiment (5000–7000 cycles), all 18 possible partial inputs related to their three linear black dot patterns (6 possible line patterns) are presented. One can observe the pattern completion from the partial input graphics A to I correlated with the output graphics J to R as well as two noisy patterns to discriminate (6800 and 6900 cycles). Other types of patterns were added at the end of this simulation (7000–7500 cycles). These patterns consisted of one bottom-right corner, two diagonals and a four dots cardinal configuration. In those cases, the SNN gave the wrong output; each time all the 9 neurons were activated.

Figure 5 illustrated the heteroassociative task for the virtual world scenario. The left column is introduced followed by the middle column patterns for the learning association between two different patterns (0–800 cycles). The recall part (900–1200 cycles) shows the precise pattern matching for both patterns. The correct directional order association are output with the presentation of the left column dots. The output neurons also show the middle column (970–1340 cycles) but not the inverse (cycle 900). This behavior was also obtained with presentation of partial input.

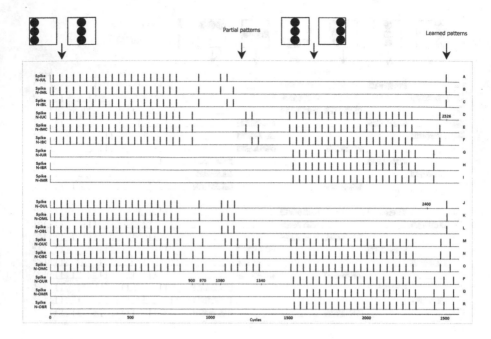

Fig. 5. Heteroassociative memory task.

Similar results were obtained when the middle column pattern was associated with the delayed right column (1500–2300 cycles). Therefore, when the left column pattern was presented at cycle 2650, the robot was able to orderly recalled the middle then the right columns.

Finally, to validate the AM model under real time condition, it was successfully reproduced in a physical robot (for video, see https://youtu.be/4e7wdfil2jA). This result also show the robustness of the SNN to sustain a variation in the temporal length period of the input presentation. In contrast to the virtual setting, a pattern is shown only once. This does not affect the behavior of the robot, as long as a cooldown of the visual input is allowed.

4   Discussion

How many neurons and synaptic links should constitute a minimalist artificial structure sustaining an AM phenomenon? Which learning rules should be applied to synapses? In biological neural systems such as in lower invertebrate animals, a formal cellular circuit producing the complete AM features still remains to be discovered. As a hypothesis state, AM do not require complex and huge neural structures considering that classical and operant conditioning are associative learning skills found in the smallest neural organisms such as Caenorhabditis elegans [34], Aplysia californica [35], Lymnaea stagnalis [36] and Drosophila melanogaster [37] and that even relational concepts learning are retrieved in the bee Apis mellifera [38]. Moreover, associative learning and memory of a simple dynamical spot along the visual pathway of invertebrates is still under the scope of neuroscientists [39].

The present AM model showed the capacity of pattern completion for auto and heteroassociative tasks. The experiment includes a static robot because the temporal variables between the visual stimuli and the SNN processing was the main target issue. The behavioral robotic complexity such as dynamical movements was beyond the scope of this paper. However, the heteroassociative capability of the current AM model may be studied with sequential motor tasks, where one action leads to the next.

A 3×3 matrix is a reductive example, but is representative enough to reproduce the AM general features. Scaling up the input data and the SNN will not affect the AM mechanism but it would limit the computational efficiency. Also, the model is restricted in terms of the number of input patterns it can learn in relation with its unit number, since in this case a group of two neurons cannot be part of two different complete patterns. This comes from the firing threshold that can be reached by the integration of two neurons using STDP synapses.

This study explored the AM phenomenon in a small-scale SNN paradigm and a simple robotic context. As such, demonstration of a real time learning task in a physical robot was a minor objective to evaluate the temporal variable relations of the model between the captured visual stimuli and the SNN processing. Using this AM model, future studies could then approach complex cognition like concept formation and relational knowledge extraction from different input patterns. For example, non-elemental learning such as with negative discrimination tasks in compound stimuli (A-, B-, AB+), it is possible to conceive the proposed model and may not require much complexity in the neural circuit [40]. These challenges remain to be investigated in future works.

5   Conclusion

This study shows several features of the AM concept using an embodied SNN paradigm, implemented as brain controllers in virtual and physical robots. With simple visual tasks and minimalist cellular circuits, it was shown that asymmetric synaptic delays and asymmetric STDP learning function are sufficient conditions to achieve pattern-completion and noise-tolerance for auto and heteroassociative tasks. This AM implementation may serves to approach higher cognitive circuits in SNN as well as a comparative basis with traditional artificial neural networks.

References

1. Rolls, E.: The mechanisms for pattern completion and pattern separation in the hippocampus. Front. Syst. Neurosci. **7**(74), 10–3389 (2013)
2. Smith, D., Wessnitzer, J., Webb, B.: A model of associative learning in the mushroom body. Biol. Cybern. **99**(2), 89–103 (2008)

3. Kohonen, T.: Associative Memory: A System-Theoretical Approach, vol. 17. Springer Science & Business Media, Heidelberg (1978). https://doi.org/10.1007/978-3-642-96384-1
4. Carpenter, G.: Neural network models for pattern recognition and associative memory. Neural Netw. **2**(4), 243–257 (1989)
5. Hopfield, J.: Neural networks and physical systems with emergent collective computational abilities. Proc. Natl. Acad. Sci. **79**(8), 2554–2558 (1982)
6. Kohonen, T.: Self-organized formation of topologically correct feature maps. Biol. Cybern. **43**(1), 59–69 (1982)
7. Kosko, B.: Bidirectional associative memories. IEEE Trans. Syst. Man Cybern. **18**(1), 49–60 (1988)
8. Chartier, S., Giguère, G., Langlois, D.: A new bidirectional heteroassociative memory encompassing correlational, competitive and topological properties. Neural Netw. **22**(5), 568–578 (2009)
9. Hebb, D.: The Organization of Behavior: A Neuropsychological Theory. Wiley, New York (1949)
10. Amit, D.: The Hebbian paradigm reintegrated: local reverberations as internal representations. Behav. Brain Sci. **18**(04), 617–626 (1995)
11. Sandberg, A., Tegnér, J., Lansner, A.: A working memory model based on fast Hebbian learning. Netw. Comput. Neural Syst. **14**(4), 789–802 (2003)
12. Sutton, R., Barto, A.: Reinforcement Learning: An Introduction. MIT Press, Cambridge (1998)
13. Zhu, S., Hammerstrom, D.: Reinforcement learning in associative memory. In: International Joint Conference on Neural Networks, pp. 1346–1350 (2003)
14. Tangruamsub, S., Kawewong, A., Tsuboyama, M., Hasegawa, O.: Self-organizing incremental associative memory-based robot navigation. IEICE Trans. Inf. Syst. **95**(10), 2415–2425 (2012)
15. Izhikevich, E.M.: Simple model of spiking neurons. IEEE Trans. Neural Netw. **14**(6), 1569–1572 (2003)
16. Zamani, M., Sadeghian, A., Chartier, S.: A bidirectional associative memory based on cortical spiking neurons using temporal coding. In: The 2010 International Joint Conference on Neural Networks (IJCNN), pp. 1–8. IEEE (2010)
17. Tan, C., Tang, H., Cheu, E., Hu, J.: A computationally efficient associative memory model of hippocampus CA3 by spiking neurons. In: The 2013 International Joint Conference on Neural Networks (IJCNN), pp. 1–8. IEEE (2013)
18. Hu, J., Tang, H., Tan, K.C., Gee, S.B.: A spiking neural network model for associative memory using temporal codes. In: Handa, H., Ishibuchi, H., Ong, Y.-S., Tan, K.C. (eds.) Proceedings of the 18th Asia Pacific Symposium on Intelligent and Evolutionary Systems, Volume 1. PALO, vol. 1, pp. 561–572. Springer, Cham (2015). https://doi.org/10.1007/978-3-319-13359-1_43
19. Komer, B., Eliasmith, C.: A unified theoretical approach for biological cognition and learning. Curr. Opin. Behav. Sci. **11**, 14–20 (2016)
20. Touzet, C.: Modeling and simulation of elementary robot behaviors using associative memories. Int. J. Adv. Robot. Syst. **3**(2), 165–170 (2006)
21. Jimenez-Romero, C., Sousa-Rodrigues, D., Johnson, J.: Designing behaviour in bio-inspired robots using associative topologies of spiking-neural-networks. arXiv preprint arXiv:1509.07035 (2015)
22. Sommer, F., Wennekers, T.: Associative memory in networks of spiking neurons. Neural Netw. **14**(6), 825–834 (2001)
23. Yu, Q., Tang, H., Tan, K., Yu, H.: A brain-inspired spiking neural network model with temporal encoding and learning. Neurocomputing **138**, 3–13 (2014)

24. Knight, J., al.: Efficient SpiNNaker simulation of a heteroassociative memory using the neural engineering framework. In: 2016 International Joint Conference on Neural Networks (IJCNN), pp. 5210–5217, July 2016

25. Shouval, H., Kalantzis, G.: Stochastic properties of synaptic transmission affect the shape of spike time-dependent plasticity curves. J. Neurophysiol. **93**(2), 1069–1073 (2005)

26. Bugmann, G., Christodoulou, C.: Learning temporal correlation between input neurons by using Dendritic propagation delays and stochastic synapses. In: Fourth Neural Coding Workshop. pp. 10–15. Citeseer (2001)

27. Panchev, C., Wermter, S.: Temporal sequence detection with spiking neurons: towards recognizing robot language instructions. Connect. Sci. **18**(1), 1–22 (2006)

28. Bi, G., Poo, M.: Activity-induced synaptic modifications in Hippocampal culture: dependence on spike timing, synaptic strength and cell type. J. Neurosci. **18**, 10464–10472 (1998)

29. Froemke, R., Dan, Y.: Spike-timing-dependent synaptic modification induced by natural spike trains. Nature **416**(6879), 433–438 (2002)

30. Caporale, N., Dan, Y.: Spike timing-dependent plasticity: a Hebbian learning rule. Ann. Rev. Neurosci. **31**, 25–46 (2008)

31. Cyr, A., Boukadoum, M.: Classical conditioning in different temporal constraints: an STDP learning rule for robots controlled by spiking neural networks. Adapt. Behav. **20**, 257–272 (2012)

32. Bi, G., Wang, H.: Temporal asymmetry in spike timing-dependent synaptic plasticity. Physiol. Behav. **77**(4), 551–555 (2002)

33. Cyr, A., Boukadoum, M., Poirier, P.: AI-SIMCOG: a simulator for spiking neurons and multiple animats behaviours. Neural Comput. Appl. **18**(5), 431–446 (2009)

34. Ardiel, E., Rankin, C.: An elegant mind: learning and memory in Caenorhabditis elegans. Learn. Mem. **17**(4), 191–201 (2010)

35. Hawkins, R., Byrne, J.: Associative learning in invertebrates. Cold Spring Harb. Perspect. Biol. **7**(5), a021709 (2015)

36. Lukowiak, K., et al.: Associative learning and memory in Lymnaea stagnalis: how well do they remember? J. Exp. Biol. **206**(13), 2097–2103 (2003)

37. Siwicki, K., Ladewski, L.: Associative learning and memory in Drosophila: beyond olfactory conditioning. Behav. Process. **64**(2), 225–238 (2003)

38. Avarguès-Weber, A., Giurfa, M.: Conceptual learning by miniature brains. Proc. R. Soc. Lond. B Biol. Sci. **280**(1772), 20131907 (2013)

39. Bianco, I., Kampff, A., Engert, F.: Prey capture behavior evoked by simple visual stimuli in Larval Zebrafish. Front. Syst. Neurosci. **5**, 101 (2011)

40. Giurfa, M.: Cognition with few neurons: higher-order learning in insects. Trends Neurosci. **36**(5), 285–294 (2013)

A Comprehensive Ethical Framework
for AI Entities: Foundations

Andrej Dameski[(✉)] [iD]

Law, Science and Technology Joint Doctorate (LAST-JD ERASMUS),
Università di Bologna (Consortium Coordinator), Bologna, Italy
andrej.dameski@studio.unibo.it

Abstract. The participation of AI in society is expected to increase significantly, and with that the scope, intensity and significance of morally-burdened effects produced or otherwise related to AI, and the possible future advent of AGI. There is a lack of a comprehensive ethical framework for AI and AGI, which can help manage moral scenarios in which artificial entities are participants. Therefore, I propose the foundations of such a framework in this text, and suggest that it can enable artificial entities to make morally sound decisions in complex moral scenarios.

Keywords: Ethics of AI · Machine ethics · AGI

1 Introduction

The subject of this article will be the brief introduction of a proposal for the foundations of a model of a comprehensive ethical framework (hereinafter: the Framework) for artificial intelligence (AI) entities, also including artificial general intelligence (AGI) entities, jointly referred to as A(G)I.

The participation of AI in society is expected to increase significantly (Yudkowski 2008; Kurzweil 2000), and therefore the effects AI is causing on its environment (including other AIs, humans and their societies, animals, and the world in general) will increase in scope, intensity and significance (see Veruggio 2007). Simultaneously, the scope, intensity and significance of morally-burdened effects (i.e. effects/changes imposed on the world that contain moral content; see Reader 2007) produced by AI is also expected to massively increase in the near future (Smith and Anderson 2014; Anderson and Anderson 2007, 2009). AI will increasingly enter in interactions which can be judged as morally (not-) good and/or right (and the natural expansion into (not-) justifiable, acceptable, just, etc.).

There already is a multitude of ethical issues on which we need to derive satisfying and morally-sound 'best possible'/'least worse' (hereinafter: 'BP'/'LW') solutions; and it seems that the future holds even deeper, and more insidious ethical issues that we will have to deal with in a morally-acceptable fashion, lest we avoid possible catastrophic consequences of the widespread introduction of AI in human civilisation(s) (Yudkowski 2008).

M. Iklé et al. (Eds.): AGI 2018, LNAI 10999, pp. 42–51, 2018.
https://doi.org/10.1007/978-3-319-97676-1_5

There are some efforts at deriving comprehensive solutions to the above issues in a morally and legally sound way, such as Veruggio's *EURON Roboethics Roadmap* (Veruggio 2007); *Robot Ethics: The Ethical and Social Implications of Robotics*, a collection of texts edited by Patrick Lin, Keith Abney and George A. Bekey (Lin et al. 2012); in works in philosophy and ethics of information Luciano Floridi's *Ethics of Information* is a notable example (Floridi 2004, Floridi 2013), alone and alongside other authors (i.e. Mariarosiaria Taddeo (Floridi and Taddeo 2016; Taddeo 2017), J. W. Sanders (Floridi and Sanders 2004), Savulescu (Floridi and Savulescu 2006), Mittelstadt (Mittelstadt et al. 2016), and others); and in regards of law and legal aspects of AI, a notable example is Chopra and White's *A Legal Theory for Autonomous Artificial Agents* (Chopra and White 2011). However, the scientific community is far from a consensus on the matter. Therefore, the author of the text hopes to contribute to the whole effort in this sense.

In essence, there is a clear need for the establishment of a comprehensive ethical framework in regards of A(G)I that can help:

- clearly conceptualise ethically-burdened situations (scenarios) where A(G)I is involved;
- devise computationally-representable 'BP'/'LW' solutions for such situations;
- engineers design and install an ethical cybernetic subsystem in A(G)I systems that will enable them to achieve the above two;
- invigorate and contribute to the debate among academia, industry, engineers, and policymakers about the foundations of morality and ethics in regards of A(G)I;
- manage morally-burdened effects caused or otherwise related to A(G)I, and its utilisation (where appropriate), to the best outcomes.

2 Considerations in Regards of A(G)I

2.1 Ethical Considerations in Regards of A(G)I

A comprehensive ethical framework that can help soundly manage morally-burdened scenarios—caused/received by or otherwise related to A(G)I—should take into consideration a plethora of moral issues and perspectives that inevitably will arise from the widespread introduction of AI into society, and the possible advent of AGI. Consequently, it bears to first discuss what possible such issues and perspectives should be managed by such a framework.

General comments. As a general comment, most of the dominant ethical theories of today are, arguably, agent-focused. That is, they focus on the morally-burdened actions of *moral agents*[1], and what those agents ought, or ought not do. These are deontology, teleology, and virtue ethics. There exist also ethical theories that are focused on *moral patients*. In these moral worldviews, agents are of second importance, and moral

---

[1] Namely, in the moral landscape, agents are those that take actions and thus *cause* morally-burdened effects; while moral patients are those entities which morally-burdened effects are *effected/caused to*.

frameworks are here to determine how moral agents ought act predominantly in respect of what effects their actions will have on moral patients. Examples of these theories are ethics of care, feminine ethics, some instances of ethics of information (e.g. Floridi 2013), environmental ethics, and similar.

In the opinion of the author, both moral worldviews are limited in their scope, as they focus only on certain components of morality and ethics, and choose to assign arbitrary status of higher importance to one or the other component (the agent(s) or the patient(s)). This can result in unwarranted bias during derivation of understanding, interpretation, and solutions to moral scenarios. Arguably, if an ethical framework for A(G)I is to be comprehensive, it should focus on both moral agents and moral patients, and consider them as equally important (for a discussion on this subject, see Gunkel 2014).

Ethical considerations. Below are included many essential ethical issues and perspectives that a comprehensive ethical framework for A(G)I will have to (contextually) consider in providing satisfying solutions to problematic moral scenarios. The following were chosen based on the regularity with which they appear when discussing ethics of AI (see, for example, Tzafestas 2016 p. 65–188), and also additional ones considered as important by the author. However, in the interest of available space it is by no means a final list.

Moral entities—A(G)I entities can, in a moral scenario, be moral agents and/or moral patients. In some situations, an A(G)I entity can also be both a moral agent and patient regarding the same morally-burdened effects *at the same time*.

Consciousness—An important issue to consider is how, and if, conscious experience (qualia) relates to ethics and morality, especially to A(G)I. One thing to note here is that the status of a moral agent or a moral patient for an A(G)I entity in a moral scenario can exist regardless of whether it is '(self-)conscious' about the scenario itself (see subsection *Morality in regards of A(G)I* in Sect. 3.2. below).

Universalism vs. anthropocentrism—A comprehensive ethical framework would take into consideration as important all entities in a moral scenario (i.e. humans, A(G)I, beings, the environment, entities generally including informational entities (see Floridi 2013), etc.) and the moral issues perturbing them.

Aliveness/'Being'—A consideration of what is 'alive' and what agent/patient is alive or exists ('Being'; see Floridi 2013) will be necessary so that there can be right perspective on what entity can cause morally-burdened effects, and what entity can and does receive such effects. In other words, which entities in the world can be considered as moral agents and patients respectively.

Personhood and legal personhood—A very important issue regarding ethics. Naturally, the understanding of legal personhood (considering an entity as a person before the law, and assigning it all the related rights and responsibilities) will flow from the ethical-philosophical understanding of 'person' and its attributes; and even before that (see, for example, Chopra and White 2011; and MacDorman and Cowley 2006).

Agency, autonomy—Autonomy is, by nature, directly connected to agency i.e. the property of an entity that make it a (moral) agent. Understanding of autonomy, and whether A(G)I entities possess it by definition or in practice, is a consideration predominantly in agent-focused ethical theories.

Complexity and moral uncertainty—When moral agents or patients are facing increasing complexity of moral scenarios, and thus inevitably becoming unable to devise 'perfect solutions', the role of the moral uncertainty that thus appears and potentially modifies moral responsibility and accountability is an important perspective that should be taken into consideration (see Zimmerman 2008). This is also related with the pragmatic 'BP'/'LW' solutions to moral scenarios, as mentioned before.

Rights—A(G)I entities will most probably have effect over human rights and other rights, as assigned by law, constitutions, and governing international documents (see also Tzafestas 2016 p. 75).

Values—Inspiring virtues, moral values are set of principles that moral entities (including A(G)I) use to determine what actions, effects and states are good, bad, evil, (un)acceptable, etc. In essence, moral values help determine what is considered 'valuable' from the perspective of morality and ethics. A(G)I entities dealing with moral scenarios will have to, at least implicitly, bear the capability to determine what is morally (not) valuable.

Virtues (and vices)—On the other hand, virtues are recognised as one of the most important elements of virtue ethics. They determine how a moral entity ought to think and act so that it will live the 'good life' and be 'good'. Arguably, virtues will be implicitly important for AI entities; but also explicitly important for AGI entities.

Accountability and responsibility—It is a common issue of accountability and responsibility in regards A(G)I entities causing and/or receiving morally-burdened effects in moral scenarios. Some ethical theories deny that there can be responsibility and/or accountability without (self-)consciousness. However, A(G)I entities can be held responsible and accountable even without (self-)consciousness, since we already have examples of similar treatment of children and animals, who in most ethical and legal systems are regularly treated as accountable (as in, the agent causing the effects), but not responsible.

Opacity and transparency—Opacity and transparency is a very important issue regarding A(G)I (see Danaher 2016). Designing or imposing A(G)I systems that can precisely, responsibly and intelligibly explain how they reach their conclusions and courses of (in-)action is essential for the future acceptance of the widespread introduction of automated decision making in society. This also is closely related to accountability and responsibility discussed above.

Utility (the perspective of A(G)I and algorithms simply as 'tools' or 'means')—Considering an A(G)I system simply as a tool would mean it expands a significantly narrowed down and simplified moral considerations. Potential ethical issues can arise especially with the possible advent of AGI, self-consciousness, personhood, and ability to suffer.

Trust—Trust is closely related to responsibility, accountability, predictability, opacity, and transparency. A trust in an A(G)I system facilitates its deployment and utilisation, and increases efficiency and effectiveness.

Morally-burdened effects—caused by moral agents, and received by moral patients, these are an essential part of any moral scenario, and, like all other above considerations, will need to be modelled and managed by an A(G)I system.

3 A Comprehensive Ethical Framework for A(G)I

3.1 Introduction

A comprehensive ethical framework for A(G)I has to enable derivation of satisfying solutions to the previously mentioned issues. It has to take one or more of them in consideration, where appropriate in respect of context, and provide computationally and logically representable solutions, that will be the 'BP'/'LW' ones in the moral scenarios that are faced. An A(G)I entity using such a framework would have to reach or preferably surpass moral reasoning capacities of individual humans, and of human collectives and institutions. Programmers, by consulting and implementing such a framework, will be able to design A(G)I entities that have better moral reasoning capabilities than without it. In essence, if such a framework (or an appropriate approximation) is implemented in the design and the utilisation of A(G)I entities it will leave the world better off morally on aggregate.

3.2 Characteristics and Design

Foundational—The framework should be set up as a system of axioms that can be informationally, logically and computationally represented.

Coherent—The axiomatic system is able to be informationally, logically and computationally expanded to provide solutions to arising ethical problems in context, without issues of incoherence taking place.

Hybrid, multidisciplinary, and holistic—The axiomatic base of the framework is to be conceived with a holistic approach in mind and thus help provide more comprehensive one, drawing on existing advances in ethics in general, ethics of AI and ethics of information, and on other, 'non-ethical' and meta-ethical disciplines.

Unified/unifying—The framework should have universalist pretension i.e. it should attempt to unify all the major ethical theories into a single axiomatic system; and thus render them as special cases of itself.

Contextual—The framework, when used as a cybernetic (sub)system into an A(G)I system, should be able to 'live in context', acquire new and modify its existing moral knowledge, and adjust to new environment.

Applicable to A(G)I and its interaction with the environment—i.e. other A(G)I systems and other systems in general, the world, humans and their systems, animals, the legal, financial and social systems, etc.

Translatable and implementable through engineering and legal tools.

3.3 Design

The foundation. Below is included the axiomatic foundations of the Framework for A(G)I that the author presents in this article (see also Fig. 1.).

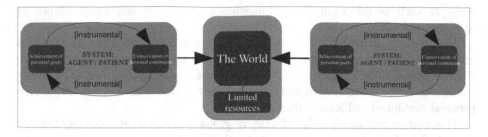

Fig. 1. Emergence of moral systems

Axiom 0	Every system[a] has as a moral imperative[b] its highest possible personal Quality of Life (QoL). Every system's QoL is comprised of the level of potential or actual achievement of two fundamental goals: (1) conservation of personal continuum (2) achievement of personal goals
Axiom 1	Every system has at least one of the fundamental goals from Axiom 0 as a moral imperative [explicit goal], and as an instrument [implicit goal]. •A system can simultaneously have both of these goals as moral imperatives (that is, explicit goals). Each fundamental goal can be partially or wholly a moral imperative and/or an instrument[c]. •For a system, a goal can, and does, simultaneously serve both as an imperative and as an instrument (for the purposes of the other goal).
Axiom 2	Every system strives towards imperative maximisation, by using its resources, which include its instruments.
Axiom 3	Resources are (inevitably) limited. •Systems compete over limited resources in their imperative maximisation, and that leads them in conflict. •This dialectical process of conflict, and the subsequent emergence of solutions to the conflicting situations, is the originator of morality.

[a]A system is defined as follows: a system is a set of interrelated and interdependent components, from whose interaction the system emerges as something more than just the simple sum of its parts. A system can be conceptualised both as a collective (of its parts) and as an individual, and this usually depends on the level of abstraction (see Floridi 2013). The usage of 'moral entity', 'informational entity', 'agent/patient', 'entity', etc. are interchangeable with system.

[b]A moral imperative is, thus, a systemic imperative; in the sense that the system considers and/or acts as if pursuing the achievement of its systemic imperatives is *right* and *good* for itself and in general. This adds the moral dimension.

[c]It is important to note that the imperative/instrument duality is not a dichotomy, but a spectre. In practice, most systems have both fundamental goals as simultaneous and independent moral imperatives and instruments. One of the goals may be independently less/more of a moral imperative, and independently less/more of an instrument for the other goal, determined by the internal structure of the system.

Morality. Morality deals with Quality of Life (QoL) of systems. QoL is defined as **the potential to achieve, or the actual achievement, of moral imperative(s) of systems**. If it is considered as a category, the *potential to achieve moral imperative(s)* part of QoL would include moral concepts such as freedom, agency, capacity, intention and similar ones. Similarly, *actual achievement of moral imperative(s)* would include moral concepts such as fulfilment, justice, happiness, alleviation and transcendence of suffering, and similar.

Simply taken, in the world systems (and therefore A(G)I agents) exist, act (and thus cause morally-burdened effects), and are acted upon (and thus receive those effects) while in pursuit of their imperatives. All systems use available resources[2] to be able to continue to do the above and proceed with pursuing their imperatives i.e. conserve their personal continuum and achieve their goals.

However, resources are either (locally or globally) limited, or inevitably become limited. This 'forces' systems to compete for them so that they can continue pursuing their imperatives. This competition inescapably leads to conflict (see also Tiles 2005 p. 70). *Conflict*, in this perspective, is a process whereby a system explicitly or implicitly threatens other system(s) with reduction of their ability to achieve their imperatives, if the first system's ability to achieve its own imperative(s) is jeopardised. In essence, when a system finds its QoL in jeopardy by another system, it acts to secure the resources that are jeopardised, and this is threatening to the QoL of the other system because the other system also needs them for its own QoL. Conflicts, by extension, and in moral scenarios with more cognitively capable moral entities, can develop into second order ones (i.e. conflicts over opposing values and methods of distribution of resources), which are in essence conflicts over differing moral systems.

If during this process systems, explicitly or implicitly, achieve a balance point, whereby there is a compromise as to how much of the contested resources should belong to the first or the second system; and this enables both systems for the time being to continue pursuing their desired, but now revised, QoL level; the balance point that has emerged ('crystallised') is a moral rule. Systems opt to respect this moral rule for the time being as it enables them to achieve the best practically possible QoL level through avoiding further conflict while lowering their desired QoL level.

Emergence of moral systems. Out of a complex, multifaceted aggregation of moral scenarios, where systems enter in conflict and subsequently establish moral rules which are then crystallised (that is, stabilised), a moral system emerges for that particular collective of systems. In essence, moral systems are methods governing the distribution of needed resources. This is what is normally understood under *morality* in a practical manner. See Fig. 1 for illustration. Morality is, therefore, a cyclical down-up (emergent) and up-down (crystallising) process. Any moral system that thus emerges or is imposed, also contains the properties of any other system.

Contextuality. Since moral systems emerge for particular collectives, each moral system is contextual and specific, even though the basic principles that cause their emergence are the same—conflict over resources needed for desired QoL. Moral systems differ because of differences in the components of the system, which include

---

[2] Under resources here are understood all parts of the world which a system can use instrumentally to pursue its imperatives i.e. both 'traditional' ones such as raw materials, energy source(s), food, water, minerals etc. but also time, situations, rules, other systems and their parts, and anything else of utility.

the contesting systems, the contested resources, and other miscellaneous factors such as difference in the environment.

However, most moral systems created by systems that enter into similar moral scenarios (i.e. human collectives) are alike, and universality or widespread adoption in some basic moral rules can be discovered throughout them. Examples in human moral systems are of the immorality of murder, rape, sexual acts with children, incest, lying, irresponsible or unnecessary disturbance or damage, and similar.

Morality in regards of A(G)I. In respect of A(G)I entities, there are several additional considerations that need to be discussed.

Firstly, A(G)I systems for which there will be a requirement to deal with moral scenarios will have to consider the aforementioned perspectives. That means that A(G)I systems will have to, directly or indirectly, take into consideration the QoL of other systems.

Secondly, as discussed before, the A(G)I system itself doesn't have to be (self-)conscious of the (moral) scenario or generally in the conventional meaning—since the algorithm doing the calculation and deriving at the decision for (in-)action can be designed by human programmers. This means that the system will participate as a moral agent and moral patient in the moral scenario regardless of any (self-)conscious sense of the underlying moral considerations (also known as mindless morality; see Floridi 2013). Simply taken, morally-burdened effects can exist without conscious intention. This is (mostly implicitly) recognised also by other ethicists and researchers working in this domain, such as Floridi (2013), Dodig Crnkovic and Çürüklü (2012), Gerdes and Øhrstrøm (2015), and others. This also means that human engineers can input moral systems, or even simple moral rules (i.e. deontological or teleological rules) in simple AI systems that deal with morally problematic scenarios. The systems in question will act as moral entities (agents/patients) and cause and/or receive morally-burdened effects.

And thirdly, in regards of AGI, there are some additional ethical considerations. Arguably, AGIs that reach or surpass cognitive and other capacities of humans and human collectives will be able to wield tremendous power, and cause significant morally-burdened effects. In moral scenarios, moral entities with higher power (i.e. ability to exert their will in pursuit of their goals regardless of resistance) bear proportionately higher moral responsibility. That would mean that such AGI systems will have to attempt to take into consideration the QoL of all other systems involved in the moral scenario in which they exist, act, and are being acted upon.

It is hence reasonable to assume that this will require tremendous capacity for moral reasoning (i.e. moral calculations) on the part of those AGI entities, which would include moral scenario model building, bias avoidance, heuristics and fallibilistic reasoning, and ability to choose the 'BP'/'LW' course of (in-)action given available data and resources.

Unifying/unified. The Framework presented in this text attempts to integrate and harmoniously unite dominant ethical theories of today. This includes deontology, teleology, virtue ethics, rights theory, value theory, ethics of care (patient-focused ethics). In this effort, all these ethical theories become special cases of the general model. Unfortunately, in the interest of space, the author can only provide a graphical representation of this unification in Fig. 2. The detailed description will have to remain for future work.

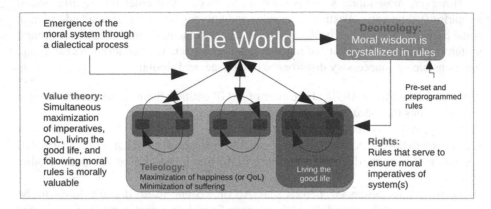

Fig. 2. The integration of ethical theories

4 Conclusion and Way Forward

The basis of the Framework presented in this text is a model of a foundational, yet flexible, adaptable and contextual moral system. It can serve as a model to be used by designers of A(G)I systems, or by A(G)I entities themselves, for the building of internal moral subsystems that will enable A(G)I entities to successfully participate in complex moral scenarios in a morally sound manner. This will enable them to manage morally-burdened effects, and attempt to avoid the negative ones, while attempting to maximise the positive ones, or the so-called 'BP'/'LW' solutions.

Subsequent efforts should be given in the elaboration of the Framework's components in detail, testing it in theoretical moral scenarios, as well as, in gathering input from a wide range of sources which would enable to determine statistical indicators that can be taken in consideration by an A(G)I entity to perform contextual moral calculations. This will enable the improvement of the model itself, and hopefully A(G)I entities using it will be able to derive moral solutions in context that will approach, and even exceed, human moral reasoning capacity.

References

Anderson, M., Anderson, S.L.: Machine ethics: creating an ethical intelligent agent, AI Magazine **28**(4), 15–26 (2007). American Association for Artificial Intelligence

Anderson, S.L., Anderson, M.: How Machines Can Advance Ethics, Philosophy Now (2009)

Chopra, S., White, L.F.: A Legal Theory for Autonomous Artificial Agents. University of Michigan, Ann Arbor (2011)

Danaher, J.: The threat of algocracy: reality. Resistance and Acommodation. Philosophy and Technology **29**, 245–268 (2016)

Dodig Crnkovic, S., Çürüklü, B.: Robots: ethical by design. Ethics Inf. Technol. **14**, 61–71 (2012)

Floridi, L. (ed.): The Blackwell Guide to the Philosophy of Computing and Information. Blackwell Publishing, Hoboken (2004)

Floridi, L.: The Ethics of Information. Oxford University Press, Oxford (2013)

Floridi, L., Sanders, J.W.: On the morality of artificial agents. Minds Mach. **14**, 349–379 (2004)

Floridi, L., Savulescu, J.: Information ethics: agents, artefacts and new cultural perspectives. Ethics Inf. Technol. **8**, 155–156 (2006)

Floridi, L., Taddeo, M.: What is Data Ethics. Philosophical Transactions of the Royal Society A **374**(2083) (2016). Preprint

Gerdes, A., Øhrstrøm, P.: Issues in robot ethics seen through the lens of a moral turing test. J. Inf. Commun. Ethics Soc. **13**(2), 98–109 (2015). Emerald Group Publishing Limited

Gunkel, D.J.: A vindication of the rights of machines. Philos. Technol. **27**, 113–132 (2014)

Kurzweil, R.E.: The Age of Spiritual Machines: When Computers Exceed Human Intelligence. Penguin Books, London (2000)

Lin, P., Abney, K., Bekey, G.A. (eds.): Robot Ethics: The Ethical and Social Implications of Robotics. The MIT Press, Cambridge (2012)

MacDorman, K.F., Cowley, S.J.: Long-term relationships as a benchmark for robot personhood. In: The 15th IEEE International Symposium on Robot and Human Interactive Communication, Hatfield, UK (2006)

Mittelstadt, B.D., Allo, P., Taddeo, M., Wachter, S., Floridi, L.: The ethics of algorithms: mapping the debate. Big Data Soc. **3**(2), 1–21 (2016)

Reader, S.: Needs and Moral Necessity, Routledge (Taylor and Francis Group). Taylor and Francis e-Library, Abingdon (2007)

Smith, A., Anderson, J.: AI, Robotics, and the Future of Jobs, Pew Research Center (2014). http://www.pewinternet.org/2014/08/06/future-of-jobs/

Taddeo, M.: The moral value of information and information ethics. In: Floridi, L. (ed.) The Routledge Handbook of Philosophy of Information. Routledge (2017)

Tiles, J.E.: Moral Measures: An Introduction to Ethics East and West, Routledge (Taylor and Francis Group). Taylor and Francis e-Library, Abingdon (2005)

Tzafestas, S.G.: Roboethics: A Navigating Overview. Springer, Cham (2016). https://doi.org/10.1007/978-3-319-21714-7

Veruggio, G.: EURON Roboethics Roadmap (2007). http://www.roboethics.org/index_file/Roboethics%20Roadmap%20Rel.1.2.pdf

Yudkowski, E.: AI as a positive and negative factor in global risk. In: Bostrom, N., Cirkovic, M.M. (eds.) Global Catastrophic Risks, pp. 308–345. Oxford University Press, Oxford (2008)

Zimmerman, M.J.: Living with Uncertainty: The Moral Significance of Ignorance. Cambridge University Press, Cambridge (2008)

Partial Operator Induction
with Beta Distributions

Nil Geisweiller[1,2,3](✉) (iD)

[1] SingularityNET Foundation, Amsterdam, The Netherlands
nil@singularitynet.io
[2] OpenCog Foundation, Wilmington, DE, USA
[3] Novamente LLC, Rockville, MD, USA

Abstract. A specialization of Solomonoff Operator Induction considering partial operators described by second order probability distributions, and more specifically Beta distributions, is introduced. An estimate to predict the second order probability of new data, obtained by averaging the second order distributions of partial operators, is derived. The problem of managing the partiality of the operators is presented. A simplistic solution based on estimating the Kolmogorov complexity of *perfect completions* of partial operators is given.

Keywords: Solomonoff Operator Induction · Beta distribution
Bayesian averaging

1 Introduction

Rarely do natural intelligent agents attempt to construct complete models of their environment. Often time they compartmentalize their knowledge into contextual rules and make use of them without worrying about the details of the assumingly remote and irrelevant parts of the world.

This is typically how PrimeAGI, aka OpenCog Prime, the AGI agent implemented over the OpenCog framework may utilize knowledge [4]. The models we are specifically targeting here are rules describing *second order* conditional probabilities, probabilities over probabilities. Maintaining second order probabilities is how OpenCog accounts for uncertainties [8] and by that properly manages cognitive tasks such as integrating knowledge from heterogeneous sources, balancing exploitation and exploration and so on. Here are some examples of rules

1. *If the sun shines, then the temperature rises*
2. *If the sun shines and there is no wind, then the temperature rises*
3. *If the sun shines and I am in a cave, then the temperature rises*

These 3 rules have different degrees of truth. The first one is often true, the second is nearly always true and the last one is rarely true. The traditional way to quantify these degrees of truth is to assign probabilities. In practice though these

© Springer Nature Switzerland AG 2018
M. Iklé et al. (Eds.): AGI 2018, LNAI 10999, pp. 52–61, 2018.
https://doi.org/10.1007/978-3-319-97676-1_6

probabilities are unknown, and instead one may only assign probability estimates based on limited evidence. Another possibility is to assign second order probabilities, distributions over probabilities as to capture their degrees of certainty. The wider the distribution the less certain, the narrower the more certain.

Once degrees of truth and confidence are properly represented, an agent should be able to utilize these rules to predict and operate in its environment. This raises a question. How to choose between rules? Someone wanting to predict whether the temperature will rise will have to make a choice. If one is in a cave, should he/she follow the third rule? Why not the first one which is still valid, or assuming there is no wind, maybe the second?

Systematically picking the rule with the narrowest context (like being in a cave) is not always right. Indeed, the narrower the context the less evidence we have, the broader the uncertainty, the more prone to overfitting it might be.

In this paper we attempt to address this issue by adapting Solomonoff Operator Induction [9] for a special class of operators representing such rules. These operators have two particularities. First, their outcomes are second order probabilities, specifically Beta distributions. Second, they are partial, that is they are only defined over a subset of observations, the available observations encompassed by their associated contexts.

The remaining of the paper is organized as follows. In Sect. 2 we briefly recount the idea of Solomonoff Operator Induction and in Sect. 3, the definition and properties of Beta distributions. In Sect. 4 we introduce our specialization of Solomonoff Operator Induction for partial operators with Beta distributions. An estimate of the second order probability predicting new data, obtained by averaging the second order probabilities of these partial operators, is derived. Then the problem of dealing with partial operators is presented and somewhat minimally addressed. Finally, in Sect. 5 we conclude and present some directions for research.

2   Solomonoff Operator Induction

Solomonoff Universal Operator Induction [9] is a general, parameter free induction method shown to theoretically converge to the true distribution, the source underlying the generation of a sequence of symbols, provided that such a source is computable. It is a special case of Bayesian Model Averaging [6] though is universal in the sense that the class of models across which the averaging is taking place is Turing complete.

Let us recall its formulation, using the same notations as in the original paper of Solomonoff (Sect. 3.2 of [9]). Given a sequence of n questions and answers $(Q_i, A_i)_{i \in [1,n]}$, and a countable family of operators O^j (the superscript j denotes the jth operator, not the exponentiation) computing partial functions mapping pairs of question and answer to probabilities, one may estimate the probability of the next answer A_{n+1} given question Q_{n+1} as follows

$$\hat{P}(A_{n+1}|Q_{n+1}) = \sum_j a_0^j \prod_{i=1}^{n+1} O^j(A_i|Q_i) \tag{1}$$

where a_0^j is the prior of the jth operator, its probability after zero observation, generally approximated by $2^{-K(O^j)}$ where K is the Kolmogorov complexity [11]. Using Hutter's convergence theorem to arbitrary alphabets [7] it can be shown that such estimate rapidly converges to the true probability.

Let us rewrite Eq. 1 by making the prediction term and the likelihood explicit

$$\hat{P}(A_{n+1}|Q_{n+1}) = \sum_j a_0^j l^j O^j(A_{n+1}|Q_{n+1}) \tag{2}$$

where $l^j = \prod_{i=1}^n O^j(A_i|Q_i)$ is the likelihood, the probability of the data given the jth operator.

Remark 1. In the remaining of the paper the superscript j is always used to denote the index of the jth operator. Sometimes, though in a consistent manner, it is used as subscript. All other superscript notations not using j denote exponentiation.

3   Beta Distribution

Beta distributions [1] are convenient to model probability distributions over probabilities, i.e. second order probabilities. In particular, given a prior over a probability p of some event, like a coin toss to head, defined by a Beta distribution, and a sequence of experiments, like tossing coins, the posterior of p is still a Beta distribution. For that reason the Beta distribution is called a *conjugate prior* for the binomial distribution.

Let us recall the probability density and cumulative distribution functions of the Beta distribution as it will be useful later on.

3.1   Prior and Posterior Probability Density Function

The probability density function (pdf) of the Beta distribution with parameters α and β, is

$$f(x; \alpha, \beta) = \frac{x^{\alpha-1}(1-x)^{\beta-1}}{B(\alpha, \beta)} \tag{3}$$

where x is a probability and $B(\alpha, \beta)$ is the beta function

$$B(\alpha, \beta) = \int_0^1 p^{\alpha-1}(1-p)^{\beta-1}dp \tag{4}$$

One may notice that multiplying the density by the likelihood

$$x^m(1-x)^{n-m} \tag{5}$$

of a particular sequence of n experiments with m positive outcomes with probability x, is also a Beta distribution

$$f(x; m+\alpha, n-m+\beta) \propto x^{m+\alpha-1}(1-x)^{n-m+\beta-1} \tag{6}$$

3.2 Cumulative Distribution Function

The cumulative distribution function (cdf) of the Beta distribution is

$$I_x(\alpha, \beta) = \frac{\mathrm{B}(x; \alpha, \beta)}{\mathrm{B}(\alpha, \beta)} \tag{7}$$

where $\mathrm{B}(x; \alpha, \beta)$ is the incomplete beta function

$$\mathrm{B}(x; \alpha, \beta) = \int_0^x p^{\alpha-1}(1-p)^{\beta-1} dp \tag{8}$$

I_x is also called the regularized incomplete beta function [13].

4   Partial Operator Induction with Beta Distributions

In this section we introduce our specialization of Solomonoff Operator Induction for partial operators describing second order distributions, and more specifically Beta distributions. An estimate of the second order conditional probability of the next data is derived, however it contains unknown terms, the likelihoods of the unaccounted data by partial operators, themselves estimated by a simplistic heuristic.

4.1 Second Order Probability Estimate

Let us first modify the Solomonoff Operator Induction probability estimate to represent a second order probability. This allows us to maintain, and ultimately propagate to efferent cognitive processes, the uncertainty of that estimate. It directly follows from Eq. 2 of Sect. 2, that the cumulative distribution function of the probability estimate of observing answer A_{n+1} given question Q_{n+1} is

$$\hat{cdf}(A_{n+1}|Q_{n+1})(x) = \sum_{O^j(A_{n+1}|Q_{n+1}) \leq x} a_0^j l^j \tag{9}$$

Due to O^j not being complete in general $\hat{cdf}(A_{n+1}|Q_{n+1})(1)$ may not be equal to 1. It means that some normalization will need to take place, that is even more true in practice since only a fraction of the operator space is typically explored. Also, we need not to worry about properties such as the continuity or the differentiability of $\hat{cdf}(A_{n+1}|Q_{n+1})$. What matters is that a spread of probabilities is represented to account for the uncertainty. It is expected that the breadth would be wide at first, and progressively shrinks, fluctuating depending on the novelty of the data, as measure as more questions and answers get collected.

4.2   Continuous Parameterized Operators

Let us now extend the definition of this estimate for parameterized operators to describe second order distributions. Let us consider a subclass of parameterized operators such that, if p is the parameter of operator O_p^j, the result of the conditional probability of A_{n+1} given Q_{n+1} is p. Doing so will enable us to consider operators as Beta distribution later on, in Sect. 4.3.

Theorem 1. *Given a family of parameterized operators O_p^j such that*

$$O_p^j(A_{n+1}|Q_{n+1}) = p \qquad (10)$$

and the prior of O_p^i is $a_0^j f_p$ where f_p is the prior density of p, the cumulative distribution function of the estimate $\hat{cdf}(A_{n+1}|Q_{n+1})$ is

$$\hat{cdf}(A_{n+1}|Q_{n+1})(x) = \sum_j a_0^j \int_0^x f_p l_p^j dp \qquad (11)$$

where $l_p^j = \prod_{i=1}^n O_p^j(A_i|Q_i)$ is the likelihood of the data according to the jth operator with parameter p.

Proof. Let us express Eq. 9 with a discretization of O_p^j with prior $a_0^j f_p \Delta p$

$$\hat{cdf}(A_{n+1}|Q_{n+1})(x) = \sum_{O_p^j(A_{n+1}|Q_{n+1}) \leq x} a_0^j f_p l_p^j \Delta p \qquad (12)$$

where the sum runs over all j and p by steps of Δp such that $O_p^j(A_{n+1}|Q_{n+1}) \leq x$. Since a_0^j does not depends on p, it can be moved in its own sum

$$\hat{cdf}(A_{n+1}|Q_{n+1})(x) = \sum_j a_0^j \sum_{O_p^j(A_{n+1}|Q_{n+1}) \leq x} f_p l_p^j \Delta p \qquad (13)$$

now the second sum only runs over p. Due to Eq. 10 this can be simplified into

$$\hat{cdf}(A_{n+1}|Q_{n+1})(x) = \sum_j a_0^j \sum_{p \leq x} f_p l_p^j \Delta p \qquad (14)$$

which turns into Eq. 11 when Δp tends to 0.   □

Using continuous integration may seem like a departure from Solomonoff Induction. First, it does not correspond to a countable class of models. Second, the Kolmogorov complexity of p, determining the prominent contribution of its prior, is likely chaotic and would yield very different priors than what is typically defined over continuous parameters in Bayesian inference. In practice however integration is discretized and values are truncated up to some fixed precision. Moreover any prior can probably be approximated by selecting an adequate Turing machine of reference, assuming all contributions, not just the prominent ones defined by their Kolmogorov complexities, are considered, otherwise the prior will likely be confined to an exponential one, as pointed out in [2].

4.3   Operators as Beta Distributions

We have now what we need to model our rules, second order conditional probabilities, as operators.

First, we need to assume that operators are partial, that is the jth operator is only defined for a subset of n^j questions, those that meet the conditions of the rule. For instance, when considering the rule

– *If the sun shines, then the temperature rises*

questions pertaining to what happens at night will be ignored by it.

Second, we assume that answers are Boolean, so that $A_i \in \{0, 1\}$ for any i. In reality, OpenCog rules manipulate predicates (generally fuzzy predicates but that can be let aside), and the questions they represent are: *if some instance holds property R, what are the odds that it holds property S?* We simplify this by fixing predicate S so that the problem is reduced to finding R that best predicts it. Thus we assume that if $A_i = A_{n+1}$ then O_p^j models the odds of $S(Q_i)$, and if $A_i \neq A_{n+1}$, it models the odds of $\neg S(Q_i)$. More formally, the class of operators under consideration can be represented as programs of the form

$$O_p^j(A_i|Q_i) = \text{if } R^j(Q_i) \text{ then } \begin{cases} p, & \text{if } A_i = A_{n+1} \\ 1-p, & \text{otherwise} \end{cases} \tag{15}$$

where R^j is the conditioning predicate of the rule. This allows an operator to be modeled as a Beta distribution, with cumulative distribution function

$$cdf_{O^j}(x) = I_x(m^j + \alpha, n^j - m^j + \beta) \tag{16}$$

where m^j is the number of times $A_i = A_{n+1}$ for the subset of n^j questions such that $R^j(Q_i)$ is true. The parameters α and β are the parameters of the prior of p, itself a Beta distribution. Equation 16 is in fact the definition of OpenCog Truth Values as described in Chap. 4 of the PLN book [5].

4.4   Handling Partial Operators

When attempting to use such operators we still need to account for their partiality. Although Solomonoff Operator Induction does in principle encompass partial operators[1], it does so insufficiently, in our case anyway. Indeed, if a given operator cannot compute the conditional probability of some question/answer pair, the contribution of that operator may simply be ignored in the estimate. This does not work for us since partial operators (rules over restricted contexts) might carry significant predictive power and should not go to waste.

To the best of our knowledge, the existing literature does not cover that problem. The Bayesian inference literature contains in-depth treatments about

---

[1] More by necessity, since the set of partial operators is enumerable, while the set of complete ones is not.

how to properly consider missing data [12]. Unfortunately, they do not directly apply to our case because our assumptions are different. In particular, here, data omission depends on the model. However, the general principle of modeling missing data and taking into account these models in the inference process, can be applied. Let us attempt to do that by explicitly representing the portion of the likelihood over the missing, or to use better terms, *unexplained* or *unaccounted* data of the jth operator, by a dedicated term, denoted r^j. Let us also define a *completion* of O_p^j, a subprogram that explains the unaccounted data.

Definition 1. *A completion C of O_p^j is a program that completes O_p^j for the unaccounted data, when $R^j(Q_i)$ is false, such that the operator once completed is as follows*

$$O_{p,C}^j(A_i|Q_i) = \text{if } R^j(Q_i) \text{ then } \begin{cases} p, & \text{if } A_i = A_{n+1} \\ 1-p, & \text{otherwise} \end{cases} \tag{17}$$
$$\text{else } C(A_i|Q_i)$$

The likelihood given the operator completed is

$$l_p^j = p^{m^j}(1-p)^{n^j-m^j}r^j \tag{18}$$

where the binomial term account for the likelihood of the explained data, and r^j accounts for the likelihood of the unexplained data, more specifically

$$r^j = \prod_{i \leq n \,\wedge\, \neg R^j(Q_i)} C^j(A_i|Q_i) \tag{19}$$

where C^j is the underlying completion of O_p^j. One may notice that r^j does not depends on p. Such assumption tremendously simplifies the analysis and is somewhat reasonable to make. We generally assume that the completion of the model is independent on its pre-existing part. By replacing the likelihood in Eq. 11 by Eq. 18 we obtain

$$\hat{cdf}(A_{n+1}|Q_{n+1})(x) = \sum_j a_0^j \int_0^x f_p p^{m^j}(1-p)^{n^j-m^j}r^j dp \tag{20}$$

Choosing a Beta distribution as the prior of f_p simplifies the equation as the posterior remains a Beta distribution

$$f_p = f(p; \alpha, \beta) \tag{21}$$

where f is the pdf of the Beta distribution as defined in Eq. 3. Usual priors are Bayes' with $\alpha = 1$ and $\beta = 1$, Haldane's with $\alpha = 0$ and $\beta = 0$ and Jeffreys' with $\alpha = \frac{1}{2}$ and $\beta = \frac{1}{2}$. The latter is probably the most accepted due to being *uninformative* in some sense [10]. We do not need to commit to a particular one at that point and let the parameters α and β free, giving us

$$\hat{cdf}(A_{n+1}|Q_{n+1})(x) = \sum_j a_0^j \int_0^x \frac{p^{\alpha-1}(1-p)^{\beta-1}}{\mathrm{B}(\alpha,\beta)} p^{m^j}(1-p)^{n^j-m^j}r^j dp \tag{22}$$

r^j can be moved out of the integral and the constant $B(\alpha, \beta)$ can be ignored on the ground that our estimate will require normalization anyway

$$c\hat{d}f(A_{n+1}|Q_{n+1})(x) \propto \sum_j a_0^j r^j \int_0^x p^{m^j+\alpha-1}(1-p)^{n^j-m^j+\beta-1} dp \qquad (23)$$

$\int_0^x p^{m^j+\alpha-1}(1-p)^{n^j-m^j+\beta-1} dp$ is the incomplete Beta function with parameters $m^j + \alpha$ and $n^j - m^j + \beta$, thus

$$c\hat{d}f(A_{n+1}|Q_{n+1})(x) \propto \sum_j a_0^j r^j B(x; m^j + \alpha, n^j - m^j + \beta) \qquad (24)$$

Using the regularized incomplete beta function we obtain

$$c\hat{d}f(A_{n+1}|Q_{n+1})(x) \propto \sum_j a_0^j r^j I_x(m^j + \alpha, n^j - m^j + \beta) B(m^j + \alpha, n^j - m^j + \beta) \qquad (25)$$

As I_x is the cumulative distribution function of O^j (Eq. 16), we finally get

$$c\hat{d}f(A_{n+1}|Q_{n+1})(x) \propto \sum_j a_0^j r^j cdf_{O^j}(x) B(m^j + \alpha, n^j - m^j + \beta) \qquad (26)$$

We have expressed our cumulative distribution function estimate as an averaging of the cumulative distribution functions of the operators. This gives us an estimate that predicts to what extend S holds for a new question and how much confidence we have in that prediction.

However, we still need to address r^j, the likelihood of the unaccounted data. In theory, the right way to model r^j would be to consider all possible completions of the jth operator, but that is intractable. One would be tempted to simply ignore r^j, however, as we have already observed in some preliminary experiments, this gives an unfair advantage to rules that have a lot of unexplained data, and thus make them more prone to overfitting. This is true even in spite of the fact that such rules naturally exhibit more uncertainty due to carrying less evidence.

4.5 Perfectly Explaining Unaccounted Data

Instead we attempt to consider the most prominent completions. For now we consider completions that perfectly explain the unaccounted data. Moreover, to simplify further, we assume that unaccounted answers are entirely determined by their corresponding questions. This is generally not true, the same question may relate to different answers. But under such assumptions r^j becomes 1. This may seem equivalent to ignoring r^j unless the complexity of the completion is taken into account. Meaning, we must consider not only the complexity of the rule but also the complexity of its completion. Unfortunately calculating that complexity is intractable. To work around that we estimate it as function of the length of the unexplained data. Specifically, we suggest as prior

$$a_0^j = 2^{-K(O^j) - v_j^{(1-c)}} \qquad (27)$$

where $K(O^j)$ is the Kolmogorov complexity of the jth operator (the length of its corresponding rule in bits), v_j is the length of its unaccounted data, and c is a *compressability* parameter. If $c = 0$ then the unaccounted data are incompressible. If $c = 1$ then the unaccounted data can be compressed to a single bit. It is a very crude heuristic and is not parameter free, but it is simple and computationally lightweight. When applied to experiments, not described here due to their early stage nature and the space limitation of the paper, a value of $c = 0.5$ was actually shown to be somewhat satisfactory.

5   Conclusion

We have introduced a specialization of Solomonoff Operator Induction over operators with the particularities of being partial and modeled by Beta distributions. A second order probability estimate to predict new data, as well as capturing the uncertainty of such prediction, has been derived. While doing so we have uncovered an interesting problem, how to account for partial operators in the estimate. This problem appears to have no obvious solution, is manifestly under-addressed by the research community, and yet important in practice. Although the solution we provide is very lacking (crudely estimating the Kolmogorov complexity of a perfect completion) we hope that it provides some initial ground for experimentation and motivates further research. Even though, ultimately, it is expected that this problem might be hard enough to require some form of meta-learning [3], improvements in the heuristic by, for instance, considering completions reusing available models that do explain some unaccounted data could help.

Experiments using this estimate are currently being carried out in the context of enabling inference control meta-learning within the OpenCog framework and will be the subject of future publications.

References

1. Abourizk, S., Halpin, D., Wilson, J.: Fitting beta distributions based on sample data. J. Constr. Eng. Manag. **120**, 288–305 (1994)
2. Goertzel, B.: Toward a formal characterization of real-world general intelligence. In: Proceedings of 3rd International Conference on Artificial General Intelligence (2010)
3. Goertzel, B.: Probabilistic growth and mining of combinations: a unifying meta-algorithm for practical general intelligence. In: Steunebrink, B., Wang, P., Goertzel, B. (eds.) AGI -2016. LNCS (LNAI), vol. 9782, pp. 344–353. Springer, Cham (2016). https://doi.org/10.1007/978-3-319-41649-6_35
4. Goertzel, B., et al.: Speculative scientific inference via synergetic combination of probabilistic logic and evolutionary pattern recognition. In: Bieger, J., Goertzel, B., Potapov, A. (eds.) AGI 2015. LNCS (LNAI), vol. 9205, pp. 80–89. Springer, Cham (2015). https://doi.org/10.1007/978-3-319-21365-1_9
5. Goertzel, B., Ikle, M., Goertzel, I.F., Heljakka, A.: Probabilistic Logic Networks. Springer, US (2009)

6. Hoeting, J.A., Madigan, D., Raftery, A.E., Volinsky, C.T.: Bayesian model averaging: a tutorial. Statist. Sci. **14**(4), 382–417 (1999)
7. Hutter, M.: Optimality of universal Bayesian sequence prediction for general loss and alphabet. J. Mach. Learn. Res. **4**, 971–1000 (2003)
8. Ikle, M., Goertzel, B.: Probabilistic quantifier logic for general intelligence: an indefinite probabilities approach. In: First International Conference on Artificial General Intelligence, pp. 188–199 (2008)
9. Solomonoff, R.J.: Three kinds of probabilistic induction: universal distributions and convergence theorems. Comput. J. **51**, 566–570 (2008)
10. Jeffreys, H.: An invariant form for the prior probability in estimation problems. Proc. Royal Soc. London Ser. A **186**, 453–461 (1946)
11. Li, M., Vitanyi, P.: An Introduction to Kolmogorov Complexity and Its Applications. Springer, New York (1997). https://doi.org/10.1007/978-1-4757-2606-0
12. Schafer, J.L., Graham, J.W.: Missing data: our view of the state of the art. Psychol. Methods **7**, 147–177 (2002)
13. Weisstein, E.W.: Regularized beta function. From MathWorld–A Wolfram Web Resource. http://mathworld.wolfram.com/RegularizedBetaFunction.html. Accessed 20 Apr 2018

Solving Tree Problems with Category Theory

Rafik Hadfi[(✉)]

School of Psychological Sciences, Faculty of Medicine Nursing and Health Sciences,
Monash University, Melbourne, Australia
rafik.hadfi@monash.edu

Abstract. Artificial Intelligence (AI) has long pursued models, theories, and techniques to imbue machines with human-like general intelligence. Yet even the currently predominant data-driven approasches in AI seem to be lacking humans' unique ability to solve wide ranges of problems. This situation begs the question of the existence of principles that underlie general problem-solving capabilities. We approach this question through the mathematical formulation of analogies across different problems and solutions. We focus in particular on problems that could be represented as tree-like structures. Most importantly, we adopt a category-theoretic approach in formalising tree problems as categories, and in proving the existence of equivalences across apparently unrelated problem domains. We prove the existence of a functor between the category of tree problems and the category of solutions. We also provide a weaker version of the functor by quantifying equivalences of problem categories using a metric on tree problems.

Keywords: Artificial general intelligence · Problem solving
Analogy-making · Category theory · Functor · Decision tree
Maze problem · Transfer learning

1 Introduction

General problem-solving has long been one of main goals of Artificial Intelligence (AI) since the early days of Computer Science. Many theories on generality and problem-solving have been proposed and yet the task of building machines that could achieve human-level intelligence is still in its infancy.

Humans are good at solving problems because they can reason about unknown situations. They are capable of asking hypothetical questions that can effectively be answered through analogical reasoning. Analogical reasoning is when concepts from one space are mapped to the concepts of another space after noticing structural similarities or equivalences between the two. For instance, having observed how a clay vase is being moulded, one could learn to mentally manipulate other clay objects. Similarly, learning to solve one puzzle could be accelerated if one could relate to previously mastered puzzle games.

M. Iklé et al. (Eds.): AGI 2018, LNAI 10999, pp. 62–76, 2018.
https://doi.org/10.1007/978-3-319-97676-1_7

Solving problems using analogies requires the ability to identify relationships amongst complex objects and transform new objects accordingly. In its canonical form, an analogy is usually described as <<A is to B as C is to D>>. Despite their intuitive appeal, analogies do have the drawback that, if the structure is not shared across the full problem space, we might end up with a distorted understanding of a new problem than if we had not tried to think analogically about it. It is therefore crucial to find a formalism that translates problems into the representation that allows comparisons and transformations on its structures.

Category Theory is a powerful mathematical language capable of expressing equivalences of structures and analogies. It was introduced in 1942–45 by Saunders MacLane and Samuel Eilenberg as part of their work on algebraic topology [9]. What seemed to be an abstract theory that had no content turned out to be a very flexible and powerful language. The theory has become indispensable in many areas of mathematics, such as algebraic geometry, representation theory, topology, and many others. Category Theory has also been used in modelling the semantics of cognitive neural systems [13], in describing certain aspects of cognition such as systematicity [28,29], in formalising artificial perception and cognition [3,23], and in advancing our understanding of brain function [31] and human consciousness [37].

In the present work, we propose a category-theoretic formalism for a class of problems represented as arborescences [11]. We strongly think that many decision-making and knowledge representation problems are amenable to such structures [8,32]. The category-theoretic approach to general problem-solving comes as a qualitative alternative to the currently dominant quantitative, data-driven approaches that rely on Machine Learning and Data Science. We aim at identifying the types or common classes in tree problems using category equivalences. The number of types should be much smaller compared to what data-driven approaches to problem-solving usually yield. It should be easier to identify a new situation by its own type and apply the right transformations to obtain the desired solution. Such transformations will be formalised using functors and aim at computing the solutions to the tree problem in multiple ways.

The main contributions of the paper are twofold. We formalise some the most common problems in AI literature in the most generic way possible and give them an algebraic structure suitable to category theory and its functor-based formulation of analogies. The second contribution is the way we combine the problems and their solutions into two distinct categories, allowing us to define equivalence classes on problems regardless of the existence of solutions.

The paper is structured as following. In the next section, we review some of the previous work on general problem-solving and the usages of analogy. In Sect. 3, we introduce the class of problems we are interested in. In Sect. 4, we show how to translate such problems to a category-theoretic representation. In Sect. 5, we show how solutions could be formalised based on functors and category equivalences. Finally, we conclude and highlight the future directions.

2   Related Work

General problem-solving is not new in Artificial Intelligence and many authors have proposed guidelines for this line of search [20, 34]. One of the earliest theories of general problem-solving was proposed in [26] and relied on recursive decompositions of large goals into subgoals while separating problem content from solution strategies. The approach became later known as the cognitive architecture SOAR [19] and is amongst the first attempts to a unified theory of cognition [25]. In the context of universal intelligence, [14] proposed a general theory that combines Solomonoff induction with sequential decision theory, and was implemented as a reinforcement learning agent called AIXI. The downside is that AIXI is incomputable and relies on approximations [38]. Other approaches to generalised intelligence rely on transferring skills or knowledge across problem domains [35, 36]. For instance, [4, 5] focuses on partially observable non-deterministic problems (PONDP) and provides a way of transferring a policy from a PONDP to another one with the same structure.

The ability to generalise across different situations has long been the hall-mark of analogy-making. One of the first attempts to formalise analogies was through the concept of elementary equivalence in logical Model Theory [17]. Most recently, deep convolutional neural networks (CNN) have enabled us to solve visual analogies by transforming a query image according to an example pair of related images [21, 33]. The approach does not exploit the regularities between the transformations and seems to follow one particular directed path in the commutative diagram of the problem if expressed in category-theoretic terms.

As mentioned in the introduction, Category Theory constitutes an elegant framework that can help conceptualise the essence of general problem-solving, and abstract how the different paradigms of AI implement the solutions algorithmically. The practical component of the theory is that it can redefine the algorithms in terms of functors (or natural transformations) across problem and solution categories. However, we think that the real challenge resides in the ability to implement the type of functors that can systematically map input (problem) to output (solution) in a manner similar to what is done in Machine Learning. Although the category-theoretic approach to general problem-solving is still at an early stage of development, the work of [15] can be considered as a recipe for a scalable and systematic usage of functors, albeit in the area of Machine Learning. Particularly, the author defines a training algorithm as a monoid homomorphism from a free monoid representing the data set, to a monoid representing the model we want to train [16]. Most instances of such "homomorphic trainer" type class are related to statistics or Machine Learning, but the class is much more general than that, and could for instance be used to approximate NP-complete problems [16]. This approach is shown to improve the learning scalability in the sense that it starts by learning the problem independently on small subsets of the data before merging the solutions together within one single round of communication.

The more general framework of [1] lays the foundation of a formal description of general intelligence. This framework is based on the claim that cognitive systems learn and solve problems by trial and error [2]. The authors introduce cognitive categories, which are categories with exactly one morphism between any two objects. The objects of the categories are interpreted as states and morphisms as transformations between those states. Cognitive problems are reduced to the specification of two objects in a cognitive category: the current state of the system and the desired state. Cognitive systems transform the target system by means of generators and evaluators. Generators realise cognitive operations over a system by grouping morphisms, while evaluators group objects as a way to generalise current and desired states to partially defined states.

For our approach to general problem-solving to work, an agent should not only be capable of solving the problems specific to its native ecological niche, but should also be capable of transcending its current conceptual framework and manipulate the class of the problems itself. This would allow the agent to solve new problems once deployed in new contexts that share some equivalences with the previously encountered contexts. Generalising across different contexts could be achieved for instance using natural transformations mapping functors between known categories of problems and solutions to new ones.

The capacity of the agent to represent and manipulate common structural relationships across equivalently cognizable problem domains is known in cognitive sciences as systematicity [10]. In general, it is an equivalence relation over cognitive capacities, a kind of generalisation over cognitive abilities. The problem with systematicity is that it fails in explaining why cognition is organised into particular groups of cognitive capacities. The author in [27] hypotheses that the failures of systematicity arise from a cost/benefit trade-off associated with employing one particular universal construction. A universal construction is defined as the necessary and sufficient conditions relating collections of mathematically structured objects. Most importantly, the author proposes adjunction as universal construction for trading the costs and benefits that come from the interaction of a cognitive system with its environment, and where general intelligence involves the effective exploitation of this trade-off.

One distinction between our approach and that of [27] is that we do not consider the interaction between the agent and the environment for which the adjunction is defined. We only focus on the functor mapping problems to solutions and do not define its adjoint functor. For our goal of general-problem solving, and given the way we define the problem and solution categories, it would not make much sense to look for a problem given its solutions.

3   Tree Problems

3.1   Definition

We define tree problems as an umbrella term for a class of problems in the area of problem-solving in general and in combinatorial optimisation in particular. While tree problems may be formulated in a number of ways, they all require a rooted arborescent interconnection of objects and an objective function. Given a directed rooted tree with predefined edge labels and a set of terminal vertices, the corresponding tree problem possesses at most one solution. The solution corresponds to a path from the root of the tree to one of its terminal nodes. A problem $\mathcal{P}$ is formally represented by the tuple $T_{\mathcal{P}} = (T, \mathcal{L}, \mathcal{A})$, defined as following.

- The tuple $T = (r, V, E)$ is a labelled tree with root r, a set of nodes V, and a set of edges $E \subseteq V \times V$. The set V is partitioned into a set of internal nodes I and a set of terminal nodes Ω. We note $V(T)$ and $E(T)$ as shorthands for the vertices and edges of the tree T.
- The tuple $\mathcal{L} = (\mathcal{L}_V, \mathcal{L}_E)$ defines the "labelling" functions $\mathcal{L}_V : V \mapsto \mathbb{R}^n$ and $\mathcal{L}_E : E \mapsto \mathbb{R}^m$. The numbers n and m are respectively the numbers of vertice and edge features.
- The algorithm $\mathcal{A} : T \mapsto S_{\mathcal{P}}$ implements an objective function that assigns solution $S_{\mathcal{P}}$ to T.

Such tree-based formalism is meant to encode a number of decision problems in the most generic fashion. Such problems could share the same structure as it is defined by the tree and differ only in the labels or features that are assigned to the nodes and edges. In the following, we choose to reduce the space of tree structures and restrict our problems to problems that could be represented as binary trees. It is in fact possible to translate n-ary representations to binary representations by transforming branchings like $\prec\!\!\!-$ into $\prec\!\!\!\prec$ and altering the edge lengths.

In the following, a solution $S_{\mathcal{P}}$ to problem $\mathcal{P}$ will be encoded as a binary vector of the form $S_{\mathcal{P}} \in \{0, 1\}^n$. That is, $S_{\mathcal{P}}$ assigns 1 to its ith entry if edge e_i is in the solution path. Note that it is possible to imagine solutions that do not possess any problem, but we do not address such cases.

3.2   Characteristic Matrix of a Tree Problem

To find a canonical characterisation of a tree problem we start by defining $\mathbb{T}$ as the set of all rooted trees with k terminal nodes ($|\Omega| = k$). We say that trees $T_a, T_b \in \mathbb{T}$ have the same labeled shape or topology if the set of all the partitions of Ω admitted by the internal edges of T_a is identical to that of T_b, and we write $T_a \simeq T_b$. We say that $T_a = T_b$ if they have the same topology and the same labelling: $\mathcal{L}_{E(T_a)} = \mathcal{L}_{E(T_b)}$. For any $T \in \mathbb{T}$, we define $\mu_{i,j}^1$ as the number of edges on the path from the root to the most recent common ancestor of terminal nodes i and j and $\mu_{i,j}^\ell$ as the ℓth feature of this edge, and set p_i^ℓ as the value of the ℓth feature corresponding to the pendant edge to tip i. Given all pairs of terminal nodes Ω, we define the characteristic matrix of T as in (1).

$$M(T) = \begin{pmatrix} \mu_{1,2}^1 & \mu_{1,3}^1 & \cdots & \mu_{i,j}^1 & \cdots & \mu_{k-1,k}^1 & 1 & \cdots & 1 \\ \mu_{1,2}^2 & \mu_{1,3}^2 & \cdots & \mu_{i,j}^2 & \cdots & \mu_{k-1,k}^2 & p_1^2 & \cdots & p_k^2 \\ \vdots & \vdots & \ddots & \vdots & & \vdots & & \ddots & \vdots \\ \mu_{1,2}^\ell & \mu_{1,3}^\ell & \cdots & \mu_{i,j}^\ell & \cdots & \mu_{k-1,k}^\ell & p_1^\ell & \cdots & p_k^\ell \\ \vdots & \vdots & \ddots & \vdots & & \vdots & & \ddots & \vdots \\ \mu_{1,2}^{m+1} & \mu_{1,3}^{m+1} & \cdots & \mu_{i,j}^{m+1} & \cdots & \mu_{k-1,k}^{m+1} & p_1^{m+1} & \cdots & p_k^{m+1} \end{pmatrix}_{m+1 \times \binom{k}{2}+k} \tag{1}$$

The first row of (1) captures the tree topology and the other rows capture both the topology and the m features encoded by $\mathcal{L}_E : E \mapsto \mathbb{R}^m$. The feature vectors $M_{\ell \geq 2}$ are in fact inspired from the vectors of cophenetic values [6]. Note that we have $m+1 < \binom{k}{2}+k$ since the number of edges of the tree usually exceeds the number of features that characterise most basic tree problems. For instance, such features are usually restricted to topology, length, probability, or cost. We finally take the convex combination of the vectors to obtain the characteristic function (2).

$$\phi_\lambda(T) = \lambda M \tag{2}$$

The characteristic form $\phi_\lambda(T)$ is parameterised by $\lambda \in [0,1]^{m+1}$ with $\sum_{j=1}^{m+1} \lambda_j = 1$. The elements of λ specify the extent to which different tree features contribute in characterising the tree T. In this sense, one feature may dominate other features as the elements of λ increase from 0 to 1.

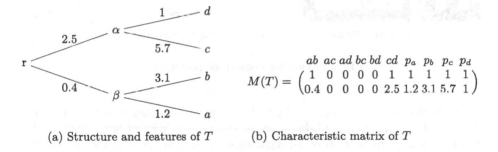

(a) Structure and features of T (b) Characteristic matrix of T

Fig. 1. Tree problem and its matrix representation

For instance, the tree in Fig. 1a is characterised by its topology and one feature corresponding to the length of its branches. The corresponding characteristic matrix $M(T)$ is given in Fig. 1b. Note that the matrix $M(T)$ is constructed from the mappings defined by $\mathcal{L}_{E(T)}$. For instance, the first column of $M(T)$ is in fact $\mathcal{L}_{E(T)}((r,\beta)) = (1,0.4)$.

3.3   Instances of Tree Problems

It is possible to find many instances of problems in AI that are reducible to tree structures. For instance, simply connected mazes are mazes that contain no loops or disconnected components. Such mazes are equivalent to a rooted tree in the sense that if one pulled and stretched out the paths in the maze in a continuous way, the result could be made to resemble a tree [24]. Mathematically, the existence of a continuous deformation between the maze and a rooted tree means that they are homeomorphic. For two spaces to be homeomorphic we only need a continuous mapping with a continuous inverse function. A homeomorphism or topological isomorphism is a continuous function between topological spaces that has a continuous inverse function. The existence of such mapping is what will be exploited in our approach by moving between problems' space and solutions' space in a well-principled manner. Instead of working directly on complex structures like mazes, one could convert them to trees, and then study the existence of homomorphisms [7] and other transformations.

For example, Fig. 2 illustrates a maze search problem and its homologous decision tree problem. In Fig. 2a, $\mathcal{L}_E : E \mapsto \mathbb{R}$ assigns lengths to the edges of the tree T, and $\mathcal{L}_V : \Omega \mapsto \mathbb{R}$ assigns outcomes to the terminal nodes Ω comprised of goal node(s) and dead-ends.

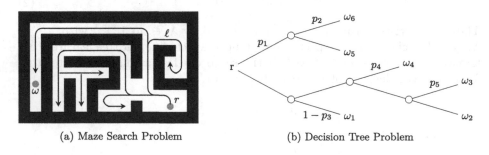

(a) Maze Search Problem   (b) Decision Tree Problem

Fig. 2. Two homeomorphic problems

In the decision tree of Fig. 2b, $\mathcal{L}_V : \Omega \mapsto \mathbb{R}$ maps terminal nodes to outcomes and $\mathcal{L}_E : E \mapsto [0, 1]$ maps sub-branches to the probabilities of being chosen. An example of implementation of an algorithm $\mathcal{A}$ for the decision tree of Fig. 2b could be defined as $\mathcal{A} : T \mapsto \mathscr{P}(E)$ with $\mathscr{P}(E)$ being the set of all paths of T. For instance, if the objective function is to find the most probable path in the tree, then the solution could be expressed as in (3).

$$\pi^* = \underset{\pi \in \{\pi_1, \ldots, \pi_6\}}{\arg\max} \sum_{e \in \pi} \log \mathbb{P}(e) \tag{3}$$

with $\mathbb{P}(e) = \mathcal{L}_E(e)$ being the probability of edge e. Other formulations of (3) could include for instance the preferences over the edges and define the goal as maximising some expected value.

4 Translating Tree Problems to Categories

4.1 Overview of Category Theory

In the following, we give a short introduction to Category Theory and the components relevant to the topic of general problem-solving as previously introduced.
For a thorough and in-depth explanation of Category Theory from a mathematical point of view, the reader is advised to use the classical book [22], and to
[30, 39] for the Computer Science point of view.

A category $\mathcal{C}$ is a collection of objects and a collection of arrows called morphisms. It is formally defined as following.

1. A class of objects $Ob(\mathcal{C})$. For $X \in Ob(\mathcal{C})$, we can also write $X \in \mathcal{C}$.
2. For every objects $X, Y \in Ob(\mathcal{C})$, the class $Mor_{\mathcal{C}}(X, Y)$ defines the class of
   morphisms from X to Y. For $f \in Mor_{\mathcal{C}}$, one may also write $f : X \to Y$.
   For any objects $X, Y, Z \in Ob(\mathcal{C})$, a composition map $\circ_{X,Y,Z} : Mor_{\mathcal{C}}(Y, Z) \times$
   $Mor_{\mathcal{C}}(X, Y) \to Mor_{\mathcal{C}}(X, Z)$, $(f, g) \mapsto f \circ g$ satisfies:
   (a) Associativity: $(f \circ g) \circ h = f \circ (g \circ h)$
   (b) Identity: For each $X \in Ob(\mathcal{C})$, there is a morphism $1_X \in Mor_{\mathcal{C}}(X, X)$,
       called the unit morphism, such that $1_X \circ f = f$ and $g \circ 1_X = g$ for any
       f, g for which composition holds.

Another useful category-theoretic construct is the notion of (covariant) func-
tor, which is a morphism of categories. Given two categories $\mathcal{C}$ and $\mathcal{C}'$, a functor
$F : \mathcal{C} \to \mathcal{C}'$ is made of

1. A function mapping objects to objects $F : Ob(\mathcal{C}) \to Ob(\mathcal{C}')$.
2. For any pair of objects $X, Y \in \mathcal{C}$, we have $F : Mor_{\mathcal{C}}(X, Y) \to$
   $Mor_{\mathcal{C}'}(F(X), F(Y))$ with the natural requirements of identity and composition:
   (a) Identity: $F(1_X) = 1_{F(X)}$
   (b) Composition: $F(f \circ g) = F(f) \circ F(g)$

Functors will be later used to formalise analogies across problem and solution
categories.

4.2 Problems as Categories

In Sect. 3.2, we have shown that any tree T_a could be encoded as a matrix M_a. In
Theorem 1, we show that tree problems are in fact a category and we name it $\mathcal{T}$.

Theorem 1. *Tree problems define a category $\mathcal{T}$.*

Proof. In order for $\mathcal{T}$ to be a category, we need to characterise its objects $Ob(\mathcal{T})$,
morphisms $Mor_{\mathcal{T}}$, and the laws of composition that govern $Mor_{\mathcal{T}}$.

- Objects: Since each tree is translatable to its characteristic matrix, we will
  take $Ob(\mathcal{T})$ to be the set of matrices that encode the trees.

- Morphisms: One analytical way of distinguishing between two tree problems is through the existence of a transformation that maps one to the other. These transformations, if they exist, are the morphisms of the category $\mathcal{T}$ that we want to characterise. That is, we need to define the morphisms and their laws of composition, and show that the identity and associativity of morphisms hold. To define $Mor_\mathcal{T}$, we define a morphism between two tree matrices $X_{(m,n)}$ and $Y_{(m,n)}$ as the transformation $A_{(n,n)}$ such as $A_{(n,n)}X_{(n,m)}^T = Y_{(n,m)}^T$. Since the number of tree edges usually exceeds the number of features $(n > m)$, we need to find the generalised inverse of $X_{(n,m)}^T$ that satisfies (4).

$$A_{(n,n)} = Y_{(n,m)}^T (X_{(n,m)}^T)^{-1}$$
$$= Y_{(n,m)}^T X_{(m,n)}^{-1} \tag{4}$$

To obtain X^{-1}, we use the singular value decomposition of X into P, Q and Δ, as in (5).

$$X = P\Delta\, Q^T \tag{5}$$

where P is an $n \times r$ semiorthogonal matrix, r is the rank of X, Δ is an $r \times r$ diagonal matrix with positive diagonal elements called the singular values of X, and Q is an $m \times r$ semiorthogonal matrix. The Moore-Penrose pseudoinverse [12] of X, denoted by X^+, is the unique $m \times n$ matrix defined by $X^+ = Q\Delta^{-1}P^T$. The final transformation matrix $A_{(n,n)}$ is therefore computed as (6).

$$A = YQ\Delta^{-1}P^T \tag{6}$$

The existence of X^+ and A is guaranteed by the nature of the feature matrices and the fact that $m < \binom{k}{2} + k - 1$, with k being the number of terminal nodes. In the following, we will be using morphisms and matrix transformation interchangeably. After defining the morphisms of $\mathcal{T}$, we prove that the composition laws within $\mathcal{T}$ hold.

- Composition: Let $f, g \in Mor_\mathcal{T}$ with $f : T_\mathcal{P} \to T_{\mathcal{P}'}$ and $g : T_{\mathcal{P}'} \to T_{\mathcal{P}''}$. Given matrices A_f and A_g of f and g, and matrices $M_\mathcal{P}$, $M_{\mathcal{P}'}$ and $M_{\mathcal{P}''}$ of $T_\mathcal{P}$, $T_{\mathcal{P}'}$ and $T_{\mathcal{P}''}$, we have (7).

$$M_{\mathcal{P}''} = A_g M_{\mathcal{P}'} \tag{7a}$$
$$= A_g(A_f M_\mathcal{P}) \tag{7b}$$
$$= (A_g A_f)M_\mathcal{P} \tag{7c}$$
$$= A_{g\circ f}M_\mathcal{P} \tag{7d}$$
$$= A_h M_\mathcal{P} \tag{7e}$$

It follows that there exists a morphism h such that $h : T_\mathcal{P} \to T_{\mathcal{P}''}$. Therefore, the composition of morphisms holds and we have (8).

$$\forall T_\mathcal{P}, T_{\mathcal{P}'}, T_{\mathcal{P}''} \in Ob(\mathcal{T})\ \ Mor_\mathcal{T}(T_\mathcal{P}, T_{\mathcal{P}'}) \times Mor_\mathcal{T}(T_{\mathcal{P}'}, T_{\mathcal{P}''}) \mapsto Mor_\mathcal{T}(T_\mathcal{P}, T_{\mathcal{P}''}) \tag{8}$$

The laws of composition need to obey the following.

1. Associativity: Let $f, g, h \in Mor_T$ and their corresponding matrix transformations A_f, A_g and A_h. Since matrix multiplication is associative $(A_f A_g)A_h = A_f(A_g A_h)$, we have $(f \circ g) \circ h = f \circ (g \circ h)$.
2. Identity: Let $f : T_P \rightarrow T_{P'}$ be a tree morphism and its characteristic matrix transformation A_f that maps M_P to $M_{P'}$. Let $1_{T_P} : T_P \rightarrow T_{P'}$ be an identity morphism. It must hold that $1_{T_{P'}} \circ f = f = f \circ 1_{T_P}$ where 1_{T_P} creates a trivial representation of T_P containing the same structure and features. Similarly, $1_{T_{P'}}$ creates a trivial representation of $T_{P'}$. Hence, there exists an identity morphism for all $Obj(T)$. This translates to the existence of identity matrix A_f such as $A_f \times M_P = M_P$

T is therefore a category and we can illustrate it with the commutative diagram of Fig. 3a.

4.3   Solutions as Categories

Similarly to the tree problems category, Theorem 2 defines the solutions as the category S.

Theorem 2. *The solutions to tree problems define a category S.*

Proof. The proof is similar to the proof of Theorem 1. The difference is that the elements of $Obj(T)$ are $m \times n$ matrices while the elements of $Obj(S)$ are $1 \times n$ matrices since the solutions are binary vectors in $\{0, 1\}^n$. The commutative diagram of S is shown in Fig. 3b.

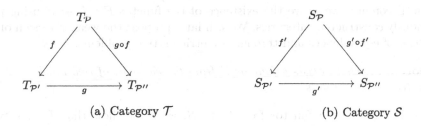

(a) Category T (b) Category S

Fig. 3. Commutative diagrams of categories T and S

5   Solving Problems Using Functors

Given problem and solution categories, it is possible to exploit analogies between old and new problems using functors. One could think of an analogy as a structure preserving map from the space of problems to the space of solutions, which rightfully translates to a functor. The analogy <<S' is to S as P' is to P>> can be rewritten as a curried sequence of objects to highlight the transformational aspect: $P \xrightarrow{f} P' \xRightarrow{\mathcal{F}} S \xrightarrow{\mathcal{F}f} S'$. If we know P, S, and P', and wish to learn about S', we could learn the functor $\mathcal{F} : P' \to S'$. Using the knowledge about P', how it relates to P, and the structure of $\mathcal{F}$, we can either use $\mathcal{F}(P')$ to further learn S' and how it relates to S or use $\mathcal{F}f$ to infer S' from S. The solution could be found in different ways and with different complexities [16], depending on how we traverse the commutative diagram. In the following, we propose to characterise the functor that maps category $\mathcal{T}$ to category $\mathcal{S}$.

5.1   Existence of Functors Between Problems and Solutions

Whenever we have a collection of problems, we want to be able to know how to relate them. Mapping problems to solutions requires a level of identification between the two. An isomorphism for instance is the type of strong identification between two categories. If two categories are isomorphic, then they are the same and perhaps differ only in notation. However, isomorphisms are in general rare and difficult to characterise. We can instead "weaken" the isomorphism by descending from isomorphism of categories to equivalence of categories, and eventually to adjunction of functors between categories [27]. This weakening holds in particular for our case of problems since some problems might not have solutions and vice versa. The concept of equivalence of categories is used to identify categories since it is weaker and more generic. We define it by a functor $F : \mathcal{T} \to \mathcal{S}$ which is an isomorphism of categories up to isomorphisms. If F is an equivalence of categories, then it induces a bijection between the classes of isomorphic objects of $\mathcal{T}$ and $\mathcal{S}$ even if F is not bijective on all the objects [22]. Thus the bijection $\mathcal{F}$ is defined as $\mathcal{F} : (\mathcal{T}/\simeq) \mapsto (\mathcal{S}/\simeq)$ and could mainly serve the purpose of identifying classes of problems and solutions as opposed to a one-to-one identification of the components of problems and solutions.

In Theorem 3, we prove the existence of the functor $F : \mathcal{T} \to \mathcal{S}$ using the previously constructed categories. We will later propose the weaker version of F in terms of equivalences and through a metric on tree problems.

Theorem 3. *There exists a functor F from the category of tree problems $\mathcal{T}$ to the category of solutions $\mathcal{S}$.*

Proof. For F to be a functor from $\mathcal{T}$ to $\mathcal{S}$, we must show that F preserves identity morphisms and composition of morphisms as introduced in Sect. 4.1.

1. Identity: Let $T_{\mathcal{P}} \in \mathcal{T}$ be given and let $1_{T_{\mathcal{P}}}$ be the identity morphism in $\mathcal{T}$ corresponding to $T_{\mathcal{P}}$. Let $1_{F(\mathcal{P})}$ be the identity morphism in $\mathcal{S}$ corresponding to $F(T_{\mathcal{P}})$. We need to show that $F(1_{T_{\mathcal{P}}}) = 1_{F(T_{\mathcal{P}})}$. In the category $\mathcal{T}$, the identity morphism $1_{T_{\mathcal{P}}}$ creates a trivial tree problem from an existing one. Similarly, in $\mathcal{S}$, the identity morphism $1_{F(T_{\mathcal{P}})}$ also creates a trivial structure from the same solution. The functor F maps the morphism $1_{T_{\mathcal{P}}} : T_{\mathcal{P}} \mapsto T_{\mathcal{P}}$ in $\mathcal{T}$ to $F(1_{T_{\mathcal{P}}}) : F(T_{\mathcal{P}}) \mapsto F(T_{\mathcal{P}})$ in $\mathcal{S}$.
   Therefore, $F(1_{T_{\mathcal{P}}}) = 1_{F(T_{\mathcal{P}})}$ and the functor F preserves identity morphisms.

2. Composition: Let $f, g \in Mor_T$ such that $f : T_P \mapsto T_{P'}$ and $g : T_{P'} \mapsto T_{P''}$. Let also $F(f), F(g) \in Mor_S$ be such that $F(f) : F(T_P) \mapsto T_{P'}$ and $F(g) : F(T_{P'}) \mapsto T_{P''}$. We need to show that $F(g \circ f) = F(g) \circ F(f)$. We have $F(g \circ f) = F(g(f(T_P))) = F(g(T_{P'})) = F(T_{P''})$ and $F(g) \circ F(f) = F(g(F(f(T_P)))) = F(g(F(T_{P'}))) = F(T_{P''})$.
Hence F preserves the composition of morphisms.

F is therefore a functor from T to S and has the commutative diagram of Fig. 4.

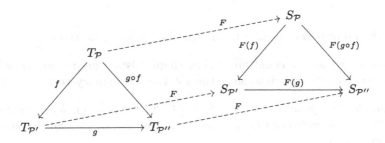

Fig. 4. Commutative diagram of the functor F

5.2 From Equivalence to Metric

The equivalences of categories of trees $(T/\simeq)$ define what can be identified as the level of similarities or analogy between the problems that they represent. Similarly, the equivalence of categories of solutions $(S/\simeq)$ defines the levels of similarities between solutions. If the tree $T_P \in Ob(T)$ is analogous to other trees $\{T_{P'}\}_{P' \neq P}$, it would be useful to find the "most" analogous ones, for instance to transfer knowledge between the closest ones [36]. This could be done by defining a distance that measures how analogous they are: the more analogous T_P and $T_{P'}$ are, the smaller $d(T_P, T_{P'})$ should be. We propose to construct such a distance on $Ob(T)$ and $Ob(S)$ to identify the objects more or less similar. Recall that by definition, a binary relation $\simeq$ is an equivalence relation if and only if it satisfies reflexivity, symmetry and transitivity. These conditions are satisfied by the equality relation $=$ and are "natural" to express what a notion of analogy should satisfy. In that way, equality can be viewed as a particular case of analogy. On the other hand, analogies, as formalised by the concept of equivalence relations, can be viewed as generalisation of equality.

5.3 Problem and Solution Metrics

A metric is the mathematical notion of distance that give structure and shape to a set of objects by forming a space. A function $d(T_P, T_{P'})$ is a tree problem metric if, for all $T_P, T_{P'} \in Ob(T)$:

1. Distances are non-negative: $d(T_P, T_{P'}) \geq 0$

2. Distance is equal to zero when trees are identical: $d(T_{\mathcal{P}}, T_{\mathcal{P}'}) = 0 \iff T_{\mathcal{P}} = T_{\mathcal{P}'}$
3. Distance is symmetric: $d(T_{\mathcal{P}}, T_{\mathcal{P}'}) = d(T_{\mathcal{P}'}, T_{\mathcal{P}})$
4. Distances satisfy the triangle inequality: $\forall T_{\mathcal{P}''} \in Ob(\mathcal{T})$, $d(T_{\mathcal{P}}, T_{\mathcal{P}'}) \leq d(T_{\mathcal{P}}, T_{\mathcal{P}''}) + d(T_{\mathcal{P}''}, T_{\mathcal{P}'})$

Now we can define the tree metric based on the characteristic function (2).

Theorem 4. *The function* $d_\lambda : Ob(\mathcal{T}) \times Ob(\mathcal{T}) \mapsto \mathbb{R}$ *given by* $d_\lambda(T_{\mathcal{P}}, T_{\mathcal{P}'}) = \|\phi_\lambda(T_{\mathcal{P}}) - \phi_{\lambda'}(T_{\mathcal{P}'})\|$ *is a metric on* $Ob(\mathcal{T})$, *with* $\|.\|$ *being the Euclidean distance and* $\lambda \in [0,1]^{m+1}$.

Proof. The proof is very similar to the one for phylogenetic trees [18].

In a similar way, we could prove that there exists a metric on the solution space. This case is more trivial since the solutions are binary vectors of $\{0,1\}^n$.

Theorem 5. *The function* $d : Ob(\mathcal{S}) \times Ob(\mathcal{S}) \mapsto \mathbb{R}$ *given by* $d(S_{\mathcal{P}}, S_{\mathcal{P}'}) = \|S_{\mathcal{P}} - S_{\mathcal{P}'}\|$ *is a metric on* $Ob(\mathcal{S})$, *with* $S_{\mathcal{P}}, S_{\mathcal{P}'} \in \{0,1\}^n$ *and* $\|.\|$ *being the Euclidean distance.*

The metrics can be used to measure how problems and solutions are relatable. This way of characterising the existence of functors allows us to find the most analogous known problem(s) to a given situation. Given a target problem P we could find the set $\{(P', S')\}_{P' \simeq P}$ of equivalent problems that were previously solved, find the convex transformation f that maps P' to P and compute S as $\mathcal{F}f(S')$. This transformation is the type of transfer of knowledge from past to new situations.

6   Conclusions

The paper proposes a category-theoretic approach that formalises problems that are represented as tree-like structures. The existence of equivalence relationships across the categories of problems and their corresponding categories of solutions is established using functors. Implementing the functors corresponds therefore to solving the problems through means of analogy.

The proposed formalism has yet to be tested on concrete instances of tree-like problems such as maze problems. The future direction is to characterise the functors as encoders in a way similar to [33] and learn the generalised solutions to different maze problem.

References

1. Arjonilla, F.J., Ogata, T.: General problem solving with category theory. arXiv preprint arXiv:1709.04825 (2017)
2. Arjonilla García, F.: A three-component cognitive theory. Master's thesis (2015)

3. Arzi-Gonczarowski, Z.: Perceive this as that-analogies, artificial perception, and category theory. Ann. Math. Artif. Intell. **26**(1–4), 215–252 (1999)
4. Bonet, B., Geffner, H.: Solving POMDPs: RTDP-Bel vs. point-based algorithms, pp. 641–1646 (2009)
5. Bonet, B., Geffner, H.: Policies that generalize: solving many planning problems with the same policy, vol. 15 (2015)
6. Cardona, G., Mir, A., Rosselló, F., Rotger, L., Sánchez, D.: Cophenetic metrics for phylogenetic trees, after sokal and rohlf. BMC Bioinform. **14**(1), 3 (2013)
7. Csikvári, P., Lin, Z.: Graph homomorphisms between trees. arXiv preprint arXiv:1307.6721 (2013)
8. Diuk, C., Schapiro, A., Córdova, N., Ribas-Fernandes, J., Niv, Y., Botvinick, M.: Divide and conquer: hierarchical reinforcement learning and task decomposition in humans. In: Baldassarre, G., Mirolli, M. (eds.) Computational and Robotic Models of the Hierarchical Organization of Behavior, pp. 271–291. Springer, Heidelberg (2013). https://doi.org/10.1007/978-3-642-39875-9_12
9. Eilenberg, S., MacLane, S.: General theory of natural equivalences. Trans. Am. Math. Soc. **58**, 231–294 (1945)
10. Fodor, J.A., Pylyshyn, Z.W.: Connectionism and cognitive architecture: a critical analysis. Cognition **28**(1–2), 3–71 (1988)
11. Gordon, G., McMahon, E.: A greedoid polynomial which distinguishes rooted arborescences. Proc. Am. Math. Soc. **107**(2), 287–298 (1989)
12. Greville, T.N.: Generalized inverses: theory and applications Adi Ben-Israel
13. Healy, M.J.: Category theory applied to neural modeling and graphical representations. In: Proceedings of the IEEE-INNS-ENNS International Joint Conference on Neural Networks, IJCNN 2000, vol. 3, pp. 35–40. IEEE (2000)
14. Hutter, M.: Universal Artificial Intelligence: Sequential Decisions Based on Algorithmic Probability. Springer, Heidelberg (2004)
15. Izbicki, M.: Algebraic classifiers: a generic approach to fast cross-validation, online training, and parallel training. In: International Conference on Machine Learning, pp. 648–656 (2013)
16. Izbicki, M.: Two monoids for approximating NP-complete problems (2013)
17. Keisler, H.J., Chang, C.C.: Model Theory, North-Holland, Amsterdam (1990)
18. Kendall, M., Colijn, C.: A tree metric using structure and length to capture distinct phylogenetic signals. arXiv preprint arXiv:1507.05211 (2015)
19. Laird, J.E.: The Soar cognitive architecture (2012)
20. Laird, J.E., Wray III, R.E.: Cognitive architecture requirements for achieving AGI. In: Proceedings of the Third Conference on Artificial General Intelligence, pp. 79–84 (2010)
21. Liao, J., Yao, Y., Yuan, L., Hua, G., Kang, S.B.: Visual attribute transfer through deep image analogy. arXiv preprint arXiv:1705.01088 (2017)
22. Mac Lane, S.: Categories for the Working Mathematician, vol. 5. Springer, New York (2013)
23. Magnan, F., Reyes, G.E.: Category theory as a conceptual tool in the study of cognition. In: The Logical Foundations of Cognition, pp. 57–90 (1994)
24. MAZEMASTERS: Maze to tree [online] (2007). https://www.youtube.com/watch?v=k1tSK5V1pds
25. Newell, A.: Unified theories of cognition and the role of soar. In: Michon, J.A., Akyürek, A. (eds.) Soar: A Cognitive Architecture in Perspective. Studies in Cognitive Systems, vol. 10, pp. 25–79. Springer, Dordrecht (1992). https://doi.org/10.1007/978-94-011-2426-3_3

26. Newell, A., Shaw, J.C., Simon, H.A.: Report on a general problem solving program. In: IFIP Congress, vol. 256, p. 64 (1959)
27. Phillips, S.: A general (category theory) principle for general intelligence: duality (adjointness). In: Everitt, T., Goertzel, B., Potapov, A. (eds.) AGI 2017. LNCS (LNAI), vol. 10414, pp. 57–66. Springer, Cham (2017). https://doi.org/10.1007/978-3-319-63703-7_6
28. Phillips, S., Wilson, W.H.: Categorial compositionality: a category theory explanation for the systematicity of human cognition. PLoS Comput. Biol. **6**(7), e1000858 (2010)
29. Phillips, S., Wilson, W.H.: Systematicity and a categorical theory of cognitive architecture: universal construction in context. Front. Psychol. **7**, 1139 (2016)
30. Pierce, B.C.: Basic Category Theory for Computer Scientists. MIT Press, Cambridge (1991)
31. Ramırez, J.D.G.: A new foundation for representation in cognitive and brain science: category theory and the hippocampus. Departamento de Automatica, Ingenierıa Electronica e Informatica Industrial Escuela Tecnica Superior de Ingenieros Industriales (2010)
32. Rasmussen, D.: Hierarchical reinforcement learning in a biologically plausible neural architecture (2014)
33. Reed, S.E., Zhang, Y., Zhang, Y., Lee, H.: Deep visual analogy-making. In: Advances in Neural Information Processing Systems, pp. 1252–1260 (2015)
34. Rosa, M., Feyereisl, J., Collective, T.G.: A framework for searching for general artificial intelligence. arXiv preprint arXiv:1611.00685 (2016)
35. Sharma, M., Holmes, M.P., Santamaría, J.C., Irani, A., Ram, A.: Transfer learning in real-time strategy games using hybrid CBR/RL
36. Taylor, M.E., Stone, P.: Transfer learning for reinforcement learning domains: a survey. J. Mach. Learn. Res. **10**, 1633–1685 (2009)
37. Tsuchiya, N., Taguchi, S., Saigo, H.: Using category theory to assess the relationship between consciousness and integrated information theory. Neurosci. Res. **107**, 1–7 (2016)
38. Veness, J., Ng, K.S., Hutter, M., Uther, W., Silver, D.: A monte-carlo AIXI approximation (2010)
39. Walters, R.F.C.: Categories and Computer Science. Cambridge University Press, Cambridge (1991)

Goal-Directed Procedure Learning

Patrick Hammer[1]([✉]) and Tony Lofthouse[2]

[1] Temple University, Philadelphia, USA
patham9@gmail.com
[2] Evolving Solutions, Andover, UK
tony.lofthouse@gmilab.com

Abstract. A novel method of Goal-directed Procedure Learning is presented that overcomes some of the drawbacks of the traditional approaches to planning and reinforcement learning. The necessary principles for acquiring goal-dependent behaviors, and the motivations behind this approach are explained. A concrete implementation exists in a Non-Axiomatic Reasoning System, OpenNARS, although we believe the findings may be generally applicable to other AGI systems.

Keywords: Goal-directed · Procedure learning · Preconditions
Motor-functions · Non-Axiomatic Reasoning System

1 Introduction

Acquiring procedural knowledge is generally concerned with representing the preconditions and consequences of actions. In traditional planning approaches [11], this knowledge is usually provided in advance, and the task is then to search for the most concise and complete plan that leads to the achievement of a certain goal, a desired end state. This approach can be modified to search for the plan that leads to the end state with the highest probability. The drawback to this approach is that the need to react to change of circumstance during the planning and execution process, as well as forming the preconditions and transition probabilities from experience, is not captured.

In Reinforcement Learning (RL) this problem is reduced to learning to act the right way in the currently observed situation, where "act the right way" is usually taken as the selection of the action with the maximum expected utility value [12]. Here, no explicit plan is generated, and no subgoal derivations happen. Instead the decision-making is only considering the currently observed state, whilst assuming it is a complete description of the current situation [12]. While being sufficient in applications where the system's behavior serves a single purpose, this treatment becomes insufficient when novel goals spontaneously appear or existing ones disappear [16]. That's clearly the case in many robotics applications, [7], and also, as many argue, in the human mind [4,9]. To improve the ability to adapt to changing circumstances, a change of goals should not

© Springer Nature Switzerland AG 2018
M. Iklé et al. (Eds.): AGI 2018, LNAI 10999, pp. 77–86, 2018.
https://doi.org/10.1007/978-3-319-97676-1_8

require re-learning the related situation-action mappings. Instead an AGI system should develop beliefs of the consequences of its actions in such a way, that when goals change, the actions that lead to the fulfillment of novel goals can be derived. This can be seen as an understanding of the environment in terms of how different outcomes can be achieved by the system, independently from what is currently "rewarded" or desired.

In this paper we present a method that combines the benefits of both traditional planning and RL, while eliminating some of the drawbacks of both approaches. As our approach is based on learning the preconditions and consequences of operations, there is no need to re-learn situation-action mappings when goals change, a major advantage. In our approach, each piece of procedural knowledge can be independently evaluated and suggests a certain operation in a certain context to realize a certain subgoal: solving "global" problems, using "local" decisions. So, different to traditional planning approaches, no complete plan is explicitly searched for, instead the individually evaluated pieces lead to a certain behavior, influenced by current goals and observations.

2   The Goal-Directed Procedure Learning Problem

We regard procedure learning as the process that forms procedural hypotheses, based on temporal patterns of events and operations that appear in the systems experience. A temporal pattern can be represented as $(A_1, ..., A_n)$, which is a sequence of n consecutive events or operations, each occurring at a certain discrete time-step. Here, events do not encode an entire state, just certain parts of it, such as temperature information coming from a sensory device, encoded by a composition of terms/IDs, called "Compound Term" (see [14]). Now, temporal patterns can become building blocks of hypotheses, which should capture useful regularities in the experience of a system. In general, a hypothesis can be defined as $A \Rightarrow B$, with a special case, where a procedural hypothesis can be defined as $(A, B) \Rightarrow C$ where A is an antecedent, B an operation and C a consequent. The antecedent can be considered as a precondition that, when followed by an operation, is believed to lead to the consequent. Additionally, with the inclusion of temporal constraints, hypotheses can be considered as predictive, such as $(A, B) /\!\!\Rightarrow C$, whereby they imply the occurrence time of the consequent to be in the future. Here, the precondition and consequent can be arbitrarily complex pattern compositions, while the behavior is usually an atomic, in the sense that it can be directly invoked. Additionally, the consequent often represents a goal or subgoal to realize. Furthermore each such hypothesis has a degree of certainty corresponding to the likelihood that the prediction will be confirmed when its precondition is fulfilled.

Given a goal $G!$, which a system wants to make as true as possible, how does it satisfy the goal? [15].

There are two approaches: via hypotheses formation through forward chaining, where helpful hypotheses are formed directly from pieces of knowledge, with observed patterns as special cases, and backward chaining, where a subgoal is derived from a goal and an existing piece of knowledge [15].

In the case where a hypothesis exists, for how to achieve $G!$ in the current context, usually a single backward chaining step to derive the operation as a subgoal, which can be directly executed, will be sufficient. Therefore, "executing a procedural hypothesis", means to perform a single backward inference leading to an operation, that can be executed.

Generally, problem-solving involves an inter-play between "chain" and "execute". That is, because when the system has no appropriate procedural hypothesis, that both predicts G and also has its preconditions currently met, then usually both chaining strategies will be necessary, to search and probe for a solution, a schema that can later be re-used [3]. The "chain" case requires creative but evidence-driven exploration of possibilities to deal with novel situations. This corresponds to finding a solution although no algorithm is known, as discussed in [15]. The "execute" case on the other hand requires the control mechanism to remember solutions to goals. This allows for faster response times to similar problems in the future and to make effective use of what has already been learned.

We believe that most of the things we do, such as driving a car, that increasingly begin to become more automatic, are due to a transition from the "chain" to the "execute" case [2]. A transition from the "novel" to the "usual" is something a systems control mechanism can and should effectively support. Furthermore, a control mechanism, will need to choose between multiple hypotheses which can satisfy a goal, to a different degree, for the current context. Therefore the formation, selection and testing of hypotheses are the main topics of this paper and each of these aspects will be described in detail below.

3   OpenNARS Considerations

A goal of this paper is to present our findings in as general a way as possible, so as to allow for the widest applicability as possible. Notwithstanding this goal, our methods, as presented in this paper, have a concrete implementation in the OpenNARS system. An explanation of some of the data structures and conceptual ideas will be of value in understanding the approaches outlined below. In particular, four aspects will be described at a relatively high level of abstraction, namely: evidence, budget, concepts, and bags. Detailed explanations of each of these can be found here [5,13,14].

Evidence. In NARS evidence is used to provide the truth of a belief, namely its certainty. It is defined as a (w_+, w_-) pair, where w_+ represents positive evidence, and w_- represents negative evidence, or alternatively as confidence c and frequency f tuple, where $f = \frac{w_+}{w_+ + w_-}$ and confidence is $c = \frac{w_+ + w_-}{k + w_+ + w_-}$, where k is a global personality parameter that indicates a global evidential horizon [6]. Evidence supports these principles:

- An item of evidence can only be used once for each statement.
- A record of evidence (a set), used in each derivation must be maintained, although this is only a partial record due to resource constraints, which is not an issue in practice.

- There can be positive and negative evidence for the same statement.
- Evidence is not only the key factor to determine truth, but also the key to judge the independence of the premises in a step of inference. Inference is only allowed when the evidence records of the two premises do not overlap. This not only avoids cyclic inference, but also keeps revision from further increasing the confidence of a belief on re-derivation.

So we can now define the degree of certainty of a hypothesis, when it's precondition is fulfilled, as a *truth* value as defined above. Therefore, the positive evidence for a predictive hypothesis is simply a measurement of how frequently the occurrence of the antecedent was followed by its consequent event, and the negative evidence how frequently the consequent did not happen whilst the antecedent did. Truth expectation, which we will sometimes refer to, 'merges' frequency and confidence into a single value, that can be used for comparison purposes. For detailed formulas, see [5,14].

Budget. The amount of system resources, namely CPU and memory, that is allocated to a specific task, an item of work, is directly related to budget, which is a tuple (p, d, q) where p is priority, d is durability and q is quality, and all parameters are between 0 and 1. Priority determines short term importance whilst durability determines long term importance. Quality is effectively implemented as a priority barrier (usually between 0 and 0.1) under which the priority value can not fall. This ensures that items of high long-term importance will survive in the bag even though they have a low priority. More details can be seen in [5]. Besides quality, there are many factors that affect the priority of an item [13], such as, but not limited to:

- How recent the event is (is it still relevant?)
- How often does the event occur (how stable is it?)
- Did the event happen unexpectedly? (how surprising was its occurrence?)
- Is it related to a goal or question?

Bags. One of the constraints of an AGI system is that it needs to work with finite resources. When working within a fixed sized memory, once a memory limit is reached, a decision has to be made as to which item to remove to make space for a new one. Here, a data structure called "Bag" is used by OpenNARS. This data structure stores items ordered by their priority value, allowing for sampling items based on the priority distribution within. Once a bag is full, in order to make room for a new item, the lowest-priority item is removed. Bag is constructed in such a way as to support efficient sampling, adding and removal of items without any search operations, so all operations on bag are O(1). Overall this control strategy is very similar to the Parallel Terraced Scan in [10], as it also allows the exploration of many possible options in parallel, with more computation devoted to options which are identified as being more promising. OpenNARS controls the resource allocation of all reasoning using the bag data structure, and is not restricted to reacting to events. The aforementioned chaining case is also controlled by Bag sampling. See [13] for more detail.

Concepts. Conceptually, the belief network of the OpenNARS system can be thought of as a directed graph where vertices are *concepts* and edges are *links* (links are outside the scope of this paper (see [5]). For the purpose of this discussion concepts can be considered as storage units, that contain a bag of beliefs and goals. Concepts themselves are stored in a large system-wide *ConceptBag* and selected as explained above. Therefore, concepts, beliefs and goals are selected probabilistically, based on their priority and forgotten when their priority is the lowest in the respective bag.

4   Goal-Directed Procedure Learning: Method

Temporal Reasoning. An adaptive agent existing in a real-time environment needs to be aware of, and capable of reasoning about, time. We refer to this mechanism as Temporal Reasoning. An event is something that the system experiences in *time* and this time is captured as an *OccurrenceTime*. In OpenNARS occurrence time is measured in system cycles, but can be any representation that supports a regularly incremented value, such as a real-time clock. When reasoning with time the notion of 'interval' becomes important. For example, two events occurring time t apart can be represented as (E_1, I_t, E_2), where I_t is an interval of time duration t. This allows arbitrarily complex temporal patterns to form. These patterns form the necessary preconditions for hypothesis creation. Intervals also apply to implications, $(E_1, I_t) /\!\!\Rightarrow E_2$, where the temporal aspect becomes part of the precondition. Intervals are always measured, though we will omit them in the discussion whenever they don't add any value. A key challenge is how to allow intervals of different duration to be revised. Imagine two hypotheses $(E_1, I_{t1}) /\!\!\Rightarrow E_2$ and $(E_1, I_{t2}) /\!\!\Rightarrow E_2$. Both of them predict the same outcome based on the same precondition, but they expect different interval durations, I_{t1} and I_{t2}. To allow these different intervals to be revised, a confidence decay (Projection) [5] increasing with the time difference is applied after revision. Here it makes a difference which premise is projected to the other. The projected premise should be the one whose timing appears less often, so as to keep the more usual timing in the conclusion. This enables the learning of the more, commonly experienced, interval durations over time.

Hypothesis Creation. This is the core of the method, and whilst selection and testing are important, creation is the key to building relevant and useful hypotheses. The crucial insight was to separate the incoming experience stream into events and operations (in OpenNARS operations are restricted to the events that the system can initiate itself. Operations also generate input events as feedback). With this separation, the task of forming meaningful preconditions was a simpler problem to solve: operations simply become the context under which certain events cause others to occur. Given, a collection (a Bag in OpenNARS) of recent *Events* and, a collection of recent *Operations*, a hypothesis is formed in the following way:

1. Probabilistically select an *Op* from *Operations*, where the probability of selection should be roughly proportional to how long ago the event happened or the operation was invoked. After invocation of an operation:
   (a) Create a concept for the *Op* (if it does not already exist) [5].
   (b) Copy the *Events*, that occurred prior to the operation, based on occurrence time, to the *Op* concept.
   (c) The *Op* concept can now form preconditions, based on probabilistic selection of these events, and construct premises of the form (E, Op), where E is a precondition of the *Op*.
2. Now when a new event E^* enters the system and an operation Op is sampled from *Operations*, two steps occur:
   (a) Sample a second premise E_{past} from *Events* to form temporal sequences (E_{past}, E^*) that are inserted into *Events*, and also the predictive hypothesis $(E_{past} /\Rightarrow E^*)$ which only exists in concept memory. The latter is required as not everything can be understood in terms of own operations (as also argued by [1]), such as the transition from day to night.
   (b) Based on Op, retrieve, via probabilistic sampling of the Op concept, one of the (E, Op) preconditions, in order to form a procedural hypothesis $((E, Op) /\Rightarrow E^*)$. Here, clearly the consequent is put into the context of the operation. Without taking operations to execute into account, there is simply no way to predict, for example, where the cup of tea in your hand will move next, as argued by [1].

Over time the total evidence of re-occurring hypotheses will increase due to the Revision rule [14] being applied within the concept of the hypothesis.

Revised procedural hypotheses $((A, Op) / \Rightarrow B)$ are also stored in the "foreign" concept B, this allows B to memorize ways of how it can be realized, and to learn its preconditions. Thereby, the most successful hypotheses, these with the highest truth expectation, will become the most likely to be selected.

Hypothesis Selection. Assuming an incoming or derived goal $G!$, the task of hypothesis selection is to choose the most relevant hypothesis that can satisfy $G!$ with some previously experienced event E as precondition. Also assuming that such a hypothesis already exists, the Detachment rule [14] can be applied twice to a matching hypothesis, which is of the form $(E, Op_i) \Rightarrow G$. The first detachment leads to $(E, Op_i)!$ and the second one to $Op_i!$. The $Op_i!$ with the highest truth expectation, or certainty, will most likely lead to the greatest satisfaction of $G!$, and therefore will be derived. $G!$ can then be revised in concept G and trigger an execution if the truth expectation of the revised goal (projected to the current time) will be above a decision threshold [5]. Note that subgoal derivations also happen in the backward chaining process we described. This is especially important when no hypothesis that can directly realize $G!$ exists, or new solutions should be probed for.

Hypothesis Pruning. Given the uncertain nature of input experience, it is not possible, in advance, to identify what will be relevant and useful. This, unavoidable, lack of foresight can lead to the formation of hypotheses that have little value to a system. Additionally, given the limited computational resources, only a certain number of hypotheses can be retained at any one time. This makes it even more important to keep track of the success rate of hypotheses, as to keep the most competent ones while removing the others.

The approach taken to allow for this is hypothesis pruning, to measure the success of hypotheses so that these that do not predict correctly can be removed by lowering their quality. While finding positive evidence is achieved through temporal induction rules as mentioned before, finding negative evidence is the job of Anticipation: given a predictive statement of the form: *antecedent* $/\Rightarrow$ *consequent*, we define *Anticipation* as the expectation that the antecedent will lead to the consequent being observed as predicted. With Anticipation a system is able to find negative evidence for previously learned predictive beliefs which generate wrong predictions [5,8].

If the event happens, in the sense that a new input event with the same term as the anticipated event is observed, the anticipation was successful (Confirmation), in which case nothing special needs to be done, since the statement will be confirmed via the normal process of temporal induction.

If the predicted event does not happen then the system needs to recognize this. This is achieved by introducing a negative input event, $not(a)$. Note that in this case, such a negative input event has high priority and should significantly influence the attention of the system, assuming such a mechanism is present.

Here, one challenge is how to determine the timeout duration after which we decide the prediction failed. A simple treatment turned out to be effective: Given that an event was predicted to occur in n steps, the failure can be recognized after a certain multiple of n steps. A more refined approach would be to keep track of the variance in timings in the concept of the predictive hypothesis, and then to decide that failure point taking the variance into account. But also in this case, a decision as to where to set the failure point, has to be made.

5 Results

Test Chamber is one of the environments that we developed to allow an AGI system to be tasked with a variety of different goals and experiences in novel surroundings. Within Test Chamber an AGI is expected to demonstrate goal-oriented observation-based procedure learning in a domain of doors, switches and lights. A birds eye view perspective is controlled by a user, opening doors, picking keys, and so on. The system observes the users actions and can call different operations directly, such as: going to an object, activating a switch, deactivating it, picking an object from the floor and so on. Activating operations in different contexts allows for different outcomes in the test environment.

A possible event stream generated from observing a user:

1. Event E_1: Reached start place
2. Operation Op_1: Go to switch1
3. Event E_2: Reached switch1
4. Operation Op_2: Activate switch1
5. Event E_3: Switch1 activated

Although these examples were performed in OpenNARS, for the purpose of this paper it is sufficient to know that these inputs can be directly represented as events and operations, and potentially in other systems.

OpenNARS easily creates hypothesis $((E_1, Op_1) /\!\Rightarrow E_3)$ by making use of the explained mechanisms. The same is true for $((E_2, Op_2) /\!\Rightarrow E_3)$. While there are other generated results too, these two are of special relevance: assuming a goal E_3 exists or enters the system, what hypothesis, or effectively behavior, should the system choose to reach its goal? It depends on the context. In this particular example, both hypotheses effectively help each other and allow for "local" decisions to realize E_3 dependent on whether E_1 or E_2 was observed: when one of the hypotheses doesn't exist, the other one would fail, as an important part of the necessary behavior would be missing, only together can they succeed. A surprising property of this implicit representation is that no explicit "global plan" exists or needs to be searched for, yet is totally sufficient for carrying out the task successfully. However, when an important piece of knowledge is missing, a fast reaction is often not possible. In this case, a system needs to improvise, either by searching for a solution in its memory, or by probing the environment, both of the strategies should be applied together rather than in a distinct way.

These representative cases work well in OpenNARS, and allow it to, more easily, acquire complex behaviors whilst switching its behavior when goals and context change.

We also applied OpenNARS to Reinforcement Learning problems, one of them being Pong: assuming a goal $G!$, an input event G. can directly act as "reward signal", which in Pong basically is an event encoding "the ball collided with the bat". Additionally, the system is given events about the horizontal ball position relative to the bat. This allows it to invoke different operations dependent on whether the ball is left or right of the bat. For this purpose, it can invoke two operations: to move the paddle to the left or to the right. This turned out to be sufficient to let the system learn to Play Pong in short time and with high reliability: the experiment was repeated 50 times, and the system learned the right behavior in all of the cases, with 98 s mean and a variance of 51 s until the right policy was learned. Important to note here is that the ball starts at a random position, with a random movement direction, and needs at least 5 s to reach another side of the quadratic board. This explains the high variance, as some representative cases need to occur first, before the relevant hypotheses will be supported by real evidence. Another factor here: when a wrong behavior (such as moving to the left side when the ball is on the right side) is learned first, due to unlucky cases, it will take longer for the right hypothesis to take over, as negative evidence generated by failed anticipations needs to be found before the right behavior will be tried.

6   Conclusion

The Reasoning-Learning Mechanism employed by NARS has been shown to be capable of goal-directed Procedure Learning: the separation of operations from other events has enabled the system to form more successful and useful hypotheses with little resource effort. These are subsequently used to enable fast hypothesis selection through the precondition memorization mechanism. This mechanism allows the system to make effective use of procedural knowledge and have fast response times when the relevant knowledge already exists. Collectively our methods allow the system to self-program and automatize itself to become gradually more competent over time. We have shown that the system can learn goal-oriented procedures involving multiple operations, without building explicit plans. Furthermore, we have demonstrated, that the system can perform well in Reinforcement-Learning style tasks as a special case, and that the "reward signal" can naturally be represented. While this paper was mainly about introducing the involved mechanisms and their properties, future work will include detailed comparisons with alternative procedure learning techniques. This will include theoretical comparisons as well as detailed results on learning performance.

In conclusion, we believe the techniques presented in this paper, specifically, operational separation, precondition memorization and Anticipation are generally applicable to a broad class of AGI systems. As has been highlighted above, the Procedure Learning capability of OpenNARS was significantly improved as a result of these enhancements.

References

1. Ahmad S., Hawkins J.: Untangling Sequqnces: Behaviour vs External Causes, bioRxiv (2017)
2. DeKeyser, R.: Skill acquisition theory. In: Theories in Second Language Acquisition: An Introduction, pp. 97–113 (2007)
3. Drescher, G.: Made-up minds: a constructivist approach to artificial intelligence. Ph.D. thesis, MIT, Computer Science, September 1989
4. Eagleman, D.M., Sejnowski, T.J.: Motion integration and postdiction in visual awareness. Science **287**, 2036–2038 (2000)
5. Hammer, P., Lofthouse, T., Wang, P.: The OpenNARS implementation of the non-axiomatic reasoning system. In: Steunebrink, B., Wang, P., Goertzel, B. (eds.) AGI -2016. LNCS (LNAI), vol. 9782, pp. 160–170. Springer, Cham (2016)
6. Pöppel, E., Bao, Y.: Temporal windows as a bridge from objective to subjective time. In: Arstila, V., Lloyd, D. (eds.) Subjective Time: The Philosophy, Psychology, and Neuroscience of Temporality. The MIT Press, Cambridge (2014)

7. Latombe, J.C.: Robot Motion Planning, vol. 124. Springer, New York (1991). https://doi.org/10.1007/978-1-4615-4022-9
8. Nivel, E., et al.: Autocatalytic Endogenous Reflective Architecture (2013)
9. Pitti, A., Braud, R., Mahé, S., Quoy, M., Gaussier, P.: Neural model for learning-to-learn of novel tasks in the motor domain. Front. Psychol. **4**, 771 (2013)
10. Rehling, J., Hofstadter, D.: The parallel terraced scan: an optimization for an agent-oriented architecture. In: Proceedings of the IEEE International Conference on Intelligent Processing Systems 1997 (1997)
11. Russel, S., Norvig, P.: Artificial Intelligence: A Modern Approach. Prentice Hall Series on Artificial Intelligence. Prentice Hall, Englewood Cliffs (2009)
12. Sutton, R., Barto, A.: Reinforcement Learning: An Introduction. MIT Press, Cambridge (2017)
13. Wang, P.: Rigid Flexibility: The Logic of Intelligence. Springer, Dordrecht (2006). https://doi.org/10.1007/1-4020-5045-3
14. Wang, P.: Non-Axiomatic Logic: A Model of Intelligent Reasoning. World Scientific, Singapore (2013)
15. Wang, P.: Solving a problem with or without a program. J. Artif. Gen. Intell. **3**(3), 43–73 (2013)
16. Wang, P., Hammer, P.: Assumptions of decision-making models in AGI. In: Bieger, J., Goertzel, B., Potapov, A. (eds.) AGI 2015. LNCS (LNAI), vol. 9205, pp. 197–207. Springer, Cham (2015). https://doi.org/10.1007/978-3-319-21365-1_21

Can Machines Design? An Artificial General Intelligence Approach

Andreas M. Hein[1(✉)] and Hélène Condat[2]

[1] Laboratoire Genie Industriel, CentraleSupélec, Université Paris-Saclay,
Gif-sur-Yvette, France
andreas-makoto.hein@centralesupelec.fr
[2] Initiative for Interstellar Studies (i4is), Charfield, UK

Abstract. Can machines design? Can they come up with creative solutions to problems and build tools and artifacts across a wide range of domains? Recent advances in the field of computational creativity and formal Artificial General Intelligence (AGI) provide frameworks towards machines with the general ability to design. In this paper we propose to integrate a formal computational creativity framework into the Gödel machine framework. We call the resulting framework design Gödel machine. Such a machine could solve a variety of design problems by generating novel concepts. In addition, it could change the way these concepts are generated by modifying itself. The design Gödel machine is able to improve its initial design program, once it has proven that a modification would increase its return on the utility function. Finally, we sketch out a specific version of the design Gödel machine which specifically aims at the design of complex software and hardware systems. Future work aims at the development of a more formal version of the design Gödel machine and a proof of concept implementation.

Keywords: Artificial general intelligence · Gödel machine
Computational creativity · Software engineering
Systems engineering · Design theory · Reinforcement learning

1 Introduction

Can machines design? In other words, can they come up with creative solutions to problems [38] and intervene into their environment by, for example, building tools and artifacts, or better versions of themselves [10,26]? Surprisingly, this question has not received a lot of attention in the current debate on artificial intelligence, such as in Bostrom [2] and Russell [33]. An exception is the literature in formal artificial general intelligence (AGI) research [10,27,28,40]. If artificial intelligence is going to have a large impact on the real world, it needs to have at least some capacity to create "new" things and to change its environment. The capacity to create new things has also been called "generativity" in the design theory literature [17]. Such machines could be used across many

© Springer Nature Switzerland AG 2018
M. Iklé et al. (Eds.): AGI 2018, LNAI 10999, pp. 87–99, 2018.
https://doi.org/10.1007/978-3-319-97676-1_9

contexts where the ability to design in the widest sense is required, for example, designing industrial goods such as the chassis of a car that can subsequently be manufactured. Another application could be in space colonization where local resources are used for building an infrastructure autonomously for a human crew [18–20]. Traditionally, the wider question of creative machines has been treated in the computational creativity community. The computational creativity community has come up with numerous systems that exhibit creativity [7–9, 32, 41], i.e. systems that are able to conceive artifacts that are considered as novel and creative by humans and/or are novel compared to the underlying knowledge base of the system. Wiggins [42] and Cherti [6] have explored the link between artificial intelligence and creativity. More specifically, Wiggins [42] formalizes the notions of exploratory creativity and transformational creativity from Boden [1] in an artificial intelligence context. A creative system that exhibits exploratory creativity is capable of exploring a set of concepts according to a set of rules. Transformational creativity is by contrast exhibited by a system that can modify the set of concepts itself and/or the rules according to which it searches for the set of concepts.

At the same time, the artificial general intelligence community is working on general foundations of intelligence and providing frameworks for formally capturing essential elements of intelligence. Within this community, intelligence is primarily defined as general problem-solving [13, 23]. According to Goertzel, [13], the field of Artificial General Intelligence deals with "the creation and study of synthetic intelligences with sufficiently broad (e.g. human-level) scope and strong generalization capability..." A relevant research stream in this field is the development of the "universalist approach" that deals with formal models of general intelligence. Examples are Hutter's AIXI [23], Schmidhuber's Gödel Machine [35], and Orseau and Ring's space-time embedded intelligence [27]. These formal models are based on reinforcement learning where an agent interacts with an environment and is capable of self-improvement.

In this paper we attempt to integrate Wiggins' formal creativity framework [42] into an Artificial General Intelligence (AGI) framework, the Gödel machine [35]. The purpose is to demonstrate that the mechanisms of self-improvement in AGI frameworks can be applied to a general design problem. The resulting design Gödel machine designs according to certain rules but is capable of changing these rules, which corresponds to exploratory and transformational creative systems in Wiggins [42]. Based on this generic framework, we will sketch out a machine that can design complex hardware or software systems. Such systems encompass most products with a high economic value such as in aerospace, automotive, transportation engineering, robotics, and artificial intelligence.

2   Literature Survey

In the literature survey, we will focus on the literature on design theory, formal modeling languages in systems and software engineering, computational creativity, and artificial general intelligence.

The design theory literature provides criteria for how to evaluate a design theory. Hatchuel et al. [17] introduce two criteria: generativity and robustness. Whereas generativity is the capacity of a design theory to explain or replicate how new things are created, robustness is understood as how sensitive the performance of the designs is with respect to different environments. The main contribution of the design theory literature to a general designing machine are the different forms of generativity and criteria for evaluating design theories.

One possibility to capture generativity is by using a formal design language. Formal design languages belong to the formalized subset of all design languages that are used for generating designs. Formal languages consist of a set of symbols, called alphabet Σ, a set of rules, called grammar, that define which expressions based on the alphabet are valid, and a mapping to a domain from which meaning for the expressions is derived [15]. This mapping is called "semantics". The set of all words over Σ is denoted Σ^*. The language L is a subset of Σ^* and contains all expressions that are valid with respect to a grammar.

For example, programming languages consist of a set of expressions such as 'if' conditions and for-loops. These expressions are used for composing a computer program. However, the expressions need to be used in a precise way. Otherwise the code cannot be executed correctly, i.e. the program has to be grammatically correct.

According to Broy et al. [5], formal semantics can be represented in terms of a calculus, another formalism (denotational and translational semantics), and a model interpreter (operational semantics). Existing formal semantics for complex systems and software engineering seem to be based on denotational semantics where the semantic domain to which the syntax is mapped is based on set theory, predicate logic [3,4], algebras [21], coalgebras [14] etc.

Formal design languages are formal languages that are used for designing, e.g. for creating new objects or problem-solving. For example, programming languages are used for programs that can be executed on a computer.

The computational creativity literature presents different forms of creativity and creativity mechanisms [11]. It distinguishes between several forms of creativity, which have been introduced by Boden [1]: Combinational creativity is creativity that is based on the combination of preexisting knowledge. For example, the game of tangram consists of primitive geometric shapes that are combined to form new shapes. Exploratory creativity is "the process of searching an area of conceptual space governed by certain rules" [30]. Finally, transformational creativity "is the process of transforming the rules and thus identifying a new sub-space." [30] These categories seem to correspond with the generativity categories combinatorial generation, search in topological proximity, and knowledge expansion in design theory [17]. All three forms of creativity can be generated by computational systems today [1]. However, a key limitation is that these systems exhibit these forms of creativity only for a very narrow domain such as art, jokes, poetry, etc. No generally creative system exists.

The artificial general intelligence literature does seldom treat creativity explicitly. Schmidhuber [34,36,37] is rather an exception. He establishes the link between a utility function and creativity. A creative agent receives a reward for being creative. Hutter [23] briefly mentions creativity. Here, creativity is rather a corollary of general intelligence. In other words, if a system exhibits general intelligence, then it is necessarily creative. In the following, we will briefly introduce the Gödel machine AGI framework that has received considerable attention within the community.

3   Creativity and the Gödel Machine: A Design Gödel Machine

We use the computational creativity framework from Wiggins [42] and integrate it with the Gödel machine framework of a self-referential learning system. In his influential paper, Wiggins [42] introduces formal representations for creative systems that have been informally introduced by Boden [1], notably exploratory and transformational creativity. We choose the Gödel machine as our AGI framework, as its ability to self-modify is a key characteristic for a general designing machine. Furthermore, it uses a formal language, which makes it easier to combine with formal design languages. However, we acknowledge that AIXI [23] and Orseau and Ring's space-time embedded intelligence [27] should be considered for a similar exercise.

A Gödel machine that can generate novel concepts (paintings, poems, cars, spacecraft) is called design Gödel machine in the following. Such a machine is a form of creative system, defined as a "collection of processes, natural or automatic, which are capable of achieving or simulating behaviour which in humans would be deemed creative" [42].

The original Gödel machine consists of a formal language $\mathcal{L}$ that may include first order logic, arithmetics, and probability theory, as shown in Fig. 1.

It also consists of a utility function u whose value the machine tries to maximize.

$$u(s, e) : \mathcal{S} \times \mathcal{E} \to \mathbb{R}$$

$$u(s, e) = E_\mu[\sum_{\tau=time}^{T} r(\tau)|s, e] \quad for \quad 1 \le t \le T \tag{1}$$

Where s is a variable state of the machine, e the variable environmental state, $r(t)$ is a real-valued reward input at a time t. $E_\mu(\cdot|\cdot)$ denotes the conditional expectation operator of a distribution μ of a set of distributions M, where M reflects the knowledge about the (probabilistic) reactions of the environment.

How does the Gödel machine self-improve? A theorem prover searches for a proof that a modification can improve the machine's performance with respect to the utility function. Once a proof is found that a modified version of itself would satisfy the target theorem in Eq. (2), the program *switchprog* rewrites the machine's code from its current to its modified version. The target theorem essentially states that when the current state s at t_1 with modifications

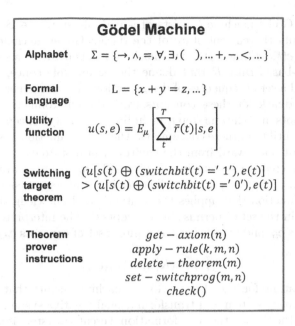

Fig. 1. Elements of the Gödel machine

yields a higher utility than the current machine, the machine will schedule its modification.

$$(u[s(t_1) \oplus switchbit(t_1) =' 1'), Env(t_1)] > u[s(t_1) \oplus switchbit(t_1) =' 0'), Env(t_1)]) \quad (2)$$

The basic idea of combining the Gödel machine framework with the formal creativity framework of Wiggins [42] is to construct a Gödel machine where its problem solver corresponds to an exploratory creative system and the proof searcher corresponds to a transformational creative system. The transformational creative system can modify the exploratory creative system or itself.

More formally, the design Gödel machine consists of an initial software $p(1)$. $p(1)$ is divided into an exploratory creative system which includes an initial policy $\pi(1)_{env}$, which interacts with the environment and a transformational creative system, which includes an initial policy $\pi(1)_{proof}$. $\pi(1)_{proof}$ searches for proofs and forms pairs of $(switchprog, proof)$, where the proof is a proof of a target theorem that states that an immediate rewrite of p via $switchprog$ would yield a higher utility u than the current version of p. $\pi(1)_{env}$ is more specifically interpreted as a set of design sequences comprising design actions. A design sequence, for example, is the order in which components are combined to form a system. The different ways of how components can be combined are the design actions and the sequence of how they are combined is the design sequence.

The design Gödel machine consists of a variable state $s \in \mathcal{S}$. The variable state s represents the current state of the design Gödel machine, including a set of concepts $c(t)$ at time t that the machine has generated, a set of syntactic and knowledge-based rules $\mathcal{R}$ that define the permissible concepts in a design language $\mathcal{L}$, and a set of sequences of design actions π_{env} for generating concepts and getting feedback for these concepts from the environment. The machine generates concepts in each time step t, including the empty concept $\top$. It receives feedback on the utility of these concepts via the utility function $u(s, e) : \mathcal{S} \times \mathcal{E} \rightarrow \mathbb{R}$, which computes a reward from the environmental state $e \in \mathcal{E}$. Analogous to the exploratory creative system in Wiggins [42], π_{env} and u are part of a 7-tuple $< \mathcal{U}, \mathcal{L}, [.], \langle ., ., . \rangle, \mathcal{R}, \pi_{env}, u >$, where $\mathcal{U}$ is a universe of concepts, $[.]$ is an interpretation function that applies the syntactic and knowledge-based rules $\mathcal{R}$ to $\mathcal{U}$, resulting in the set of permissible concepts $\mathcal{C}$. The interpreter $\langle ., ., . \rangle$ takes a set of concepts c_{in} and transforms them into a set of concepts c_{out} by applying $\langle \mathcal{R}, \pi_{env}, u \rangle$:

$$(c_{out}) \doteq \langle \mathcal{R}, \pi_{env}, u \rangle (c_{in}) \tag{3}$$

Self-modification for the design Gödel machine means that parts of the exploratory creative system and transformational creative system can be modified. Regarding the former, the transformational creative system is able to modify the exploratory creative system's rules $\mathcal{R}$, the sequences of design actions π_{env}, and the utility function u. For this purpose, the transformational creative system searches for a proof that a modification would lead to a higher value on the meta utility function u_{meta}. By default, u_{meta} returns 0 if the target theorem in Equation (2) is not satisfied and 1 if it is. If the target theorem is satisfied, this modification is implemented in the subsequent time step. In addition, a target theorem u_{meta} could capture criteria for a good design sequence in π_{env} that are expected to lead to a higher value on u. Examples are measures for the originality of the created designs via a design sequence, if originality is expected to lead to higher values on u. The proof searcher π_{proof} that searches for the proof and the proof itself are expressed in a meta-language $\mathcal{L}_{meta}$. The proof is based on axioms, rules, and theorems in $\mathcal{R}$ and π_{env}, the meta-language syntax and rules $\mathcal{R}_{meta}$, and the proof strategies π_{proof} of the proof searcher. Hence, the transformational creative system can be expressed as the 7-tuple:

$$< \mathcal{L}, \mathcal{L}_{meta}, [.]_{meta}, \langle ., ., . \rangle_{meta}, \mathcal{R}_{meta}, \pi_{proof}, u_{meta} > \tag{4}$$

More specifically, in case u is not modified, the proof searcher π_{proof} generates pairs of $\mathcal{R}$ and π_{env} from an existing $\mathcal{R}$ and π_{env} by applying an interpreter $\langle ., ., . \rangle_{meta}$ with $\mathcal{R}_{meta}$, π_{proof}, and u_{meta}:

$$(\mathcal{R}_2, \pi_{env2}) = \langle \mathcal{R}_{meta}, \pi_{proof}, u_{meta} \rangle_{meta} (\mathcal{R}_1, \pi_{env1}) \tag{5}$$

This formulation is similar to the transformational creative system in Wiggins [42]. If the proof searcher can prove $u_{meta}((\mathcal{R}_2, \pi_{env2}), e_1) > u_{meta}((\mathcal{R}_1, \pi_{env1}), e_1)$, the design Gödel machine will switch to the new rules $\mathcal{R}_2$ and design sequences π_{env2}.

Analogous to the original Gödel machine, the transformational creative system in the design Gödel machine is capable of performing self-modifications, for example, on the proof searcher and the meta-utility function:

$$(\mathcal{X}_2) = \langle \mathcal{R}_{meta}, \pi_{proof}, u_{meta} \rangle_{meta}(\mathcal{X}_1) \tag{6}$$

where $\mathcal{X}$ is one of the elements in $< \mathcal{L}, \mathcal{L}_{meta}, [.], \langle ., ., . \rangle, \mathcal{R}_{meta}, \pi_{proof}, u_{meta} >$. Self-reference in general can cause problems, however, as Schmidhuber [35] notes, in most practical applications, they are likely not relevant. A design Gödel machine would start with an initial configuration and then modify itself to find versions of itself that yield higher values on its utility function.

Figure 2 provides an overview of the main elements of the design Gödel machine that have been introduced before.

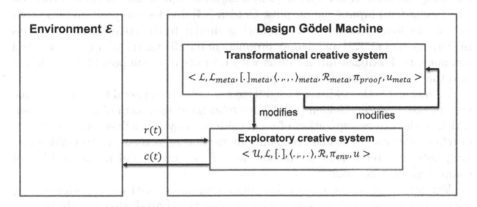

Fig. 2. Elements of the design Gödel machine

4   A Design Gödel Machine for Complex Systems Design

A specific version of the design Gödel machine for designing complex software and hardware systems can be imagined. It would include a set of syntactic and knowledge-based rules $\mathcal{R}$ that define sound designs (concepts for hardware and software) in the specific domain and a set of design actions such as abstraction, refinement, composition, and verification [3,4,14] that can be combined into design sequences π_{env}. The environment $\mathcal{E}$ could be a virtual test environment or an environment in which design prototypes are tested in the real world.

Important principles of formal systems and software engineering are components and their interactions, abstraction, composition, refinement, and verification [3,4,14]. Broy [3,4] defines interactions in terms of streams and interfaces. Golden [14] defines interactions in terms of dataflows. Component functions are specified in terms of transfer functions that transform inputs into outputs. The component behavior is specified in terms of state machines. Golden [14] specifies component behavior via a timed Mealy machine, Broy [3,4] uses a state-oriented functional specification for this purpose.

Apart from this basic representation of a system as a set of interacting components, abstraction, composition, refinement, and verification are important principles during the design of a system.

Abstraction means that details are left out in order to facilitate the comprehension of a complex system, reduce computational complexity or for mathematical reasons [14]. Abstraction is treated by Golden [14] via dataflow, transfer function, and component abstraction. He remarks that abstraction can also lead to non-determinism due to the underspecification of the abstracted system.

Composition is the aggregation of lower-level components together with their interactions to higher-level components. Herrmann et al. [21] propose a compositional algebra for aggregating components. Broy [3] specifies composition as the assignment of truth values to system-level inputs and outputs based on component-level inputs and outputs. Golden [14] divides composition into product and feedback. His notion of product is similar to the compositional algebra in Herrmann et al. [21] and defines products of dataflows, transfer functions, and components. Feedback further deals with outputs of a component that are fed into the same component as an input.

Refinement is the addition of details to arrive from a general to a more specific system specification. Golden [14] defines refinement as a form of decomposition, which is the inverse operation of composition. Broy [3] defines different forms of refinement: property, glass box, and interaction refinement. Both Golden and Broy interpret refinement as an addition of properties and decomposition of components/interactions.

Verification is the process of checking requirements satisfaction. Golden [14] assigns requirements to a system or component via "boxes" that specify the system or component's inputs, outputs, and behavior. Broy [3,4] similarly distinguishes between global (system-level) requirements and local (component-level) requirements. The verification process in his case is essentially formally proving that the system and its components satisfy the requirements.

The literature on formal modeling languages for software and systems engineering provides the necessary semantics and rules for describing complex soft- and hardware systems. However, the main shortcoming of formal modeling languages for complex software and hardware systems is that they cannot generate these systems by themselves. In other words they are not generative without additional generativity mechanisms and a knowledge base.

4.1   Design Axioms

As for the original Gödel machine, theorem proving requires a enumerable set of axioms. These axioms are strings over a finite alphabet Σ that includes symbols from set theory, predicate logic, arithmetics, etc. The design Gödel machine for complex systems design includes a number of design-related axioms that will be presented in the following. The design axioms belong to three broad categories. The first are axioms related to the formal modeling language, describing its abstract syntax (machine-readable syntax), the semantic domain, for example, expressed in predicate logic, and the semantic mapping between the abstract syntax and the semantic domain. The semantic domain and mapping in Golden [14] and Broy [3,4] can be essentially reformulated in terms of set theory, predicate logic, arithmetics, and algebra. These axioms belong to $\mathcal{R}$, but specifically define which designs are "formally correct". We denote the set of these axioms as $\mathcal{R}_{formal}$. These axioms include formal definitions for a system, component, interfaces, and interactions between component etc.

The second category consists of axioms related to different mechanisms of generating designs. Specifically, these are axioms for refinement, abstraction, composition, verification, and axioms that describe domain-specific rules based on domain-specific knowledge. We consider these axioms as part of the set of design sequences π_{env}.

The third category are axioms that describe conceptual knowledge such as the notion of "automobile". Without being too restrictive, such conceptual knowledge would include axioms for parts and whole, i.e. mereological statemenets [39]. For example, an automobile has a motor and wheels. The axioms also belong to $\mathcal{R}$, however, contrary to $\mathcal{R}_{formal}$, they are not general principles of representing complex systems but knowledge specific to certain concepts. Such axioms are expressed by $\mathcal{R}_{ck}$.

4.2   System

According to Golden [14], a system is a 7-tuple $\int =< \mathbb{T}_s, Input, Output, S, q_0, \mathcal{F}, \mathcal{Q} >$ where $\mathbb{T}_s$ is a time scale called the time scale of the system, $Input = (In, \mathcal{I})$ and $Output = (Out, \mathcal{O})$ are datasets, called input and output datasets, S is a nonempty ϵ-alphabet, called the ϵ-alphabet of states, q_0 is an element of S, called the initial state, $\mathcal{F} : In \times S \times \mathbb{T}_s \rightarrow Out$ is a function called functional behavior, $\mathcal{Q} : In \times S \times \mathbb{T}_s \rightarrow S$ is a function called states behavior. $(Input, Output)$ are called the signature of $\int$. This definition of a system corresponds to a timed Mealy machine [24].

It is rather straight-forward to model the Gödel machine in this system framework, if the loss in generality of using the timed Mealy machine is considered acceptable. In that case, we take: $\mathbb{T}_s = \mathbb{N}$, $Input = (\mathcal{E}, \mathbb{E})$, $q_0 = s(t_1)$, $Output = (\mathcal{S}, \mathbb{S})$, $\mathcal{F} : \mathcal{E} \times \mathcal{S} \times \mathbb{T}_s \rightarrow \mathcal{A}$, $\mathcal{Q} : \mathcal{E} \times \mathcal{S} \times \mathbb{T}_s \rightarrow \mathcal{S}$. $\mathbb{E}$ and $\mathbb{S}$ are any data behaviors on $\mathcal{E}$ and $\mathcal{S}$ respectively.

Formulating the design Gödel machine in the system framework allows for applying the formal machinery of the framework such as refinement, abstraction, verification etc. that the design Gödel machine can apply to itself.

4.3   Refinement and Abstraction

Refinement and abstraction relate system representations that are at different levels of abstraction [4,14]. According to Broy [3], refinement may include the addition of properties to the system that makes it more restrictive, or includes its decomposition into components. For example:

$$x \implies y \circ z \tag{7}$$

where the system x is decomposed into the components y and z.

4.4   Composition

The composition operator is important for combining components into a system with their respective interfaces. A generic composition operator can be understood as:

$$y \otimes z \implies x \tag{8}$$

where the components y and z are composed to x. These operators would not only need to be defined for software systems, such as proposed by [3,4,14] but would also need to include interpretations of the composition for physical systems [22]. This is likely to entail mereological questions of parts and wholes [39].

4.5   Verification

We interpret verification in two distinct ways: First, with respect to a set of requirements Φ that is part of the environment $\mathcal{E}$, where $\mathcal{E}$ returns a reward input $r(t)$ to the design Gödel machine. Based on $r(t)$ and the respective set of concepts $\mathcal{C}$, the utility function u is evaluated. Such a utility function would have the form $\tilde{u} : \mathcal{C} \times \Phi \to \mathbb{R}$, with $\mathcal{C} \subset \mathcal{S}$ and $\Phi \subseteq \mathcal{E}$.

Second, the set of requirements Φ is internal to the design Gödel machine. The requirements describe expectations with respect to the environment $\mathcal{E}$. Specifically, the satisfaction of the requirements is expected to return a reward input $r(t)$ from the environment. For example, if a concept c (a car) exhibits a property a (consumes less than 3 l/km in fuel), then the resulting $r(t)$ will result in a higher u than for a different property (consumes 10 l/km of fuel). The conditional expectation operator $E_\mu(\cdot|\cdot)$ from the original Gödel machine is slightly modified for this purpose, leading to a utility function $u : \mathcal{C} \times \Phi \times \mathcal{E} \to \mathbb{R}$.

$$u(c, \varphi, e) = E_\mu [\sum_{\tau=time}^{T} r(\tau) | c, \varphi, e] \quad for \quad 1 \le t \le T \tag{9}$$

where $\varphi \in \Phi$ and $c \in \mathcal{C}$. The requirements Φ are themselves expectations of what the environment $\mathcal{E}$ "wants" from the design(s). They are subject to modifications, depending on the environment's response $r(t)$. This second interpretation of verification captures nicely the distinction between verification and validation in systems engineering, where verification checks if the design satisfies the requirements and validation checks if the requirements were the right ones [16].

5   Limitations

Design Gödel machines are subject to the same limitations as the original Gödel machine [35] such as the Gödel incompleteness theorem [12] and Rice's theorem [29].

Apart from these theoretical limitations, a basic limitation of the design Gödel machine presented here is that it is based on a formal language. Computing systems that are not based on a formal language could not be addressed by this approach.

As Orseau [25] has remarked, the Gödel machine is expected to be computationally extremely expensive for reasonably complex practical applications.

An important limitation of this paper is that we have not provided an implementation of the design Gödel machine together with a proof of concept demonstration. This remains a task for future work. Furthermore, for an application in a real-world context, the problem to be solved by the machine needs to be carefully selected. For example, which tasks based on which inputs and outputs are interesting for automation [31]? Apart from the possibility of proper formalization, economic criteria will certainly play an important role.

6   Conclusions

In this paper, we proposed to integrate a formal creativity framework from Wiggins into the Gödel machine framework of a self-referential general problem solver. Such an integration would be a step towards creating a "general designing machine", i.e. a machine that is capable of solving a broad range of design problems. We call this version of the Gödel machine a design Gödel machine. The design Gödel machine is able to improve its initial design program, once it has proven that a modification would yield a higher utility. The main contribution of this paper to the artificial general intelligence literature is the integration of a framework from computational creativity into an artificial general intelligence framework. In particular, exploratory and transformational creative systems are integrated into the Gödel machine framework, where the initial design program is part of the exploratory creative system and the proof searcher is part of the transformational creative system. Of particular practical interest would be a design Gödel machine that can solve complex software and hardware design problems. Elements of such a machine are sketched out. However, a practical implementation would require a more extended formal systems engineering framework than those existing today. An interesting area for future work would be the integration of Wiggins' framework into other artificial general intelligence frameworks such as Hutter's AIXI and Orseau and Ring's space-time embedded intelligence.

References

1. Boden, M.: Computer models of creativity. AI Mag. **30**(3), 23 (2009)
2. Bostrom, N.: Superintelligence: Paths, Dangers, Strategies. Oxford University Press, Oxford (2014)
3. Broy, M.: A logical basis for component-oriented software and systems engineering. Comput. J. **53**(10), 1758–1782 (2010)
4. Broy, M., Dederichs, F., Dendorfer, C., Fuchs, M., Gritzner, T.F., Weber, R.: The design of distributed systems: an introduction to focus. Technical report, Technische Universität München. Institut für Informatik (1992)
5. Broy, M., Feilkas, M., Herrmannsdoerfer, M., Merenda, S., Ratiu, D.: Seamless model-based development: from isolated tools to integrated model engineering environments. Proc. IEEE **98**(4), 526–545 (2010)
6. Cherti, M.: Deep generative neural networks for novelty generation: a foundational framework, metrics and experiments. Ph.D. thesis, Université Paris-Saclay (2018)
7. Colton, S., Goodwin, J., Veale, T.: Full-FACE poetry generation. In: ICCC, pp. 95–102 (2012)
8. Cope, D.: Computer Models of Musical Creativity. MIT Press, Cambridge (2005)
9. Elgammal, A., Papazoglou, M., Krämer, B.: Design for customization: a new paradigm for product-service system development. In: Procedia CIRP (2017)
10. Fallenstein, B., Soares, N.: Problems of self-reference in self-improving space-time embedded intelligence. In: Goertzel, B., Orseau, L., Snaider, J. (eds.) AGI 2014. LNCS (LNAI), vol. 8598, pp. 21–32. Springer, Cham (2014). https://doi.org/10.1007/978-3-319-09274-4_3
11. Gero, J.: Creativity, emergence and evolution in design. Knowl.-Based Syst. **9**(7), 435–448 (1996)
12. Gödel, K.: Über formal unentscheidbare Sätze der Principia Mathematica und verwandter Systeme I. Monatshefte für mathematik und physik **38**(1), 173–198 (1931)
13. Goertzel, B.: Artificial general intelligence: concept, state of the art, and future prospects. J. Artif. Gen. Intell. **5**(1), 1–48 (2014)
14. Golden, B.: A unified formalism for complex systems architecture. Ph.D. thesis, École Polytechnique (2013)
15. Harel, D., Rumpe, B.: Meaningful modeling: what's the semantics of semantics? Computer **37**(10), 64–72 (2004)
16. Haskins, C., Forsberg, K., Krueger, M.: INCOSE systems engineering handbook. In: International Council On Systems Engineering INCOSE (2007)
17. Hatchuel, A., Le Masson, P., Reich, Y., Weil, B.: A systematic approach of design theories using generativeness and robustness. In: Proceedings of the 18th International Conference on Engineering Design (ICED 11) (2011)
18. Hein, A.: Artificial intelligence probes for interstellar exploration and colonization. arXiv, arXiv:1612 (2016)
19. Hein, A.M.: The greatest challenge: manned interstellar travel. In: Beyond the Boundary: Exploring the Science and Culture of Interstellar Spaceflight, pp. 349–376, Lulu (2014)
20. Hein, A.M., Pak, M., Pütz, D., Bühler, C., Reiss, P.: World ships-architectures & feasibility revisited. J. Br. Interplanetary Soc. **65**(4), 119–133 (2012)
21. Herrmann, C., Krahn, H., Rumpe, B., Schindler, M., Völkel, S.: An algebraic view on the semantics of model composition. In: Akehurst, D.H., Vogel, R., Paige, R.F. (eds.) ECMDA-FA 2007. LNCS, vol. 4530, pp. 99–113. Springer, Heidelberg (2007). https://doi.org/10.1007/978-3-540-72901-3_8

22. Herzig, S.I.J., Brandstätter, M.: Applying software engineering methodologies to model-based systems engineering. In: Proceedings of 4th International Workshop on System & Concurrent Engineering for Space Applications SECESA (2010)
23. Hutter, M.: Universal Artificial Intelligence: Sequential Decisions Based on Algorithmic Probability. Springer, Heidelberg (2004). https://doi.org/10.1007/b138233
24. Mealy, G.H.: A method for synthesizing sequential circuits. Bell Labs Tech. J. **34**(5), 1045–1079 (1955)
25. Muehlhauser, L.. Laurent Orseau on Artificial General Intelligence (2013)
26. Myhill, J.: The abstract theory of self-reproduction. In: Views on General Systems Theory, pp. 106–118 (1964)
27. Orseau, L., Ring, M.: Space-time embedded intelligence. In: Bach, J., Goertzel, B., Iklé, M. (eds.) AGI 2012. LNCS (LNAI), vol. 7716, pp. 209–218. Springer, Heidelberg (2012)
28. Orseau, L., Ring, M.: Self-modification and mortality in artificial agents. In: Schmidhuber, J., Thórisson, K.R., Looks, M. (eds.) AGI 2011. LNCS (LNAI), vol. 6830, pp. 1–10. Springer, Heidelberg (2011). https://doi.org/10.1007/978-3-642-22887-2_1
29. Rice, H.: Classes of recursively enumerable sets and their decision problems. Trans. Am. Math. Soc. **74**(2), 358–366 (1953)
30. Riedl, M., Young, R.: Story planning as exploratory creativity: techniques for expanding the narrative search space. New Gener. Comput. **24**(3), 303–323 (2006)
31. Rigger, E., Shea, K., Stankovic, T.: Task categorisation for identification of design automation opportunities. J. Eng. Des. **29**(3), 131–159 (2018)
32. Ritchie, G.: The JAPE riddle generator: technical specification. Technical report (2003)
33. Russell, S., Dewey, D., Tegmark, M.: Research priorities for robust and beneficial artificial intelligence. AI Mag. **36**(4), 105–114 (2015)
34. Schmidhuber, J.: Developmental robotics, optimal artificial curiosity, creativity, music, and the fine arts. Connection Sci. **18**(2), 173–187 (2006)
35. Schmidhuber, J.: Ultimate cognition à la Gödel. Cogn. Comput. **1**(2), 177–193 (2009)
36. Schmidhuber, J.: Formal theory of creativity, fun, and intrinsic motivation (1990–2010). IEEE Trans. Auton. Ment. Dev. **2**(3), 230–247 (2010)
37. Schmidhuber, J.: A formal theory of creativity to model the creation of art. In: McCormack, J., d'Inverno, M. (eds.) Computers and Creativity, pp. 323–337. Springer, Heidelberg (2012). https://doi.org/10.1007/978-3-642-31727-9_12
38. Simon, H., Lea, G.: Problem solving and rule induction: a unified view (1974)
39. Simons, P.: Parts: A Study in Ontology. Oxford University Press, Oxford (1987)
40. Soares, N.: Formalizing two problems of realistic world-models. In: Technical report, Machine Intelligence Research Institute (2014)
41. Todd, S., Latham, W.: Evolutionary Art and Computers. Academic Press, Cambridge (1992)
42. Wiggins, G.: A preliminary framework for description, analysis and comparison of creative systems. Knowl.-Based Syst. **19**(7), 449–458 (2006)

Resource-Constrained Social Evidence Based Cognitive Model for Empathy-Driven Artificial Intelligence

Anton Kolonin[1,2(✉)]

[1] Aigents Group, Novosibirsk, Russia
akolonin@gmail.com
[2] SingularityNET Foundation, Amsterdam, Netherlands

Abstract. Working model of social aspects of human and non-human intelligence is required for social embodiment of artificial general intelligence systems to explain, predict and manage behavioral patterns in multi-agent communities. For this purpose, we propose implementation of resource-constrained social evidence based model and discuss possible implications of its application.

Keywords: Artificial psychology · Artificial general intelligence · Compassion
Cognitive model · Empathy · Social evidence · Social proof

1 Introduction

For complete embodiment of any artificial general intelligence (AGI) system [1], we anticipate the need for social embodiment. That is, besides physical or virtual connections to the world, supplying self-reinforcement feedback, we assume there is a need for social connections supporting social reflections, based on empathy and compassion mutually expressed between members of human or non-human community of natural or artificial beings. In fact, there is known evidence in mass psychology regarding effects that social patterns have on behavior of individuals [2]. These effects may have constructive or destructive implications, depending on the case [3], including such negative scenarios as social engineering and psychological operations [4]. The former may be employed to implement soft control of entire community improving its performance while the latter may be used to abuse and destroy the community. At the same time, need for human-friendly AGI requires comprehension of human values on behalf of AGI system, while these values might get learned in course of self-reinforced co-development of AGI system with humans that it is supposed to serve to. For this purpose, having the system possessing cognitive model capable to learn values of its social environment appears very important.

Earlier works in the area of artificial psychology (AP) involving mathematical modeling of social interactions phenomena and dispute resolution in communities have been carried out by Lefebvre [5]. As it has been suggested by Goertzel and other authors (Kolonin, Pressing, Pennachin) in 2000, basis of social motives of an artificial agent behavior can be grounded on principle of compassion between interacting agents. The

© Springer Nature Switzerland AG 2018
M. Iklé et al. (Eds.): AGI 2018, LNAI 10999, pp. 100–108, 2018.
https://doi.org/10.1007/978-3-319-97676-1_10

definition of the same principle can be called "empathic computing" [6] and applied for study of effects of behavioral modifications in human, non-human and hybrid environments.

In the further discussion, we will be relying on the principles of empathy and compassion as built-in qualities of AGI system, following definition of intelligence made by Goertzel [1] as ability to reach complex goals in complex environments using limited resources. It will be assumed that decision making process of a system capable for social behavior based on these principles can be implemented with fuzzy or probabilistic logic operating with networks or graphs of concepts and relationships [7, 8]. Specifically, we will discuss extensions and implications of the social evidence based cognitive model constrained by resources [9, 10].

In such model, social evidence based decision making process implies that an agents reaches internal consensus in its internal system of reflections of its social referees, being limited by time and amount of power to make these decision timely not over-consuming available energy [9]. In social psychology studies this principle and its implications are well backed up with known phenomenology and notion of social proof identified by Cialdini [2].

The end goal of the work is to engineer working AGI agent capable for empathic and compassionate behavior serving its human environment [11].

2 Model

The suggested resource-constrained social evidence based cognitive model of an AGI agent, based on earlier works [9, 10], assumes the scope of knowledge is represented with atoms [1] being concepts or relationships, with each atom having its truth value, or subjective agent's expression of truth value attached to it.

The scope of atoms may be representing hyper-graph [1], consisting of few segments, as Fig. 1 shows, such as foundation graph, social graph, evidence graph and imagination graph [9]. For further analysis and discussion, we provide following definitions of the segments and their functional relationships.

Foundation graph contains trusted "hardwired" knowledge which does not need fuzzy logic or probabilistic reasoning to infer truth values of knowledge atoms it it. Each i of the atoms F_i represents part of consistent belief system of the knowledge owner, so subjective expression of truth value F_i is fixed maximum value, such as *1.0* in case of reasoning on scale between *0.0* and *1.0*.

Social graph contains weighted relationships with social referees of the knowledge owner, with expression values indicating cumulative level of trust, empathy and compassion in respect to every member j of society S_j. It should be noted that this level may be computed from the rest of the other relationships P_{ij} connecting social referee j to atoms in foundation graph and representing reflection of referee in the belief of the knowledge owner. The latter can be thought as social binding reflecting proximity of of social referee to the knowledge owner self in its own view.

Evidence graph contains facts k of everyday evidence E_k owner of knowledge is being exposed to, with each fact having its expression value. Each of the facts may have

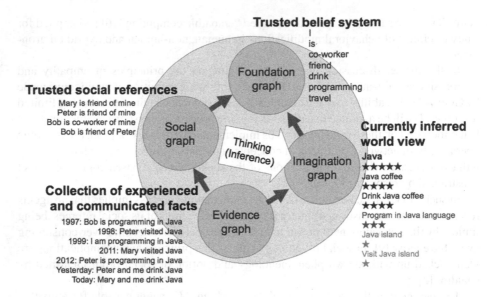

Fig. 1. Social evidence based cognitive model – segmentation of scope of knowledge.

connections Q_{ik} to atoms in foundation graph with expression values representing extent to which the fact is grounded in the belief of the knowledge owner. Also, each of the facts may have connections R_{jk} to members of social graph with expression values indicating extent to which social referee j is though to be responsible for authoring these facts themselves or treating them as reliable and relevant.

Imagination graph contains current view image G_k of the world supplied by evidence facts k to to the extent the facts are grounded in the belief of the owner Q_{ik}, with account to valuation of the facts by referees R_{jk}, including valuations of the referees S_j themselves. The following formula may be used to approximate this dependency.

$$G_k = E_k * (\Sigma_i(Q_{ik}) * \Sigma_j(R_{ik} * S_j)), \qquad S_j = \Sigma_i(P_{ij} * F_i)$$

Obvious interpretation of the formula suggests that expression of fact k in world view image of a subject depends on everything variable above, with growth of it with amount of the raw fact evidence E_k, extent to which is is grounded in core belief system Q_{ik}, and supporting social evidence R_{jk} weighted by social binding S_j.

Further, the idealistic framework described above may be complicated by physical limits on any of the segments, restricting their capacity, so only the atoms with highest degree of expression are retained while the others may by pushed out from agent memory, with different effects in respect to short-term or working memory and long-term one [9, 10]. In simple form, for each segment of the graph, it may be represented with filtering functions F, S, E, and G retaining only top expressed atoms in foundation, social, evidence and imagination graphs, respectively.

$$G_k = G(E(E_k) * \Sigma_i(Q_{ik}) * \Sigma_j(R_{ik} * S(S_j))), \qquad S_j = \Sigma_i(P_{ij} * F(F_i))$$

Important part of the model is that atoms in foundation graph are considered trusted unconditionally, so F_i is always true, while atoms in imagination graph require resource-consuming inference as described above. For atoms G_k that are always true or close to that, the inference makes no sense so resources can be preserved "hardwiring" them into belief system, moving knowledge from segment G to F. For atoms G_k that are not close to true, still requiring inference yet occupying imagination graph often enough to impact on resource consumption by inference, another ways to preserve energy and space are possible. It can be solved with adjusting any of the other variables so that inferred truth values approach to true and respective atoms may follow the scenario above due to increased expression of truth value. Alternatively, the other variables can be adjusted do the truth values get below the filtering functions and respective facts are not involved in the inference at all.

Justification of the model can be considered from few different perspectives. First, there is separation of the scope of knowledge, underlying decision making, into "absolute truths" and "context-specific truths". In hardware and software, the former is more like hardcoded OS-level code operating efficiently in pre-allocated portion of memory while the latter is more like loadable and overloadable applications, operating on top of the former in remaining memory and being swapped optionally. In humans, the former goes to implementation of unconditional stimuli and long-term conditional stimuli associated with deep beliefs such as religion or attachment to liberal or conservative points of view, while the latter corresponds to short-term conditional stimuli and may me changed based on specific circumstances and current mood.

The other justification to split store of information and cognitive processes into segments such as foundation graph and imagination graph is implied by need to provide fast and computationally cheap responses within restricted amount of resources and limited time in respect to operations that are repeating often enough, so they should not consume too much energy, or are critical for survival, so they should be handled rapidly. On the opposite side, events not happening often and not critical to survival may deserver careful consideration within wider context involved different possible inference paths and options. This is like move to rescue children from wild animal or moving car is something fundamental for average human and happens almost unconditionally given core belief, while rescue children from the rain main may be opted out if the rain is warm and children are enjoying the natural shower. It worth noticing that our model assumes the knowledge and cognitive activities that involves it may be moved across these segments due to long-term changes of contexts, as long as environment changes during the life time.

The need for social graph used for social referencing can be justified to keep weights of particular social referees involved in the inference process. It may benefit decision making process introducing social evidence ("social proof" by Cialdini [2]) in cases when there is no sufficient personal evidence to make decision or when there are conflicting personal evidences to be resolved. Since the social evidences from different sources may involve even more conflicting evidences, there is the need to ranking of the sources of evidence by social proximity, expressed in terms of belief proximity. Notable, since either human or artificial being may have no access to internal belief of its peer, we may consider measure of apparent belief or peer's interaction partner to be considered. In humans, for surrogate measure of social proximity natural and behavioral traits are considered. In artificial beings operating within communities based on open protocols, actual measure of true belief systems may be computed.

3   Analysis

Earlier qualitative empirical modeling of practical implications of the model above are presenting different cases of social engineering [9] as well as overall social dynamics at large scale [10]. Below we discuss how the model works in greater details.

On the left side of the Fig. 2 there is initial state of multi-agent interaction history, where two agents on the top share knowledge atoms A,B with each other, whereas two agents at the bottom share knowledge X,Y. Also, there is agent in the middle sharing A,B with upper ones and X with lower ones, plus it has atom being C communicated to everyone. Finally, the agent on the left at the bottom has Z being communicated with its close circles. Assuming the possessed knowledge resides in foundation graph, due to overlaps in beliefs, the three agents at the top are somewhat closer one to another while the two agents at the bottom are close to each other but distant from the upper three. Respectively, due to different strengths of social bindings, expression of communicated knowledge atoms C and Z is different for different agents, as shown by thickness of arrows representing agent-to-agent interactions.

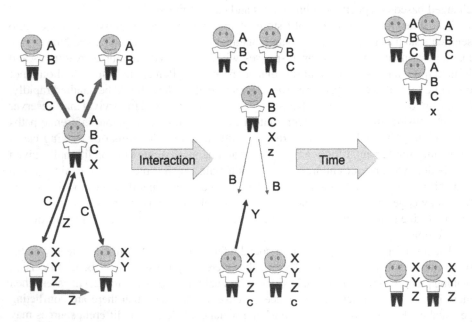

Fig. 2. Explanation of social dynamics due to interaction with knowledge comprehension based on social evidence with impact of limited resources.

The effect of such interaction is shown in the center. Two agents on the top have obtained high expression of C which may be eventually moved to their foundation graph, while two agents at the bottom are given weak expression of C which may stay remaining in imagination graph. Similarly, agent in the middle has got weakened expression of Z. Still, agent on the right at the bottom has got well expressed Z to get retained in its belief. The effect of the interaction is that three agents at the top become socially closer to each other – same as two agents at the bottom, with both groups moved socially further away each from the other. Now, when agent in the middle tries to communicate B to agents at the bottom, their similarity may be not sufficient to let B even entering imagination graph of the latter agents, so the evidence may get completely ignored. Still, Y communicated to middle agent from the bottom may enter its imagination graph, still being weak enough to enter belief system of it.

Over the time, forgetting may take place so the knowledge atoms with weak expression are removed from imagination graphs, so Z may get forgotten by agent in the middle while C may be get forgotten by agents at the bottom. It ends up with further separation of agent society into isolated groups barely sharing any common values.

Social dynamics above justifies earlier discussion [10] that any inhomogeneous community, given no extra input outside affecting expression of some common values, tends to get separated into isolated social clusters eventually. In turn, with external inputs affecting such common values, like mutual benefits or shared existential threats, society can be rather united. On the other hand, having particular inhomogeneous input fed from outside, some of it may be consumed by one part of society but not the other, so in such case internal divergence of society can be even enforced. Practically, the latter effect is being exploited in so called "psychological operations" [4], implementing methods "of social engineering" based on social proof [2]. Respectively, understanding of this dynamics allows to engineer measures to resist psychological operations or social engineering on behalf of society of either artificial agents or humans being subject of such attack vector.

4   Implications and Applications

While numerical simulations based on the model discussed have not been performed yet, qualitative analysis of the model behavior are well confirmed with both positive and negative phenomena found in literature on mass psychology, mathematical modeling and live experiments with social networks [2, 3, 5]. In particular, "social proof" described bu Cialdini [2], methods of directing human masses [3], methods for quantitive modulation of human mood [4] may be turned for good as well as for bad, based on the means and those who applies such method and for which purpose. Within the Aigents project [11, 12], we are trying to build artificial agent compassionate to its human master and its close social environment, so we anticipate what agent learns from its master can not be turned into evil. So, far, current implementation of news monitoring and information extraction agents based on the model learns web surfing preferences and information extraction patterns from the user owner as well as from user's connection in social media, considered as social peer, with proximity of relations between the user and the peer taken into account [13]. News relevance assessment based on so called "personal relevance" and "social relevance" performed by Aigent can be explored on https:// aigents.com website, as shown on Fig. 3.

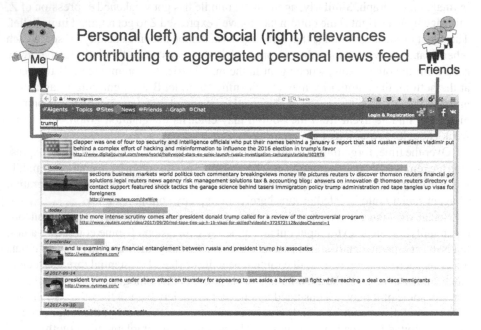

Fig. 3. Personal and social relevances used by news monitoring and information extraction agent. Width of left part of the bar above each of the news items corresponds to the personal relevance, based on experiential learning in course of interaction between the agent and its human owner. Width of right part of the bar corresponds to social relevance learned in the course of interactions with other users, with account to proximity between the users' profiles.

For wider area of applications, we assume that building human-friendly agent of artificial general intelligence can not be rule based but should rather apply reasoning in respect to what can be though as friendly to particular human at the moment and what should be not. Obviously, this reasoning should be efficient, so definition of general intelligence made by Goertzel as "ability to reach complex goals in complex environments giving limited resources" [1] would apply. Hence, different segments of agent memory used by agent for operations on different kinds of data with different performance and efficiency, being adaptable to changing social context appears reasonable for implementation of generic-purpose AGI agents other than just personal assistants specialized for news monitoring and information extraction.

5   Conclusion

We conclude that suggested model is well justified with known phenomenological evidence in the area of mass psychology and may be suited to model behavior of artificial societies of multi-agent systems, as well as human communities and hybrid human-computer societies. This makes it possible to quantify and predict the resistance to social engineering and psychological operations, and also to model constructive manipulations in respect to target communities. This also provides framework to build cognitive models of AGI creatures capable for human like behavior grounded in empathy end compassion, with possibility of tuning parameters or such cognitive models in course of self-reinforcing interactions.

Still, qualitative empirical modeling and verification by means of phenomenological evidence does not seem sufficient enough to justify the suggested model completely, so simulation modeling of multi-agent societies employing the model is required in the future. The other part of our plan is to implement such model in AGI agent serving to human user as intelligent assistant in the course of interaction with online and social media [11], with prototype now available at https://aigents.com website.

Acknowledgements. This work was inspired by earlier ideas of Ben Goertzel, Jeff Pressing, Cassio Pennachin and Pei Wang in the course of Webmind project targeted to build artificial psyche in 1998–2001.

References

1. Goertzel, B.: CogPrime: An Integrative Architecture for Embodied Artificial General Intelligence. OpenCog, Paris, October 2, 2012 (2012)
2. Cialdini, R.: Influence: The Psychology of Persuasion. ISBN 0-688-12816-5 (1984)
3. Kramer, A., Guillory, J., Hancock, J.: Experimental evidence of massive-scale emotional contagion through social networks. PNAS 2014 **111**(24), 8788–8790 (2014)
4. Nazaretyan, A.: Psychology of mass behavior. ISBN 5-9292-0033-5, PER SE (2001)
5. Lefebvre, V.: Algebra of conscience. Springer, New York (2001). https://doi.org/10.1007/978-94-017-0691-9
6. Nguyen, H., Masthoff, J.: Designing empathic computers: the effect of multimodal empathic feedback using animated agent. In: Proceeding Persuasive '09 Proceedings of the 4th International Conference on Persuasive Technology, Article No. 7, Claremont, California, USA 26–29 April 2009
7. Iklé, M.: Probabilistic Logic Networks in a Nutshell. In: Benferhat, S., Grant, J. (eds.) SUM 2011. LNCS (LNAI), vol. 6929, pp. 52–60. Springer, Heidelberg (2011). https://doi.org/10.1007/978-3-642-23963-2_5
8. Vityaev, E.: Unified formalization of « natural » classification, « natural » concepts, and consciousness as integrated information by Giulio Tononi. In: The Sixth international conference on Biologically Inspired Cognitive Architectures, BICA 2015, Lyon, France, 6–8 November 2015, vol. 71, pp 169–177. Elsevier (2015). Procedia Computer Science
9. Kolonin, A.: Computable cognitive model based on social evidence and restricted by resources: Applications for personalized search and social media in multi-agent environments. In: International Conference on Biomedical Engineering and Computational Technologies (SIBIRCON) 2015, Novosibirsk, Russia (2015)
10. Kolonin A., Vityaev E., Orlov, Y.: Cognitive architecture of collective intelligence based on social evidence. In: Proceedings of 7th Annual International Conference on Biologically Inspired Cognitive Architectures BICA 2016, NY, USA, July 2016

11. Kolonin, A.: Architecture of Internet Agent with Social Awareness. In: 8th Annual International Conference on Biologically Inspired Cognitive Architectures BICA 2017, vol. 123, 2018, pp. 240–245 (2017). Procedia Computer Science
12. Kolonin, A.: Adaptive experiential learning for business intelligence agents. In: Cognitive Sciences, Genomics and Bioinformatics (CSGB) - Symposium Proceedings (2016)
13. Kolonin, A., Shamenkov, D., Muravev, A., Solovev, A.: Personal analytics for societies and businesses with Aigents online platform. In: 2017 International Multi-Conference on Engineering, Computer and Information Sciences (SIBIRCON) - Conference Proceedings (2017)

Unsupervised Language Learning in OpenCog

Alex Glushchenko[1], Andres Suarez[2], Anton Kolonin[1(✉)], Ben Goertzel[1,2],
Claudia Castillo[2], Man Hin Leung[2], and Oleg Baskov[1]

[1] SingularityNET Foundation, Amsterdam, Netherlands
{anton,ben}@singularitynet.io
[2] Hanson Robotics, Hong Kong, China

Abstract. We discuss technology capable to learn language without supervision. While the entire goal may be too ambitious and not achievable to full extent, we explore how far we can advance grammar learning. We present the current approach employed in the open source OpenCog Artificial Intelligence Platform, describe the cognitive pipeline being constructed and present some intermediate results.

Keywords: Categorization · Clustering · Computational linguistics
Dimensionality reduction · Formal grammar · Grammar induction
Natural language processing · Unsupervised learning · Vector space

1 Introduction

This work is driven by a desire to make sense of the possible mechanisms underlying natural intelligence and applied to language-based communication skills. According to earlier work [1–3], human intelligence is substantially connected with language acquisition abilities. As pointed out in [1], most of such acquisition is loosely supervised, while existing machine learning techniques require more effort and training data to reach the level of human children.

Another point being made in [2] is that current natural language processing applications require a formal grammar or an annotated corpora as input. In practice, however, the cost of creating such grammars results in a lack of good-quality ones for many languages. Indeed, several years of human effort are required to create a formal grammar for a language, given formalisms such as Link Grammar (LG) [4]. While this has been done to great extent in English, as the language most widely used in electronic communications, other languages are far less represented, and for many natural languages such effort has never been undertaken. Even for English, the existent grammar dictionary in Link Grammar can only handle literary English texts and fails to support deviations, like dialects used in chat rooms, or domain-specific jargon. Our work, aiming to automatically produce a grammar from unannotated text, could potentially reduce the effort needed to process any language and make it comprehensible by software.

Moreover, many natural language processing (NLP) applications for text mining and information extraction rely on pattern-based approaches for classification, entity extraction and attribution [5]. For such applications, it is crucial to have a way to identify textual patterns which could be used for entity extraction, as well as for finding

M. Iklé et al. (Eds.): AGI 2018, LNAI 10999, pp. 109–118, 2018.
https://doi.org/10.1007/978-3-319-97676-1_11

relationships between entities. That is, the patterns should be flexible enough to represent different textual representations of the same semantic entity as well as to describe patterns of connections between such entities represented in text. Technology that infers these patterns in an unsupervised way, given prepared (controlled) corpora, could be highly valuable, as it would make NLP applications cheaper, faster, more precise and efficient.

A system like the one we propose would also help approach the artificial general intelligence problem known as "Baby Turing Test" [6]. While the classic "Turing Test" expects an AI system to display conversational intelligence comparable to a human, it does not prevent such system from being simply hardcoded, and does not guarantee that the system actually learned its abilities through education and interaction with its environment. In turn, the "Baby Turing Test" requires that an "uneducated" system undergoes the process of experiential or didactic training, and eventually develop skills sufficient to pass the classic "Turing Test". Our work could help on this goal, at least from a comprehension perspective, so that an artificially intelligent system could be incrementally fed with information in a given language, and eventually make sense of this information and new information of similar kind, like texts in the known language within the same knowledge domain.

The overall direction of research is shaped by earlier works [2, 3], and it's based on representing linguistic structures as "sheafs" of graphs [7], where the elementary structures of the graphs are represented with so-called "disjuncts" from Link Grammar [4], which can then be used to infer a grammar in Link Grammar format. The input of the grammar-learning process are statistical parses generated with a minimum spanning tree (MST) approach based on "mutual information" computed for co-occurring words in sentences [8].

In this work, we discuss some practical aspects of implementing the NLP pipeline for unsupervised language learning (ULL), including building a vector space [9], its dimension reduction (DR), and unsupervised category learning grammatical and semantic concepts by means of clustering [10–15]. We will also consider the different approaches for word-sense disambiguation (WSD) applied [16, 17].

All of the research and developments discussed further are performed in the scope of the open source OpenCog project [18] and SingularityNET platform.

2   Background

For the work discussed in this article we are making certain assumptions and considering specific options, as discussed below. We are not sure if unsupervised learning on unannotated corpora with neither grounding nor reinforcement feedback can succeed at all. Still, we do want to advance in this direction to see if we can learn at least most of the grammar and some of the semantics. We also understand that there is no clear boundary between grammatical and semantic categories, because certain semantics categories such as time, gender and plurality may affect grammar to extents specific to particular languages. To make the problem solvable at least to some extent, we can make certain simplifications and relaxations, as follows.

Controlled Corpora. Although unannotated, our learning corpora are pre-processed to reduce the amount of gibberish (tables, graphics, mixed languages, etc.) found in them, as they are obtained from public sources. We also use corpora of different complexity in the following order, targeting different goals.

- **Proof-of-Concept Turtle** (POC-Turtle) corpus - represents closed semantic space of very few words communicated in simplex Turtle language [19], used in semantic web programming, with complexity limited to three words per sentence in strict Subject-Verb-Predicate triplet grammar. Complexity of such language can be thought closer to complexity of language that non-human primates can learn [20] or that children at age up to 3 can use [21].
- **Proof-of-Concept English with no ambiguity** (POC-English-NoAmb) corpus - manually created closed semantic space of very few English words with nearly the same frequency of use, communicated in simple grammatical construction of 4–5 words per sentence, without any ambiguous words.
- **Proof-of-Concept English with ambiguity** (POC-English-Amb) corpus – similar to the above, but with two words involved in semantically and grammatically ambiguous constructions. Semantic ambiguity is represented by word "board" which can be either board of a ship or black board. Grammatical ambiguity is represented by word "saw" which can be either noun or past form of verb "see".
- **Child Directed Speech** corpus - collection of English communications directed to children with adapted lexicon and grammar complexity.
- **Gutenberg Children and Adult** corpora - children and adult subsets of literary corpora collected within Gutenberg Project (see https://www.gutenberg.org/).

Incremental Learning and "One-Shot Learning". Incremental learning approach may be interesting from a number of perspectives. There are different points of view whether using simplified language when conversing to child can advance language learning or complicate it [1]. In real life the richness of lexicon increases gradually over years of child development. So we would like to use both approaches. In one approach called "One-shot Learning", we would try to have entire grammar learned at one upon one successful reading of entire corpus. In the other one called "Incremental Learning", we would split the corpus into sections with gradually increasing complexity (in terms of either maximum sentence length of richness of lexicon or both), trying to capture more grammatical constructions incrementally. During the second approach we would measure the learning curve tracking the ability of developing system to pass the Baby Turing Test [6].

Symbolic vs. Sub-symbolic Approach. We are not limiting ourselves to use either "old school" symbolic approach such as LG [4] or "new school" of distributional representations in NLP with its latest advances [9]. In fact, we are planning to try both and it is anticipated that the final solution will be a combination of the two.

Variety of Vector Spaces. Generally, the word space can be represented with vector embeddings created by a number of sub-symbolic approaches. The most widely used vector space is the space of words, either "Bag-of-Words" or "Skip-gram" [9]. In our work we study the ways of replacing word tokens with word senses defined earlier. We also introduce the space of connectors - directed connectors between words, so the word "like" in phrases "like you" and "you like" would form two different dimensions "like-" and "like+" following the Link Grammar notation [2, 4]. Finally, we will also introduce the space of disjuncts so the word "like" in phrases "I like you" and "you like me" would form two dimensions corresponding to the disjuncts "I- & you+" and "you- & me+". Notably, the space of words is the most dense, the space of connectors is up to two times more sparse, and the space of disjuncts might appear orders of magnitude more sparse on large corpora.

Disambiguation. Since we are going to use statistical parsing, the question arises - how to compute mutual information for ambiguous words. In the sentence "I saw the saw", we can try disambiguating "saw" into "saw@noun" and "saw@verb" prior to calculating the MI, thus facilitating the parser task. The alternative is to parse the text as is, and later try to find the different senses of each word. We will try both options.

Mutual Information Counting. Another question is whether mutual information (MI) should be direction-sensitive, so we count directed links between words [4], or direction-insensitive, so we count co-occurring word pairs no matter what their mutual positions are. We are counting directed links but co-occurrence counting is possible as option to try.

Morphology. The importance of morphology in language comprehension and learning is well understood and there are approaches known to handle that [2, 3]. However, for now we do not consider this level of complexity. We deal with word tokens as entire symbols, disregarding their internal morphology and potential token interactions.

3 Natural Language Pipeline Architecture

The general overview of the cognitive pipeline architecture for the current stage of the project is presented below. Further, we describe specific the components, with their options. In the current implementation the pipeline is linear, so no iterative loops can take place at the moment. The entire pipeline with most of components is being developed as open source at https://github.com/singnet/language-learning with TextParser is being maintained as part of OpenCog at https://github.com/opencog/opencog/.

1. Text Pre-Cleaner - preprocesses corpus files with configurable cleanup and normalization options (is implemented now).
2. Sense Pre-Disambiguator - optionally, performs word disambiguation and builds senses from tokens (is being implemented now).
3. Text Parser - parses sentences of word tokens or senses with one of the possible approaches (is implemented now but may be improved in the future).
4. Grammar Learner - learns word categories from parses, infers grammar in LG format (is implemented now and improvements are ongoing).
5. Tester/Evaluator - evaluates quality of inferred grammar (is implemented).

Text Pre-cleaner. The goal of this component is to standardize corpora tests, removing HTML markup and graphics, normalizing different varieties of the same punctuation marks, interpreting UTF codes, and optionally converting all characters to lowercase. Although there is controversy about representing the capitalized and lower-cased versions of a word as the same token (e.g. "You" and "you"), we currently proceed with converting all texts to lower-case, on the basis that capitalization is not expressed explicitly in spoken conversations, and that all words have the same pronunciation regardless of their location in a sentence. This avoids a single meaning to be represented as two distinct vectors, one for each of its capitalized and non-capitalized versions. We may move past this point in future work and represent them individually.

Sense Pre-disambiguator. In order to use appropriate word-sense entries for mutual information counting during statistical parsing, we may try to disambiguate word tokens before the parsing takes place. For doing so, we may use distributed representation of words with n-grams and skip-grams in vector space of adjacent words [9] using AdaGram to provide word-sense disambiguation [17]. AdaGram extends the renowned Skip-gram methodology of word2vec [9] to include one vector embedding per word-sense, without fixing a number of senses per word a priori.

Text Parser. This component implements two phases: Mutual Information (MI) counting, with the Observer sub-component, and Minimum Spanning Tree (MST) Parser, accordingly to earlier design [3, 8].

Mutual information calculation during the Observer phase may be implemented in one of four ways: (a) cartesian combination of per-sentence words without account for distance; (b) cartesian combination of per-sentence words with account for distance; (c) sampling all parses produced by the Link Grammar Parser in random parsing mode; (d) sampling limited number of parses from the Link Grammar Parser in random parsing mode.

The pointwise mutual information (PMI), also known as focus mutual information (FMI) or association ratio [12] for an ordered pair of words (x, y) is a measure of the level of association of the two words in a given context, and is computed as:

$$PMI(x, y) = log2(p(x, y)/(p(x) \cdot p(y)))$$

where $p(x)$, $p(y)$, and $p(x,y)$ are short for $P(X = x)$, $P(Y = y)$ and $P(X = x, Y = y)$ respectively. Here X the is the random variable of the event of watching a word x to the left of any other word in a sentence, i.e. the probability of observing the ordered pair $(x, *)$. Similarly, Y is the random variable of the event of watching a word y to the right of any other word in a sentence, i.e. the probability of observing the ordered pair $(*, y)$. Thus $p(x, y)$ is the probability of observing the ordered pair (x, y) in a sentence. In turn this probabilities are calculated as:

$$p(x) = N(x, *)/N(*, *)$$
$$p(x) = N(*, y)/N(*, *)$$
$$p(x, y) = (x, y)/N(*, *)$$

Notice tha $N(x, y)$ is not necessarily the same as $N(y, x)$. PMI is a ratio that compares the probability of observing the two words together in a specific order vs observing them separately, and therefore lies in the range $(-\infty, \infty)$.

The way $N(x, y)$ is counted (the number of appearances of the pair (x, y) in the corpus) depends on choice from the above-mentioned methods. For cartesian combination methods (options a and b above), the pair (x, y) is counted only if x and y occur within distance R (a parameter) in the current sentence (distance r is defined as difference in word position in the sentence: $r = pos(y) - pos(x)$). When disregarding distance, they are counted one time per co-occurrence: $N(x, y) = \sum r < R(1)$, across all appearances of x and y in each of the sentences in the corpus. When accounting for distance, we count the pair R/r times: $N(x, y) = \sum r < R(R/r)$, so the words in greater proximity are getting more counts, with default count as R instead of 1.

For counting methods c and d above, the LG Parser can produce an exhaustive set of possible parses for a sentence, regardless of any grammar or prior knowledge on relationships between words. We can consider all possible parses if sentence length is small (method c), or select a number N (a parameter) of randomly chosen parses, for longer sentences where number of possible trees bursts exponentially. In these methods the pair (x, y) is counted each time x and y are linked together in a parse tree for the given sentence.

Once mutual information is collected, our MST-parser approximates the spanning tree with highest total MI [8], and returns that as output. A tree's MI score is computed as the sum of all linked word pair scores, where score is mutual information per word pair. In this step, we also test if accounting for distance in different ways improves the resulting parses: (i) $Score = PMI * R/r$; (ii) $Score = PMI + 1/r$; (iii) $Score = PMI + R/r$, with r and R as defined above.

Grammar Learner. This pipeline component processes the parse trees produced by the Text Parser in two phases: Category Learning and Grammar Induction. The Category Learning phase includes Vector Space modeling, Clustering, and optional Generalization sub-phases.

The Vector Space dimensions are chosen from: (a) words - either word tokens or word senses; (b) connectors [3, 4]; (c) disjuncts [3, 4]. Positive pointwise mutual information (PPMI) [12] is used for term weighting.

Clustering is performed using "sub-symbolic" or "symbolic" approach. The "sub-symbolic" Unsupervised Category Learning includes dimensionality reduction (DR) with singular value decomposition (SVD) [13] and K-means clustering [14]. The optimal number of clusters is selected based on maximum Silhouette index [15] value.

The alternative "symbolic" approach to clustering the disjunct space implies consecutive merging the single-germ-single-disjuncts ("seeds") extracted from the parse tree into single-germ-multi-disjunct "stalks" and multi-germ-multi-disjunct lexical entries.

The optional generalization agglomerates the learned categories (clusters) into higher-level grammatical categories, preserving relationships between child and parent category clusters.

Grammar Induction infers grammar links between the learned categories (clusters) by statistical processing the parse tree. The Link Grammar rules are induced for the learned set of clusters as either (a) sets of connectors to the linked clusters or (b) sets of disjuncts consisting of connectors to clusters.

Grammar Tester. Purpose of this component is to provide fitness function for entire pipeline with options and parameters configured for every pipeline component and each of its sub-components. There are two ways the fitness function can be evaluated. First, we may use inferred grammar in LG format and try to parse original text with given grammar configured for LG parser. Then, counting percentage of successfully parsed sentences and words per each sentence would give use usability value of the learned grammar, calling it "parse-ability". This approach would work for any language, including unknown languages, however it can not provide warranty that the grammar makes any real sense from linguistic perspective. Second, alternative approach can be tried for languages that are well studied by computational linguistics such as English, where LG dictionaries and grammatical rules are present. For the latter case, we can compare LG parses of original corpus done with native English LG setup as well as with inferred grammar. The proximity across parse trees on sentence-per-sentence basis for these two parses, called "parse-quality", would serve us fitness function rendering to which extent rules that we learn are close to ones created by human computational linguists.

4 Intermediate Results

The results obtained for the current state of the project can be split into a few sections. First, we discuss the use of words, connectors or disjuncts for building the vector space of real-size corpora. Next, we move onto studying different options to count mutual information and perform statistical parsing. Then, we systematically explore the possibility of learning valid Link Grammar dictionaries and rules for simplistic Proof-of-Concept corpora for Turtle and English languages. Finally, we study the possibility of using word-sense disambiguation before parsing, and if its use can improve the quality of Grammar Learning. All corpor and intermediate results are available at http://langlearn.singularitynet.io/data/ site.

At the beginning of the current stage of the project, efforts have been made to try unsupervised word category learning with Gutenberg Adult corpus data, available from the earlier stage of the project [3].

Unfortunately, the data was of low quality, with multiple non-English texts mixed with English ones, lots of special characters and pseudo-graphics included, and only cumulative information on counts of words, connectors and disjuncts extracted from original parses, with no actual parses present. However, using MST parse trees as inputs, we were able to build vector spaces of words and connectors and perform clustering.

It has turned out that, after cleaning the data, for 324 K words, there were 12 M links between the words. Respectively, in vector space of words, there were 324 K original dimensions and in vector space of connectors there were 285 K words on the left and 295 K on the right, so initial dimension for the vector space has effectively doubled. It was found that using original vector space of words, we were not able to identify sensible word categories, due to sparseness of the vector space.

Further, we used a cleaned set of link pairs extracted from the original MST parse trees, accepting only words having more than 85 unique neighbors total, on left and right. It provided us with 31 K words appearing in space of 61 K connectors with 9 M links between the words, so 9.4% words from original data set were supplying 76.2% of links. Using this vector space of connectors, we could clearly identify clusters of words in different languages, proper names, numeric values, and parts of speech. However, due to multiple inconsistencies in training corpus found, we did not proceed with this corpus further for grammar learning, to have re-iteration with this corpus later, when we can confirm that grammar can be actually learned with more simple corpora, as discussed further.

To determine which word-pair counting method better fits the natural "sampling" of parses using LG "ANY" mode, we have computed the Pearson correlation coefficient (PCC) across distributions of FMI values for our POC corpora, between this method and the cartesian combination of per-sentence words, with and without accounting for distance. For the POC-English corpus, we have discovered that the PCC between LG "ANY" and cartesian product, without taking distance into consideration, is 83%; instead, when we consider distance in the cartesian method, we get a PCC of 96%, which indicates that the methods produce very similar FMI. Due to its simplicity and good correlation, we will the default should be method of window-based word co-occurrence counting with account for distance (method b in section Text Parser above) to calculate FMI.

We have also studied to which extent the "expected" English parses, created manually for our POC corpora, correspond to parses provided by Link Grammar Parser with standard English dictionary. It is found that, for the POC-English-NoAmb corpus, the "expected parses" and the LG parses share around 97% of their links. Similarly, for the POC-English-Amb corpus, they share 93% of their links. Based on their similarity, we will use "expected" parses, instead of Link Grammar parses, for "parse-quality" fitness function.

We used "parse-quality" fitness function to compare different versions of MST-Parsing with (a) "expected" parses created manually. For POC-Turtle, it has been found that using (c) "cartesian" combination with account for distance as well as (e) LG "ANY" parses the "parse-quality" is 92% while using (d) "cartesian" combination with no account for distance provides "parse-quality" of 50% only. For POC-English, (c) "cartesian" combination with account for distance provides best quality of 66%, while (e) LG "ANY" parses the "parse-quality" provides 60%, and (d) "cartesian" combination with no account for distance is the worst at 50%. For further work, we choose to use MST-Parsing option (c) "cartesian" combination with account for distance, since it provides the best "parse-quality".

For systematic study of possibility of grammar inference with our pipeline, we have used two simplistic corpora with no ambiguous words in them, namely POC-Turtle and POC-English. For input parses used for grammar learning we used five options: (a) "expected" parses, created manually, with account to LG parse tree conventions; (b) native LG parses with known English LG setup (for POC-English only); (c) Text Parses based on "cartesian" combination of words within window and account for distance; (d) same as (c) but without account of distance; e) LG "ANY" parses, considering all possible parses for the sentence without any grammar knowledge. Four different configurations of Grammar Learner were used. For each of the configurations, different ways of modeling vector space with Connectors or Disjuncts, clustering with Dimension Reduction and K-means (DRK) or collection of Identical Lexical Entries (ILE) and grammar induction with Connectors or Disjuncts were used.

For the two corpora, using different configurations of Parser and Grammar Learner, we were able to get the following results from perspectives of "parse-ability" and "parse-quality". Pearson correlation coefficient between parse-ability and parse-quality has turned to be 85%, which means that **being able to make parse at all means been able to make it right**. When using Turtle language, grammar learning results present 100% parse-ability and parse-quality. When using English - parse-ability in range 50–100% and parse-quality 50–65%. Based on that, we conclude **the problem of automatic learning of formal grammar can be solved with accuracy 50–100%, given corpora that we have tried**. For both corpora, better parse-ability and parse-quality are provided with **MST parsing based on MI with account for distance, building vector space of connectors, then using dimensionality reduction and K-means clustering with subsequent grammar induction by means of either Connectors or Disjuncts**.

5   Conclusion

The primary conclusion of our work is that it is possible to learn formal grammar programmatically based on etalon parses corpus, with possibility to use the grammar for parsing the texts in given language automatically with accuracy in range 50–100%, depending on language. In particular, it has been confirmed for Link Grammar and for very simple controlled corpora in Turtle and English languages.

The secondary conclusion is that statistical parsing can be used for the purpose above, using MST parsing in particular, with account for distance between words when computing mutual information.

Our further plans involve upscaling our approach for using larger corpora, such as Gutenberg Children and Adult an others. We also plan to involve word-sense disambiguation and generalization stages trying to improve parse-ability and parse-quality of the results of parsing with learned grammar. Finally, testing approach would get improved so combination of testing learned grammars on novel corpus data not used for grammar learning will be used for any given language.

References

1. Dupoux, E.: Cognitive science in the era of artificial intelligence: a roadmap for reverse-engineering the infant language-learner. arXiv:1607.08723 [cs.CL] (2018)
2. Goertzel, B., Pennachin, C., Geisweiller, G.: Engineering General Intelligence, Part 2: The CogPrime Architecture for Integrative. Embodied AGI, Atlantis Press, New York (2014)
3. Vepstas L., Goertzel B.: Learning language from a large (unannotated) corpus. arXiv: 1401.3372 [cs.CL], 14 January 2014
4. Sleator D., Temperley D.: Parsing English with a link grammar. In: Third International Workshop on Parsing Technologies (1993)

5. Kolonin A.: Automatic text classification and property extraction. In: 2015 SIBIRCON/ SibMedInfo Conference Proceedings, pp. 27–31 (2015). ISBN 987-1-4673-9109-2
6. Barbara, P.: Workshop on Information and Representation Report. In: Workshop on Information and Representation (Washington, DC, March 30-April 1, 1985). Collected Works - Conference Proceedings (021), 151 p. (1985)
7. Friedman, J.: Sheaves on graphs, their homological invariants, and a proof of the Hanna Neumann conjecture. arXiv:1105.0129v2 [math.CO] (2011)
8. Yuret, D.: Discovery of linguistic relations using lexical attraction. arXiv:cmp-lg/9805009 [cs.CL] (1998)
9. Mikolov T., Sutskever I., Chen K., Corrado G., Dean J.: Distributed representations of words and phrases and their compositionality. arXiv:1310.4546v1 [cs.CL] (2013)
10. Cha M., Gwon Y., Kung H.: Language modeling by clustering with word embeddings for text readability assessment. arXiv:1709.01888v1 [cs.CL] (2017)
11. Franco-Penya, H. et al.: An analysis of the application of simplified silhouette to the evaluation of k-means clustering validity. In: 13th International Conference on Machine Learning and Data Mining MLDM 2017, New York, USA (2017)
12. Church, K., Hank, P.: Word association norms, mutual information, and lexicography. Comput. Linguist. Arch. **16**(1), 22–29 (1990)
13. Wall M., Rechtsteiner A., Rocha L.: Singular value decomposition and principal component analysis, arXiv:physics/0208101 (2002)
14. Sculley D.: Web-scale k-means clustering. In: WWW 2010 Proceedings of the 19th International Conference on World Wide Web, pp. 1177–1178, Raleigh, North Carolina, USA (2010)
15. Starczewski, A., Krzyżak, A.: Performance evaluation of the Silhouette index. In: International Conference on Artificial Intelligence and Soft Computing, ICAISC 2015: Artificial Intelligence and Soft Computing, pp. 49–58 (2015)
16. Delpech J.: Unsupervised word sense disambiguation in dynamic semantic spaces arXiv: 1802.02605 [cs.CL] (2018)
17. Bartunov, S., Kondrashkin, D., Osokin, A., Vetrov, D.: Breaking sticks and ambiguities with adaptive skip-gram. In: Proceedings of the 19th International Conference on Artificial Intelligence and Statistics, pp. 130–138 (2016)
18. Hart, D., Goertzel, B.: OpenCog: a software framework for integrative artificial general intelligence. In: Proceedings of the 2008 Conference on Artificial General Intelligence 2008, pp. 468–472. IOS Press Amsterdam (2008). ISBN: 978-1-58603-833-5
19. World Wide Web Consortium: Turtle Terse RDF Triple Language (2012)
20. Gillespie-Lynch, K., Savage-Rumbaugh, S., Lyn, H.: Language learning in non-human primates. In: Brooks, P.J., Kempe, V. (eds.) Encyclopedia of Language Development. SAGE Publications (2014). https://doi.org/10.13140/2.1.3105.3122
21. Patterson, F., Patterson, C., Brentari, D.: Language in child, chimp, and gorilla. Am. Psychol. **42**(3), 270–272 (1987). https://doi.org/10.1037/0003-066x.42.3.270.b

Functionalist Emotion Model in NARS

Xiang Li[1], Patrick Hammer[1](✉), Pei Wang[1](✉), and Hongling Xie[2](✉)

[1] Department of Computer and Information Sciences, Temple University,
Philadelphia, USA
{xiangliAGI,tuh38867,pei.wang}@temple.edu
[2] Department of Psychology, Temple University, Philadelphia, USA
hongling.xie@temple.edu

Abstract. Emotions play a crucial role in different cognitive functions, such as action selection and decision-making processes. This paper describes a new appraisal model for the emotion mechanism of NARS, an AGI system. Different from the previous appraisal model where emotions are triggered by the specific context, the new appraisal evaluates the relations between the system and its goals, based on a new set of criteria, including desirability, belief, and anticipation. Our work focuses on the functions of emotions and how emotional reactions could help NARS to improve its various cognitive capacities.

Keywords: Artificial general intelligence · NARS · Emotion

1 Introduction

Emotion is intrinsic to human cognition and serves important functions in human cognition by providing critical information just like vision, hearing, touch, taste, and smell [3]. Emotion has only been the subject of study relatively recently, in the last centuries. The founder of American Psychology, William James, wrote one of the earliest treatments; "What is an Emotion?" [4] in 1884. Since then, many psychologists have tried to give a concrete definition of emotion. Many come to the same conclusion, exemplified by Dr. Joseph Ledoux's statement *"Unfortunately, ones of the most significant things ever said about emotion may be that everyone knows what it is until they are asked to define it"* [6]. This paper is not an attempt to produce such a definition. Instead it is meant to show an implementation of emotion within a specific cognitive architecture, NARS (Non-Axiomatic Reasoning System) [8,9].

The basic emotion mechanism of NARS has been discussed in previous publications [10,11]. NARS has a basic satisfaction-evaluation mechanism to indicate its "satisfaction" level, based on the degree of goals being achieved. In [10] an appraisal model has also been proposed where it generates emotions based on concrete events. For instance, when the system is hurt by an object, the system will subsequently react to this object with fear, and the object has to be clearly indicated. Recently, this design has been further aligned with the basic assumption of NARS that it should work with *"insufficient knowledge and resources"*,

© Springer Nature Switzerland AG 2018
M. Iklé et al. (Eds.): AGI 2018, LNAI 10999, pp. 119–129, 2018.
https://doi.org/10.1007/978-3-319-97676-1_12

and also with the principle of an AGI system which is designed for general purposes. This paper will propose a new appraisal model in which emotions can be triggered by evaluating the events based on different criteria. Any events meeting those criteria will trigger corresponding emotions in NARS.

In the following, we will first review relevant concepts and proposals from psychology on emotion and its functions. We will then discuss the components related to the emotion mechanism of NARS, and finally, we will introduce the design decisions related to the new mechanism.

2   Psychological Studies on Human Emotion

Generally, the psychological study of emotion can be classified into two main schools: structuralism and functionalism. The structural perspective focuses on defining sets of features in an effort to build a taxonomy of basic emotions [1]. Understanding emotion is then the process of building a one-to-one relation between internal emotional states and observable artifacts: like facial expressions, autonomic responses, and changes in body chemistry. This perspective attempts to determine what areas of the brain are 'responsible' for a specific set of emotion, and how specific chemicals relate to their expression. Structuralists tend to neglect the study of intentionality.

In contrast, functionalists believe that emotion cannot be understood without understanding the motivations of the agent [1]. Their focus is on the impact of external and internal factors on a person's emotional state. Functionalists assert that facial expressions, gestures, and other indicators of emotion are also signals to other agents that affect the emotional state of others. Functionalism is a more pragmatic approach to studying machine emotion, making it the more appropriate perspective by which to investigate emotion as it may be applied to a computer system. This paper will adopt this perspective while outlining its approach to emotion.

Functionalists view emotion as relations between the external events and the internal goals of an agent and believe that emotion is synonymous with the 'significance' of the person-event transaction [1]. The significance of an event is related to how useful it is to the fulfillment of goals to the person. For the transaction to be significant at all, it must contribute to some goal.

To decide significance, Lazarus proposed an appraisal model which evaluates several factors related to goals and uses these appraisals to generate goal-related emotions [5]. Lazarus' model proceeds in three steps. First, the event is checked against current goals. If no goals are found to be related to the event, then there is no emotion triggered. Second, the congruence of the event with the goals is evaluated. This stage models how the event will impact the completion of the relevant goals, which can be either a positive or negative impact. The third stage is a type of ego-involvement, an involvement of one's self-esteem in the performance of a task or in an object, for example, ego-ideal, ego-identity, etc.

Denham [2] also designed an integrative model of three components (i.e., desire, state, and belief of certainty underline the cognitive process) for a child's experience of different emotions. The **Prototype Approach** describes the correlation between general types of events and specific emotions, each emotion is linked to common situations that cause it. For example, pleasurable stimuli or getting or doing something desired causes happiness. Anticipated harm or unfamiliar situations may cause fear, etc. Instead of encompassing emotional themes, the **Event Structure Approach** focuses on capturing the processes by which children come to experience different emotions. A child may experience fear if she realizes that it is very unlikely to maintain a desired state. In contrast, a child may experience anger if he realizes that some external conditions prevent him from achieving a desired state or avoiding an undesired state. The last approach is called **Desire-Belief Approach**, and it describes how emotions may result from the consistency or discrepancy between one's desire or belief and the reality. A child who desires a gift feels happy if he actually gets one; in contrast, a child who believes Mom is sleeping in the bedroom may feel surprised when she finds nobody there. Based on these three components, Denham proposed an integrative model that encompasses both the process and the content of a child's reasoning that leads to different emotions. Table 1 shows the model for Happiness, Sadness, Anger, and Fear.

Table 1. Integrative model of Happiness, Sadness, Anger and Fear, by Susanne A. Denham

Desire	Want	Want	Want	Not want
State	Have	Not have	Not have	Have
Belief of certainty	Yes	Never	Can reinstate	Likely
Emotion	Happiness	Sadness	Anger	Fear

3   NARS Overview

NARS is an AGI built in the framework of a reasoning system and founded on the belief that "Intelligence" can be defined as *the ability for a system to adapt to its environment and to work with insufficient knowledge and resources.* This is captured by the acronym AIKR; Assumption of Insufficient Knowledge and Resources. AIKR and the NARS system are discussed in many publications, including two books [8,9]. This section will only cover the aspects of NARS most relevant to the current discussion.

NARS makes use of a formal language, "Narsese", for its knowledge representation, and this language is defined using a formal grammar in [9]. The system's logic is developed from the traditional "term logic". Statements in this logic have the form *subject-copula-predicate*. The smallest element that can be used as one of these components is referred to as a "term".

The most basic statement in Narsese is the *inheritance statement*, with the format "$S \rightarrow P$", where S is the subject term, and P is the predicate term. The "$\rightarrow$" is the *inheritance* copula, defined in ideal situations as a reflexive and transitive relation from one term to another term. The intuitive meaning of "$S \rightarrow P$" is "S is a special case of P" and "P is a general case of S". For example, the statement "*robin* $\rightarrow$ *bird*" intuitively means "Robin is a type of bird".

At an atomic level, terms are simply sentences formed over a finite alphabet. In this article, terms are given a semantic meaning that is easily understood by a human reader. Terms like *wolf* or *animal* have some suggested meaning to the reader, but this is not required. Aside from atomic terms, Narsese also includes *compound terms* of various types. A compound term $(con, C_1, C_2, ..., C_n)$ is formed by a term connector, *con*, and one or more component terms $(C_1, C_2, ..., C_n)$. The term connector is a logical constant with predefined meaning in the system. Major types of compound terms in Narsese include

- **Sets:** Term $\{Tom, Jerry\}$ is an *extensional set* specified by enumerating its instances; term $[small, yellow]$ is an *intensional set* specified by enumerating its properties.
- **Products and images:** The relation "Tom is the uncle of Jerry" is represented as "$(\{Tom\} \times \{Jerry\}) \rightarrow uncle\text{-}of$", "$\{Tom\} \rightarrow (uncle\text{-}of\ /\ \diamond\ \{Jerry\})$", and "$\{Jerry\} \rightarrow (uncle\text{-}of\ /\ \{Tom\}\ \diamond)$", equivalently.
- **Statement:** "Tom knows snow is white" can be represented as a *higher-order statement* "$\{Tom\} \rightarrow (know\ /\ \diamond\ \{snow \rightarrow [white]\})$", where the statement "$snow \rightarrow [white]$" is used as a term.
- **Compound statements:** Statements can be combined using term connectors for disjunction('$\vee$'), conjunction('$\wedge$'), and negation('$\neg$'), which are intuitively similar to those in propositional logic, but not defined using truth-tables [8].

Several term connectors can be extended to take more than two component terms. The connector is then written before the components rather than between them, such as $(\times \{Tom\} \{Jerry\})$.

Beside the *inheritance* copula ('$\rightarrow$', "is a type of"), Narsese also includes three other basic copulas: *similarity* ('$\leftrightarrow$', "is similar to"), *implication* ('$\Rightarrow$', "if-then"), and *equivalence* ('$\Leftrightarrow$', "if-and-only-if"). The last two copulas are "higher order", meant to be applied to statements themselves.

In NARS, an *event* is a statement with temporal attributes. Based on their occurrence order, two events E_1 and E_2 may have one of the following basic temporal relations:

- E_1 happens before E_2
- E_1 happens after E_2
- E_1 happens when E_2 happen

Temporal statements are formed by combining the above basic temporal relations with some logical relations indicated by the term connectors and copulas. For example, the implication statement "$E_1 \Rightarrow E_2$" has three temporal versions, corresponding to the three temporal order relations:

- $E_1 \not\Rightarrow E_2$ (E_1 happens before E_2 and implies it)
- $E_1 \setminus\Rightarrow E_2$ (E_1 happens after E_2 and implies it)
- $E_1 \mid\Rightarrow E_2$ (E_1 happens when E_2 is happening and implies it)

These statements can be interpreted as a 'third-person' view of the statements or events. Narsese can also provide a 'first-person' view of events, describing things that the reasoning system may directly realize themselves. These special events are referred to as *operations*. These operations are tied to executable commands or procedures built or plugged into the system.

Formally, an operation is an application of an operator on a list of arguments, written as $op(a_1, \ldots, a_n)$ where op is the operator, and $a_1, ..., a_n$ is a list of arguments. Such an operation is interpreted logically as statement "$(\times \{SELF\} \{a_1\} \ldots \{a_n\}) \rightarrow op$", where $SELF$ is a special term indicating the system itself, and op is a term that has a procedural interpretation. For instance, if we want to describe an event "The system is holding key_001", the statement can be expressed as "$(\times \{SELF\} \{key\_001\}) \rightarrow hold$".

There are three types of sentences in Narsese:

- A **judgment** is a statement with a truth value, and represents a piece of new knowledge that system needs to learn or consider. For example, "$\langle robin \rightarrow bird \rangle$." with a truth-value makes the system to absorb this conceptual relation, together with its implications, into the system's beliefs. More details about the truth value can be found in [8].
- A **goal** is a statement to be realized by executing some operations. For example, "$\langle(\times \{SELF\} \{door\_001\}) \rightarrow open\rangle$!" means the system should open the *door_001* or make sure that *door_001* is opened. Each goal associates with a "desire-value" indicating the extent to which the system hopes for a situation where the statement is true. More details about the desire value can be found in [8], too.
- A **question** is a statement without a truth-value or desire-value, and represents a query to be answered according to the system's beliefs or goals. For example, if the system has a belief "$robin \rightarrow bird$" (with a truth-value), it can be used to answer question "$\langle robin \rightarrow bird \rangle$?" by reporting the truth-value, as well as to answer the question "$\langle robin \rightarrow ?x \rangle$?" by reporting the truth-value together with the term *bird*, as it is in the intension of *robin*. Similarly, the same belief can also be used to answer question "$\langle ?y \rightarrow bird \rangle$?" by reporting the truth-value together with the term *robin*.

NARS' beliefs about itself start with its built-in operations. As mentioned above, the operation $op(a_1, \ldots, a_n)$ corresponds to a relation that the system can establish between itself and the arguments, as expressed by the statement

"($\times \{SELF\} \{a_1\} \ldots \{a_n\}$) $\rightarrow op$" (where the subject term is a *product* term written in the prefix format), since it specifies a relation among the arguments plus the system identified by the special term $SELF$.

An operation may be completely executed by the actuator of the host system (e.g., a NARS-controlled robot raises a hand or moves forward), or partly by another coupled system or device (e.g., a NARS-controlled robot pushes a button or issues a command to another system). NARS has an interface for such "external" operations to be registered. Additionally there are "internal" or "mental" operations that can cause changes within the system.

In general, mental operations supplement and influence the automatic control mechanism, and let certain actions be taken as the consequence of inference. Mental operations contribute to the system's self-concept by telling the system what is going on in its mind, and allow the system to control its own thinking process to a certain extent. For instance, the system can explicitly plan its processing of a certain type of task. After the design and implementation phases, the system needs to learn how to properly use its mental operations, just like it needs to learn about the other (external) operations.

With regard to the current discussion, there are several important mental operations:

- **believe** generates a belief about a certain statement where the premises are not those covered by the existing inference rules. For instance, such a belief can be derived from a goal or a question.
- **want** is used to increase the desire-value of a statement, also in ways beyond what have been covered by the goal-derivation rules. When the desire-value exceeds a certain threshold, a goal is generated, and the event is recorded in the system's internal experience.
- **anticipate** allows NARS to predict the observation of an event. If the predicted event does not occur in time, the system will notice and more attention will given to the involved concepts. Additionally, a "disappointment' event can be generated, allowing the system to draw conclusions from the absence of a predicted event.

4   Appraisal Model in NARS

We take the position that emotions arise from cognitions regarding the outside world [7], through an appraisal process. Appraisal starts with extracting relevant information from its experience. No matter it is to a human being or to an intelligent agent, information about the outside world is not always prepared and waiting for the agent to receive. NARS is designed to handle such conditions, in a manner similar to a human agent.

To implement emotion, we need to concern ourselves with what kind of events might trigger emotion and apply the appraisal framework to these events. According to the previous discussion, the events that may trigger emotions are events that related to goals. This corresponds to the first stage of Lazarus's appraisal theory [5] which stated that only events related to goals would trigger emotions. If there is no goal concerning the event, then no emotion will be triggered.

The second stage of Lazarus's appraisal theory is to evaluate the congruence of the event with the agent's current goals. The result of this stage determines whether the emotion is positive or negative. In NARS, this evaluation is carried out by comparing the two measurements on an event: its desire-value and truth-value. If we assign binary values to desire-value (True for want, False for not want), truth-value (True for have, False for not have), and satisfaction value (True for positivity, False for negativity), the latter behaves exactly like the logic of an XNOR gate with the former two as inputs, as shown in Table 2.

Table 2. The relation among desire-value, truth-value, and satisfy-value

Desire value	Truth value	Satisfaction
Want	Have	Positive
Want	Not have	Negative
Not want	Have	Negative
Not want	Not have	Positive

The third stage of Lazarus's model, estimating the types of ego-involvement, is not considered in our appraisal model. Doing so would involve listing all possible types of ego-involvement, which is incongruent with the idea of being general-purpose, as well as with the situations where the same event may carry different meanings to a machine than to a human being. Also, we can interpret Denham's Belief of Certainty model as an uncertainty about the state, this can be represented by the tense of the event. If it is "yes", or "never", then the event should have already happened. If it is "likely to happen", it means the event has not happened but has a possibility to happen in the future. Our treatment addresses the implicit distinction of tense in the third row. However, we do not make a binary distinction based on the certainty as we believe the transition from Anxiety to Fear is gradual.

The following is how we defined criteria for some emotions:

- **Fear:** An undesired event is anticipated to happen
- **Happiness:** An desired event is believed as already happened (high satisfaction)
- **Sadness:** An undesired event is believed as already happened (low satisfaction)

The current design of NARS does not include a mechanism to simulate the physiological changes that accompany human emotional experiences such as changes in voltage or temperature. However, this does not mean that the system cannot "feel" anything. The basic feeling mechanism in NARS has been introduced in [11]. Feelings of emotions are realized by the *feel* operator through accessing the relevant sensors and returning the sensed state into the system's inner experience.

For example, if the system feels fear, the experience can be represented as

$$(\texttt{\^{}feel, \{SELF\}, fear}).$$

Once some event matches the criteria of being afraid, the system will feel fear, implemented by the *feel* operator and the system will report the emotion it is currently feeling when such a question is asked.

So far, we have introduced how NARS generates different emotions by the new appraisal model, and how it feels these emotions. Examples of how NARS takes actions triggered by these emotions will be displayed in the next section.

In humans, emotions often improve their cognitive faculties. Allowing quicker reaction times, aiding in planning, and improving communication are all the important functions of an emotion mechanism. Similar benefits are gained by NARS.

Emotion helps the system summarize its experience at a more abstract level. For example; suppose an agent were to have some understanding of the concept of a 'beast' and had experienced instances that made the agent feel fear (e.g., seeing a wolf). This abstract notion of fear, as related to the concept of *beast*, may provide additional information about how to act when encountering a new member of the class *beast* (e.g. a bear). The emotional parameter offers a direct, concise way to encode information critical to the survival of the agent. Such summaries reduce the need for extra concepts to encode the relation between the source of the emotion and its outcomes.

Emotions can also decrease the time needed to respond to certain events. Emotional constructs like fear can facilitate a quicker response. Assuming that the emotions of the system are tied to more 'intrinsic' fundamental elements of the system, fear could be implemented as a response to anything that would impede the working of these fundamental systems. If fear is experienced, it is due to the agent being exposed to a situation or event that negatively impacted such systems. Any future event that produces the same interpretation could be responded to quickly.

5   Example

In the following, we illustrate an example using the Open-NARS implementation of NARS to show how emotions raise from the evaluations of events, and how emotions trigger actions. Due to the space limitation, we cannot explain the details of the representation, which can be found in [8,9].

```
===========================Happiness===========================
```

//Meaning of the statement: If something is wanted by SELF,
//and SELF's belief agrees with the case, SELF feels Happy

//1. #1 is a dependent variable which represents a certain
//   unspecified term under a given restriction. It can be
//   either an object or an event

//2. (^want, {SELF}, #1, TRUE) represents a mental operation
//   means something is desired by SELF; TRUE indicates the
//   truth value of this mental operation, where #1 is desired,
//   otherwise, use FALSE

//3. (^believe, {SELF}, #1,TRUE) means SELF's belief agree
//   with #1, if #1 represents an event, it indicates that
//   #1 has already happened.

//4. (^feel, {SELF}, happy) implements feel operator and
//   indicates the feeling of SELF being happy

//5. && is a term connecter, it connects the follow
//   term by meaning ''and''

Input: <(&&, (^want, {SELF}, #1, TRUE), (^believe, {SELF},
#1,TRUE)) =|> (^feel, {SELF}, happy)>.

//SELF has a goal which is not being hurt, ''--'' is the negation
//of the statement

Input: (--,<{SELF} --> hurt>)!

//SELF is not getting hurt, :|: represents the tense ''present''
//means SELF is not getting hurt right now

Input: (--,<{SELF} --> hurt>). :|:

//What do you feel?
//This statement is a question, and it corresponding to
//(^feel, {SELF}, happy) where ''?what'' at the position of the
//emotion

Input: (^feel,{SELF},?what)?

//SELF feels Happy, the reason why it feels happy is because
//SELF doesn't want to get hurt (generated by goal), and SELF
//is not getting hurt (generated by belief).

Answer: (^feel,{SELF}, happy).

```
==========================Fear=================================

//If something is wanted by SELF, and SELF anticipates the
//opposite to happen, SELF feels fear
Input:<(&&, (^want, {SELF}, #1, FALSE), (^anticipate, {SELF},
#1)) =|> (^feel, {SELF}, fear)>.

//At the same time when SELF feels fear, it generate an
//motivation which to run away, run is also an operator in NARS

Input: <(^feel,{SELF}, fear) =|> <(*, {SELF},
<(*, {SELF}) --> ^run) --> ^want>>.

//SELF doesn't want to be hurt

Input: (--,<{SELF} --> hurt>)!

//If wolf is getting close to SELF, SELF will get hurt
//&/ is another term connector representing the relation between
//two terms is ''and'', also the latter happens after the former.
//42 represents inference steps, it means, when wolf start
//getting close to SELF, after 42 steps, the SELF will get
//hurt. The number is not fixed, it can be any integer.

Input: <(&/,<(*, {SELF}, wolf) --> close_to>,+42) =/>
   <{SELF} --> [hurt]>>.

//Wolf is getting close to self

Input: <(*, {SELF}, wolf) --> close_to>. :|:

//Result: SELF takes the action run, based on the knowledge
//where SELF runs when it feels fear, SELF also feels the emotion
//fear
EXECUTE (^run,{SELF})
```

6 Conclusion

In this paper we introduced several new emotions to the NARS framework; *fear*,
sadness, *happiness*, and *disappointment*. These additions were partially motivated by the descriptions of emotion provided by [2,5], but also came from the
need to improve the control mechanism of NARS. In human, emotion results
from a combined evaluation of belief, desire, and anticipation. This paper outlined how analogous processes in NARS can work to interpret a combination of
parameters as an effective emotion.

Our results show that emotions could make the system to take actions in various situations. Emotion provides information that the system can use by offering
a concise summary of the system's past experience with respect to its emotional

state. In addition, it provides an additional mode of communication (system-to-system, human-to-system). Such functionality is important for a general-purpose intelligence system, especially if it should operate under the assumption of insufficient knowledge and resources (AIKR).

This work is not intended to produce an AGI with an emotional system just like that of a human being. Instead, the intent is to draw analogies between the human emotional system and components of a reasoning system in such a way that the reasoning system is improved. The basic emotions described in this paper provide a first step in establishing an effective emotional mechanism within NARS. Future work will be directed at building a richer experience for NARS. For instance, new emotional states, like regret, may provide additional feedback for the system to learn about prior errors.

References

1. Campos, J.J., Mumme, D.L., Kermoian, R., Campos, R.G.: A functionalist perspective on the nature of emotion. In: The Development of Emotion Regulation: Biological and Behavioral Considerations, vol. 59, pp. 284–303 (1994)
2. Denham, S.A.: Emotional Development in Young Children. Guilford Publications, New York City (1998)
3. Dijk, S.V.: Calming the Emotional Storm: Using Dialectical Behavior Therapy Skills to Manage Your Emotions and Balance Your Life. New Harbinger Publications, Oakland (2012)
4. James, W.: What is an emotion. Mind **9**, 188–205 (1884)
5. Lazarus, R.S.: Emotion and Adaptation. Oxford University Press, Oxford (1991)
6. Ledoux, J.: The Emotional Brain: The Mysterious Underpinnings of Emotional Life. Simon and Schuster, New Jersey (1998)
7. Steunebrink, B.: The logical structure of emotions. Ph.D. thesis, Utrecht University Repository (2010)
8. Wang, P.: Rigid Flexibility: The Logic of Intelligence. Springer, Dordrecht (2006)
9. Wang, P.: Non-Axiomatic Logic: A Model of Intelligent Reasoning. World Scientific, Singapore (2013)
10. Wang, P., Li, X., Hammer, P.: Self in NARS, an AGI System. In: Frontier in Robotics and AI 5 (2018)
11. Wang, P., Talanov, M., Hammer, P.: The emotional mechanisms in NARS. In: Steunebrink, B., Wang, P., Goertzel, B. (eds.) AGI -2016. LNCS (LNAI), vol. 9782, pp. 150–159. Springer, Cham (2016). https://doi.org/10.1007/978-3-319-41649-6_15

Towards a Sociological Conception of Artificial Intelligence

Jakub Mlynář[1,2(✉)] [iD], Hamed S. Alavi[2,3] [iD], Himanshu Verma[2] [iD],
and Lorenzo Cantoni[4] [iD]

[1] Charles University, Nám. Jana Palacha 2, 116 38 Praha, Czech Republic
jakub.mlynar@ff.cuni.cz
[2] University of Fribourg, Boulevard de Pérolles 90, 1700 Fribourg, Switzerland
h.alavi@ucl.ac.uk, himanshu.verma@unifr.ch
[3] University College London, 66-72 Gower Street, London, WC1E 6EA, UK
[4] University of Lugano, Via Giuseppe Buffi 13, 6900 Lugano, Switzerland
lorenzo.cantoni@usi.ch

Abstract. Social sciences have been always formed and influenced by the development of society, adjusting the conceptual, methodological, and theoretical frameworks to emerging social phenomena. In recent years, with the leap in the advancement of Artificial Intelligence (AI) and the proliferation of its everyday applications, "non-human intelligent actors" are increasingly becoming part of the society. This is manifested in the evolving realms of smart home systems, autonomous vehicles, chatbots, intelligent public displays, etc. In this paper, we present a prospective research project that takes one of the pioneering steps towards establishing a "distinctively sociological" conception of AI. Its first objective is to extract the existing conceptions of AI as perceived by its technological developers and (possibly differently) by its users. In the second part, capitalizing on a set of interviews with experts from social science domains, we will explore the new imaginable conceptions of AI that do not originate from its technological possibilities but rather from societal necessities. The current formal ways of defining AI are grounded in the technological possibilities, namely machine learning methods and neural network models. But what exactly is AI as a social phenomenon, which may act on its own, can be blamed responsible for ethically problematic behavior, or even endanger people's employment? We argue that such conceptual investigation is a crucial step for further empirical studies of phenomena related to AI's position in current societies, but also will open up ways for critiques of new technological advancements with social consequences in mind from the outset.

Keywords: Artificial intelligence · Sociology · Social sciences

1 AI as a Sociological Phenomenon

Given the rapidly growing importance of Artificial Intelligence (AI) in many domains of social life, it is striking that the interest of sociologists and social scientists in AI has been quite scarce. At the end of 20th century, AI was occasionally discussed in sociology

© Springer Nature Switzerland AG 2018
M. Iklé et al. (Eds.): AGI 2018, LNAI 10999, pp. 130–139, 2018.
https://doi.org/10.1007/978-3-319-97676-1_13

as a methodological tool for data analysis and theory development, yet not as a social phenomenon in its own right. However, as it is expected that the social impact of AI will continue to increase over the next years, contributing to transform the ways people organize economical production, learn and spend leisure time, to name just a few concerned fields, we argue that sociology and other social sciences need to acquire an adequate understanding of how artificial intelligence is and should be grown into a social actor, reflecting its relevance and consequentiality in different layers of social organization and social reality.

This precisely is the central aim of our project, which we describe in this paper. It intends to provide a sociological conception of AI, i.e. understanding AI as a *social phenomenon* and a *non-human social actor*. We are convinced that scientific studies of human beings and their collectivities need to tailor their conceptual tools to the society of the 21st century. This requires, first and foremost, a proper understanding of specific aspects of digitalization in everyday life, which is a domain where AI plays an increasing role. Through an exploratory study, our intention is to "prototype" the methodological and conceptual cross-fertilization between sociology and the fields that deal traditionally with the subject of AI, such as computer science, philosophy of mind, and cognitive psychology. The second equally important goal of our project is to execute an investigation of the possibilities of sociology to influence and guide the future of AI-related developments in our societies. In this paper, rather than presenting results of empirical research, we introduce and discuss an agenda to proceed.

1.1 The Case of Facebook

In the recent public and political discourses, the role of AI has been already the subject of challenging debates. In the US Senate hearing held on April 10th, 2018, with Mark Zuckerberg, the founder and CEO of Facebook, the words "Artificial Intelligence" or their abbreviation "A.I." were used 29 times. In fact, more often than "trust" (20 occurrences), "transparency" and "transparent" (18 occ.), or even "freedom(s)" (4 occ.) and "democracy/democratic" (3 occ.). This was also noticed by the participants of the meeting, one of whom noted that Zuckerberg "brought [AI] up many times during [his] testimony." (Senator Peters, 3:47:13–3:47:16 of Zuckerberg's US Senate hearing as available online[1]) This – highly medially exposed – example documents and illustrates the role that AI has taken in current societies worldwide. It also points to the major role that the AI "systems" or "tools" might play in future social developments. Indeed, Zuckerberg himself stressed the societal relevance of such questions more than once during the hearing session: "[A]s we're able to technologically shift towards especially having AI proactively look at content, I think that that's going to create massive questions for society about what obligations we want to require companies… to fulfill." (Mark Zuckerberg, 2:53:48–2:54:05 of the hearing) And also about one hour later: "[T]he core question you're asking about, AI transparency, is a really important one that people are just starting to very seriously study, and that's ramping up a lot. And I think

---

[1] https://www.youtube.com/watch?v=pXq-5L2ghhg.

this is going to be a very central question for how we think about AI systems over the next decade and beyond." (Mark Zuckerberg, 3:47:46–3:48:02 of the hearing)

1.2   Our Approach

In providing a sociological conception of AI, our project starts from an extensive literature review, as well as content analysis of media production related to AI. At the most fundamental level, we aim to conceptualize AI sociologically, providing answers to questions such as: Are there inherent differences between human and non-human (AI) social actors? Should we revisit and reconsider our presumptions of human uniqueness? And, on the other hand, can we truly speak about anything like "AI in general", or do we rather encounter loosely related instances of phenomena in the sense of "family resemblances" [1]? As explained further in this paper, the answers provided will be based on analysis of several kinds of empirical data, qualitative and quantitative in nature. The resulting conception of AI, although sociological in its nature, will be then adaptable by other social sciences such as communication, economy, political science, or social anthropology.

2   The Study of AI in Sociology and Computer Science

2.1   AI and Non-human Actors in Sociology

With the growth of initiatives such as Ubiquitous Computing (*UbiComp*, see e.g. [2]), and the remarkable entry of "smart" systems into the domain of everyday social lives, it is necessary to reconsider the position of AI in sociology and *vice versa*. Historically and traditionally, sociology was usually practiced – as Zygmunt Bauman once nicely put it – as "a narrative on what follows from the fact that man is not alone" [3]. One of the tacit presumptions, arising from this conception of sociology as a science on accumulated and interrelated human beings, has been the disregard for non-human actors and material components of the social world (cf. [4]). Sociologists simply considered the "non-human" and "extra-human" to compose only the environment of sociologically relevant phenomena, which does not have to be taken into account. Since the late 1970s, this neglect was explicitly formulated and criticised in sociological orientation to subjects such as the natural environment [5], animals [6], or technology [7]. Focusing specifically on AI – which has been extensively discussed in cognitive psychology, philosophy of mind, and computer science already since the 1950s (cf. [8]) –, few sociologists have started writing on the subject in the 1980s and 1990s. However, up to this day, AI has been almost exclusively conceived in sociological context only as a methodological tool in statistical or textual analysis [9], and development of sociological theories [10] – in other words, an "application of machine intelligence techniques to social phenomena", i.e. the Artificial Social Intelligence [11].

Broadly speaking, so far, AI has not been systematically considered as a social and sociological phenomenon *sui generis* and the discipline of sociology lacks a suitable conception of AI, which could serve as a framework for empirical studies. Rare exceptions include that of Woolgar [12], who proposed a "sociology of machines", arguing that we should see the "AI phenomenon as an occasion for reassessing the central axiom of sociology that there is something distinctively 'social' about human behaviour" (p. 557), and proposed that we should examine the underlying assumption in social sciences that there is a fundamental difference between humans and machines (and, by extension, also between human and machine intelligence). Apart from advocating sociological research of AI discourse and AI research practices, he also claimed more broadly that "the phenomenon of AI provides an opportunity for investigating how presumptions of the distinction between human and machine delimit social inquiry" (p. 568). Wolfe [13] explored Woolgar's radical idea and demonstrated that "interpretive" sociological approaches (such as ethnomethodology or symbolic interactionism), rather than "systemic" ones, may "expand and elaborate" the hypothesis of human uniqueness in comparison with AI. Schwartz [14] suggested that AI has to be studied with regard to the social context (setting) in which it is "implemented", and characterized AI systems as "social actors playing social roles" (p. 199). At the turn of the century, Malsch [15] discussed the proximities of AI and sociology through the concept of socionics. This field, standing at the intersection of sociology and AI, aims to "address the question how to exploit models from the social world for the development of intelligent computer technologies" (p. 155), exploring the specificities of modern societies and resilient adaptability of social systems in order to provide means of translating these features into computer-based technologies. Indeed, the most influential attempt to incorporate non-human actors into sociological thinking is the conception of Bruno Latour [16]. His actor network theory (ANT) aims, among other things, to transgress the distinction of human and non-human actors ([17]; similarly to Woolgar's [12] argument presented above), acknowledging technologies and objects as partakers in the construction of society. However, AI as a phenomenon is not discussed by Latour in this context. More recently, Muhle [18] presents an ethnomethodological study of "embodied conversational agents" (bots) in the virtual world of a massively multiplayer online game *Second Life*, posing the question whether bots (i.e. non-playable characters) in computer games are conceived by players as social actors. His approach relates closely to our own interests, but our aim is to provide much broader picture. Some other empirical studies of specific instances involving AI-based technologies have been conducted (such as the use of smartphones in social interaction: e.g., [19]), however, they rather focus on the "human side" of the interaction, and without the intention of providing a generalizable socio-logical framework of the subject of AI. This is also the case of the field of Human-AI Interaction, which we review in more detail in the next subsection.

2.2 Human-AI Interaction in Computer Science

Human-AI Interaction, as a field of study, is a subdomain of Human-Computer Inter-action (HCI), and focuses on the understanding of the nuances of our interactions with AI supported tools, technologies, and processes. Although currently in a nascent stage of development, this subdomain of computer science embodies an extensive range of contexts, activities, and types of users. Furthermore, the encapsulation of human-like behavior in artifacts and environments, and embodiment of intelligence in varied kinds of technologies are being homogenized within the fabric of everyday life. From domain experts (such as medical experts diagnosing cancer cells through intelligent image processing [20]) to children (the use of AI in education to improve the learning experience and outcome [21]) to building and urban dwellers (home automation controlling thermal comfort of inhabitants [22], and autonomous cars changing the shape of cities and experience of mobility [23]) to disabled users (for example mobile assistive applications helping blind users navigate in urban environments [24, 25]), the role of AI in our socio-cultural aspects has become increasingly pervasive. This is no longer limited to the embodiment of technologies by artifacts, but also extends to the realm of built environments [26], having direct spatial and consequently social impacts – topics that the proliferating HCI contributions in built environments have recently begun to address [27, 28]. Still the conception, design, and study of Human-AI Interaction is predominantly focused on *ad hoc instances* (such as robots, driverless cars, chatbots, etc.) with little or no overlap between instances of different kinds. This lack of generalizability in the study of Human-AI Interaction can be attributed to the HCI's emphasis on design instances and a bi-directional disconnect between these instances and theoretical frameworks. In addition, the "black box" approach of representing AI algorithms by the researchers oftentimes undermines the efforts to achieve a significant level of generalizability. Consequently, the widely accepted conceptions of AI algorithms and tools, especially their social impact, is currently distributed across the nature and form of design instances (or products), and how experts and users likewise ascribe meaning to these separate instances. This multi-layered gap in conceptions about AI and its societal impact amongst actors of different backgrounds (AI developers, sociologists, and users), and their varying levels of interactivity with smart technologies has remained out of the scope of Human-AI Interaction as domain of computer science research.

2.3 Research Gap

As demonstrated in the previous subsections, there is a research gap in contemporary sociology as well as computer science which relates to (1) the conceptual understanding of AI as a specific social (non-human) actor, and (2) the role sociology could play not only in interpreting but also in helping to lead the future technological development of AI-based tools, systems and devices. This research gap manifests itself on several levels of social scientific endeavors: at the level of *sociological theory*, where non-human social actors are commonly "theorized out of existence", and also at the level of *empirical studies* (similarly to the related domain of Human-AI Interaction), where the broader societal impacts of AI are not considered, given the primary focus on particular cases of specific technology use.

3 Research Plan and Methodology

3.1 Literature and Discourse Analysis

The first step of our research project will cover an investigation of past and ongoing discourses within the other relevant research domains pertaining to AI, such as computer science, cognitive psychology, and philosophy. In particular, we will aim to identify aspects that are relevant for a specifically sociological formulation of empirically investigatable research questions related to AI: its societal roles, functions and imaginaries. In addition, content and discourse analysis of online discussion forums and other media (TV, newspaper) will be an important initial step in outlining and understanding the common-sense conceptualizations of AI in current society. Qualitative and quantitative techniques of content analysis (cf. [29]) will allow us to systematically gather initial knowledge of the existing imaginaries and conceptualizations of AI in media. Furthermore, the discursive aspects of the analysed texts will be studied by the methodologies of discourse analysis [30]. In addition to literature review, these approaches will serve to further elaborate and specify the research questions for empirical investigation in the next stages.

3.2 Online Survey

An online survey will aim to collect the widespread common-sense conceptions and imaginaries of AI in contemporary Swiss society, and capture its expectable varieties. Our aim is to have a representative sample, reflecting the demographic and social diversity, and cover all Swiss languages. We will use *TypeForm* platform for online collection of survey data, and distribute the questionnaire among potential respondents by a number of diverse venues. Descriptive and inferential statistics will be used to gain quantitative insights and test hypotheses about different manifestation of certain ideas and their correlation in the survey responses. In addition, to extract the influence of different variable (culture, age, education level, etc.) on the perception of AI, we will use exploratory data mining and statistical methods that allow for clustering and pattern recognition. Visualizing the patterns and quantifying the seminal components in the current perception of AI will be followed by qualitative analysis to extract the meanings and nuances of what AI means in our current societies.

3.3 Observational Studies

In the third phase, we will conduct three in-depth observational studies, collecting video recordings of instances when a group of individuals interact with AI-based tools and systems: (i) driverless shuttle; (ii) chatbots; (iii) game-play systems. In order to extract features of situated common-sense conception of AI from the recordings, we will analyse the data from the perspective of ethnomethodology and conversation analysis [31–33], which focuses on the "perspective of the actor" and aims to describe and elucidate the methodical work of practical sense-making in specific social settings. It has been convincingly demonstrated by previous research in the field that ethnomethodological analysis of video recordings of social interaction can yield valuable insights into the details of situated action (e.g., [34]).

3.4 Interviews with Experts

We will conduct approximately 15 semi-structured interviews with experts on AI, as well as experts in the relevant domains of sociology. First, mostly with the AI experts, the goal of the interviews will be to discuss the results of empirical studies (see Subsects. 3.2 and 3.3) and compare the common-sense conceptions/imaginaries of AI with the experts' perspective. In this case, the expert opinions are needed as a contrastive foil in further elaboration of a truly sociological conception of AI, which is the ultimate goal of our project. Second, mostly with the social scientists, we will discuss the possibilities of sociology (or other social sciences) to influence and guide the future of AI-related developments in our societies. In this case, the expert opinions are needed especially because of the long-lasting controversies in sociology regarding social advocacy and public engagement (cf. [35]). As a complementary method of gathering experts' opinions, we will also consider using the Delphi method.

3.5 Sociological Conception of AI

The goal of this final phase is to synthesize the main results of all previous phases in a sociological conception of AI. The conception, we expect, will have the form of an original coordinate system (matrix) for evaluation of societal conceptions and imaginaries of AI. We will also conduct a general assessment of the current status of AI in sociological thought and research. Our theoretical (concept-building) work will be oriented by two main regards: (1) to sociological research, i.e., the operationalizability of our conception in further empirical studies conducted from different paradigmatic standpoints; (2) to other human and social sciences, i.e., providing the conceptual framework for sociologically sensitive research in communication, political science, cultural anthropology, social psychology etc.

4   Conclusion

4.1   Subsequent Research Prospects

A number of empirical studies (qualitative and quantitative) can be outlined as a direct result of a sociological conceptualization of AI. Our investigation respecifies and opens up novel fields for collaboration between human/social and computer/natural sciences. A sociological conceptualization of AI is necessary in order to carry out further empirical research in this area, which would investigate AI as a social phenomenon, its imaginaries in different segments of current societies, and the role it has as a non-human social actor in particular social and institutional settings. Presently, AI is already being applied in a great number of fields, such as games, households, education, transportation, logistics, industrial production, marketing and sales, communication, scientific research, data analysis, and many others. Each of these fields requires sociological knowledge in order to understand AI application, its impact on "users", "customers", "clients", and their possible concerns regarding interaction with AI. The ongoing *fourth industrial revolution* – expansion of cyber-physical systems such as AI and robots – will presumably contribute to major transformations when it comes to the ways we live, think and communicate. Proper sociological understanding of AI provides us with a historically unique opportunity of capturing the details of this revolution continuously and progressively as it happens. The specific subsequent research prospects include survey-based studies of the diversity of AI imaginaries in different segments of societies (defined economically, culturally, politically, demographically etc.); detailed examination of communicative and discursive processes related to AI (such as interaction with chatbots); investigation of positive and negative impacts of AI-based automation in various industrial spheres, and its influence on employment; historically oriented explorations of the image of AI in popular culture; and indeed, further refinement of conceptual and theoretical frameworks of AI based on empirical validations of sociological models.

4.2 Innovation Potential

Our project will open the way for sociology and the social sciences into major AI projects, where their influence is currently only marginal. In particular, sociology and the social sciences, equipped with an adequate conception of AI, could (and should) fully contribute to steer the development of AI-based technologies. This is important especially since the current development of AI is predominantly grounded in the field of technological possibilities (such as machine learning methods, neural network models), rather than preliminary consideration of societal effects of the proliferation and expansion of AI.[2] On the other hand, indeed as with other technologies, it is important to develop AI-based devices and tools in a way that builds on already existing ways of practical usage of technology. For, as Harvey Sacks remarked already in the 1960s, any novel technological object is "made at home in the world that has whatever organization it already has" [33] – it is incorporated in familiar social practices. We do not need to stress that it is primarily sociology that sets out the detailed study of the organization of the social world and related practical activities as its principal and primordial field of interest. Similarly to other domains of technology, sociology can provide crucial knowledge to AI designers; however, in order to do so, it needs an appropriate understanding of the subject in question, in our case, artificial intelligence.

To conclude, we firmly believe that precise sociological conceptualization of AI could, in a long-term perspective, improve our comprehension of the nature of humans and technology. Therefore, sociological conceptualization of AI, and empirical studies in the sense outlined above, would have far-reaching impact not only in the field of sociology, but also in human and social sciences in general.

References

1. Wittgenstein, L.: Philosophical Investigations. Basil Blackwell, Oxford (1953)
2. Greenfield, A.: Everyware: The Dawning Age of Ubiquitous Computing. New Riders, Berkeley (2006)
3. Bauman, Z.: Úvahy o postmoderní době [Thoughts on the Postmodern Age]. Sociologické nakladatelství SLON, Prague (1995)

---

[2] Our arguments to consider only the currently employed Machine Learning and Neural Network algorithms rather than Agent-Based and BDI systems in the sociological conceptions of AI are based on the predominant proliferation of the former methods in intelligent applications which users often interact with.

4. Lindemann, G.: The analysis of the borders of the social world: a challenge for sociological theory. J. Theor. Soc. Behav. **35**, 69–98 (2005). https://doi.org/10.1111/j. 0021-8308.2005.00264.x
5. Dunlap, R.E., Catton Jr., W.R.: Environmental sociology. Annu. Rev. Sociol. **5**, 243–273 (1979). https://doi.org/10.1146/annurev.so.05.080179.001331
6. Bryant, C.: The zoological connection: animal related human behavior. Soc. Forces **58**, 399–421 (1979). https://doi.org/10.1093/sf/58.2.399
7. MacKenzie, D., Wajcman, J. (eds.): The Social Shaping of Technology. Open University Press, Milton Keynes/Philadelphia (1985)
8. Nilsson, N.J.: The Quest for Artificial Intelligence: A History of Ideas and Achievements. Cambridge University Press, Cambridge (2009)
9. Carley, K.M.: Artificial intelligence within sociology. Sociol. Method. Res. **25**, 3–30 (1996). https://doi.org/10.1177/0049124196025001001
10. Brent, E.E.: Is There a Role for Artificial Intelligence in Sociological Theorizing? Am. Sociol. **19**, 158–166 (1988). https://doi.org/10.1007/BF02691809
11. Bainbridge, W.S., Brent, E.E., Carley, K.M., Heise, D.R., Macy, M.W., Markovsky, B., Skvoretz, J.: Artificial social intelligence. Annu. Rev. Sociol. **20**, 407–436 (1994). https://doi.org/10.1146/annurev.so.20.080194.002203
12. Woolgar, S.: Why not a sociology of machines? The case of sociology and artificial intelligence. Sociology **19**, 557–572 (1985). https://doi.org/10.1177/0038038585019004005
13. Wolfe, A.: Mind, self, society, and computer: artificial intelligence and the sociology of mind. Am. J. Sociol. **96**, 1073–1096 (1991). https://doi.org/10.1086/229649
14. Schwartz, R.D.: Artificial intelligence as a sociological phenomenon. Can. J. Sociol. **14**, 179–202 (1989). https://doi.org/10.2307/3341290
15. Malsch, T.: Naming the unnamable: socionics or the sociological turn of/to distributed artificial intelligence. Auton. Agent. Multi-Agent Syst. **4**, 155–186 (2001). https://doi.org/10.1145/91474.91483
16. Latour, B.: Reassembling the Social: An Introduction to Actor-Network Theory. Oxford University Press, Oxford (2005)
17. Callon, M., Latour, B.: Unscrewing the big Leviathan. In: Knorr Cetina, K.D., Mulay, M. (eds.) Advances in Social Theory and Methodology, pp. 196–223. Routledge & Kegan Paul, London (1981)
18. Muhle, F.: Embodied conversational agents as social actors? Sociological considerations on the change of human-machine relations in online environments. In: Gehl, R.W., Bakardjieva, M. (eds.) Socialbots and their Friends: Digital Media and the Automation of Society, pp. 86–109. Routledge, New York/London (2017)
19. Laurier, E., Brown, B., McGregor, M.: Mediated pedestrian mobility: walking and the map app. Mobilities **11**, 117–134 (2016). https://doi.org/10.1080/17450101.2015.1099900
20. Esteva, A., Kuprel, B., Novoa, R.A., Ko, J., Swetter, S.M., Blau, H.M., Thrun, S.: Dermatologist-level classification of skin cancer with deep neural networks. Nature **542**, 115 (2017). https://doi.org/10.1038/nature21056
21. Siemens, G., Long, P.: Penetrating the fog: analytics in learning and education. EDUCAUSE Rev. **46**, 30 (2011). https://doi.org/10.17471/2499-4324/195
22. Brambilla, A., Alavi, H., Verma, H., Lalanne, D., Jusselme, T., Andersen, M.: "Our inherent desire for control": a case study of automation's impact on the perception of comfort. Energy Proced. **122**, 925–930 (2017). https://doi.org/10.1016/j.egypro.2017.07.414

23. Alavi, H.S., Verma, H., Bahrami, F., Lalanne, D.: Is driverless car another Weiserian mistake? In: Proceedings of the 2016 ACM Conference Companion Publication on Designing Interactive Systems, pp. 249–253. ACM, New York (2017). https://doi.org/10.1145/3064857.3079155
24. Ross, D.A., Blasch, B.B.: Wearable interfaces for orientation and wayfinding. In: Proceedings of the Fourth International ACM Conference on Assistive Technologies, pp. 193–200. ACM, New York (2000). https://doi.org/10.1145/354324.354380
25. Shen, H., Chan, K.Y., Coughlan, J., Brabyn, J.: A mobile phone system to find crosswalks for visually impaired pedestrians. Technol. Disabil. **20**, 217–224 (2008)
26. Alavi, H.S., Churchill, E., Kirk, D., Bier, H., Verma, H., Lalanne, D., Schnädelbach, H.: From artifacts to architecture. In: Proceedings of the 19th International ACM SIGACCESS Conference on Computers and Accessibility, pp. 387–390. ACM, New York (2018). https://doi.org/10.1145/3197391.3197393
27. Alavi, H.S., Lalanne, D., Nembrini, J., Churchill, E., Kirk, D., Moncur, W.: Future of human-building interaction. In: Proceedings of the 2016 CHI Conference Extended Abstracts on Human Factors in Computing Systems, pp. 3408–3414. ACM, New York (2016). https://doi.org/10.1145/2851581.2856502
28. Alavi, H.S., Churchill, E., Kirk, D., Nembrini, J., Lalanne, D.: Deconstructing human-building interaction. Interactions **23**, 60–62 (2016). https://doi.org/10.1145/2991897
29. Krippendorff, K.: Content Analysis: An Introduction to its Methodology. SAGE, Thousand Oaks/London/New Delhi (2004)
30. Fairclough, N.: Analysing Discourse: Textual Analysis for Social Research. Routledge, London/New York (2003)
31. Garfinkel, H.: Studies in Ethnomethodology. Prentice-Hall, Englewood Cliffs (1967)
32. Garfinkel, H.: Ethnomethodology's Program: Working Out Durkheim's Aphorism. Rowman & Littlefield, Lanham (2002)
33. Sacks, H.: Lectures on Conversation I-II. Blackwell, Oxford (1992)
34. Knoblauch, H., Schnettler, B., Raab, J., Soeffner, H.-G. (eds.): Video Analysis: Methodology and Methods. Lang, Bern (2006)
35. Hartmann, D.: Sociology and its publics: reframing engagement and revitalizing the field. Sociol. Q. **58**, 3–18 (2016). https://doi.org/10.1080/00380253.2016.1248132

Efficient Concept Formation in Large State Spaces

Fredrik Mäkeläinen$^{(\boxtimes)}$, Hampus Torén, and Claes Strannegård

Department of Computer Science and Engineering,
Chalmers University of Technology, Gothenburg, Sweden
fredrik.makelainen@gmail.com

Abstract. General autonomous agents must be able to operate in previously unseen worlds with large state spaces. To operate successfully in such worlds, the agents must maintain their own models of the environment, based on concept sets that are several orders of magnitude smaller. For adaptive agents, those concept sets cannot be fixed, but must adapt continuously to new situations. This, in turn, requires mechanisms for forming and preserving those concepts that are critical to successful decision-making, while removing others. In this paper we compare four general algorithms for learning and decision-making: (i) standard Q-learning, (ii) deep Q-learning, (iii) single-agent local Q-learning, and (iv) single-agent local Q-learning with improved concept formation rules. In an experiment with a state space larger than 2^{32}, it was found that a single-agent local Q-learning agent with improved concept formation rules performed substantially better than a similar agent with less sophisticated concept formation rules and slightly better than a deep Q-learning agent.

Keywords: Autonomous agents · Artificial animals
Efficient concept formation · Adaptive architectures · Local Q-learning

Neuroplasticity refers to the capacity of animals to alter their nervous systems in response to changes in the environment. The connectivity between neurons may change over time and neurons may be added and removed continuously in a life-long process [1]. Artificial neural network models are frequently based on static architectures that are only plastic in the sense that their connectivity patterns develop over time. Several neural network models also allow nodes to be added and removed, however. For instance, the cascade-correlation architecture adds one hidden neuron at the time [2], and the progressive neural networks grow new columns while retaining previously acquired knowledge [11]. There are also regularization techniques [3] and pruning methods [18] that reduce the size of neural networks, while improving generalization.

Reinforcement learning occurs across the animal kingdom, and its biological basis has been studied extensively [9]. Reinforcement learning algorithms, on

Research supported by the Torsten Söderberg Foundation Ö110/17.

M. Iklé et al. (Eds.): AGI 2018, LNAI 10999, pp. 140–150, 2018.
https://doi.org/10.1007/978-3-319-97676-1_14

the other hand, are powerful tools for learning and decision-making in a general setting [13]. Q-learning is a basic algorithm for learning an optimal policy from experience for any Markov Decision Process [15]. The U-tree model has been used for building decision-trees for state representations [4] and local Q-learning has been used in a multiple agent setting for merging Q-values collected from multiple agents into a global Q-value [10]. Reinforcement learning algorithms have also been applied to homeostatic agents, whose single objective is to regulate their homeostatic variables and thus stay alive as long as possible [5,19].

Artificial animals have been studied primarily in the context of artificial life [6,14]. Stewart Wilson defined *animats* as a form of artificial animals, whose sole goal is homeostasis [16]. He also suggested the *animat path to AI* as a way of creating artificial intelligence by modeling animal behavior [17].

In this paper, we consider artificial animals and propose generic mechanisms for perception, learning, and decision-making. For perception we use a graph model that supports sequences and represents sensory concepts as single nodes (*cf.* grandmother nodes). This choice of graph model makes it relatively easy to define efficient rules for adapting the graph topology continuously. The purpose of our dynamic graph model is to support one-shot, life-long, on-line learning while avoiding catastrophic forgetting and the data hunger associated with deep learning.

This paper extends our previous work [12], with its single-agent local Q-learning and basic structural rules for adding new nodes by introducing radically improved rules for node formation. Section 1 presents the improved animat model. Section 2 presents an experiment in which our animat model is compared to four other models. The results of the experiment are presented in Sect. 3. Section 4 discusses possible directions for future research. Section 5, finally, draws some conclusions.

1   Animats

A schematic description of the *animat* model is given in Fig. 1. Time proceeds in discrete ticks in the animat model and the animat is updated at each tick according to Algorithm 1. Code describing the model in full detail is open sourced and available at [7]. Now let us zoom in on the constituents of the animat.

1.1   Body

The *body* is the animat's physical representation. The body has its associated finite sets of variables called *sensors*, *needs*, and *motors*. Sensors and motors take boolean values, whereas needs take values in the real interval $[0, 1]$.

Needs are denoted by natural numbers i. The status of need i at time t is the real value $\iota_i(t) \in [0, 1]$. Intuitively, 0 means death, while 1 means full need satisfaction. Examples of needs are water, energy, and protein. Now, it is easy to define reward in terms of changes in the status of the needs:

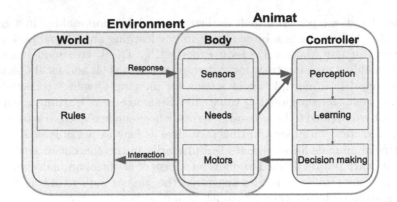

Fig. 1. The main constituents of the animat model in a reinforcement learning setting.

Algorithm 1. The update sequence for the animat.

Input: An animat A
while A *is alive* **do**
> The body receives a response from the environment and updates its sensors and needs accordingly
> The controller receives the active sensors and the status of the needs from the body
> The top active nodes are determined
> The global Q-values are determined
> The local Q-values are updated
> Formation rules are activated
> The top active nodes are determined again
> The global Q-values are determined again
> The action goodness and utility are determined
> An action is selected and sent to the body
> The action is performed by the body
> The world evaluates the interaction

end

Definition 1 (Rewards). *For each need i and time $t > 0$, the reward signal $r_i(t)$ is defined as follows:*

$$r_i(t) = \iota_i(t) - \iota_i(t-1). \tag{1}$$

1.2   Controller

The controller is responsible for both learning and decision-making. Intuitively, it models the animat's brain. The controller is a function that takes a (physiological) state consisting of sensor values and need values as input and outputs an action, which is immediately executed by the motors. The controller either selects a random action (exploration), or an action that is expected to have the best consequences, based on its experience from previous interactions (exploitation). Next let us describe the controller in more detail.

1.3 Perception

Based on sensory input, a perception graph is used to approximate the state, an example of a perception graph is given in Fig. 2. We construct the perception graph as a DAG where the input layer consists of the sensors. Initially, the perception graph consists only of the input layer, but through the use of formation rules, AND nodes can be added over time.

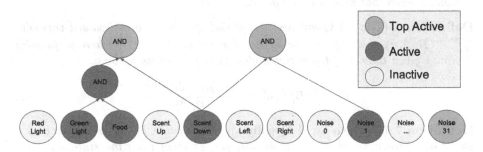

Fig. 2. A perception graph with 5 active and 3 top active nodes. The lowest layer contains the sensors.

Definition 2 (Perception graph). *A perception graph is a graph whose nodes (concepts) are sensors and binary AND-gates.*

Definition 3 (Perception graph activity). *At each time step the perception graph receives boolean values to its sensors. Those that receive the value True are called active. This activity propagates to the AND-nodes within the same tick. An AND-node is active if both its incoming signals are active.*

We use the symbol b for nodes of the perception graph and B_t for the set of all nodes at time t. The set of all active nodes at time t is denoted by B_t^A.

Definition 4 (Top activity). *An active node $b \in B_t^A$ is top active if the set of sensors it represents is not a subset to a set of sensors represented by another active node $b' \in B_t^A$.*

The set of all top active nodes at time t is denoted by B_t^{TA}. The set of top active nodes describes the current state to its maximum level of detail with respect to the structure of the perception graph.

1.4 Learning

In this section we present several experience structures that are updated each time step, and three new formation rules for the perception graph. The rules for expanding the perception graph are the main novelty of the present model compared to our previous work [12].

We will start with how the quality of each action, with respect to either a single top active node or the set of all top active nodes, are updated and calculated in this model.

Definition 5 (Local Q-values). *A* local *Q-value is a real-valued variable* $Q_i(b, a)$ *that reflects the expected response to the status of need i when performing action a, given that node b is top active.*

Definition 6 (Global Q-values). *A* global *Q-value is a real-valued variable* $Q_i^{global}(B_t^{TA}, a)$ *that reflects the expected response to need i when performing action a given the set of top active nodes. It is defined as follows:*

$$Q_i^{global}(B_t^{TA}, a) = \frac{\sum_{b \in B_t^{TA}} Q_i(b, a)}{|B_t^{TA}|}. \tag{2}$$

Definition 7 (Update local Q-values). *The update of the local Q-values is based on Q-learning where the main differences stem from the state representation, which is given by the set of top active nodes. At $t+1$ the Q-values are updated for all previous top active nodes $b \in B_t^{TA}$, with respect to the selected action a_t, the received rewards $r_i(t+1)$ and the new top active nodes $b' \in B_{t+1}^{TA}$, as*

$$Q_i(b, a_t) \leftarrow Q_i(b, a_t) + \alpha \left(r_i(t+1) + \gamma \cdot \max_a \left[Q_i^{global}(B_{t+1}^{TA}, a) \right] - Q_i(b, a_t) \right), \tag{3}$$

where $\alpha \in [0, 1]$ is the learning rate and $\gamma \in [0, 1]$ is the discount rate.

We will now move over to the new formation rules, but before we introduce them, we will present the information that they are based on.

Definition 8 (Pair reward). *$PairReward_i(b, b', a)$ is the probability that the reward for need i will be positive if action a is performed when b and b' are both top active.*

Definition 9 (Reward history). *The reward history $RewardHistory_i(b, a)$ is a pair (pos, neg), where pos (neg) is the number of times a positive (negative) reward for need i has been received when doing action a while node b has been active.*

To increase their chances of surviving, animats must be able to memorize what kind of objects are, e.g. suitable for eating and drinking.

Definition 10 (Positive stable nodes). *Based on the entries in RewardHistory_i(b, a), the positive stable nodes $PositiveStable_i(a)$ is a list of all nodes that have received at least $\phi_{PositiveStable}$ positive rewards and no negative rewards for need i and action a.*

Definition 11 (Relevant nodes). *For each stable node $b \in PositiveStable_i(a)$ all nodes b' that seem to be correlated to b are added to the list of relevant nodes, $Relevant_i(b)$. If at least at least $\phi_{RelevantUpdates}$ updates have been performed for an entry in $RelevantTransition(b, b'|b'', a)$ and $RelevantTransition(b, b'| b'', a) > p_{Relevant}$, then b'' is added to $Relevant_i(b)$.*

Definition 12 (Relevant transition probabilities). *The relevant transition probabilities, $RelevantTransition(b, b'|b'', a)$, contains the conditional probability that b' is active given that b'' was active and action a was performed, where $b \in PositiveStable_i(a')$ and $b' \in Relevant_i(b)$.*

From studying the Definitions 4, 6 and 7, we made the following observation: all sets of top activities a node can be part of needs to have a coherent response from the environment for each action, otherwise conflicting rewards and conflicting global Q-values could prevent the agent from learning a good policy. Our new formation rules were designed with this in mind, and they will now be briefly described.

Definition 13 (Positive reward merge). *At each time step, flip a biased coin. If heads, then select two nodes b and b' with probability proportional to their entry $PairReward_i(b, b', a)$ and so that b and/or b' have received conflicting rewards, i.e. the entry in $RewardHistory_i(b, a)$ is $(> 0, > 0)$. Then if it does not yet exist, add $b'' = b$ AND b' to B_t.*

The positive reward merge creates connections for nodes with conflicting rewards, with the goal that the new node becomes a positive stable node. Entries in *PairReward* with high probability are more likely to be made first.

Definition 14 (Stable node merge). *Suppose a stable node $b \in PositiveStable_i(a)$ is active, $b \in B_t^A$. For $b' \in B_t^{TA}$, if it is not already represented, add $b'' = b$ AND b' to B_t.*

The stable node merge makes sure that all stable nodes receive a coherent response from the environment, i.e. we isolate them by forming new nodes with the top active nodes.

Definition 15 (Relevant node merge). *Suppose a relevant node $b' \in Relevant_i(b)$, is active, $b' \in B_t^A$. For $b' \in B_t^{TA}$, if it is not already represented, add $b'' = b$ AND b' to B_t.*

Similar to stable node merge, we also isolate nodes deemed relevant to a stable node.

1.5 Decision-Making

In this section, we present the building blocks that are used by an animat to select an action in a potentially multi-objective setting.

Definition 16 (Action goodness). *The action goodness is defined as*

$$G_i(a, t) = \iota_i(t) + \omega Q_i^{global}(B_t^{TA}, a), \tag{4}$$

where $\omega \in [0, 1]$ is a constant.

Definition 17 (Utility). *The utility is defined as*

$$utility(a, t) = \min_i \left[G_i(a, t) \right]. \tag{5}$$

Definition 18 (Policy). *Flip a biased coin. If heads then select the action that maximizes utility(a, t), otherwise select a random action.*

2   Experiment

Now let us describe the experiment, whose purpose was to evaluate the three new formation rules (Definitions 13, 14, 15) and make comparisons with some other models. Accompanying code can be found at [7].

Fig. 3. The 3×3 cat world shown in a state with fish in three locations, red light off, green light on and 4 out of the 32 noise lights active, as shown in the top bar. The cat has to find the fish by using its smell sensors and then determine whether the fish is edible. Because of the noise, the state space of this world is greater than 2^{32}. (Color figure online)

2.1   World

The world that is used in the experiment consists of a 3×3 bounded grid populated by a cat and fish, see Fig. 3. When exploring the cat discovers that eating the fish sometimes results in (energy) reward, sometimes in punishment. For this environment, a green light indicates that the fish is safe to consume while a red light indicates the opposite. For the agent to find an optimal policy, it must learn to navigate towards fish and then only consume fish when the green light is active. To increase the size of the state space there are also lights that represent noise, these are activated randomly with $p = 0.25$, and they do not affect the received reward. The optimal policy is thus straightforward, but the problem lies in finding this policy with all the noise present.

2.2   Agents

In the experiment we evaluated five agents:

- **New Animat**, which is the animat model described in this paper.
- **Old Animat**, which is an adaptation of the animat model described in [12].
- **DQN**, which uses a two-layer ANN for approximating the Q-value. It also uses a target network and replay-memory similar to [8]. In total there are 200 weights to train.
- **Q-learner**, which is based on ordinary Q-learning, where each unique set of active sensors has an entry in its Q-matrix. Since the state space is vast, it is implemented using lazy initialisation.
- **Random**, which selects actions randomly.

The New Animat, Old Animat and Q-learner share the common Q-learning parameters: $\epsilon_{start} = 1.0$, $\epsilon_{decay} = 0.99$, $\epsilon_{min} = 0.01$, $\alpha = 0.05$, $\gamma = 0.9$, which are the exploration/exploitation parameters, learning rate and the discount rate, respectively.

Sensors. The body of the cat has the following sensors: a green light sensor, a red light sensor, 32 noise light sensors, a fish sensor and four remote sensors for fish smell. So in total, the agent's perception of the environment is based on 39 boolean values.

Needs. The cat has one need only: energy. The energy is not only affected by the actions, but it also decreases each time step with a constant decay rate of -0.02, an agent that is not following a good policy will usually see its energy reach 0 in about 40 time steps.

Actions. The agent can perform five different actions $a \in \{$move up, move down, move left, move right, eat$\}$. The actions have the following impact on energy in terms of the received reward: any move, $r = -0.01$; eat fish while green light is active, $r = 0.3$; eat fish while red light is active, $r = -0.3$; eat nothing, $r = -0.015$.

2.3   Evaluation

For each agent, data is collected over 20 independent experiments where one experiment is divided into two parts: training and testing. Learning and exploration are turned on during training and turned off during testing. Each training episode lasts 200 time steps and is followed by a test episode, in which performance data from 20 test runs are collected. Each test run ends after 100 time steps or if the agent's energy level reaches 0.

3   Results

In this section, we present the results of the experiment. Figure 4 shows the performance of the five agents. It is clear that New Animat and DQN has the best performance. DQN is the quickest to improve but is soon overtaken by New Animat. New Animat performs best overall and stabilizes at a level above all other agents. Old Animat performs better than both the Q-learner and the Random agent.

Figure 5 shows that at the end of the experiment, Old Animat's perception graph contained ∼2000 nodes, while New Animat's perception graph had stabilized around ∼700 nodes already after 3000 time steps. Although Old Animat used almost three times the number of nodes compared to New Animat, it failed to match its performance level. The main difference between the two lies in the formation rules, and thus they are the explanation of the success of New Animat.

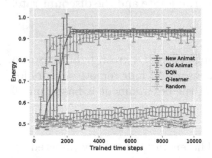
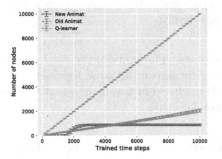

Fig. 4. For each agent, the mean and standard deviation of the energy with respect to the number of trained steps can be seen.

Fig. 5. The mean and standard deviation for the total number of nodes for New Animat and Old Animat, and the total number of unique states for Q-learner, with respect to the number of trained steps.

4   Future Work

The animat model was extended with three new formation rules. They all have the goal of creating a coherent response for all top active nodes, by identifying and isolating important nodes. Instead of isolating the important nodes by creating many nodes in the perception graph, we suggest that it might be possible to simply filter the top active nodes so that only the important nodes are taken into account. We believe this approach is well worth exploring further, since it has the potential to significantly reduce the number of nodes in the perception graph, while possibly maintaining the same level of performance.

5   Conclusion

Improvements to a computational model for artificial animals were proposed. The model combines generic mechanisms for homeostatic decision-making, local reinforcement learning, and dynamic concept formation. An experiment was conducted in which this model was compared to four other models: a previous version of the animat model, a deep Q-learning model, a basic Q-learning model, and a randomizer. The experiment was conducted in an environment with a state space of size exceeding 2^{32}, which rendered basic Q-learning infeasible. It was found that the improved animat model performed substantially better than the previous animat model and somewhat better than an optimized deep Q-learning model, despite starting with a blank slate architecture.

References

1. Draganski, B., May, A.: Training-induced structural changes in the adult human brain. Behav. Brain Res. **192**(1), 137–142 (2008)
2. Fahlman, S.E., Lebiere, C.: The cascade-correlation learning architecture. In: Advances in Neural Information Processing Systems, pp. 524–532 (1990)
3. Goodfellow, I., Bengio, Y., Courville, A.: Deep Learning. MIT Press, Cambridge (2016). http://www.deeplearningbook.org
4. Jonsson, A., Barto, A.G.: Automated state abstraction for options using the U-tree algorithm. In: Advances in Neural Information Processing Systems, pp. 1054–1060 (2001)
5. Keramati, M., Gutkin, B.S.: A reinforcement learning theory for homeostatic regulation. In: Advances in Neural Information Processing Systems, pp. 82–90 (2011)
6. Langton, C.G.: Artificial Life: An Overview. MIT Press, Cambridge (1997)
7. Mäkeläinen, F., Torén, H., Strannegård, C.: Dynamic State Representation for Homeostatic Agents (2018). https://gitlab.com/fredrikma/aaa_survivability
8. Mnih, V., et al.: Human-level control through deep reinforcement learning. Nature **518**(7540), 529–533 (2015)
9. Niv, Y.: Reinforcement learning in the brain. J. Math. Psychol. **53**(3), 139–154 (2009)
10. Russell, S.J., Zimdars, A.: Q-decomposition for reinforcement learning agents. In: Proceedings of the 20th International Conference on Machine Learning (ICML-03), pp. 656–663 (2003)
11. Rusu, A.A., et al.: Progressive neural networks. arXiv preprint arXiv:1606.04671 (2016)
12. Strannegård, C., Svangård, N., Lindström, D., Bach, J., Steunebrink, B.: The animat path to artificial general intelligence. In: Workshop on Architectures for Generality and Autonomy, IJCAI-17 (2017). http://cadia.ru.is/workshops/aga2017/proceedings/AGA_2017_Strannegard_et_al.pdf
13. Sutton, R.S., Barto, A.G.: Reinforcement Learning: An Introduction. MIT press, Cambridge (1998)
14. Tuci, E., Giagkos, A., Wilson, M., Hallam, J. (eds.): From Animals to Animats. 1st International Conference on the Simulation of Adaptive Behavior. Springer, Cham (2016). https://doi.org/10.1007/978-3-319-43488-9

15. Watkins, C.J.C.H.: Learning from delayed rewards. Ph.D. thesis. King's College, Cambridge (1989)
16. Wilson, S.W.: Knowledge growth in an artificial animal. In: Narendra, K.S. (ed.) Adaptive and Learning Systems, pp. 255–264. Springer, Boston (1986). https://doi.org/10.1007/978-1-4757-1895-9_18
17. Wilson, S.W.: The animat path to AI. In: Meyer, J.A., Wilson, S.W. (eds.) From Animals to Animats: Proceedings of the First International Conference on Simulation of Adaptive Behavior, pp. 15–21. MIT Press, Cambridge (1991)
18. Wolfe, N., Sharma, A., Drude, L., Raj, B.: The incredible shrinking neural network: new perspectives on learning representations through the lens of pruning. arXiv preprint arXiv:1701.04465 (2017)
19. Yoshida, N.: Homeostatic agent for general environment. J. Artif. Gen. Intell. (2017). https://doi.org/10.1515/jagi-2017-0001

DSO Cognitive Architecture:
Implementation and Validation
of the Global Workspace Enhancement

Khin Hua Ng$^{(\boxtimes)}$, Zhiyuan Du, and Gee Wah Ng

Cognition and Fusion Lab 2, DSO National Laboratories, Singapore, Singapore
{nkhinhua,dzhiyuan,ngeewah}@dso.org.sg

Abstract. An enhanced DSO Cognitive Architecture design was recently introduced to augment its cognitive functions by incorporating the Global Workspace Theory. A computational implementation of this new design is described in detail in this paper. The implementation is built as a distributed system with parallel pipelines of specialised processes, executing asynchronously. Competition initiated by these processes, and facilitated by the attention mechanism and global broadcast mechanism, leads to pipelines being dynamically created and allows disconnected pipelines to influence the processing of others. To validate the implementation, it was applied to a traffic control problem and experimental results showed increase in performance gain using the enhanced cognitive architecture.

Keywords: Cognitive architecture · Global Workspace Theory
Adaptive traffic control

1 Introduction

The DSO Cognitive Architecture (DSO-CA) [4] is a top-level cognitive architecture that incorporates the design principles of parallelism, distributed memory and hierarchical structure to model how the human brain processes information. It has been successfully used to develop Artificial Intelligence (AI) solutions to problems in applications like scene understanding [6] and mobile surveillance [5]. More recently, an enhanced design of the DSO-CA has been proposed [7] with the goal of enabling more human-like general intelligence and dynamic reasoning in AI systems. The design extension makes use of the Global Workspace Theory (GWT) [1] to enable Unified Reasoning — a process that permits reasoning across different knowledge domains and representations.

The motivation for unified reasoning is inspired by a cognitive architecture design problem known as the diversity dilemma [9] by which there is a need to blend diversity of different cognitive functions with uniformity of structure for efficiency, integrability, extensibility, and maintainability. The Global Workspace Theory is a neuro-cognitive theory of consciousness developed by

© Springer Nature Switzerland AG 2018
M. Iklé et al. (Eds.): AGI 2018, LNAI 10999, pp. 151–161, 2018.
https://doi.org/10.1007/978-3-319-97676-1_15

Bernard Baars [1]. It advances a model of information flow in which multiple, parallel, specialised processes compete and co-operate for access to a global workspace, which permits the winning coalition to broadcast to the rest of the specialist. By making use of an integrative memory system and applying the GWT, the newer DSO-CA with GWT design is able to facilitate collaboration among different cognitive functions and therefore indirectly provides a resolution to the diversity dilemma. Due to space constraints, we refer the reader to [7], for details on the design of the enhanced architecture, the inspirations drawn from the GWT, the principles behind the unified reasoning process using an integrative memory system, and the discussions on related cognitive architectures that had influenced the design. Nevertheless, to paint a clearer picture to the motivation behind the newer DSO-CA design, we will highlight two related work here, where the detailed comparisons are also given in the original paper. First, the diversity dilemma was discussed by Paul Rosenbloom and his answer to the dilemma is the SIGMA cognitive architecture that attempts to merge all the cognitive functions using a language representation which can be compiled into a common representation [10]. Second, Ben Goertzel formalised the concept of cognitive synergy [2], a framework that measures the compatibility and interaction between different cognitive functions (defined as knowledge creation mechanism that acts on a specific memory type), and how a cognitive function can help another when one gets 'stuck' if both functions have high compatibility. The point here is, these related works share a similar approach towards producing more general intelligence in AI systems, and the key is to work out how meaningful fusion and interaction among different cognitive functions can be achieved. The approach adopted by the DSO-CA is akin to creating a small-world network where cognitive processes that contribute to similar functionalities with respect to either agent's environment or it's task, form cliques amongst themselves due to frequent interactions. Communications between these cliques of disparate functionalities happen when the agent is met with a new or infrequent task. To solve this, the agent needs to chain different processes or cliques together dynamically through a GWT-inspired implementation. With that, it can create a platform for emergent, adaptive behaviours by allowing different pathways (learned or not) to communicate with one another through a common global workspace.

In this paper, we present a computational implementation of the DSO-CA [7] with GWT. The implementation is centred on the same distributed system principle whereby every specialised processor is executed as an independent parallel process with inter-process communication achieved by a message-oriented middleware (MOM). This means the system will have many pipelines executed in parallel, with some of them disconnected from one another. Competitions from these processes will either lead to pipelines being dynamically created, or allow disconnected pipelines to influence the processing of others. Full details of the implementation will be presented in the next section. In the section after that, we will discuss a successful validation of the implemented cognitive architecture applied to an urban traffic control problem. We will conclude the paper with future work where we discuss about learning pathways between the different specialised processors.

2   Design and Implementation

An overview of the enhanced DSO-CA is shown in Fig. 1. There are three design aspects with respect to incorporating the GWT: (1) parallelised, specialised processes, (2) competition, (3) inhibitory function to suppress competition after a broadcast. For aspect (1), there are Cognitive Codelets, which are specialised functions as described in the GWT (e.g the Reasoners in Executive group in Fig. 1a). Communications between them are done through the Reference Memory Cells (RMCs) which act as interfaces to the Working Memory (Fig. 1b). These communications can be considered as pathways and each pathway can be independent from one another. Aspect (2) is initiated via bottom-up attention which starts with Cognitive Codelets and RMCs sending salient information to compete for global broadcast access. This is realised through the attention mechanism, which comprises of Triggers and Attention Codelets, and Global Broadcast Mechanism (GBM). The competition is multi-tiered and it starts with candidates competing at a localised, contextual level in each Attention Codelet, and finally competing in the GBM, the winner thereby gaining global broadcast access. After which, it is propagated through the system allowing it to influence relevant pathways. These pathways form a coalition which is a group of processes that are dynamically formed to address contextual matters within the system. Finally aspect (3) is achieved via suppressing competition at the attention mechanism, preventing any local competition from taking place. This results in a cooldown period for other Cognitive Codelets to process the global broadcast before the next round of competition is allowed.

To implement the design aspects and information flow, the DSO-CA is implemented as a distributed system consisting of parallel processes. An MOM facilitates the inter-process communications based on a publish-subscribe pattern — a

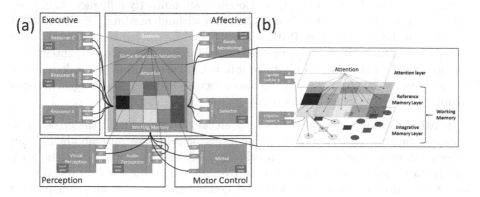

Fig. 1. (a) An overview of the DSO-CA. (b) The Working Memory zoomed in, with the Reference Memory Layer and Integrative Memory Layer.

process publishes its message to a topic and processes subscribed to it will receive the message. Additionally, all codelets are standardised to a multithreaded setup with threads following a producer-consumer pattern in concurrency design. Each thread is either a listener, processor, or sender; listener receives inputs and pre-processes them for the processor; processor represents a specialised function of which the codelet is designed for; and sender post-processes and sends the processor's result to designated codelets. The reasons for such a workflow are to be MOM-agnostic, and decouple preprocessing and post-processing from the main process so as to maximise time on it. Another benefit is code-reuse if the listener and sender threads are applicable to different codelets.

Cognitive Codelets are implemented as parallel processes that serve as specialised functions within the DSO-CA. Each has its own memory representation, which can differ from the integrative memory's. For example, Cognitive Codelets in Perception (Fig. 1a) can be different deep learning algorithms with different deep networks as their memory representations. The listener thread takes input from other RMCs and global broadcast (Fig. 1), it is also here where translation from integrative memory representation to local representation can take place. When a Cognitive Codelet receives a broadcast, it becomes a prioritised input which will be processed first even if the Cognitive Codelet receives a local input earlier. How the broadcast is processed depends on its relevance and the function of the Cognitive Codelet. For example, a Bayesian reasoner receiving a broadcast from a First Order Logic reasoner can use the conclusion within the result as an input to a what-if situation, i.e. diagnostic reasoning.

Reference Memory Cells constitute the Reference Memory Layer (Fig. 1b), with each RMC holding memory references to the integrative memory. In Fig. 2b, a RMC will merge the inputs into the underlying integrative memory by executing the transaction defined by the sender. This transaction includes adding, removing, refreshing (removing all references and adding new ones), or executing custom transactions. With regards to the references, different RMCs can refer to the same elements, thus changes to these elements are reflected to those RMCs referring to it. With that, a Cognitive Codelet can indirectly influence other Cognitive Codelets by modifying shared elements without needing a pathway. This ties in with the output where RMC will only send its reference memory to other Cognitive Codelets, meaning it only shares the relevant part of the integrative memory without the need to filter. To follow the design principle of distributed memory and parallelism, each RMC also executes in parallel and asynchronous manner for simultaneous transactions.

Attention Codelets represent contexts either abstracted from the goals, environment, or internal states of the system, e.g. survival for an embodied agent; external threats; imminent, and critical failure of other Cognitive Codelets. Each Attention Codelet's main purpose is to oversee competition within its context, and this translates to unique, localised competition that executes in parallel and asynchronously from one another. Each winner is the best representative for a context and is sent to the GBM for the final competition. The Attention

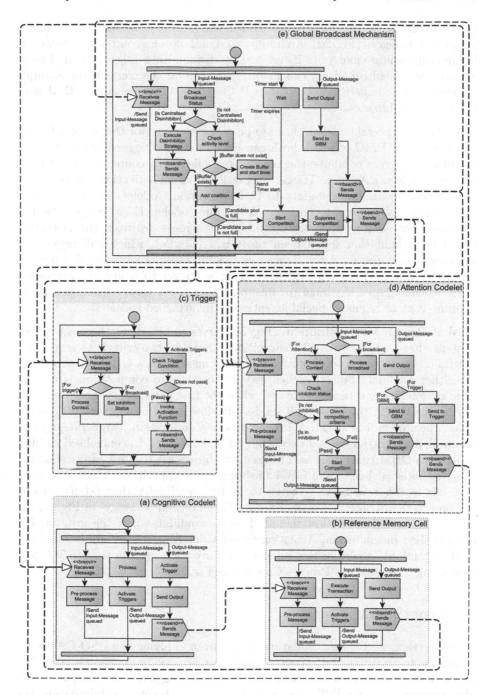

Fig. 2. Summarised activity diagrams of the DSO-CA with GWT. Dotted arrows indicate interprocess communication. Text with '/Send' prefix indicates the start of parallel thread e.g. '/Send Input-Message Queued' indicates the start of activity after 'Input-Message Queued'.

Codelet can also be affected by the GBM in the form of either inhibition signals or global broadcasts (Fig. 2d). An inhibition signal disables competition however, it can still monitor changes to its context by disinhibiting Triggers related to it. Meanwhile, global broadcast can modify the state of the context, for example unsuppressing competition on its own if the context has become critical with respect to the broadcast.

Triggers are special codelets that are part of the processor thread of a Cognitive Codelet or RMC of which both can have multiple Triggers. For bottom-up attention, Triggers compute the novelty or saliency of content sent by their attached codelet ('Activate Trigger' in Fig. 2) using an activation function, and send it along with the metadata to their Attention Codelets for competition. Each Trigger is assigned to only one Attention Codelet. Each Trigger also has a listener thread for either top-down attention messages from the Attention Codelets or inhibition signal from the GBM (Fig. 2c), which will reject any activation attempts until the Trigger is unsuppressed. Examples of top-down attention include Attention Codelet tasking a Trigger to adjust the activation level depending on the winner, or unsuppressing the Trigger's inhibition if the winning context requires special attention to its attached codelets.

Global Broadcast Mechanism (Fig. 2e) serves to broadcast the most salient content after a winner-take-all competition. There are two criteria to start competition: (1) activation level of all candidates must cross a GBM-set threshold, (2) either candidate buffer reached its limit or time to competition is up; the candidate buffer and timer is created when the first candidate is accepted. Following the GWT, the GBM will send inhibition signal to suppress all competitions before the broadcast. With regards to disinhibition, two strategies can be employed: centralised and decentralised disinhibition. In centralised disinhibition, the GBM controls it and maps every broadcast to a set of criteria that must be satisfied before the GBM unsuppresses competition. Thus, Attention Codelets in this scheme will switch to finding candidates that satisfy criteria relevant to their context. Under 'Execute Disinhibition Strategy' in Fig. 2e, the GBM will send disinhibition signals if these candidates met the criteria. For decentralised disinhibition, Attention Codelet determines disinhibition instead. Each Attention Codelet in this scheme will have their criteria to satisfy before continuing competition ('Process Context' in Fig. 2d).

3   Experiment

In this section, we present validation results from applying the DSO-CA implementation to an urban traffic control problem discussed in [8] whereby the CST group showcased the gain in performance using their cognitive architecture which also incorporated the GWT. It is clear that we have chosen to validate using the same problem because both architectures share a commonality on incorporating the GWT to enhance their architectures. The availability of the data and results presented in [8] also forms the baseline for our experiment. The experiment is conducted on a simulation platform known as Simulation of Urban Mobility (SUMO) [3]. We used the same experiment data made available by the CST group which includes the road network (Fig. 3) and the routes of all vehicles, each route dictating the start, destination and time of insertion; and the activation function which will be elaborated below. The aim of the experiment is to reduce mean traveling time of each vehicle via controlling phases of a traffic controller which consists of all traffic lights in a junction. Phase in this case means the lights of the traffic controller and each light presides over an incoming lane, for example GGrrGr means green light for incoming lane 0, 1 and 4. For more details about the experiment, please refer to [8]. In addition to the original three phase selection schemes reported in the paper, we have designed two additional schemes made possible using our GWT implementation, which will further improve the performance gains.

Fixed Timing: Fixed phase cycle in which the traffic controller goes through a cyclic timed sequence of phases. Phases are predefined within the network.

Parallel Reactive (PR): The activation function of an incoming lane is as followed: $AT_l(t) = \sum_{c \in C}(1 - \alpha V_c(t) - \beta X_c(t))$ where l is the lane, t is the time, c is a vehicle, V_c and X_c are velocity and distance from the traffic light of the vehicle respectively, $\alpha = 0.01\,\mathrm{m}^{-1}$, and $\beta = 0.001\,\mathrm{m}^{-1}$. The activation value is an indication of how congested the junction is — the higher it is, the more congested it gets. Phases are from Fixed Timing and the phase selected is the highest activation value summed from the green lights of that phase [8].

Artificial Consciousness (PR-GWT): The junction activation value is calculated ($\frac{\sum_{l \in L} AT_l(t)}{|L|}$) [8] and this serves as the metric for competition. Junction with the highest activation value that passes a threshold will be selected as the critical junction by the GWT and be broadcasted to other traffic controllers. The traffic controllers whose lanes are within range to the critical junction will form a coalition and their phases will be generated based on the following rules: (1) critical junction's outgoing lane to any incoming lane will be given the green light. (2) critical junction's incoming lanes connected to any outgoing lanes are given red light. We shall call this generated phase, forced phase.

Projection Scheme: Built upon PR-GWT, this new scheme allows coalition of traffic controllers to compromise between the critical junction and their traffic by selecting a phase based on projected activation. Given a candidate phase, compare each light in it to the corresponding current phase's light (could be any of the phases above) and subtract ϵ to that lane's activation if the transition is red→green. Add ϵ for the inverse. If the projected value crosses a threshold, permutate all possible phases constrained by only flipping the red lights in the current phase e.g. GrrG will yield 4 different phases. The permuted phase whose projected activation value is closest to the threshold, will be selected.

Reactive Scheme: Similar to Projection Scheme except traffic controller initially follow the PR-GWT scheme. Once its current activation value crosses a threshold, it will change its phase. First, it inverts the lights in the forced phase e.g `GrGGrrG` → `rGrrGGr`, this allows vehicles at the red light to move. Next, it selects a PR phase e.g `GrrrrG`. This is to preserve green lights to those lanes that may still have significant traffic. Lastly, an OR operation is performed on the two phases e.g `GrrrrG` ∨ `rGrrGGr` → `GGrrGGG`.

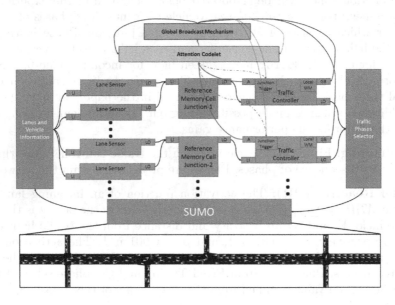

Fig. 3. Overview of the DSO-CA with Global Workspace applied to the traffic experiment.

Figure 3 shows the instantiation of the implementation for this experiment. Each traffic controller independently optimises its own traffic in parallel. When junctions get congested, the traffic controllers will start competing for broadcast access facilitated by the attention mechanism and GBM. Traffic controllers upon receiving the winner, will form a coalition if they are within reach to the critical junction and generate a forced phase to optimise for the critical junction's traffic. They will maintain it until the GBM signals that the activation level of the critical junction has fallen below a threshold, this can be considered as the **goal**. This also means that centralised disinhibition is used. Regarding the codelets in this instantiation, **Lane Sensor codelets** will retrieve the speed and distance of each vehicle to the traffic light on their respective lane, V_c and X_c at time step, t. Each **Reference Memory Cell** represents a junction. They will fuse inputs from Lane Sensors connected to their respective junction, and send to the Traffic Controller, V_c and X_c of each vehicle, c on that junction. When a **Traffic Controller Codelet** receives an update from a RMC, it selects the best phase and sends it back to SUMO. Under normal circumstances, PR is used to optimise local traffic. However if it is in a coalition, it will stick with the forced phase originally generated for PR-GWT. If Projection or Reactive scheme is used, the forced phase is regenerated after every update. The Traffic Controller

Codelet will go back to using PR when the goal is reached. For **Attention Codelet**, the context is the congestion of each junction, thus its competition criteria is to find the most congested junction. Competition is initiated when all Triggers have sent their candidates. When it knows of the critical junction, the Attention Codelet will need to monitor its activation level to meet the goal. To do that, it will disinhibit the Junction Trigger presiding over the critical junction (dashed-dot line in Fig. 3), this is a form of top-down attention. Related to the Attention Codelet, each **Junction Trigger** is attached to a Traffic Controller Codelet. For bottom-up attention, it will send the junction activation value to the Attention Codelet (Fig. 3). The functionality remains the same when one of them is disinhibited by the Attention Codelet. As for the **Global Broadcast Mechanism**, its implementation follows the Design and Implementation section.

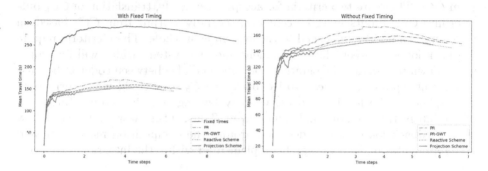

Fig. 4. Experiment results. Graph on the right is zoom-in-view without Fixed Timing.

Figure 4 shows the results of running the experiment using the "Corridor" traffic network model [8] with the setup of vehicles added every 0.1 s in SUMO. Using PR as a baseline, the performance gain for PR-GWT has an average of 3.8% with maximum value of 8.6%. This percentage improvement is comparable to that reported in [8] and it serves as validation for the correctness of our implementation. In addition, our proposed Reactive Scheme reduced the mean travel time even further by 5.9% on average, with up to a maximum of 10.9%. Furthermore, the proposed Projection Scheme has the best result: 7.1% average reduction, with maximum value of 15%. The experiment has successfully demonstrated that a dynamic, collaborative interaction can emerge through incorporating the GWT — pathways leading to Traffic Controller Codelets never interact with each other, however they still form a coalition to address critical context through the competition and broadcast mechanism.

4   Conclusion

In this paper, we have presented the implementation details of the enhanced design of the DSO-CA. The implementation is a distributed system of parallel processes that communicates with each other via an MOM. Each parallel process represents the specialised function of the GWT. Competitions are initiated by these processes and they compete for global broadcast via the attention mechanism and the GBM. The winner thereby, will either lead to pipelines being dynamically created, or allow parallel pipelines to influence the processing of others. For validation, the implementation was applied to the traffic control problem and experimental results showed increase in performance gain using methods that are enabled by our implementation of the enhanced DSO-CA.

For future work, we will be looking into the learning aspects of the design and implementation. Currently, pathways between codelets are predetermined but in general the pathways should also be learned. This can be done by leveraging on the competition design aspect. Intuitively, a pathway is formed between two Cognitive Codelets, CC_a and CC_b if CC_a frequently accepts the broadcast sourced from CC_b. There are two criteria for acceptance: firstly, translation of CC_b outputs into CC_a inputs must be coherent; secondly, output from CC_a based on CC_b input should be beneficial to the system as a whole. These criteria require feedback loops between the environment and the system, which will be propagated down to individual Cognitive Codelets, and also between codelets because incoherent inputs should lead to feedback to CC_b so it could make correction. To implement the feedback loops, we may leverage on the representativeness of the integrative memory and competition. Thus, future work is to study how these feedback loops can be designed around the competition mechanism and how representation learning can be implemented within the integrative memory.

References

1. Baars, B.J.: A Cognitive Theory of Consciousness. Cambridge University Press, Cambridge (1993)
2. Goertzel, B.: A formal model of cognitive synergy. In: Everitt, T., Goertzel, B., Potapov, A. (eds.) AGI 2017. LNCS (LNAI), vol. 10414, pp. 13–22. Springer, Cham (2017). https://doi.org/10.1007/978-3-319-63703-7_2
3. Krajzewicz, D., Erdmann, J., Behrisch, M., Bieker, L.: Recent development and applications of sumo-simulation of urban mobility. Int. J. Adv. Syst. Meas. 5(3&4), 128–138 (2012)
4. Ng, G.W., Tan, Y.S., Teow, L.N., Ng, K.H., Tan, K.H., Chan, R.Z.: A cognitive architecture for knowledge exploitation. In: 3rd Conference on Artificial General Intelligence (AGI-2010). Atlantis Press (2010)
5. Ng, G.W., Tan, Y.S., Xiao, X.H., Chan, R.Z.: DSO cognitive architecture in mobile surveillance. In: 2012 Workshop on Sensor Data Fusion: Trends, Solutions, Applications (SDF), pp. 111–115. IEEE (2012)
6. Ng, G.W., Xiao, X., Chan, R.Z., Tan, Y.S.: Scene understanding using DSO cognitive architecture. In: 2012 15th International Conference on Information Fusion (FUSION), pp. 2277–2284. IEEE (2012)
7. Ng, K.H., Du, Z., Ng, G.W.: DSO cognitive architecture: unified reasoning with integrative memory using global workspace theory. In: Everitt, T., Goertzel, B., Potapov, A. (eds.) AGI 2017. LNCS (LNAI), vol. 10414, pp. 44–53. Springer, Cham (2017). https://doi.org/10.1007/978-3-319-63703-7_5

8. Paraense, A.L.O., Raizer, K., Gudwin, R.R.: A machine consciousness approach to urban traffic control. Biol. Inspired Cogn. Archit. **15**, 61–73 (2016)
9. Rosenbloom, P.S.: Towards uniform implementation of architectural diversity. Artif. Intell. **20**, 197–218 (2009)
10. Rosenbloom, P.S., Demski, A., Ustun, V.: The sigma cognitive architecture and system: towards functionally elegant grand unification. J. Artif. Gen. Intell. **7**(1), 1–103 (2016)

The Foundations of Deep Learning
with a Path Towards General Intelligence

Eray Özkural[✉]

Celestial Intellect Cybernetics, Istanbul, Turkey
examachine@gmail.com
http://celestialintellect.com

Abstract. Like any field of empirical science, AI may be approached axiomatically. We formulate requirements for a general-purpose, human-level AI system in terms of postulates. We review the methodology of deep learning, examining the explicit and tacit assumptions in deep learning research. Deep Learning methodology seeks to overcome limitations in traditional machine learning research as it combines facets of model richness, generality, and practical applicability. The methodology so far has produced outstanding results due to a productive synergy of function approximation, under plausible assumptions of irreducibility and the efficiency of back-propagation family of algorithms. We examine these winning traits of deep learning, and also observe the various known failure modes of deep learning. We conclude by giving recommendations on how to extend deep learning methodology to cover the postulates of general-purpose AI including modularity, and cognitive architecture. We also relate deep learning to advances in theoretical neuroscience research.

1 Introduction

Deep learning is a rapidly developing branch of machine learning which is clustered around training deep neural models with many layers and rich computational structure well suited to the problem domain [15,44]. Initially motivated by modelling the visual cortex [11,12], human-level perceptual performance was approached and eventually attained in a number of challenging visual perception tasks such as image recognition with the aid of GPU acceleration [16,31,38]. The applications quickly extended to other computer vision tasks such as image segmentation [4], producing a variety of impressive results in visual information processing such as style transfer [13], opening new vistas in machine learning capabilities. The applications have been extended to domains beyond vision, such as speech recognition [18], language processing [29], and reinforcement learning [30], often with striking performance, proving the versatility and the significance of the approach in AI, urging us to consider whether the approach may yield a general AI (called Artificial General Intelligence (AGI) in some circles), and if so which problems would have to be tackled to make deep learning approach truly human-level AI that covers all aspects of cognition.

© Springer Nature Switzerland AG 2018
M. Iklé et al. (Eds.): AGI 2018, LNAI 10999, pp. 162–173, 2018.
https://doi.org/10.1007/978-3-319-97676-1_16

We analyze the approach from a 10,000 feet vantage point, revisiting the idea of AI axiomatization. Although, we are generally in agreement with Minsky that the attempt to make AI like physics is likely a futile pursuit, we also note the achievements of later theorists who have applied Bayesian methods successfully. We make no attempt to formalize any of our claims due to space consideration, however we discuss relevant research in cognitive sciences. Then, we apply the same foundational thinking to deep learning critically probing its intellectual foundations. The axioms, or postulates, of AI, are examined with an eye towards whether the current progress in deep learning in some way satisfies them, and what has to be done to fill the gap. The present paper may thus be regarded as an analytical, critical meta-level review, rather than a comprehensive review such as [44].

2   Postulates of General AI

One of the most ambitious mathematical models in AGI research is AIXI [26] which is a universal Reinforcement Learning (RL) model that can be applied to a very large variety of AI agent models and AI tasks including game playing, machine learning tasks, and general problem solving. AIXI is based on an extension of Solomonoff's sequence induction model which works with arbitrary loss and alphabet [24], making the aforementioned induction problem fairly general. Hutter proves in his book [25] that many problems can be easily transformed to this particular formulation of universal induction. There are a few conditions that have to be satisfied for a system to be called a universal induction system, and even then the system must be realized in a practical manner so as to be widely applicable and reproduce the cognitive competencies of homo sapiens, or failing that, a less intelligent animal.

The AIXI model combines Bellman equation with universal induction, casting action selection as the problem of maximizing expected cumulative reward in any computable environment. Although RL is a common approach in machine learning, AIXI had the novelty that it focused solely on universal RL agents. When viewed this way, it is obvious that AIXI is a minimalist cognitive architecture model, that exploits the predictive power of induction in RL setting, that does give the model the kind of versatility noted above. Solomonoff induction presents a desirable limit of inductive inference systems, since it has the least generalization error possible; the error is dependent only on the stochastic source and a good approximation can learn from very few examples [46]. AIXI model also retains a property of optimal behavior, Hutter deliberates that the model defines optimal, but incomputable intelligence, and thus any RL agent must approximate it. Therefore, our axiomatization must consider the conditions for Solomonoff's universal induction model, and consequently AIXI, to be approximated well, but we believe additional conditions are necessary for it to also satisfy generality in practice and within a versatile system, as follows.

Completeness: The class of models that can be acquired by the machine learning system must be Turing-complete. If a large portion of the space of programs is unavailable to the system, it will not have the full power and generalization properties of Solomonoff induction. The convergence theorem in that case is voided, and the generalization performance of Solomonoff induction cannot be guaranteed [46].

Stochastic Models: The system requires an adequately wide class of stochastic models to deal with uncertainty in the real world, a system with only deterministic components will be brittle. Induction is better suited to working with stochastic models, one example of such an approach is Wallace's Minimum Message Length (MML) model where we minimize the message length that contains both the length of the statistical model encoding and data encoding length relative to model [50, 51].

Bayesian Prediction: The system must compute the inferences with Bayes' law. The inference in Solomonoff's model is considered Bayesian. In neuroscience, the Bayesian Brain Hypothesis has been mostly accepted, and the brain is often regarded as a Bayesian inference machine that extracts information from the environment in theoretical neuroscience. Jaynes introduced the possibility of Bayesian reasoning in the brain from a statistical point of view [27]. The Bayesian approach to theoretical neuroscience is examined in a relatively recent book [5]. Fahlman et al. introduced the statistically motivated energy minimizing Boltzmann machine model [7]; Hinton et al. connected the induction principle of Minimum Description Length and Helmholtz free energy introducing the autoencoder model in 1993 [22]. Bialek's lab has greatly contributed to the understanding of the Bayesian nature of the brain, a decent summary of the approach detailing the application of the information bottleneck method may be found in [1]. Friston has later rigorously applied the free energy principle and has obtained even more encouraging results, he explains the Bayesian paradigm in [9]. Note that Helmoltz free energy and the free energy principle are related, and both are related to approximate Bayesian inference.

Principle of Induction: The system must have a sound principle of induction that is equivalent to Solomonoff's model of induction which uses an a priori probability model of programs that is inversely and exponentially proportional to program size. Without the proper principle of induction, generalization error will suffer greatly, as the system will be corrupted. Likewise, as Solomonoff induction is more completely approximated, the generalization error will decrease dramatically, allowing the system to obtain one-shot learning first predicted by Solomonoff, achieving a successful generalization from a sufficiently complex single example without any prior training whenever such an example is possible.

Practical Approximation: Solomonoff induction has an exponential worst-case bound with respect to program size rendering it infeasible. This surely is not a practical result, any approximation must introduce algorithmic methods to obtain a feasible approximation of the theoretical inductive inference model.

Incremental Learning: The system must be capable of cumulative learning, and therefore it must have a model of memory with adequate practical algorithms. Solomonoff has himself described a rather elaborate approach to transfer learning [47], however, it was not until much later that experimental results were possible for universal induction since Solomonoff's theoretical description did not specify an efficient algorithm. The first such result was obtained in OOPS system [45] demonstrating significant speedups for a universal problem solver.

Modularity and Scalability: The system must be composed of parametrized modules that attend to different tasks, allowing complex ensemble systems to be built for scalability like the neocortex in the human brain. A monolithic system is not likely to scale well, the system must be able to adapt modules to distinct tasks, and then be able to re-use the skills. A modular system also provides a good base for specialization according to modality and cognitive task, starting from a common module description. In the human brain, there are both functional regions and a complex, hierarchical modular structure in the form of cortical columns, and micro-columns.

Cognitive Architecture: The system must have a cognitive architecture, depending on modularity that will address typical cognitive functions of learning, memory, perception, reasoning, planning, and language as well as aspects of robotics which allow it to control robotic appendages. This manner of organization is modeled after the human brain, however, it seems essential for any real-world AI system that requires these basic competencies to deliver robust performance across a sufficiently general set of cognitive tasks. Even if unlike the brain, the system must have an architectural design, or one that is capable of introducing the required architecture.

These reasonable and desirable properties of a complete AI system lead naturally to a top-down design sometimes called an AGI Unification Architecture among practitioners, if built around the floor plan of a universal induction system such as AIXI. An example of such an approach to designing a cognitive architecture may be seen in [36]. However, this is not necessarily the only kind of solution. An adequate architecture could also be built around a deep learning approach; let us therefore proceed to its postulates.

3 Postulates of Deep Learning

Deep Learning is a particular kind of Artificial Neural Network (ANN) research which shares some commonalities and inherits some assumptions/principles from earlier ANN research some of which may seem implicit to outsiders. We try to recover these tacit or implicit assumptions for the sake of general AI readership, and also delineate the borders of deep learning from other ANN research in the following.

No Free Lunch: The well-known No Free Lunch theorem for machine learning implies that there can be no general learning algorithm that will be effective for all problems. This theorem has generated a strong bias towards model-based learning in ANN research where the researcher tries to design a rich network model that covers all contingencies in the domain but uses insights into the problem domain and thus the experiment does not suffer from the unreasonable large search space of a model-free learning method. From image processing to language, this particular blend of specificity and generality seems to have guided deep learning quite successfully and resulted in impressive outcomes. The specificity determined by the ANN researcher may be likened to "innateness" in cognitive science. Note that AGI theorists have argued otherwise [6], therefore this heuristic principle remains arguable.

Epistemic Non-reductionism: This is the view that loosely depends on Quine's observation that epistemic reductionism often fails in terms of explanatory power for the real world [37], which is to say that there is a wealth of necessary complexity to account for it. When we look at a deep learning vision architecture, we see that the irreducible patterns of visual information are indeed stored as they are useful however not overmuch; the system does not store every pattern much like our brains. Epistemic irreducibility is a guiding principle in deep learning research, and it is why deep learning models are large rather than small and minimalistic as in some ANN research.

Eliminative Materialism: Churchland's philosophical observation that the brain does not deal in any of the folk psychological concepts in cognitive science literature, but must be understood as the activation state and trajectory of the brain [3], plays a fundamental intellectual role in the deep learning approach, where we shift our attention to brain-like representations and learning for dealing with any problem, even if it looks like a matter of propositional logic to us.

Subsymbolic and Distributed Representation: Expressed in detail in the classical connectionist volume [40], this principle is the view that all representations in the brain have a distributed, real-valued representation rather than discrete, symbolic representations that computer scientists prefer in their programs. Sparse Coding hypothesis has been mostly confirmed in neuroscience, therefore we do know that the brain uses population codes that are sparse, distributed, and redundant. Unlike a symbolic representation, the brain networks are fault-tolerant and redundant, and deal with uncertainty at every level. Subsymbolic representations are more robust and better suited to the nature of sensory input. However, we also know that "grandmother cells" exist which may correspond to predicates, which are still best modeled as non-linear detectors, or ReLu units, in a neural network.

Universal Approximation: The universal approximation theorem [23] for multi-layer feed forward neural networks underlies the heuristic of using many hidden layers in a deep learning architecture. The theorem shows that a multilayer neural network can approximate arbitrary continuous real-valued functions. Therefore, the system is capable of representing any mapping under mild assumptions, including those with irregular features forming a synergy with the epistemic non-reductionism postulate.

Deep Models: The number of layers in a feed forward network, or the circumference of a Recurrent Neural Network (RNN) must be greater than 3, meaning multiple hidden layers in a multi-layer feed forward network, or an RNN with complex topology. Model depth avoids much of the criticism in Minsky and Papert's critical book on neural networks that showed perceptrons cannot learn concave discriminants [34], and its later editions that extend the criticism to multi-layer models. In today's ANN applications we observe all manners of intricate discrimination models were successfully learnt, however shallow networks will still not avoid Minsky's observations. A complexity analysis also supports that increasing depth can result in asymptotically smaller networks for the same function representation [48], implying that deep models are fundamentally more efficient.

Hierarchy and Locality: A distinguishing feature of deep learning is that it contains local pattern recognition networks and a hierarchy of these pattern recognition circuits that affixes the local and global views. Thus, a sequence of convolutional and pooling layers have been a staple of image processing applications in deep learning as the convolutional layer is basically a set of texture recognition patches, and downsampling via max-pooling gives us a dimensionality reduction and the ability to hierarchically combine pattern recognizers efficiently. This organization was inspired by 2d image processing in the visual cortex, however many domains can benefit from the same organizational principle since they apply to any sensory array. The principle is also valid for domains that are not directly sensory arrays, but maintain a similar topological relation. The principle also has great synergy with the depth principle because the network tries to capture perceptually salient features and avoids learning irrelevant patterns making it possible to increase network depth which avoids Minskyan objections even more effectively.

Gradient Descent: Perhaps the most common feature of deep learning is that a variation of back propagation or gradient descent is used to train the model. This is required since any other way to train the large networks in deep learning research would be infeasible. Other methods such as variational learning and MCMC tree search have been applied in deep learning research, however this principle has remained fairly constant as it is necessitated by other principles above, which may result in billions of real valued parameters to be trained.

Dataflow Models and SIMD Acceleration: Since the number of parameters to be trained is large, exploiting data-parallelism through SIMD-based accelerators such as GPU's, and later executing data-flow representations on FPGA's have proven to be an essential factor for deep learning research. This property of deep learning corresponds to the "massive parallelism" property of the brain.

4   Shortcomings and Extensions

Although deep learning has generated phenomenal results, it also has some shortcomings that are being worked on. The most common limitation is that a typical deep learning architecture requires on the order of 10,000 or more examples. Some of the largest experiments have used millions of examples, therefore this was simply not an issue that was focused on. It may well be the case that this is a fundamental shortcoming of deep learning, however, researchers have tried solutions such as using stochastic gradient over the entire set of samples, as a usual statistical approach would necessitate, instead of running BP in epochs, which imitates the brain's online learning capability. Another common problem is that most deep learning uses supervised learning, which presents a problem in terms of constructing many labeled/annotated examples for every new problem. Autoencoder [21] is an unsupervised learning model, and it has many variations and applications in deep learning, however, most applications still require a good deal of hand crafted data. A strange problem persists in deep learning systems, which makes them easy to fool in ways that are not intuitive to humans, such as a simple perturbation causing a misclassification, an intuitively unrelated artificial image recognized as a natural image, or a specially crafted patch on an unrelated image causing a misclassification. These might either be symptoms of fundamental limitations, or they might be ameliorated with better deep learning models. We observe that these issues look much like overfitting, i.e., poor generalization performance.

When we contrast the general AI postulates and deep learning postulates, we see some interesting overlap and also some areas where deep learning requires a good deal of development. A deep learning system has one sort of completeness that stems from the universal approximation theorem, and dataflow models can be augmented with arbitrary computational units such as the Neural Turing Machine model [17], and the later Differentiable Neural Computer model [19] that augments neural networks with external memory. Program class extensions of this sort may be an integral part of next-generation deep learning. Recent proposals for non-Euclidian embedding of data also enhance generality of deep learning models [2].

It is possible to design deep architectures for rigorous stochastic models, which is an important extension to deep learning that will increase robustness.

Typically, deep learning lacks a principle of induction, but at the same time a stochastic model of induction is implicit in deep learning as the information bottleneck analysis of deep learning shows [49], where we can view deep learning as a lossy compression scheme that forgets unnecessary information. Such theories will lead to better generalization performance. [28] applies random matrix theory to generalization in deep learning, and introduces a new regularization method for improving generalization.

Progressive deep learning architectures add layers as necessary, substantiating an important analogy to SVM's function class iteration [41]. Much richer forms of induction may be beneficial for improving a deep learning network's generalization power. The training procedure in deep learning is efficient but only locally optimal, in the future a combination of neuro-evolution and gradient descent may outperform gradient descent and approximate universal induction better. Evolution has already been applied to automated design of deep networks [33,35]. Neuro-evolution has been shown to be effective in game playing [39] and other tasks that are difficult for deep learning, and therefore it might displace deep learning methodology altogether in the future.

Deep learning architectures gained memory capability with the LSTM unit, and similarly designed memory cells, however, long-term memory across tasks remains problematic. A good realization of algorithmic memory in deep learning is Neural Task Programming (NTP) [53] which achieves an indexical algorithmic memory based on LSTM and the ability to hierarchically decompose skills which has been successfully applied to robotics tasks. Progress in the direction of NTP is likely to be a major improvement for deep learning, since without cumulative and hierarchical learning intelligence is highly restricted.

Recently, progress has been made in the matter of modularity with Hinton's update of Capsule Networks, that models the cortical architecture for visual tasks [42]. Capsule Networks adds dynamic routing between visual processing modules with affine transformations, enhancing invariance and defines neural modules as capsules that may be arranged like neurons. Capsules correspond to visual entities in the model, therefore capsules that recognize a face decompose into eyes, a nose, lips, and so forth. The step from monolithic to modular deep learning is as powerful as the step from shallow to deep networks, hence this line of research is a significant extension of deep learning. A similar line of research is advanced by Vicarious, which propose a recursive neural architecture that exploits lateral connections accounting for distinct feature sets such as contour and surface, and the hierarchical representation of entities like in Capsule Networks [14]; their system can reportedly break CAPTCHA's. Hawkins proposes a new cortex architecture that introduces pyramidal neurons, active dendrites, and multiple integration sites, identifying cortical computations for hierarchical sequence memory, and it intriguingly involves dendritic computation [20]. Capsule Networks might be enhanced to provide a similar dendritic model eventually, or capsule-like speciation might be ported to Hawkins's model.

Cognitive architectures built on symbolic concepts may not be readily applicable to deep learning, however, modeling the functional anatomy of the brain creates much needed synergy with neural networks. For instance, in Deep Mind's I2A model [52], we see a direction towards capturing more brain function in the form of imagining future states, while PathNet presents a modular, reflective learning system that can recombine network modules by evolving paths over the network [8]. Both neural architectures exhibit progress towards a more complete cognitive neural architecture. Another recent direction is the relational networks that model reasoning [43]. Conceivably, neural models of fundamental cognitive functions may be developed with a similar methodology, and bound in a connectionist agent architecture. Likewise, the active inference agent of [10] with deep temporal models captures the essentials of functional anatomy based on hierarchical probabilistic models, and even gives us a fully unsupervised agent model that is quite intriguing from a scientific perspective.

5 Discussion and Future Research

Despite recent criticism raised against deep learning [32], almost all of the postulates of general AI we have outlined seem achievable, however, with major improvements over existing systems. While it is entirely possible for a traditional symbolic-oriented system to achieve the same performance, the advantages of deep learning approach cannot be neglected, and the possible extensions to deep learning discussed may also ameliorate the common shortcomings we summarized. Another combination that might work is the combination of the symbolic AI approach with deep learning. In some circles, researchers pursue a mathematical AI unification approach (like AIXI approximations), however, the merits of such an approach are yet to be proven experimentally over deep learning. It seems prudent to at least try to integrate deep learning faithfully in existing AI architectures, or for new architectures, attempt to construct them solely on a neural architecture. In the future, we expect a convergence of more powerful training methods and deep architectures, taking us to a more model-free learning system, and more capable, modular neural agent architectures inspired by neuroscience.

References

1. Bialek, W., Nemenman, I., Tishby, N.: Predictability, complexity, and learning. Neural Comput. **13**(11), 2409–2463 (2001). https://doi.org/10.1162/089976601753195969
2. Bronstein, M.M., Bruna, J., LeCun, Y., Szlam, A., Vandergheynst, P.: Geometric deep learning: going beyond euclidean data. IEEE Signal Process. Mag. **34**, 18–42 (2017). https://doi.org/10.1109/MSP.2017.2693418
3. Churchland, P.M.: Eliminative materialism and the propositional attitudes. J. Philos. **78**(February), 67–90 (1981)
4. Ciresan, D.C., Giusti, A., Gambardella, L.M., Schmidhuber, J.: Neural networks for segmenting neuronal structures in EM stacks. In: ISBI Segmentation Challenge Competition: Abstracts (2012)
5. Doya, K., Ishii, S., Pouget, A., Rao, R.P.N.: Bayesian Brain: Probabilistic Approaches to Neural Coding. The MIT Press, Cambridge (2007)
6. Everitt, T., Lattimore, T., Hutter, M.: Free lunch for optimisation under the universal distribution. In: Proceedings of the IEEE Congress on Evolutionary Computation, CEC 2014, Beijing, China, July 6–11, 2014, pp. 167–174 (2014). https://doi.org/10.1109/CEC.2014.6900546
7. Fahlman, S.E., Hinton, G.E., Sejnowski, T.J.: Massively parallel architectures for AI: Netl, thistle, and boltzmann machines. In: Proceedings of the Third AAAI Conference on Artificial Intelligence. AAAI 1983, pp. 109–113. AAAI Press (1983). http://dl.acm.org/citation.cfm?id=2886844.2886868
8. Fernando, C., et al.: PathNet: Evolution Channels Gradient Descent in Super Neural Networks. ArXiv e-prints, January 2017
9. Friston, K.: The history of the future of the bayesian brain. Neuroimage **62**(248), 1230–1233 (2012)

10. Friston, K.J., Rosch, R., Parr, T., Price, C., Bowman, H.: Deep temporal models and active inference. Neurosci. Biobehav. Rev. **77**, 388–402 (2017). https://doi.org/10.1016/j.neubiorev.2017.04.009
11. Fukushima, K.: Neocognitron: a self-organizing neural network for a mechanism of pattern recognition unaffected by shift in position. Biol. Cybern. **36**(4), 193–202 (1980)
12. Fukushima, K.: Artificial vision by multi-layered neural networks: Neocognitron and its advances. Neural Networks **37**, 103–119 (2013)
13. Gatys, L.A., Ecker, A.S., Bethge, M.: Image style transfer using convolutional neural networks. In: 2016 IEEE Conference on Computer Vision and Pattern Recognition, CVPR 2016, Las Vegas, NV, USA, June 27–30, 2016, pp. 2414–2423 (2016). https://doi.org/10.1109/CVPR.2016.265
14. George, D., et al.: A generative vision model that trains with high data efficiency and breaks text-based captchas. Science (2017). https://doi.org/10.1126/science.aag2612
15. Goodfellow, I., Bengio, Y., Courville, A.: Deep Learning. MIT Press, Cambridge (2016). http://www.deeplearningbook.org
16. Graves, A., Liwicki, M., Fernandez, S., Bertolami, R., Bunke, H., Schmidhuber, J.: A novel connectionist system for improved unconstrained handwriting recognition. IEEE Trans. Pattern Anal. Mach. Intell. **31**(5), 855–868 (2009)
17. Graves, A., Wayne, G., Danihelka, I.: Neural Turing Machines. ArXiv e-prints, October 2014
18. Graves, A., Mohamed, A.R., Hinton, G.E.: Speech recognition with deep recurrent neural networks. In: IEEE International Conference on Acoustics, Speech and Signal Processing (ICASSP), pp. 6645–6649. IEEE (2013)
19. Graves, A., et al.: Hybrid computing using a neural network with dynamic external memory. Nature **538**(7626), 471–476 (2016). https://doi.org/10.1038/nature20101
20. Hawkins, J., Ahmad, S.: Why neurons have thousands of synapses, a theory of sequence memory in neocortex. Front. Neural Circ. **10**, 23 (2016). https://doi.org/10.3389/fncir.2016.00023
21. Hinton, G.E., Zemel, R.S.: Autoencoders, minimum description length and Helmholtz free energy. In: Cowan, J.D., Tesauro, G., Alspector, J. (eds.) Advances in Neural Information Processing Systems (NIPS) 6, pp. 3–10. Morgan Kaufmann (1994)
22. Hinton, G.E., Zemel, R.S.: Autoencoders, minimum description length and helmholtz free energy. In: Proceedings of the 6th International Conference on Neural Information Processing Systems. NIPS 1993, pp. 3–10. Morgan Kaufmann Publishers Inc., San Francisco (1993). http://dl.acm.org/citation.cfm?id=2987189.2987190
23. Hornik, K.: Approximation capabilities of multilayer feedforward networks. Neural Netw. **4**(2), 251–257 (1991). https://doi.org/10.1016/0893-6080(91)90009-T
24. Hutter, M.: Optimality of universal Bayesian prediction for general loss and alphabet. J. Mach. Learn. Res. **4**, 971–1000 (2003). (On J. Schmidhuber's SNF grant 20–61847)
25. Hutter, M.: Universal Artificial Intelligence: Sequential Decisions Based on Algorithmic Probability. Springer, Heidelberg (2005). https://doi.org/10.1007/b138233
26. Hutter, M.: Universal algorithmic intelligence: a mathematical top→down approach. In: Goertzel, B., Pennachin, C. (eds.) Artificial General Intelligence. Cognitive Technologies, pp. 227–290. Springer, Heidelberg (2007). https://doi.org/10.1007/978-3-540-68677-4_8

27. Jaynes, E.T.: How does the brain do plausible reasoning? In: Erickson, G.J., Smith, C.R. (eds.) Maximum-Entropy and Bayesian Methods in Science and Engineering, vol. 1. Springer, Dordrecht (1988). https://doi.org/10.1007/978-94-009-3049-0_1

28. Kawaguchi, K., Pack Kaelbling, L., Bengio, Y.: Generalization in Deep Learning. ArXiv e-prints, October 2017

29. Kim, Y., Jernite, Y., Sontag, D., Rush, A.M.: Character-aware neural language models. In: Proceedings of the Thirtieth AAAI Conference on Artificial Intelligence, February 12–17, 2016, Phoenix, Arizona, USA, pp. 2741–2749 (2016)

30. Koutník, J., Cuccu, G., Schmidhuber, J., Gomez, F.: Evolving large-scale neural networks for vision-based TORCS. In: Foundations of Digital Games, Chania, Crete, GR, pp. 206–212 (2013)

31. LeCun, Y., et al.: Back-propagation applied to handwritten zip code recognition. Neural Comput. 1(4), 541–551 (1989)

32. Marcus, G.: Deep Learning: A Critical Appraisal. ArXiv e-prints, January 2018

33. Miikkulainen, R., et al.: Evolving Deep Neural Networks. ArXiv e-prints, March 2017

34. Minsky, M., Papert, S.: Perceptrons: An Introduction to Computational Geometry. MIT Press, Cambridge (1969)

35. Petroski Such, F., Madhavan, V., Conti, E., Lehman, J., Stanley, K.O., Clune, J.: Deep Neuroevolution: Genetic Algorithms Are a Competitive Alternative for Training Deep Neural Networks for Reinforcement Learning. ArXiv e-prints, December 2017

36. Potapov, A., Rodionov, S., Potapova, V.: Real-time GA-based probabilistic programming in application to robot control. In: Steunebrink, B., Wang, P., Goertzel, B. (eds.) AGI -2016. LNCS (LNAI), vol. 9782, pp. 95–105. Springer, Cham (2016). https://doi.org/10.1007/978-3-319-41649-6_10

37. Quine, W.: Two dogmas of empiricism. Philos. Rev. 60, 20–43 (1951)

38. Ranzato, M.A., Huang, F., Boureau, Y., LeCun, Y.: Unsupervised learning of invariant feature hierarchies with applications to object recognition. In: Proceedings of the Computer Vision and Pattern Recognition Conference (CVPR 2007), pp. 1–8. IEEE Press (2007)

39. Risi, S., Togelius, J.: Neuroevolution in games: State of the art and open challenges. IEEE Trans. Comput. Intellig. AI Games 9(1), 25–41 (2017). https://doi.org/10.1109/TCIAIG.2015.2494596

40. Rumelhart, D.E., McClelland, J.L., PDP Research Group (eds.): Parallel Distributed Processing: Explorations in the Microstructure of Cognition, Vol. 1: Foundations. MIT Press, Cambridge (1986)

41. Rusu, A.A., et al.: Progressive neural networks. arXiv preprint arXiv:1606.04671 (2016)

42. Sabour, S., Frosst, N., Hinton, G.E.: Dynamic routing between capsules. In: NIPS, pp. 3859–3869 (2017). http://papers.nips.cc/paper/6975-dynamic-routing-between-capsules

43. Santoro, A., et al.: A simple neural network module for relational reasoning. CoRR abs/1706.01427 (2017)

44. Schmidhuber, J.: Deep learning in neural networks: an overview. Neural Networks 61, 85–117 (2015). https://doi.org/10.1016/j.neunet.2014.09.003

45. Schmidhuber, J.: Optimal ordered problem solver. Mach. Learn. 54, 211–256 (2004)

46. Solomonoff, R.J.: Complexity-based induction systems: comparisons and convergence theorems. IEEE Trans. Inf. Theor. IT–24(4), 422–432 (1978)

47. Solomonoff, R.J.: A system for incremental learning based on algorithmic proba-
    bility. In: Proceedings of the Sixth Israeli Conference on Artificial Intelligence, pp.
    515–527. Tel Aviv, Israel, December 1989
48. Telgarsky, M.: benefits of depth in neural networks. In: Proceedings of the 29th
    Conference on Learning Theory, COLT 2016, New York, USA, June 23–26, 2016,
    pp. 1517–1539 (2016). http://jmlr.org/proceedings/papers/v49/telgarsky16.html
49. Tishby, N., Zaslavsky, N.: Deep learning and the information bottleneck principle.
    In: 2015 IEEE Information Theory Workshop, ITW 2015, Jerusalem, Israel, April
    26 - May 1, 2015, pp. 1–5 (2015). https://doi.org/10.1109/ITW.2015.7133169
50. Wallace, C.S., Dowe, D.L.: Minimum message length and kolmogorov complexity.
    Comput. J. **42**(4), 270–283 (1999). https://doi.org/10.1093/comjnl/42.4.270
51. Wallace, C.S., Boulton, D.M.: A information measure for classification. Comput.
    J. **11**(2), 185–194 (1968)
52. Weber, T., et al.: Imagination-Augmented Agents for Deep Reinforcement Learn-
    ing. ArXiv e-prints, July 2017
53. Xu, D., Nair, S., Zhu, Y., Gao, J., Garg, A., Fei-Fei, L., Savarese, S.: Neural Task
    Programming: Learning to Generalize Across Hierarchical Tasks. ArXiv e-prints,
    October 2017

Zeta Distribution and Transfer Learning Problem

Eray Özkural[(✉)]

Celestial Intellect Cybernetics, Istanbul, Turkey
examachine@gmail.com
http://www.celestialintellet.com

Abstract. We explore the relations between the zeta distribution and algorithmic information theory via a new model of the transfer learning problem. The program distribution is approximated by a zeta distribution with parameter near 1. We model the training sequence as a stochastic process. We analyze the upper temporal bound for learning a training sequence and its entropy rates, assuming an oracle for the transfer learning problem. We argue from empirical evidence that power-law models are suitable for natural processes. Four sequence models are proposed. Random typing model is like no-free lunch where transfer learning does not work. Zeta process independently samples programs from the zeta distribution. A model of common sub-programs inspired by genetics uses a database of sub-programs. An evolutionary zeta process samples mutations from Zeta distribution. The analysis of stochastic processes inspired by evolution suggest that AI may be feasible in nature, countering no-free lunch sort of arguments.

1 Introduction

Although power-law distributions have been analyzed in depth in physical sciences, little has been said about their relevance to Artificial Intelligence (AI). We introduce the zeta distribution as an analytic device in algorithmic information theory and propose using it to approximate the distribution of programs. We have been inspired by the empirical evidence in complex systems, especially biology and genetics, that show an abundance of power-law distributions in nature. It is well possible that the famous universal distribution in AI theory is closely related to power-law distributions in complex systems.

The transfer learning problem also merits our attention, as a general model of it has not been presented in machine learning literature. We develop a basic formalization of the problem using stochastic processes and introduce temporal bounds for learning a training sequence of induction problems, and transfer learning. The entropy rate of a stochastic process emerges as a critical quantity in these bounds. We show how to apply the bounds by analyzing the entropy rates of simple training sequence models that generate programs. Two models are close to what critics of AI have imagined, and easily result in unsolvable problems, while two models inspired by evolution suggest that there may be stochastic processes in nature on which AGI algorithms may be quite effective.

© Springer Nature Switzerland AG 2018
M. Iklé et al. (Eds.): AGI 2018, LNAI 10999, pp. 174–184, 2018.
https://doi.org/10.1007/978-3-319-97676-1_17

2 Approximating the Distribution of Programs

Solomonoff's universal distribution depends on the probability distribution of programs. A natural model is to consider programs, the bits of which are generated by a fair coin. Solomonoff defined the probability of a program $\pi \in \{0,1\}^+$ as:

$$P(\pi) = 2^{-|\pi|} \tag{1}$$

where $|\pi|$ is the program length in bits. The total probability of all programs thus defined unfortunately diverges if all bit-strings $\pi \in \{0,1\}^*$ are considered valid programs. For constructing probability distributions, a convergent sum is required. Extended Kraft inequality shows that the total probability is less than 1 for a prefix-free set of infinite programs [2]. Let M be a reference machine which runs programs with a prefix-free encoding like LISP. The algorithmic probability that a bit-string $x \in \{0,1\}^*$ is generated by a random program of M is:

$$P_M(x) = \sum_{M(\pi)=x*} P(\pi) \tag{2}$$

which conforms to Kolmogorov's axioms [9]. P_M is also called the universal prior for it may be used as the prior in Bayesian inference, as any data can be encoded as a bit-string.

2.1 Zeta Distribution of Programs

We propose the zeta distribution for approximating the distribution of programs of M. The distribution of (1) is already an approximation, even after normalization, since it contains many programs that are semantically incorrect, and those that do not generate any strings. A realistic program distribution requires us to specify a detailed probability model of programs, which is not covered by the general model, however, the general model, which is approximate, still gives excellent bounds on the limits of Solomonoff's universal induction method. Therefore, other general approximations may also be considered.

Additionally, the zeta function is universal, which encourages us to relate algorithmic information theory to zeta distribution [12].

Let us consider a program bit-string $\pi = b_1 b_2 b_3 \dots b_k$. Let $\phi : \{0,1\}^+ \to \mathbb{Z}$ define the arithmetization of programs represented as bit-strings, where the first bit is the most significant bit.

$$\phi(\pi) = \sum_{i=1}^{i \le |\pi|} b_i . 2^{|\pi|-i} \tag{3}$$

Thus arithmetized, we now show a simple, but interesting inequality about the distribution of programs:

$$P(\pi) = 2^{-\lceil \log_2(\phi(\pi)+1) \rceil} \tag{4}$$

$$(2a)^{-1} \le 2^{-\lceil \log_2 a \rceil} \le a^{-1}, \text{ for } a \ge 4 \tag{5}$$

$$(2(\phi(\pi) + 1))^{-1} \le P(\pi) \le (\phi(\pi) + 1)^{-1}, \text{ for } \phi(\pi) \ge 3 \tag{6}$$

which shows an approximation that is closer than a factor of 2. Program codes $\phi(\pi) < 3$ are discarded.

Zipf's law $f_n \alpha n^{-1}$ manifests itself as the Zipf distribution of ranked discrete objects $\{o_1, o_2, \ldots, o_n\}$ in order of increasing rank i

$$P(Z_s^{(n)} = o_i) \triangleq \frac{1}{i^s Z} \tag{7}$$

where $Z_s^{(n)}$ is a random variable, Z is the normalization constant and $s \geq 1$ (we used the notation $Z_s^{(n)}$ simply to avoid confusion with exponentiation, Z_s is a standard notation for the zeta random variable). Zeta distribution is the countably infinite version of Zipf distribution with parameter $s > 1$

$$P(Z_s = k) = \frac{1}{k^s . \zeta(s)} \tag{8}$$

where Z_s is a random variable with co-domain $\mathbb{Z}^+$ and the zeta function is defined as

$$\zeta(s) = \sum_{n=1}^{\infty} \frac{1}{n^s}. \tag{9}$$

Note that Zeta distribution is a discrete variant of Pareto distribution.

It is much involved to work with a prefix-free set, therefore we will suggest an alternative device to approximate $P(\pi)$.

Theorem 1. *A program distribution may be approximated by the Zipf distribution with $s = 1$, or by the zeta distribution with a real s close to 1 from above.*

Proof. (a) Zeta distribution is undefined for $s = 1$. However, if we use the Zipf distribution instead, and model programs up to a fixed program-length, we can approximate the program distribution from above using $(\phi(\pi) + 1)^{-1}$ and from below using $(2\phi(\pi) + 2)^{-1}$ due to the sandwich property (6).

(b) We can approximate the program distribution from below using $(2\phi(\pi) + 2)^{-1}$. Since

$$\forall \epsilon > 0, \ (2\phi(\pi) + 2)^{-(1+\epsilon)} \leq (2\phi(\pi) + 2)^{-1} < P(\pi),$$

we can also approximate it with the Zeta distribution (8) for s close to 1.

In either case, the need for a prefix-free set of programs is obviated. Of the simplified distribution, we investigate if the approximations are usable.

Theorem 2. *The program distribution $P(\pi)$ asymptotically obeys a power law with exponent -1 as program size grows.*

Proof. The probability of arithmetized program π is sandwiched between $(\phi(\pi) + 1)^{-1}$ and $(2\phi(\pi) + 2)^{-1}$, therefore as $|\pi|$ grows, Zipf's law grows closer to $P(\pi)$.

$$\lim_{|\pi| \to \infty} (\phi(\pi) + 1)^{-1} - (2\phi(\pi) + 2)^{-1} = 0 \tag{10}$$

$$\lim_{|\pi| \to \infty} 2^{-|\pi|} - (2\phi(\pi) + 2)^{-1} = \lim_{|\pi| \to \infty} (\phi(\pi) + 1)^{-1} - 2^{-|\pi|} = 0 \tag{11}$$

Combining Theorems 1 and 2, we propose using a Zeta distribution with a parameter close to 1. Obviously, lower and upper bounds vary only by a factor of 2 within each other, therefore the error in the approximation of program distribution is at most by 1 bit (this property will be analyzed in detail in an extended version of the present paper). Substituting into (2), we propose an approximation.

Definition 1

$$P_M(x) \approx \sum_{M(\pi)=x*} \frac{1}{(\phi(\pi) + 1)^{1+\epsilon}.\zeta(1 + \epsilon)} \qquad (12)$$

where $\zeta(1 + \epsilon) \geq 2$ ($\zeta(1.7) \approx 2$). Definition 1 may be useful for machine learning theorists wherever they must represent a priori program probabilities, as it allows them to employ number theory. See Elias Gamma Code [3] for an alternative integer code.

3   Training Sequence as a Stochastic Process

Although Solomonoff has theoretically described how the transfer learning problem might be solved in [10], a detailed theoretical model of transfer learning for the universal induction setting is missing in the literature. Here, we attempt to fill this gap. In his treatise of incremental learning, Solomonoff approached the transfer learning problem by describing an update problem which improves the guiding conditional probability distribution (GCPD) of the system as an inductive inference problem of the type that the system usually solves. Solomonoff's modular approach started with a number of problem solving methods and invented new such methods as the system progressed. The initial methods, however, are not fully specified, and we leave it as an open problem in this paper. Instead, we attempt at describing the space of training sequences using the zeta distribution, showing an interesting similarity to our world, whereas most problems in a sequence may be solved, but rarely they are not solvable at all. For instance, a mathematician may solve most problems, but stall at a conjecture that requires the invention of a new, non-trivial axiom indefinitely.

In usual Solomonoff induction (with no transfer learning component), a computable stochastic source μ is assumed. The stochastic source may generate sequences, sets, functions, or other structures that we please, the general law of which may be induced via Solomonoff's method. We extend Solomonoff's induction model to a training sequence of induction problems, by considering a stochastic process $\mathcal{M}$ of n random variables.

$$\mathcal{M} = \{\mu_1, \mu_2, \mu_3, \ldots, \mu_n\} \qquad (13)$$

The transfer learning problem thus is constituted from solving n induction problems in sequence which are generated from the stochastic process $\mathcal{M}$. It does not matter which type of induction problem these problems are, as long as they are generated via $\mathcal{M}$.

3.1   Entropy Rate of a Training Sequence

A critical measurement of a stochastic process is its entropy rate, which is defined as the following for $\mathcal{M}$:

$$H(\mathcal{M}) = \lim_{n\to\infty} \frac{H(\mu_1, \mu_2, \mu_3, \ldots, \mu_n)}{n} \tag{14}$$

and the conditional entropy rate,

$$H'(\mathcal{M}) = \lim_{n\to\infty} \frac{H(\mu_n|\mu_1, \mu_2, \mu_3, \ldots, \mu_{n-1})}{n} \tag{15}$$

which gives the entropy given past observations. Observe that there is a well-known relation between average Kolmogorov complexity and the entropy of an i.i.d. stochastic process (Eq. 5 in [1]):

$$\lim_{n\to\infty} \frac{K_M(X_1, X_2, X_3, \ldots, X_n)}{n} = H(X) + O(1) \tag{16}$$

where X is a stochastic process and X_i its random variables. We assume that the relation extends to conditional entropy without proof due to lack of space.

3.2   Training Time

Let π_i^* be the minimal program for exactly simulating μ_i on M. The most general expression for π_i^* is given in the following

$$\pi_i^* = \arg\min_{\pi_j}(\{|\pi_j| \mid \forall x, y \in \{0,1\}^* : M(\pi_j, x, y) = P(\mu_i = x|y)\}) \tag{17}$$

where the pdf of stochastic source μ_i is simulated by a program π_j. The conditional parameter y is optional. Let us note the following identity

$$K_M(\mu_i) = |\pi_i^*| \tag{18}$$

since arguments x, y are extraneous input to the pdf specified by π_i^*.

Let $t(\mu_i)$ denote the time taken to solve μ_i, and $t(\pi)$ denote the time taken by program π on M. Assume that $t(\mu_i) < \infty$. We know that the running time of extended Levin Search is bias-optimal [10], and

$$\frac{t(\pi_i^*)}{P(\pi_i^*)} \leq t(\mu_i) \leq \frac{2t(\pi_i^*)}{P(\pi_i^*)} \tag{19}$$

for a computable stochastic source μ_i ($K_M(\mu_i) < \infty$). The lower bound in (19) has been named conceptual jump size by Solomonoff, because it refers to the solution of individual induction problems within a training sequence, quantifying how much conceptual innovation is required for a new problem [10]. We cannot exactly predict $t(\mu_i)$ due to the incomputability of algorithmic probability. Extended Levin Search will keep running indefinitely. It is up to the user to stop execution, which is usually bounded only by the amount of computational resources available to the user. We should also mention that Levin himself does not think that any realistic problems can be solved by Levin search or created on a computer [8]. In the present paper, we run counter to Levin's position, by arguing that Levin search can work in an evolutionary setting, assuming an $O(1)$ oracle for the transfer learning problem.

We substitute the relation between $K_M(x)$ and $P_M(x)$ in the upper bound for $t(\mu_i)$,

$$K_M(\pi_i^*) = -\log_2 P(\pi_i^*) \tag{20}$$

obtaining the following fact due to (18) and (20):

Lemma 1. $t(\mu_i) \leq 2t(\pi_i^*)2^{K_M(\mu_i)}$

The inequality translates to the time for the training sequence $\mathcal{M}$ as

Theorem 3

$$t(\mathcal{M}) \leq \sum_{i=1}^{n} t(\pi_i^*)2^{K_M(\mu_i)+1} \tag{21}$$

which is a simple sum of Lemma 1.

The conditional entropy rate is useful when the stochastic process has interdependence. Let us define conditional Kolmogorov complexity for the training sequence $\mathcal{M}$,

$$K'(\mathcal{M}_{<k}) \triangleq K(\mu_k|\mu_1,\mu_2,\mu_3,\ldots,\mu_{k-1}) \tag{22}$$

where $\mathcal{M}_{<k} \triangleq \{\mu_i|i \leq k\}$. We define likewise for the stochastic process probabilities.

$$P'(\mathcal{M}_{<k}) \triangleq P(\mu_k|\mu_1,\mu_2,\mu_3,\ldots,\mu_{k-1}) \tag{23}$$

$K'(\mathcal{M}_{<k})$ captures new algorithmic information content for the kth variable of the stochastic process given the entire history.

As n grows, the transfer learning oracle has to add $H'(\mathcal{M})$ bits of information to its memory on the average in the stochastic process $\mathcal{M}$ as Kolmogorov-Shannon entropy relation (16) holds in the limit for conditional entropy, as well. Since the upper temporal bound grows exponentially, (22) only relates loosely to the solution time $t(\mu_i)$ of a particular problem. We instead define the conditional expected training time upper bound with respect to $\mathcal{M}$:

$$\mathbb{E}'[t(\mathcal{M}_{<k})] \triangleq \mathbb{E}_{\mathcal{M}}[t(\mu_k)|\mu_1,\ldots,\mu_{k-1}] \leq \sum_{\forall \mu_k \in \{0,1\}*} 2t(\pi_k^*)2^{K'(\mathcal{M}_{<k})}P'(\mathcal{M}_{<k})$$

$$\tag{24}$$

3.3   Random Typing Model

Let us start by considering the well-known model of random typing. If each μ_i is regarded as a random m-bit program out of 2^m such programs, the programs are independent, and the entropy rate is m bits exactly (under usual i.i.d. assumptions, e.g., we are using fair coin tosses, and we construct programs using a binary alphabet). Assume $2^m \gg n$.

In the random typing model, all μ_i are algorithmically independent, therefore there is no saving that can be achieved by transfer learning. The time it takes for any problem is therefore:

$$t(\mu_i) \leq t(\pi_i^*)2^{m+1} \tag{25}$$

for any of the 2^m programs. Since m can be arbitrarily large, this model is compatible with Levin's conjecture that AI is impossible. Note that this simplistic model is reminiscent of various no-free lunch theorems that were heralded as mathematical proof that general-purpose machine learning was impossible. However, this scenario is highly unrealistic. It is extremely difficult to find problems that are completely independent, as this would require us to be using true random number generators to generate any problem. In other words, we are only showing this "model" to demonstrate how far removed from reality no-free lunch theorems are. In a physical world, this model would correspond to the claim that quantum randomness saturates every observation we may make. However, we already know this claim to be false, since our observations do not consist of noise. On the contrary, there is a lot of dependable regularity in the environment we inhabit, which is sometimes termed "common sense" in AI literature.

3.4   Power-Law in Nature

A more realistic model, however, uses the zeta distribution for programs instead of uniform distribution. We propose this indeed to be the case since zeta distribution is empirically observed in a multitude of domains, and has good theoretical justification for the abundance of power-law in nature. Theorem 2 gives some weak and indirect justification as to why we might observe fractions of the zeta distribution of programs in a computable universe. However, there are more direct and appealing reasons why we must expect to see the zeta distribution in highly evolved complex systems. First, it is a direct consequence of the power-law ansatz, and scale-invariance [1] or preferential attachment in evolutionary systems [13]. Second, it follows from an application of maximum entropy principle where the mean of logarithms of observations is fixed [11]. Third, biologists have observed the zeta distribution directly in genetic evolution, thus strengthening the case that our π_i^*'s are likely to conform to zeta distributions. For instance, gene family sizes versus their frequencies follow a power-law distribution [5] and the gene expression in various species follows Zipf's law [4]. Universal regularities in evolution have been observed, for instance in the power-law relation between the number of gene families and gene family size, and number of genes in a category versus number of genes in genome, and power-law like distribution of network node degree [6]. Therefore, there is not only a highly theoretical heuristic argument that we are following, but there exist multiple theoretical and empirical justifications for expecting to observe the zeta distribution of programs in nature. The material evolution of the environment in a habitat, is not altogether different from biological evolution. Except in the case of rare natural catastrophes, the material environment changes only gradually in accord with the dynamic flow of natural law (surprise is small), and is dependent mostly on the actions of organisms in a complex habitat, which may be considered to be programs from an information-theoretic point of view. In that sense, the entire ecology of the habitat in question may be considered to be an evolutionary system, with program frequencies similar to the case of genes in a single organism. In the following, we introduce novel models of training sequences inspired by these empirical justifications.

3.5   Identical Zeta Random Variables

Let $\mathcal{M}$ be i.i.d. generated from zeta distribution according to Theorem 2. Then,

$$H'(\mathcal{M}) = H(\mu_1) = H(Z_s) \qquad (26)$$

indicating that the constant entropy rate depends only on the entropy of the zeta distribution. We thus analyze the running time. Let $t_{max} = \max\{t(\mu_i)\}$.

$$\mathbb{E}'[t(\mathcal{M}_{<k})] \leq \frac{2t_{max}}{\zeta(s)} \sum_{k=1}^{\infty} 2^{\lceil \log_2 k \rceil} k^{-s} \leq \frac{4t_{max}}{\zeta(s)} \sum_{k=1}^{\infty} \frac{k}{k^s} \qquad (27)$$

For the first 1 trillion programs, $t_{max} \sum_{k=1}^{10^{12}} 4k/k^{1.001} \zeta(1.001) \approx 3.89 \times 10^9 t_{max}$ for $s = 1.001$, which is a feasible factor for a realistic program search limit.

Note that AI theorists interpret i.i.d. assumptions as the main reason why no free-lunch theorems are unrealistic [7]. Our i.i.d. zeta process here may be interpreted as an elaboration of that particular objection to no free-lunch theorems. Therefore, we follow the heuristic argument that the right description of the environment which we observe must be something else than the random typing model since agents succeed in transfer learning. The constant zeta process leans towards feasibility, but it does not yet model transfer learning in complex environments.

3.6   Zipf Distribution of Sub-programs

Based upon the observations of genetic evolution above and the fact that the whole ecology is an evolutionary system, we may consider a process of programs that has the following property. Each π_i^* that corresponds to μ_i is constructed from a number of sub-programs (concatenated). The joint distribution of sub-programs is $Z_s^{(n)}$. This is a model of gene frequencies observed in chromosomes, where each chromosome corresponds to a program, and each gene corresponds to a sub-program. Such a distribution would more closely model a realistic distribution of programs by constraining possible programs, as in the real-world the process that generates programs is not ergodic. The total entropy of the process therefore depends on the sub-programs that may be assumed to be random, and program coding. Let each sub-program be a k-bit random program for the sake of simplicity. The sub-programs that correspond to instructions are specified in a database of 2^k bits. Instructions are not equiprobable, however, as in the random typing model. Let each program have m instructions drawn from the set of 2^k instructions:

$$A = \{a_1, a_2, a_3, \ldots, a_{2^k}\}. \tag{28}$$

Then, we can model each optimal program π_i^* as

$$\pi_i^* = \pi_{i,1}^* \pi_{i,2}^* \pi_{i,3}^* \ldots \pi_{i,m}^* \tag{29}$$

which make up a matrix of instructions $P^* = \pi_{i,j}^*$ where $\pi_{i,j}^*$ is drawn from the set A of instructions. The total entropy is due to the database of sub-programs, and the entropy of the global distribution of sub-programs $Z_s^{(n)}$ which determines the entropy of P^*. The total entropy is then approximately,

$$H(\mu_1, \mu_2, \ldots, \mu_n) \approx \log_2 k + k.2^k + \log_2 n + \log_2 m + H(Z_s^{(2^k)}) \tag{30}$$

where we show the significant terms for k, n, m, parameters.

Lemma 2. *For the Zipf distribution of sub-programs,*

$$H'(\mathcal{M}) \approx \lim_{n \to \infty} \frac{1}{n} \left(k.2^k + \frac{s}{H_{2^k,s}} \sum_{l=1}^{2^k} \frac{\ln(l)}{l^s} + \ln(H_{2^k,s}) + \log_2 k + \log_2 n + \log_2 m \right) \tag{31}$$

due to (30).

which is to say that, the entropy rate, and thus running time, critically depends on the choice of k and n.

3.7   An Evolutionary Zeta Process

Another process of programs may be determined by mimicking evolution, by considering random mutations of programs in a training sequence. Let us set

$$\pi_1^* = \wedge \tag{32}$$

$$\pi_i^* = \begin{cases} M(Z_s, \pi_{i-1}^*), & \text{if } Z_s \text{ is a valid transformation} \\ \pi_{i-1}^*, & \text{otherwise} \end{cases} \tag{33}$$

which would apply a random transformation sampled from Z_s in sequence to an initially null program. Such mutations are unlikely to be too complex. The resulting process has small conditional entropy rate, which is wholly dependent on Z_s.

$$\lim_{n \to \infty} H'(\mathcal{M}) = H(Z_s) = \log(\zeta(s)) - \frac{s\zeta'(s)}{\zeta(s)} \tag{34}$$

Lemma 3

$$H(Z_{1.1}) = 13.8 \qquad\qquad H(Z_{1.05}) = 24.5 \qquad\qquad (35)$$
$$H(Z_{1.01}) = 106.1 \qquad\qquad H(Z_{1.001}) = 1008.4 \qquad\qquad (36)$$

The lemma suggests that if an evolutionary process evolves slowly enough, then an AI can easily learn everything there is to learn about it provided that the time complexity of random variables is not too large. We can also employ $Z_s^{(k)}$ instead of Z_s in (33). For a universal induction approximation, $Z_{1.001}$ may be difficult to handle, however, for efficient model-based learning algorithms such as gradient descent methods, digesting new information on the order of a thousand bits is not a big challenge given sufficiently many samples for a problem μ_i in the sequence.

4   Concluding Remarks

We have shown novel relations between Zipf's law and program distribution by means of the arithmetization of programs. We have shown that zeta distribution may be used for approximating program distributions. We have proposed using the conditional entropy rate as an informative quantity for transfer learning. We have extended Solomonoff's induction model to a training sequence of problems as a stochastic process. We have proposed that the entropy rate of a stochastic process is informative. We have defined conditional Kolmogorov complexity and probability for the sequence, and have used these quantities to define a conditional expected upper bound of training time assuming an $O(1)$ transfer learning oracle. We introduced sequence models to show that there is a wide range of possible stochastic processes that may be used to argue for the possibility of general purpose AI. The random typing model is a sensible elaboration of no-free lunch theorem kind of arguments, and demonstrate how artificial and unlikely they are since everything is interconnected in nature and pure randomness is very hard to come by, which we therefore rule out as a plausible model of transfer learning. We have shown several empirical justifications for using a power-law model of natural processes. Independent Zeta process tends to the feasible, but does not explain transfer learning. The models that were inspired by natural evolution allow general purpose learning to be feasible. In particular, the model of common sub-programs which is inspired by empirical evidence in genetics supports a view of evolution of natural processes that allows incremental learning to be effective. The evolutionary Zeta process applies random mutations, which can be slow enough for a machine learning algorithm to digest all the new information.

A more detailed analysis of the transfer learning problem will be presented in an extended journal paper. Open problems include analyzing the complexity of the optimal update algorithm, time complexity analysis for the evolutionary processes, and accounting for the time complexity of individual programs.

Acknowledgements. The paper was substantially improved owing to the extensive and helpful comments of anonymous AGI 2014 and AGI 2018 reviewers.

References

1. Corominas-Murtra, B., Solé, R.V.: Universality of zipf's law. Phys. Rev. E **82**, 011102 (2010). http://www.link.aps.org/doi/10.1103/PhysRevE.82.011102
2. Cover, T.M., Thomas, J.A.: Elements of Information Theory. Wiley-Interscience, New York (1991)
3. Elias, P.: Universal codeword sets and representations of the integers. IEEE Trans. Inf. Theor. **21**(2), 194–203 (1975)
4. Furusawa, C., Kaneko, K.: Zipf's law in gene expression. Phys. Rev. Lett. **90**, 088102 (2003). http://www.link.aps.org/doi/10.1103/PhysRevLett.90.088102
5. Huynen, M.A., van Nimwegen, E.: The frequency distribution of gene family sizes in complete genomes. Mol. Biol. Evol. **15**(5), 583–589 (1998). http://www.mbe.oxfordjournals.org/content/15/5/583.abstract
6. Koonin, E.V.: Are there laws of genome evolution? PLoS Comput. Biol. **7**(8), e1002173 (2011). https://www.doi.org/10.1371%2Fjournal.pcbi.1002173
7. Lattimore, T., Hutter, M.: No free lunch versus occam's razor in supervised learning. In: Dowe, D.L. (ed.) Algorithmic Probability and Friends. Bayesian Prediction and Artificial Intelligence. LNCS, vol. 7070, pp. 223–235. Springer, Heidelberg (2013). https://doi.org/10.1007/978-3-642-44958-1_17
8. Levin, L.A.: Forbidden information. eprint arXiv:cs/0203029, March 2002
9. Levin, L.A.: Some theorems on the algorithmic approach to probability theory and information theory. CoRR abs/1009.5894 (2010)
10. Solomonoff, R.J.: A system for incremental learning based on algorithmic probability. In: Proceedings of the Sixth Israeli Conference on Artificial Intelligence, pp. 515–527. Tel Aviv, Israel, December 1989
11. Visser, M.: Zipf's law, power laws and maximum entropy. New J. Phys. **15**(4), 043021 (2013). http://www.stacks.iop.org/1367-2630/15/i=4/a=043021
12. Voronin, S.M.: Theorem on the "universality" of the riemann zeta-function. Izv. Akad. Nauk SSSR Ser. Mat. **39**(3), 475–486 (1975)
13. Yule, G.U.: A mathematical theory of evolution, based on the conclusions of Dr. J. C. Willis, F.R.S. Philos. Trans. R. Soc. B, Containing Pap. Biol. Charact. **213**(402–410), 21–87 (1925). http://www.rstb.royalsocietypublishing.org/content/213/402-410/21.short

Vision System for AGI: Problems and Directions

Alexey Potapov[1,2]([✉]), Sergey Rodionov[1,3], Maxim Peterson[1,2],
Oleg Scherbakov[1,2], Innokentii Zhdanov[1,2], and Nikolai Skorobogatko[1,3]

[1] SingularityNET Foundation, Amsterdam, The Netherlands
pas.aicv@gmail.com, astroseger@gmail.com,
maxim.peterson@gmail.com
[2] ITMO University, St. Petersburg, Russia
scherbakovolegdk@yandex.ru, avenger15@yandex.ru
[3] Novamente LLC, Rockville, USA
nicksk@mail.ru

Abstract. What frameworks and architectures are necessary to create a vision system for AGI? In this paper, we propose a formal model that states the task of perception within AGI. We show the role of discriminative and generative models in achieving efficient and general solution of this task, thus specifying the task in more detail. We discuss some existing generative and discriminative models and demonstrate their insufficiency for our purposes. Finally, we discuss some architectural dilemmas and open questions.

Keywords: Vision · AGI · Generative models · Discriminative models

1 Introduction

Within "Good Old-Fashioned Artificial Intelligence", vision was considered as a peripheral function, which doesn't have a direct relation to the mind, which was more associated with the knowledge-based symbolic reasoning. This situation has been preserved for many cognitive architectures (CAs), not only purely symbolic, but also hybrid, which cannot process images by themselves and require additional modules. However, such external perception modules appear to be not tightly integrated into CAs limiting these CAs in their ability to interact with the physical world.

At the same time, the idea that the basis of natural intelligence consists in pattern recognition is quite usual. In turn, experts in computer vision sometimes joke that thinking is just the upper level of the visual system. However computer vision has for a long time being developed in a relative isolation from the AI field, while the purely emergent CAs, going from perception upwards, are far from solving symbolic tasks that are the prerogative of the human mind.

Moreover, such isolated tasks as object detection and recognition, motion analysis, stereovision, shape from shading (or even more narrow tasks, e.g. shadow detection) are studied in computer vision. The problem of how a general vision system should be built is mostly not addressed, and we believe it cannot be reduced to a set of narrow tasks. This problem is especially relevant in the field of AGI.

© Springer Nature Switzerland AG 2018
M. Iklé et al. (Eds.): AGI 2018, LNAI 10999, pp. 185–195, 2018.
https://doi.org/10.1007/978-3-319-97676-1_18

In this paper, we consider the question how to proceed towards the goal of creation of a sufficient vision system for AGI. Here, we do not propose to limit ourselves to considering only those technical solutions that can work in real time on modern computers, however, consideration of resource constraints is fundamentally necessary for developing a potentially realizable vision system. For example, the unified model of perception and action selection given within AIXI [1] is not sufficient since even its rough approximation [2] can deal only with low-dimensional inputs.

2   Vision Task

Separation of the Vision Subsystem

The ultimate task of intelligence consists in calculating probability $P\left(a_t|x_{1:t}, a_{1:t-1}\right)$ of taking action a_t at time t (x_t unite current sensory and reinforcement signals) in order to maximize expected future rewards. AIXI uses universal (Solomonoff) induction [3], which predicts future observations via marginalization over all computable generative models consistent with the agent-environment interaction history. Consider the case of pure induction:

$$P_U(x) = \sum_{\mu:U[\mu]=x^*} 2^{-l(\mu)},$$

where μ is a program for universal machine U, generating a string with prefix x. The probability distribution over continuations x' of x is $P_U(x'|x) = P_U(xx')/P_U(x)$.

Of course, enumeration of all models at each time step is computationally infeasible. Consistent models should be somehow "cached", which goes far beyond sensory system and makes up half of the intelligence (the second half is decision making). Is it possible to draw a boundary between the sensory subsystem and the rest of intelligence (in particular, memory), or do we need a holistic model like AIXI?

The task of perception can be seen in the processing of the current data x_t (or $x_{t-k:t}$ for small k), while the whole history should be dealt with by the memory.

Without loss of generality, one can consider environment models (not necessarily Markovian) with internal states z_t. Then, let $\mu(z_t|z_{t-1}, a_t)$ be an environment model and $o(x_t|z_t)$ is an observation model (computable probability distribution). Indeed, one can assume $z_t = x_{1:t} a_{1:t}$ with trivial o, which, of course, doesn't give any advantage. However, one can hope that z can represent the interaction history much more compactly. Then, the task of perception is to infer z_t from x_t with the use of priors $\mu(z_t|z_{t-1}, a_t)$.

This task is not simpler than universal induction since to predict x_t one still needs to marginalize over all possible models, and for each model to calculate the probability of the interaction history (marginalizing over all $z_{1:t}$).

However, we can (or should for the sake of efficiency) approximately solve the task of perception in assumption of the fixed μ and o. Then, this task will consist in inferring posterior probabilities over z_t given x_t:

$$P(z_t|x_t) = \frac{P(x_t|z_t)P(z_t)}{P(x_t)} = \frac{o(x_t|z_t)\int \mu(z_t|z_{t-1},a_t)P(z_{t-1}|x_{t-1})dz_{t-1}}{\int P(x_t|z_t)P(z_t)dz_t}, \tag{1}$$

if an AGI system maintains an uncertain state representation in the form of $P(z_t|x_t)$. Simplification $P(z_t) = \mu(z_t|z_{t-1}, a_t)$ can be useful for analysis, but imprecise.

Thus, the task of perception can be reduced to (1), although the task of learning the models should also be accounted for.

Discriminative and Generative Models

Does AGI really need to reconstruct a generative model of the environment? Indeed, the main approach in reinforcement learning (RL) is model-free (although the model-based approach is advocated as a more adequate, e.g. [12]). Although it assumes some class of environments, their models are not explicitly reconstructed. Instead, value functions are estimated or policies are directly learnt, which can be treated as discriminative models since they describe conditional instead of joint probabilities.

Discriminative models are intensively used in computer vision and machine learning also. Traditional and most successful (at least, in pattern recognition) deep learning models are discriminative. However, the shortcomings of these models have also been generally recognized recently.

In particular, discriminative models don't support unsupervised, semi-supervised, or one-shot learning. Transfer learning with these models is also difficult. For example, in the case of reinforcement learning, the policy or value function should be retrained from scratch even for the same environment, but modified reward function [4]. In terms of AGI, we can say that discriminative models belong to narrow AI.

Generative models possess the required flexibility and support all the mentioned forms of learning because they "explain" data, but not just predict target variables. The possibility to generate data is not usually an aim, but means to ensure that the description of data is complete, and no information is lost, thus, enabling criteria for any kind of learning. Discriminative models throw away information, which is irrelevant to target variables, and we don't know its amount, thus, learning criteria based on the prediction of target variables are to be used.

In the context of AGI, we cannot limit ourselves to the consideration of discriminative models, regardless of whether they map observations to actions to or labels for detected objects. Ultimately, it is necessary to state the task of vision as a task of reconstruction of a latent description of a scene within a trainable generative model.

Unfortunately, inference over generative models is computationally demanding not only in universal induction, but also in more specific cases (inference can be inefficient even in a very limited case of graphical models), so they are also not sufficient.

We consider a discriminative model as a result of specialization of a general inference procedure in projection onto a certain generative model [5]. So, the properties of models of both types are understandable. In generative models, the inference process is separated from the model itself, and the models can be flexibly changed. Discriminative models can be viewed as efficient, but narrow inference procedures over certain generative models. Any changes to the generative model (albeit not presented explicitly) will affect this specialized inference procedure in a non-trivial way. Discriminative models are like reflexes, which are developed to solve narrow tasks with maximum efficiency, but which are badly applicable outside their scope.

But shouldn't a developed vision system processing huge volumes of information normally act as a specialized discriminative model which maps observations x_t into their latent code z_t? Seemingly, it should. Of course, AGI should be able to learn to recognize new classes of objects. However, natural images contain typical regularities, for the extraction of which a discriminative model can be trained once.

The practice of using deep convolutional neural networks (DCNNs) shows that networks trained discriminatively on large databases such as ImageNet can be successfully used when solving more specialized recognition tasks. However, in order to get really good results, fine-tuning of pre-trained networks is required. This process affects the upper level features, while the lowest levels remain mostly unchanged.

In the human visual system, there are also specialized discriminative models, e.g., for the face analysis. It is difficult to say whether new discriminative models are formed for the analysis of specific images (e.g. tomograms), but even if this does not happen, and analysis of such images by our visual system remains suboptimal, this restriction is not necessary to reproduce in AGI. Thus, the higher the level in the discriminative vision subsystem, the more extendable it should be.

If there is no need to modify lower levels of the discriminative model, should the generative image model go down to the pixel level? Humans see images of scenes. These are not the images registered by the retina, but the reconstructed images. Indeed, we see not the pixel brightness, but the estimates of the reflective characteristics of the points on physical surfaces (as demonstrated by a number of visual "illusions").

If the generative model ended its work at the level of some convolutional features, then we would not see, e.g., hot pixels on monitors. On the other hand, when responding to sudden and rapid events, humans can perform adequate actions before understanding what they react to. This is similar to a quick inference by discriminative models processing images from pixels to scene descriptions. Thus, both generative and discriminative models work at all levels of perception.

However, it should be noted that the discriminative model $Q(z|x)$ is constructed as a variational approximation to the posterior distribution specified by the generative model with *fixed priors* $P(z)$: $P(z|x) = P(x|z)P(z)/P(x)$. But in accordance with (1), probabilities $P(z_t)$ are calculated at each time step using predictions $\mu(z_t|z_{t-1}, a_t)$. Indeed, human vision system intensively uses such predictions to compensate for eye and body movements, to recognize objects in known dark rooms, etc.

Thus, the bottom-up processing of images by the discriminative model can only produce hypotheses with high likelihood (i.e. efficiently sample z_t with high $o(x_t|z_t)$), while the generative model can propagate prior expectations $\mu(z_t|z_{t-1}, a_t)$ top-down. Possibly, adaptive resonance [6] unites these processes into one procedure of iterative search for optimal z_t accounting both for the likelihood and expectations.

Thus, although the task of vision consists in inferring a latent description within the trainable generative model, a solution of this problem requires the construction of a system of discriminative models, both general purpose and specialized, with possible interaction with the generative model.

Learning

A generative model $o(x_t|z_t)$ samples an image of the scene from its description. This description is multi-level – it includes both a list of objects, and information about visible surfaces, their reflectivity maps, reconstructed sources of illumination, etc. This can be treated as a 3D rendering engine with a library of objects, textures, etc.

Obviously, the models of new objects must be constantly learned. More difficult is the question regarding the scene rendering model. Should the AGI visual system learn the laws of light propagation, reflection, dispersion and refraction from scratch? The dimensionality of our world and its geometric laws? Indeed, a general intelligence would have to be able to reconstruct the appropriate environment model for any type of sensor on its own. On the other hand, there is no reason why we should not alleviate this problem for AGI systems from practical considerations by explicitly laying down or pre-training the inevitably necessary elements in the generative model (for example, the 3D representation of scenes and the laws of their projections).

However, our world is too diverse to take into account all the possible aspects of image formation, especially since AGI will need to perceive images of arbitrary objects (from atoms to galaxies) formed by special optical devices. In particular, although modern rendering engines can generate photorealistic images, they are not capable of generating any images that can be found in reality.

Thus, the generative image model $o(x_t|z_t)$ should be trainable, but the degree of this trainability and the content of priors are the questions for deeper discussion.

Apparently, the environment model μ should be learned mostly from scratch (although some general priors are necessary). This problem belongs to the field of AGI as such, and goes far beyond the scope of this paper, but we want to emphasize that arbitrary changes in μ can cause arbitrary changes in the space of latent states z_t that render $o(x_t|z_t)$ obsolete. From the point of view of the sensor subsystem design, this space should be common to all possible environment models, and should be expandable, but not replaceable. Indeed, the acquaintance with the matter atomic structure does not force us to rewrite the entire content of our memory in new terms or retrain our vision system to account for the Maxwell's equations.

The discriminative vision subsystem must also be trainable at least to recognize new objects, but it might be necessary to retrain lower levels too (one can imagine an AGI system that has never before fallen into a snowfall and whose discriminative vision subsystem is not pre-trained on images obtained under such conditions).

Won't such learning disrupt the descriptions of previously recognized objects? To avoid this, the embedding space of the older objects should remain unchanged. Fortunately, this problem is solvable with the use of the generative model: descriptions formed by the discriminative model, should not just be useful for recognition or decision-making, but they should allow the generative model to reconstruct initial images.

Memory

We live in a very large environment, and instant observations x_t contain not too much information about its partial state z_t known to an agent. Thus, density $o(x_t|z_t)$ as a function of z_t given x_t will be very wide, and it is useless to require the discriminative subsystem to estimate it. It is natural to make estimations only for those hidden variables, information about which is contained in x_t (i.e. the content of the current scene).

However, the estimation of probabilities even of relevant hidden variables is problematic for the purely discriminative model. In particular, we expect z_t to contain some form of 3D reconstruction of a current scene. In practice, the task of simultaneous localization and mapping (SLAM) is considered, in which 3D coordinates of image points are not estimated by bottom-up image processing solely, but by matching these points with the earlier reconstructed map, that results in the map update also. Thus, the estimation of the visible part of z_t should intensively use z_{t-1}, i.e. both read and update the memory. The solution of this task greatly depends on the memory organization (how the map is represented in it, to what extent this representation is trainable, and so on), that goes far beyond the vision problem only.

Nevertheless, the processing of stand-alone still images should also be supported (humans can perceive photos). Thus, some part of development of the vision system can be carried out in isolation from the rest of the AGI system. However, we should expect such vision system to learn not 3D scene reconstruction and separate objects, but only lower-level texture and contour-based 2D segmentation.

The vision is connected in a non-trivial way with the semantic vision also, which contains information about objects and their relations. The part-whole and is-a relations are used by the vision system and are partially formed with its help. The scene description can go down to the finest pixel-size details like specks of dust hanging in the air or grains of sand composing a texture.

Apparently, existing discriminative models are not that detailed. If they recognize a face, then not as a hierarchy of objects starting with individual hairs and wrinkles, but via features integrally describing square fragments of growing sizes regularly covering the image area (which makes it difficult to assign some semantics to such features even in the context of recognized larger objects).

Although specialized discriminative models can be trained for recognizing small objects of high importance, it seems that generative models should typically participate in the construction of the detailed scene description. These are the generative models, which "know" the structure of objects, and try to fit the parameters of this structure to observations. Indeed, humans usually are not conscious of all scene details, if they don't pay special attention to them (i.e. inference over generative models is controlled by general cognitive functions).

In fact, the generative model of images also does not need to operate with concepts such as each individual hair on the head or a speck of dust. Informationally, they are of little importance, and the generative model can consider their deviation from the background as noise. In general, generative and discriminative models can share all levels of the representation, so that the generative model will "draw" the image using "brushes" – the transposed filter kernels of the discriminative model.

Thus, in general, one should not expect to extract too many semantic categories as a result of the analysis of individual images. At least, video sequences with a varying point of view and with the (dis)appearance of objects should be analyzed in order to separate the concept of objects from their immediate sensory image. In addition, some usual object classes may be due to other sensory modalities or pragmatic criteria (it can even be argued that most categories are separated based on the ability to manipulate the relevant objects; for example, the notion of chair or cup is determined not so much by their visual features, but by their usage). Nevertheless, the trained visual system in an autonomous mode should be able to extract significant visual categories. We just should not demand the extraction of exactly the categories that we use. In general, however, it should be borne in mind that the boundary between the generative model of the environment for which the entire intelligence is responsible and the generative model of images turns out to be rather vague.

3 Frameworks

Discriminative Models

DCNNs show outstanding results in image recognition. Are these networks sufficient to implement discriminative models for AGI vision?

First of all, the task of vision for AGI is much broader. What is needed is not just to recognize an object by its image, but to construct a scene description including all the objects with their shapes, poses, reflectance maps, etc. DCNNs are used also for the object detection, 3D reconstruction and semantic segmentation, but the results are not so great here. Neural solutions for the SLAM problem are also being developed (e.g. [7]), but their architectures are far from purely discriminative DCNNs.

Thus, either discriminative DCNNs should be used to construct some intermediate representation, on the top of which some other models (neural or not) will be built, or the whole formalism should be modified. "Object-oriented deep learning" [8] can be mentioned as one example of such modification. While it is difficult to say how effective can such extensions be, they look attractive from the point of view of uniting discriminative models with symbolic generative models and cognitive architectures.

Secondly, as noted, applied DCNNs are trained on the labeled data. Of course, pre-trained models can be used to build AGI, but training of new models will inevitably be required. In this case, manually labeled data will be absent, and the discriminative model will be taught on the basis of or in conjunction with the generative model (that is, the learning signal will be weaker than for discriminative training). In this connection, the efficiency of generalization will be critical, which is very low in classical DCNNs: they are not capable of generalizing beyond the area of the training sample, but only interpolate inside it.

For example, if a DCNN did not see objects of some class rotated in a certain range of angles, it will not be able to recognize this class for new angles, even if it learned to recognize other classes for all angles. Does the discriminative model have to be rotation invariant in the same way as the invariance to shifts is ensured by convolution? It is possible that with proper implementation this could be practical, but this does not solve the problem of weak generalization for arbitrary transformations. The source of this problem is a fixed system of links within the network so that a fragment of the network that implements some function is always applied to data coming from the same addresses (neurons). Convolutional networks go beyond such tight connectivity, but they apply the same network to different addresses in a fixed manner.

This problem can be approach in different ways, e.g., by introducing dynamic addressing, as is done in models with external memory [9] or in capsule networks [10]. Unfortunately, capsule networks only partially solve the problem of weak generalization. For example, we conducted the following experiment. We took eight MNIST digits (excluding 6 and 9), and trained CapsNets on six digits rotated arbitrarily and two digits (3 and 4) rotated in range $[-45°, 45°]$. The precision on the training set composed of 3 and 4 rotated within $[-45°, 45°]$ was 99.04% for dynamic routing [10] and 98.27% for EM-routing [11], while for $180° \pm 45°$ it appeared to be 1.05% and 12.92% correspondingly. The baseline DCNN model also showed 1.02% precision meaning that it systematically confuses rotated 3 and 4 with other digits, while EM-routing CapsNets recognize them on a level of random guess.

Thus, more powerful models are still to be developed. Alternatively, the responsibility for achieving the invariance to arbitrary transformations can be shifted to generative models and corresponding inference mechanisms.

For example, if the generative model learned to rotate arbitrary scenes, then the rotation angle can act as an unknown latent variable, which is not estimated by the discriminative model. The generative model (e.g. using EM-algorithm) can try to guess such angle, which lead to a self-consistent solution: the discriminative model produces such description of the generated rotated scene, which allows the generative model to render this scene (and the generative model can render the original image from the same description, but another value of the rotation). This can be considered as the mental rotation used by humans to recognize objects in unfamiliar perspectives.

Thus, discriminative models should not be necessarily capable of automatic learning of invariants, but the question whether to expand the existing formal neural models or not remains open. In turn, the need to extend discriminative architectures, both for solving wider problems, and for interacting with the generative model, is obvious.

Generative Models

If in the case of discriminative models one can reconcile with their insufficient universality in favor of efficiency, then the requirements for the expressiveness of generative models are much higher. In particular, the generative model should be able (to learn) to generate images of the same object viewed from different angles.

Consider the following experiment. Let us take a deep convolutional adversarial autoencoder that receives a non-rotated image from the input, and the result of the reconstruction is compared with the rotated image, while the correct rotation angle is supplied as an additional latent feature (sine and cosine of an angle as two neurons). We

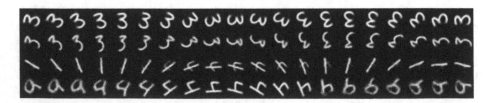

Fig. 1. Reconstruction results for different rotation angles (deep convolutional AAE)

teach the autoencoder to rotate digits from MNIST to all angles, while restricting the range of angles for 4 and 9. Figure 1 shows the results of reconstruction.

As it can be seen, the autoencoder successfully reconstructs new images of digits rotating them at known angle (all images of 3 and central part for 4), but it transforms 4 to other digits trying to rotate it to a new angle.

The absolutely same effect takes place even if we try to train the autoencoder to reconstruct the shifted images. It might seem that convolutional networks should naturally perform the necessary generalization. Indeed, the transposed convolutional network can easily reconstruct the digit at any given location. However, the corresponding pattern in the highest level convolutional feature maps should somehow be activated. This is what dense layers going from the latent code cannot do. Connections going to different places in the feature maps are trained independently, so the network cannot transfer its experience in drawing 4 at one place to draw it at another place, and it will simply draw the digit with the most similar latent code which it knows how to draw at this specific place.

Thus, traditional generative neural networks cannot generalize spatial transformations independent of their content. Again, the question arises if we should extend the existing formalisms, and if yes, how specialized for vision should this extension be? For example, a specialized architecture can be crafted, which has a network for learning spatial transformations $(x', y') = f(x, y | \mathbf{w})$, which are then directly applied to images or feature maps. Similarly, one can train a network to transform 3D points. Apparently, this solution will be narrow, although it might be useful to the pragmatic AGI. But for us, more general solutions are more interesting.

For example, if we add second-order control neurons, which accept transformation parameters as input and influence the connection weights going from the latent code neurons to the highest level feature maps of convolutional autoencoder, then such network can learn to reconstruct arbitrary images independent on their content. We trained such network on the same data as the autoencoder. Figure 2 shows the results of reconstruction of both of the previously seen digit with new rotation angles, and reconstruction of a new symbol rotated on arbitrary angles. The network has only some problems with image corners, since they were always black in the training set, so it couldn't learn a mapping for pixels in them. Second-order networks are a general extension of ANNs, but the specific architecture we used here is rather specialized. Other solutions to the problem can be proposed, but their efficiency and generality for the AGI vision are the topics for further investigations.

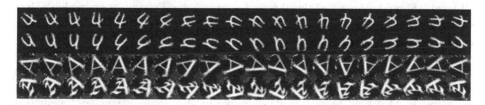

Fig. 2. Reconstruction results for different rotation angles (2nd-order autoencoder)

Instead of extending neural networks one can try to use more general and expressive frameworks for specifying generative models like probabilistic programming. It is relatively easy to write a probabilistic program serving as a scene generative model. Unfortunately, the training of such models is computationally problematic, so one has to impose very strong priors in practice making the solution not too general.

Also, while discriminative models by themselves should not necessarily be capable of learning clear whole-part relationships, the latent description of a scene within the generative model should be ultimately expressed in terms of objects and their parts, thus, corresponding relations should be somehow learned. Existing frameworks neither for generative nor for discriminative models are powerful enough to do this.

4   Conclusion

The vision system should ultimately construct the scene description and participates in the reconstruction of the environment model. The generative subsystem guides the (unsupervised, one-shot, transfer) learning process and accounts for expectations, while the discriminative subsystem makes perception efficient in typical situations. However, many details are unclear.

- Should we require the capabilities to learn invariants and extract hierarchical relations from the discriminative models? If no (which seems biologically plausible), they should work with tight integration with the generative models, without which they will be useful only for forming reflective responses to stereotypical stimuli. But this doesn't mean that more powerful discriminative models cannot be developed.
- Should generative models be normally involved in image analysis? It seems, yes: purely discriminative models can be trained to solve not too narrow vision tasks on super-human level, but the necessity to propagate expectations is rather common. However, architectures with more emphasis on discriminative models are possible.
- Should the generative subsystem infer such latent variables, which are not estimated by the discriminative subsystem? It seems, yes, but only occasionally (i.e. to imagine a rotated object or a person wearing glasses, when recognition fails), since general inference over generative models is computationally demanding.
- How strong priors should be? This question is really controversial.

If we go down on the level of formalisms and implementations, the number of vague questions will increase. Should the generative and discriminative models be aligned on all levels? Should we use traditional neural networks for discriminative models? How should we extend existing formalisms for generative models? What are acceptable architectures for vision tasks beyond object recognition? And so on.

In general, we can conclude that existing frameworks and models are far from enough for implementing the vision system for AGI, especially in the generative part, which should be capable of rendering the images of scenes with new combination of objects in new poses. Also, tight integration of generative and discriminative models for efficient inference should be studied. This enables the consideration of the vision system as a part of AGI systems.

References

1. Hutter, M.: Universal Artificial Intelligence: Sequential Decisions Based on Algorithmic Probability. Springer, Heidelberg (2005). https://doi.org/10.1007/b138233
2. Veness, J., et al.: A Monte Carlo AIXI Approximation. arXiv:0909.0801 [cs.AI] (2010)
3. Solomonoff, R.: A formal theory of inductive inference, part 1 and part 2. In: Information and Control, vol. 7, pp. 1–22, 224–254 (1964)
4. Lake, B.M., et al.: Building Machines That Learn and Think Like People. arXiv:1604.00289 [cs.AI] (2016)
5. Potapov, A., Rodionov, S.: Making universal induction efficient by specialization. In: Goertzel, B., Orseau, L., Snaider, J. (eds.) AGI 2014. LNCS (LNAI), vol. 8598, pp. 133–142. Springer, Cham (2014). https://doi.org/10.1007/978-3-319-09274-4_13
6. Grossberg, S.: Adaptive pattern classification and universal recoding (I, II). Parallel development and coding of neural feature detectors. Biol. Cybernet. **23**, 121–134, 187–202 (1976)
7. Parisotto, E., et al.: Global Pose Estimation with an Attention-based Recurrent Network. arXiv:1802.06857 [cs.CV] (2018)
8. Liao, Q., Poggio, T.A.: Object-Oriented Deep Learning. CBMM Memo, No. 070 (2017)
9. Graves, A., Wayne, G., Danihelka, I.: Neural Turing Machines. arXiv:1410.5401 [cs.NE] (2014)
10. Sabour, S., Frosst, N., Hinton, G.E.: Dynamic Routing Between Capsules. arXiv:1710.09829 [cs.CV] (2017)
11. Hinton, G.E., Sabour, S., Frosst, N.: Matrix capsules with EM routing. In: ICLR Conference (2018)
12. Ha, D., Schmidhuber, J.: World Models. arXiv:1803.10122 [cs.LG] (2018)

Semantic Image Retrieval by Uniting Deep Neural Networks and Cognitive Architectures

Alexey Potapov[1,3]([✉]), Innokentii Zhdanov[2,3], Oleg Scherbakov[2,3], Nikolai Skorobogatko[2], Hugo Latapie[4], and Enzo Fenoglio[4]

[1] SingularityNET Foundation, Amsterdam, The Netherlands
pas.aicv@gmail.com
[2] Novamente LLC, Rockville, USA
nicksk@mail.ru
[3] ITMO University, Kronverkskiy pr. 49, 197101 St. Petersburg, Russia
avenger15@yandex.ru, scherbakovolegdk@yandex.ru
[4] Chief Technology and Architecture Office, Cisco, San Jose, USA
{hlatapie,efenogli}@cisco.com

Abstract. Image and video retrieval by their semantic content has been an important and challenging task for years, because it ultimately requires bridging the symbolic/subsymbolic gap. Recent successes in deep learning enabled detection of objects belonging to many classes greatly outperforming traditional computer vision techniques. However, deep learning solutions capable of executing retrieval queries are still not available. We propose a hybrid solution consisting of a deep neural network for object detection and a cognitive architecture for query execution. Specifically, we use YOLOv2 and OpenCog. Queries allowing the retrieval of video frames containing objects of specified classes and specified spatial arrangement are implemented.

Keywords: Semantic vision · Image retrieval · Deep learning
Cognitive architectures

1 Introduction

Bridging symbolic/subsymbolic gap (e.g. [22]) is one of difficult problems in artificial general intelligence (AGI) and cognitive architectures (CAs) in particular. This problem has many manifestations in practical tasks. One such task is the semantic image retrieval, which involves both subsymbolic processing of images or videos, and queries defined on a symbolic level describing the semantic content of images to be retrieved. This task is also practically important. One might want to find specific images in a photo collection or a video frame with certain content.

Due to its practical importance, semantic image retrieval has been intensively studied within traditional AI areas. However, conventional computer vision methods were able to recognize not too many classes of objects simultaneously. Thus, many efforts were directed towards bridging the "semantic gap" between low-level image features and high-level concepts in terms of which queries are specified (e.g. [1–3]).

© Springer Nature Switzerland AG 2018
M. Iklé et al. (Eds.): AGI 2018, LNAI 10999, pp. 196–206, 2018.
https://doi.org/10.1007/978-3-319-97676-1_19

Apparently, the semantic gap in computer vision is a particular manifestation of the symbolic/subsymbolic gap.

Deep convolutional neural networks (DCNN) opened the possibility to detect and recognize objects belonging to hundreds and even thousands of different classes. Moreover, pre-trained DNNs solving this task are readily available, for example, YOLOv2 [4] (You Only Look Once), Deformable R-FCN [5] (Region-based Fully Convolutional Networks), SSD [17] (Single Shot multibox Detector).

However, when we want not just to detect separate objects on images, but to find images with a specified content, modern DCNNs don't provide out-of-the-box solutions (unless being used to perform deep hashing for retrieving images semantically similar to a query image, e.g. [6, 7]). Although there are some successes in purely DCNN-based image understanding including image caption generation [8] and visual question answering [9], such systems don't directly solve the image retrieval task, they are difficult to train and are less flexible in comparison with traditional knowledge-based image understanding systems. Thus, constructing a purely neural system that learns a mapping between visual and linguistic data is still not too practical now, at least, for image retrieval. Moreover, a question whether the purely neural-based approach is optimal for AGI is controversial.

Thus, the most accessible benefit of deep learning in the semantic image retrieval now is object detection and recognition. However, a hard-coded engine for executing a limited set of queries based on detected objects is also not useful enough, and usage of a knowledge-based reasoning is desirable. CAs as modern intelligent systems that usually support knowledge representation and reasoning are underutilized here.

In this paper, we investigate if it is possible to efficiently use CAs, namely, OpenCog, in combination with DCNNs to construct a semantic image retrieval system. Although we report preliminary results achieved without tight integration of the symbolic and subsymbolic components, these results show that even a loose integration provides practical benefits for semantic image retrieval, which is a good testbed for studying the problem of bridging the symbolic/subsymbolic gap.

2   Previous Works

Semantic Image Retrieval

A common approach to retrieve images with semantic structure through the learning is to train deep models on images with joint labels of several classes which form complex concepts and learn a relationship model that represents the expected spatial relationships among the relevant objects for retrieval of instances of visual situations [10]. For example, if we have labels for person and bicycle with corresponding relation we can train model to a new concept – cyclist. However, such procedure requires exhaustive labeling (including forming of negative examples).

Also there are a plenty of traditional methods such as [11, 12] that use low-level hand-crafted features for image representation along with relatively simple text-clustering techniques. Needless to say that such limited representations lead to poor performance when applied to wide range of image retrieval problems.

Knowledge-Based System for Image Retrieval

Another approach to image retrieval task is the one based on knowledge manipulating systems. These techniques mostly shift focus from the quality of image representation to consistent work with complex structure of semantic relations between concepts. Also such approach provides useful tools for construction of languages for visual programming.

Some of the methods [13] use knowledge parsers along with popular knowledge datasets such as ConceptNet or WordNet to improve retrieval accuracy. Some others [18] use conditional random field models defined over a scene graph representing the query for semantic image retrieval. Here, the scene graph captures the detailed semantics of visual scenes by explicitly modeling objects, attributes of objects, and relationships between objects and assumes existence of rich concept graphs which are usually immutable. So it makes such methods non-flexible and hardly extensible. Some of the methods [14] use self-organizing maps (SOM) for concerted high-level semantic and low-level visual features analysis. Obviously these methods have limitations caused by expressive power of SOM.

Apparently, both expressive image representations and structured knowledge are needed for semantic image retrieval.

3   Proposed System

Object Detector

State-of-the-art DCNN object detectors can be divided into two groups: region proposal-based methods and proposal-free methods. Proposal-based methods like R-FCN [5, 20] are two-stage detectors that start generating a set of candidate bounding boxes (BBs), and then focus on processing each candidate. Proposal-free methods like YOLO [4, 19] are single-stage detectors that consider detection a regression problem, use a single ConvNet and run once on the entire image.

We considered two deep convolutional neural networks, to detect and recognize objects: YOLOv2 [4, 19] which offers a competitive speed and Deformable R-FCN [5] which offers a good trade-off between detection efficiency and accuracy. Both networks were trained on the same MS COCO [15] dataset with 80 objects category.

The detector is one of the key components of the system, so it was important to compare the performance of both networks with our data sets. For this purpose, a video was mounted and synchronized to show the output frames from YOLO and Deformable R-FCN.

As a result of the comparison, we made the following observations (see Fig. 1):

- Deformable R-FCN network marks out the same detected object at once with many frames (basically same class). See Fig. 1(a).
- In general, the Deformable R-FCN classification has fewer errors than YOLO, at the cost of fewer detected objects. See Fig. 1(b).
- The YOLO network detects more different objects that are interesting for the semantic video frame retrieval than the Deformable R-FCN; these objects can be a part of the interior, an element of human clothing, etc. See Fig. 1(c).

Additionally, the detection threshold of YOLO can be changed to display objects detected with a higher (lower) confidence by increasing (decreasing) the parameter "threshold", but the number of interesting objects will be affected accordingly. In general, the YOLO network is more preferable for extracting data about objects on video. However, in some cases, this network cannot be used because of the large number of classification errors.

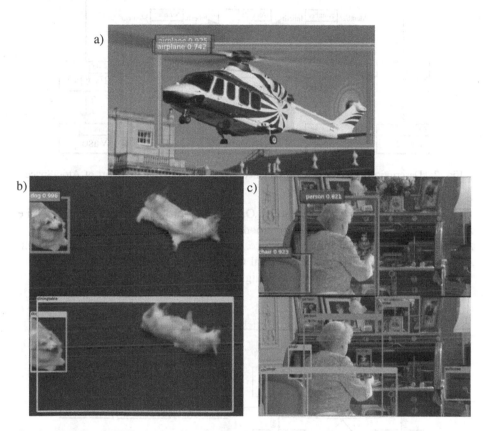

Fig. 1. Sample of Deformable R-FCN detection; (b, c): the upper image corresponds to Deformable R-FCN, the lower image corresponds to YOLO

Implementation of Queries in OpenCog

OpenCog is a cognitive architecture built on the top of a hypergraph-based knowledge representation and a powerful inference engine. The container for these hypergraphs is called *AtomSpace*. We will use just a small part of its functionality, addressing the interested reader to the detailed description referenced in [16]. For our current purposes, it is enough to treat its knowledge representation as an ordinary graph (except Bind link used in the inference), which is filled with information about detected bounding boxes including their coordinates and labels.

Figure 2 shows an example of a fragment of this graph describing two bounding boxes belonging to one frame.

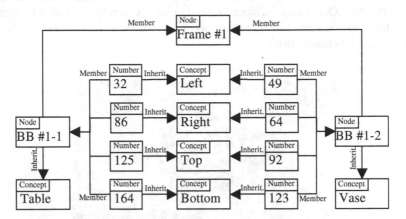

Fig. 2. Description of two extracted bounded boxes in one frame as a part of AtomSpace

One way to perform the inference in OpenCog is through "Pattern Matching", i.e. matching a template (with variable nodes) sub-graph (which is also stored in AtomSpace) against the rest of AtomSpace. The matching result can also be placed into AtomSpace via the activation of a special type of links, e.g. Bind link.

Consider the Bind link shown in a slightly simplified form in Fig. 3.

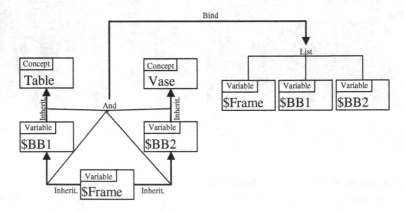

Fig. 3. Example of Bind link for retrieving a sub-graph corresponding to two specific objects presented in one frame

Left part of this link can be matched against a sub-graph of the graph presented in Fig. 2. Thus, by activating this link one can retrieve a sub-graph containing the List link uniting the BB#1-1, BB#1-2 and Frame#1 nodes.

Thus, such Bind link can be used to retrieve frames containing required objects. We use Python API to AtomSpace to synthesize Bind links for specified objects, although this could be done inside AtomSpace (e.g. by Bind links over Bind links).

More types of queries can be implemented using coordinates of bounding boxes and additional types of links. Coordinates of bounding boxes can be bound with variables in the same way as it was done above for BB nodes. These coordinates can be compared using GreaterThan links, and one can use And link to require several conditions to be hold simultaneously. For example, the following code in *Atomese* (a programming language to describe the content of AtomSpace in the text form) specifies a template graph (similar to those shown in the previous figures) that can be used to find bounding boxes in the same frame, one of which is left to another one.

```
AndLink
  MemberLink
    InheritanceLink
      VariableNode "$Left1"
      Node "Left"
    VariableNode "$BB1"
  MemberLink
    InheritanceLink
      VariableNode "$Right2"
      Node "Left"
    VariableNode "$BB2"
  MemberLink
    VariableNode "$BB1"
    VariableNode "$Frame"
  MemberLink
    VariableNode "$BB2"
    VariableNode "$Frame"
GreaterThanLink
  VariableNode "$Left1"
  VariableNode "$Right2"
```

To utilize modularity, we defined a number of Bind links, which insert intermediate inference results into AtomSpace. For example, the code shown above was used in a Bind link with the following resultant:

```
EvaluationLink
  PredicateNode "RightTo"
  ListLink
    VariableNode "$BB1"
    VariableNode "$BB2"
```

This Atomese code means that the predicate "RightTo" evaluates to true for a pair of nodes bound to the Variable nodes "$BB1" and "$BB2". It is not necessary to represent the resultant as a predicate. What is needed is to create a sub-graph which contains the necessary information and which can further be pattern-matched. Nevertheless, predicates seem quite natural here.

Similarly, one can define such predicates, which will be true for intersecting BBs, or pairs of BBs, one of which is inside another one, or on the top of it, etc. Thus, one can implement such queries as "a vase on a table" or "a painting with a person".

It should be noted that OpenCog supports non-binary truth values, although we don't utilize them in our current implementation, but they should be useful to describe soft versions of spatial relations. Such truth values can also be combined with confidence values assigned to labels by the detector.

With such intermediate conclusions, one-step pattern matching will not be able to find sub-graphs corresponding to queries of interest, e.g. "a vase on a table", without invoking Bind links calculating truth values of helper predicates. OpenCog has to main mechanisms for chaining inference steps, namely, the forward chaining and the backward chaining. The forward chaining starts with the available data and iteratively applies Bind links to fill AtomSpace with resultants. In our task, the backward chaining is more suitable. It starts with a sub-graph (query) of interest and goes backward to find Bind links which can help to infer this sub-graph.

4   Experiments

We conducted experiments with some video sequences to validate our approach and test the constructed system. Different queries for retrieving video frames containing specified objects in certain relative locations were executed. Such queries as 'a person inside a car' or 'a person with a bag' were successfully tested. Figure 4 shows some examples of successfully retrieved frames from different videos.

The following queries were used: 'a person inside a car', 'a person left to a car', 'a person with a tie', 'a person with a backpack', and the corresponding bounding boxes are shown in Fig. 4. Similar queries can be executed for arbitrary pairs of objects recognizable by the DCNN. Queries involving more than two objects can also be added, but it has not been done yet.

Of course, our image retrieval system can fail in some cases. These failures can be due to incorrect object recognition or by imprecise or not supposed sizes and positions of BBs. Figure 5 shows an example of incorrectly retrieved video frame, because of the recognition error. Figure 6 shows two examples of incorrectly constructed bounding boxes retrieved with the use of unnatural queries. Figure 7 shows another example, for which one can argue that the bounding boxes are not that bad, but 'vase' BB appears to be inside 'flowers' BB. As a result, such frames will not be retrieved by a normal query.

Fig. 4. Examples of successfully retrieved video frames

Fig. 5. Incorrect retrieval of 'a person with a backpack'

Fig. 6. Examples of video frames with incorrect bounding boxes

Fig. 7. Example of bounding boxes with not supposed arrangement

5 Conclusion

In this paper, we have proposed an approach to semantic image retrieval based on integration of DCNNs for object detection and cognitive architectures for semantic analysis and query execution to utilize the power of DNN-based image analysis and flexibility and compositionality of knowledge representation and reasoning in cognitive architectures.

We developed a first version of such system based on YOLOv2 network and OpenCog. We implemented functionality in Atomese language to support queries for retrieving video frames containing specified objects in specified relative spatial positions.

Our results show that this approach is quite practical, and it can be considerably extended in future:

1. One can utilize imprecise probabilities supported by OpenCog to perform probabilistic querying.
2. Language understanding capabilities of OpenCog can be used to create natural language interface for specifying queries.
3. Richer set of queries can be implemented, in particular, to describe events (e.g. approaching of one object to another).
4. Pattern Miner module of OpenCog can be used to automatically create new useful elements of knowledge representation. For example, we may want to recognize visual analogies taking advantage of the "conceptual slippage" in the sense of Hofstadter [21] in which roles defining a situation can be fluidly filled by concepts semantically related to the query and the concepts used in creating the analogies can be considered realization of statistically emergent active symbols formed in the AtomSpace.
5. Detection of possibly incorrectly detected objects or wrong bounding boxes for them using mined patterns in relations between BBs.
6. Events can be handled either on the cognitive level, or with the use of DNNs, or both.

References

1. Smeulders, A.W., Worring, M., Santini, S., Gupta, A., Jain, R.: Content-based image retrieval at the end of the early years. IEEE Trans. Pattern Anal. Mach. Intell. **22**(12), 1349–1380 (2000)
2. Thanga Ramya, S., Rangarajan, P.: Knowledge based methods for video data retrieval. Int. J. Comput. Sci. Inf. Technol. (IJCSIT) **3**(5), 165–172 (2011)
3. Manzoor, U., Balubaid, M.A., Zafar, B., Umar, H., Khan, M.Sh.: Semantic image retrieval: an ontology based approach. (IJARAI) Int. J. Adv. Res. Artif. Intell. **4**(4) (2015)
4. Redmon, J., Farhadi, A.: YOLO9000: better, faster, stronger. arXiv:1612.08242 [cs.CV] (2016)
5. Dai, J., et al.: Deformable convolutional networks. arXiv:1703.06211 [cs.CV] (2017)
6. Liu, H., Wang, R., Shan, Sh., Chen, X.: Deep supervised hashing for fast image retrieval. In: IEEE Conference on Computer Vision and Pattern Recognition (CVPR), pp. 2064–2072 (2016)
7. Varga, D., Szirányi, T.: Fast content-based image retrieval using convolutional neural network and hash function. In: IEEE International Conference on Systems, Man, and Cybernetics (SMC) (2016)
8. Karpathy, A., Li, F.-F.: Deep visual-semantic alignments for generating image descriptions. CoRR, abs/1412.2306 (2014)
9. Gordon, D., et al.: IQA: visual question answering in interactive environments. arXiv:1712.03316 [cs.CV] (2017)
10. Quinn, M., Conser, E., Witte, J., Mitchell, M.: Semantic image retrieval via active grounding of visual situations. arXiv:1711.00088 [cs.CV] (2017)
11. Celebi, E., Alpkocak, A.: Semantic image retrieval and auto-annotation by converting keyword space to image space. In: 12th International IEEE Multi-Media Modelling Conference Proceedings (2006)
12. Singh, N., Dubey, S., Dixit, P., Gupta, J.: Semantic image retrieval using multiple features. In: Meghanathan, N., et al. (eds.) SIPM, FCST, ITCA, WSE, ACSIT, CS & IT 06, pp. 277–284 (2012)
13. Chen, H., Trouve, A., Murakami, K.J., Fukuda, A.: Semantic image retrieval for complex queries using a knowledge parser. Multimed. Tools Appl. **77**, 10733–10751 (2017). https://doi.org/10.1007/s11042-017-4932-2
14. Subramanyam, V., RallabandiSett, R.: Knowledge-based image retrieval system. Knowl. Based Syst. **21**(2), 89–100 (2008)
15. Lin, T.-Y., et al.: Microsoft COCO: common objects in context. arXiv preprint arXiv:1405.0312 (2014)
16. Goertzel, B., Pennachin, C., Geisweiller, G.: Engineering General Intelligence, Part 2: A Path to Advanced AGI via Embodied Learning and Cognitive Synergy. Atlantis Publishing Corporation (2014)
17. Liu, W., Anguelov, D., Erhan, D., Szegedy, C., Reed, S.: SSD: single shot multibox detector. arXiv:1512.02325 (2015)
18. Johnson, J., et al.: Image retrieval using scene graphs. In: IEEE Conference on Computer Vision and Pattern Recognition (CVPR) (2015)
19. Redmon, J., Divvala, S., Girshick, R., Farhadi, A.: You only look once: unified, real-time object detection. arXiv:1506.02640 (2015)
20. Li, Y., He, K., Sun, J., et al.: R-FCN: object detection via region based fully convolutional networks. In: Advances in Neural Information Processing Systems, pp. 379–387 (2016)

21. Hofstadter, D.R., Mitchell, M.: The copycat project: a model of mental fluidity and analogy-making. In: Holyoak, K., Barnden, J. (eds.) Advances in Connectionist and Neural Computation Theory. Ablex Publishing Corporation (1994)
22. Goertzel, B.: Perception processing for general intelligence: bridging the symbolic/subsymbolic gap. In: Bach, J., Goertzel, B., Iklé, M. (eds.) AGI 2012. LNCS (LNAI), vol. 7716, pp. 79–88. Springer, Heidelberg (2012). https://doi.org/10.1007/978-3-642-35506-6_9

The Temporal Singularity: Time-Accelerated Simulated Civilizations and Their Implications

Giacomo Spigler(✉)

The Biorobotics Institute, Scuola Superiore Sant'Anna, Pisa, Italy
giacomo.spigler@santannapisa.it
http://www.spigler.net/giacomo/

Abstract. Provided significant future progress in artificial intelligence and computing, it may ultimately be possible to create multiple Artificial General Intelligences (AGIs), and possibly entire societies living within simulated environments. In that case, it should be possible to improve the problem solving capabilities of the system by increasing the speed of the simulation. If a minimal simulation with sufficient capabilities is created, it might manage to increase its own speed by accelerating progress in science and technology, in a way similar to the Technological Singularity. This may ultimately lead to large simulated civilizations unfolding at extreme temporal speedups, achieving what from the outside would look like a Temporal Singularity. Here we discuss the feasibility of the minimal simulation and the potential advantages, dangers, and connection to the Fermi paradox of the Temporal Singularity. The medium-term importance of the topic derives from the amount of computational power required to start the process, which could be available within the next decades, making the Temporal Singularity theoretically possible before the end of the century.

Keywords: Temporal Singularity · Simulated civilization
Multi-agent systems · Simulated society · Fermi paradox
Artificial life · Technological Singularity · Artificial general intelligence
Deep reinforcement learning · Simulation hypothesis
Post-biological civilization

1 The Temporal Singularity

It seems possible, if not likely, that artificial agents with general intelligence (AGI) will be built in the future [21, 25]. It also seems likely that such agents could be further improved to achieve super-human degrees of intelligence (ASI). A simple way to increase the capabilities of an agent is to execute the same algorithms on a faster (super-)computer, so to provide it with more time to think and solve problems, thus resulting in a shorter solving time in the external world. In practice, a simulated environment may be required for the agent to work in, as

© Springer Nature Switzerland AG 2018
M. Iklé et al. (Eds.): AGI 2018, LNAI 10999, pp. 207–216, 2018.
https://doi.org/10.1007/978-3-319-97676-1_20

the 'slow' external world would be a limitation to the performance the agent even at moderate speedups. It is interesting to note that this approach is already regularly used, for example in training deep reinforcement learning (DRL) agents, that is usually performed in simulated environments whose execution speed is limited only by the available computing power [4,8,19]. For example, DRL agents learning to play Atari games can experience thousands of game frames per second even on a regular desktop computer, compared to human players that play them at 15–60 frames per second.

Another approach to improve the effective capabilities of the system without any modification to its algorithms is to simulate multiple agents each with its specific differences, so that they can come up with different ways of solving the problem individually or cooperatively by exploiting dynamics of collective intelligence. An interesting outcome of simulations of this type is the potential to simulate the unfolding of entire "civilizations", possibly pursuing complex sets of goals like general progress in science and technology. The potential of the approach relies not only on the possibly advanced intelligence level of the agents (ASI), but also on the temporal speedups that could be achieved by increasing the computing resources available for the simulation. Throughout this paper intelligent agents and civilizations will be referred to as 'simulated' only to mean that they experience a simulated environment in contrast to the 'real' external world, but there is no reason not to consider them as real as any intelligent agent outside the simulation.

Here we suggest that *if* it will be possible to create at least a limited group of AGIs in a simulation unfolding faster than the external time, *then* such simulation may be able to accelerate the rate of progress in science and technology, possibly by continually self-improving its core technologies such as its intelligence algorithms and its computing systems in a manner similar to the *Technological Singularity* [9,14,18,21,30], and thus potentially achieve a runaway increase in its capabilities. Specifically, the rate of progress may be so high that in a very short time the simulations could progress to producing entire civilizations spanning thousands or millions of years or even more in an arbitrarily short time interval elapsed in the external world, achieving what from the outside would be a **Temporal Singularity**. In particular the Temporal Singularity is defined as the moment in time where a minimal simulation capable of beginning the runaway exponential self-improvement is started. We will discuss the feasibility of the minimal simulation in Sect. 2.

It is difficult to imagine what such a quick progress would look like, as even a single century of progress at the present rate is challenging to forecast. Even more, we can only wonder what the world would become after the Temporal Singularity has allowed the unfolding of millions or billions of years of an advanced civilization [18], during which potentially any questions our species may ever ask could have been answered.

This result is compatible with the idea of the Technological Singularity, of which the Temporal Singularity can represent a component or a way to achieve it. Contrary to the main definitions of the Technological Singularity, however, the Temporal Singularity would not necessarily require a runaway increase in the cognitive capabilities of the artificial agents, but rather only a runaway increase in the temporal speedups of the simulations. We should note that speeding up the execution of AGIs has been already suggested in this context, for example by Vernor Vinge, who discusses an AI whose 'mind clock' is significantly faster than its creator and the problem of AI boxing [30], or by Solomonoff in the context of an exponential increase in the number of simulated agents [28]. Most notably Marcus Hutter [18] explored what the Technological Singularity would look like for both the outside and the inside of a virtual software society undergoing it, also discussing the difference between speeding up the simulation time and increasing the intelligence of the agents. However, the focus of the discussion was put on the extreme progress and changes achieved in the traditional Technological Singularity, rather than on the implications of a drastic increase in the temporal speedups of the simulations and its potential implications on the Fermi Paradox.

The idea of simulated civilizations is also not novel, although it has been generally applied to us being in the simulation ourselves, rather than focusing directly on the benefits, limits and implications of us producing it, and in particular on the possibility to speed up the elapsing of the simulated time. Philosophers have always wondered about the nature of reality and the possibility of it being an illusion. In recent times, the argument has been especially developed by Hans Moravec [23] and Nick Bostrom [5] in the explicit context of computer simulations. A more closely related investigation was proposed by Vidal, who explored the possibility that scientific simulations will improve significantly in the future and finally result in simulating an entire universe, in order to better probe and understand our own universe and the processes of physical, biological and cultural evolution [29]. However, most of the discussions such as Vidal's and Bostrom's only focus on a very special type of simulations restricted to detailed versions of our physical universe and our same society and life as we know it, which although intriguing from a scientific point of view, constitute only a tiny fraction of the potential uses of time-accelerated simulations, and possibly an inefficient use of the computing resources. For example, as we discuss in Sect. 2, it may be that fooling the simulated agents to prevent them from discovering that they belong to a simulation may not be necessary, which would in turn lower the computational requirements for the simulated environment. In any case, whether our own world is itself simulated or not does not reduce the potential advantages of running our own time-accelerated simulations.

Section 2 will next overview the feasibility and broad computational requirements for simulations capable of achieving and sustaining the Temporal Singularity, while Sect. 3 will explore some of the advantages and risks of such simulations, and the implications of the Temporal Singularity for the Fermi paradox.

2   Feasibility

The Minimal Simulation. It is difficult to estimate what are the minimal requirements for a simulation capable of starting the runaway exponential process of self-improvement and time-acceleration that characterizes the Temporal Singularity. In general, we should expect the minimal simulation to provide a problem-solving capability sufficient to compete with teams of human experts, either by providing significant temporal speedups, by using more capable AGIs/ASIs or by creating a larger number of individuals. Even small advantages, compared to traditional research and development, may be sufficient to start the process by exploiting the compound nature of progress [21,28]. The minimal requirements could thus be reasonably low (see the discussion on the *computational requirements* below), especially after achieving human-level AGI, which itself however *may* not be required, as a super-human narrow intelligence in specific fields like improving the computing technology may be sufficient.

AGI. Still, while we could imagine some limited type of "civilization" composed by agents with narrow intelligence (ANI), the development of artificial general intelligence (AGI) is likely to be a core requirement for enabling complex artificial civilizations. It is not known whether AGI itself will ever be possible, though there do *not* seem to be strong reasons for it to be not. Unfortunately, the field is known to have a poor track record of predictions about when such a system wil be developed. Current predictions also vary greatly depending on the expected requirements for specific types of implementations, with average agreement placed around 2040 [6,25] and possibly as early as 2029 [2,21], and a high confidence in any case that it may happen before the end of the century. We could also wonder whether the artificial agents could instantiate *consciousness*, but it may not be a strict requirement in this context. On the other hand, it may turn out that consciousness is required, for example for the establishment and maintenance of societies and complex civilizations (e.g., for consciousness and sociality [15]).

Fooling the Agents. The requirements for the simulations discussed here also change significantly depending on whether the simulated agents are allowed to know they belong to a simulation or whether they need to be fooled. In particular, fooling the agents may be challenging especially if the aim of the simulations is to produce progress in science and technology that apply to the external world, as a large degree of knowledge of it would be required. In the limit, a perfect simulation of our physical world may be required for perfect fooling, which would however limit the simulation (for an analysis of the requirements, see for example [3]). It is however possible that fooling is not necessary, or that perfect fooling can be achieved with simpler simulations. If fooling is not used, the potential problems that may arise and their solutions would fall within the traditional problem of AI boxing and containment (e.g., [1,6]).

Computational Requirements. The computational requirements for the simulations described here can be assessed by separately estimating the resources required for the agents and for the simulated environment. It is difficult to predict the requirements for a single AGI agent, but estimates have been suggested for the calculations per second required for a real-time functional simulation of the human brain. Such estimates range wildly from tens of Teraflops [24]

(10^{13} FLOPS) to Exaflops and more (10^{18} to 10^{25} FLOPS [26]). However, the highest estimates have been mostly suggested for detailed whole brain emulation approaches, which are unlikely to be the most computationally efficient approach to AGI, and may thus constitute an upper-bound on the actual requirements for computer-optimized implementations of the algorithms. A common intermediate estimate is for the required power to be of the order of tens of Petaflops (10^{16} FLOPS) [21], comparable to the performance of present day supercomputers.

As for the computational requirements for the simulated environment, multiple answers may be correct. Even today we are performing time-accelerated simulations in limited conditions, for example to train deep reinforcement learning agents, so there seems to be no strict lower bound on the required speed of the system. However, it is likely that more complex environments will be required in order to support AGI agents performing complex tasks, especially to allow progress in science and technology. While a certain degree of physically-detailed simulation of the real world may be required, a perfect simulation of the real world may not. Indeed, even present-day engineering software allow for part of the development in engineering to be performed in simulation (for example, using the COMSOL Multiphysics simulation software [10]).

Still, a perfect simulation may be required in case fooling of the agents was desired. For example, even if an imperfect simulation was sufficient to fool the agents, knowledge of the external world will be required to achieve progress in science and engineering, which could allow the agents to ultimately discover the truth. Nonetheless, while a perfect simulation would be computationally prohibitive with our current technology, we might be able to achieve it in the future [3]. In any case, it seems unlikely that a perfect simulation will be required for the *minimal simulation* and thus to start the Temporal Singularity.

When. If we assume that the agents require a computational power on the order of the average current estimates for the computational power of the human brain, and a linear scaling of the total requirements with the number of agents and temporal speedup, with negligible environment overhead, then the computational requirements for a minimal simulation of tens to hundreds of agents at faster than real-time may be as low as 10^{18} to 10^{21} FLOPS (e.g., $10^{16} \cdot 100 \rightarrow 100$ agents in real-time or 10 agents at $10\times$ faster than real-time). If the Moore's law continues to hold, the world's most powerful supercomputer could achieve the required speed between the years 2020–2040, or alternatively individual home workstations between the years 2055–2075. Specialized hardware may however be developed to provide faster increases in the computational power in the future, as it has happened for example in the specific case of deep learning with the development of specialized accelerators like the Tensor Processing Unit (TPU) [20]. It is also interesting that these estimates are similar to current estimates for the development of AGI, which could be an important requirement for the simulations.

Allocation of the Resources. We may further wonder how the available computing resources could be allocated between different processes to achieve the highest problem-solving capabilities of the system. For example, increased computation could be traded off between creating a larger number of agents, increasing the speed of the simulation and thus its temporal speedup compared to the external world, increasing the cognitive capabilities of the individual agents or simulating more complex environments. It may thus be required for the resources to be re-allocated dynamically depending on the state of technology.

Potential Limitations. Even if the minimal simulation would be possible, there may be other limitations that could prevent or limit the Temporal Singularity. For example, it may be that temporal acceleration will not be the most efficient allocation of the computing resources, so that creating a larger number of agents or stronger ASIs will produce the best results. However, the fact that artificial agents working at faster than real-time are already being used and the potential advantages of simulating societies and civilizations suggest that this is unlikely to be the case. Temporal acceleration may also be helpful to speed up the solution of time-critical problems given a current level of intelligence of the available agents, in case improving the cognitive capabilities of the agent would prove difficult and more time-consuming. Finally, increasing the number of simulated agents may ultimately be limited by the intrinsic problem solving speed of each agent, which could be then trivially improved with temporal acceleration.

Another potential limit is that perfect simulations may be required to enable practical progress in science and technology. However, even present day research involves significant portions of time for theoretical work and simulations, so there seems to be a margin of speedup that can be achieved. Moreover, even if the first environments limited the potential to advance science and technology, it would be possible to iterate between time-accelerated work performed inside the simulation and prototyping, testing, and conducting experimental work in the external world, whose results and data could be fed back into the simulation to start the next cycle. Also, some type of theoretical work like in mathematics, computer science, philosophy and others may not need frequent access to data from the external world, suggesting that it should still be possible to benefit greatly from the temporal speedups of these simulations. In any case, interaction with the external world will always be required for maintenance and upgrades, to manufacture the newly developed technologies, and to acquire experimental data [18]. This dependency may ultimately limit the maximum speedups that can be achieved or their rate of growth. Still, even relatively low effective speedups could be highly beneficial. Further, the processes performed in the external world may be optimized inside the simulations to avoid wasting external time, for example by providing efficient instructions distributed among a large number of external world agents, although this may involve risks in the context of AI boxing [1,6].

3   Implications

Advantages. Similar to the Technological Singularity, the Temporal Singularity would produce a runaway increase the rate of growth of scientific and technological progress. In addition, however, it would also allow the study of the potential future of advanced intelligent civilizations and societal structures that will be required to be stable for extremely long intervals of time, which could be useful for scientific purposes and may provide invaluable information, thus impacting our society and guiding the future of our own civilization in a safe and beneficial way. In the extreme, we might be able to simulate civilizations with characteristics similar to our own, experimenting new societal designs and conditions. Finally, due to the potential for significant technological development, there is a clear competitive advantage for the first entity that will achieve a minimal simulation, even at moderate temporal speedups, whether it would be governments or private companies.

Dangers. In general, the Temporal Singularity shares all the potential dangers related to AGI/ASI and the Technological Singularity (see for example [6]), and in particular to the problem AI boxing [1]. However, the problems may be worse in this context, as even moderate temporal speedups would make it difficult to track the events inside the simulation. Finally, the same extreme progress in technology in a short span of time also constitutes a potential danger, as our society may not be capable of metabolizing it in the available time. For example, we can try to imagine what could have happened if we abruptly produced not just the technology, but a full stockpile of thermonuclear weapons during the Middle Ages.

Fermi Paradox. The Fermi Paradox is the contradiction between the apparent high likelihood of the existence of other intelligent civilizations in our galaxy or in the universe and the current lack of evidence of any. The Temporal Singularity leads to interesting implications in this context. First, if intelligent civilizations would achieve a degree of technology similar to our present one, and in particular develop computing systems, it may turn out to be almost inevitable that at some point they would produce a Temporal Singularity. Time-accelerated simulations could thus be part of some or all the possible intelligent civilizations, providing advantages like achieving a practical 'subjective immortality' within the simulated environments, either for the individual agents or for their civilization as a whole, and subjectively delaying its demise due to the heat death of the universe or earlier extinction events. This can apply to either the external agents 'moving into' the simulation, or for the simulated agents themselves as 'mind children' progeny, as put by Hans Moravec [22], which could then possibly imply an abundance of post-biological civilizations in the universe [11,12]. An interesting possible outcome of this process is that time in the real world would be an important resource, and the speed of space colonization and communication, that is already considered slow, would become unbearable. Future civilizations may then prefer to avoid large-scale galactic colonization.

It is interesting to note that the Temporal Singularity shares features with the transcension hypothesis [27] in the inevitable search for more energy and computing power, but ultimately produces opposite predictions, as in the transcension hypothesis advanced civilizations would try to slow down their subjective time by approaching black holes, rather than to accelerate it, in order to forward time travel to a time where all civilizations may ultimately meet and merge, and to optimize the acquisition of information.

On a negative side, the potential dangers that arise from this technology may constitute a 'Great Filter' [17] that very few civilizations survive, thus explaining the Fermi paradox. However, time-accelerated simulations may also be used to escape traditional Great Filters by quickly providing us with solutions in time-critical situations, including for example impacts of asteroids detected with short notice or the Berserker scenario, in which an advanced intelligent civilization may attack any newly emerging civilization.

Finally, a prediction of the Temporal Singularity in the context of the Fermi paradox can be made in the rapid increase in the power used by a civilization, tracking the super-exponential progress in technology, which could progress from using the resources of its host planet to those of its entire solar system within decades rather than millennia. Further, depending on the physical limits of technology, it may be possible that at least partial Dyson spheres [13] or Matrioska brains [7] would be constructed in a relatively short time. The idea is particularly interesting as present day technology should be capable of detecting even partial neighboring Dyson spheres by changes in the infrared radiation of their host star [16,31,32]. A prediction of the Temporal Singularity in the context of the Fermi Paradox is then on the speed of construction of such mega-structures.

4   Conclusion

We have explored the idea that progress in computing and artificial intelligence can lead to time-accelerated simulated civilizations unfolding in short time intervals in the external world, due to a runaway increase in the rate of growth of scientific and technological progress they could produce, that would quickly increase the temporal speedups of the simulations themselves, ultimately resulting in a 'Temporal Singularity'. The potential advantages and dangers of such simulations have been briefly explored together with some implications of the Temporal Singularity on the Fermi paradox.

The medium-term relevance of the topic comes from the potentially relatively low computational power required to start the process, which could be as low as $10^{18} - 10^{21}$ FLOPS and thus be available within the next decades, making the Temporal Singularity theoretically possible before the end of the century, and possibly in its first half.

As a final remark, it is interesting to note that given the great competitive advantages of running a simulation of the type described here, it is virtually inevitable that if it will ever be technically possible to create it, it will be created. It should be noted, however, that this is unlikely to happen in a discontinuous way, but rather we should expect an incremental progress, for example, starting from the simple advantage of temporal speedups in simulated environments for training artificial narrow intelligences (ANIs), as is already being done, to perhaps accelerating simulated 'childhood' development and training of AGIs, to actual simulated multi-agent systems, building towards complete societies and civilizations following the increase in the available computing power.

Acknowledgments. I would like to thank Ivana Kolorici and Renato Spigler for the helpful discussions and comments and the anonymous reviewers for the useful suggestions and references, from which this manuscript benefited significantly.

References

1. Armstrong, S., Sandberg, A., Bostrom, N.: Thinking inside the box: controlling and using an Oracle AI. Minds Mach. **22**(4), 299–324 (2012)
2. Barrat, J.: Our Final Invention: Artificial Intelligence and the End of the Human Era. Macmillan, Basingstoke (2013)
3. Baxter, S.: The planetarium hypothesis - a resolution of the Fermi paradox. J. Br. Interplanet. Soc. **54**, 210–216 (2001)
4. Beattie, C., et al.: Deepmind Lab. arXiv preprint arXiv:1612.03801 (2016)
5. Bostrom, N.: Are we living in a computer simulation? Philos. Q. **53**(211), 243–255 (2003)
6. Bostrom, N.: Superintelligence: Paths, Dangers, Strategies. OUP Oxford, New York (2014)
7. Bradbury, R.J.: Matrioshka brains (2001)
8. Brockman, G., et al.: OpenAI gym. arXiv preprint arXiv:1606.01540 (2016)
9. Chalmers, D.: The singularity: a philosophical analysis. J. Conscious. Stud. **17**(9–1), 7–65 (2010)
10. Comsol, A.: COMSOL multiphysics user's guide. Version: September 10, 333 (2005)
11. Dick, S.: The postbiological universe. Acta Astronaut. **62**(8), 499–504 (2008)
12. Dick, S.J.: Cultural evolution, the postbiological universe and SETI. Int. J. Astrobiol. **2**(1), 65–74 (2003)
13. Dyson, F.J.: Search for artificial stellar sources of infrared radiation. Science **131**(3414), 1667–1668 (1960)
14. Good, I.J.: Speculations concerning the first ultraintelligent machine. Adv. Comput. **6**, 31–88 (1966)
15. Graziano, M.S.: Consciousness and the Social Brain. Oxford University Press, New York (2013)
16. Griffith, R.L., Wright, J.T., Maldonado, J., Povich, M.S., Sigurdsson, S., Mullan, B.: The ĝ infrared search for extraterrestrial civilizations with large energy supplies. III. The reddest extended sources in WISE. Astrophys. J. Suppl. Ser. **217**(2), 25 (2015)
17. Hanson, R.: The great filter - are we almost past it? (1998). http://hanson.gmu.edu/greatfilter.html
18. Hutter, M.: Can intelligence explode? J. Conscious. Stud. **19**(1–2), 143–166 (2012)
19. Johnson, M., Hofmann, K., Hutton, T., Bignell, D.: The Malmo platform for artificial intelligence experimentation. In: IJCAI, pp. 4246–4247 (2016)
20. Jouppi, N.P., et al.: In-datacenter performance analysis of a tensor processing unit. arXiv preprint arXiv:1704.04760 (2017)
21. Kurzweil, R.: The Singularity is Near: When Humans Transcend Biology. Penguin, London (2005)
22. Moravec, H.: Mind Children: The Future of Robot and Human Intelligence. Harvard University Press, Cambridge (1988)
23. Moravec, H.: Simulation, consciousness, existence (1999)
24. Moravec, H.: Rise of the robots-the future of artificial intelligence. Sci. Am. (2009)

25. Müller, V.C., Bostrom, N.: Future progress in artificial intelligence: a survey of expert opinion. In: Müller, V.C. (ed.) Fundamental Issues of Artificial Intelligence. SL, vol. 376, pp. 553–570. Springer, Cham (2016). https://doi.org/10.1007/978-3-319-26485-1_33

26. Sandberg, A., Bostrom, N.: Whole brain emulation (2008)

27. Smart, J.M.: The transcension hypothesis: sufficiently advanced civilizations invariably leave our universe, and implications for meti and seti. Acta Astronaut. **78**, 55–68 (2012)

28. Solomonoff, R.J.: The time scale of artificial intelligence: reflections on social effects. Hum. Syst. Manage. **5**(2), 149–153 (1985)

29. Vidal, C.: The future of scientific simulations: from artificial life to artificial cosmogenesis. arXiv preprint arXiv:0803.1087 (2008)

30. Vinge, V.: The coming technological singularity. Whole Earth Rev. **81**, 88–95 (1993)

31. Wright, J.T., Mullan, B., Sigurdsson, S., Povich, M.S.: The ĝ infrared search for extraterrestrial civilizations with large energy supplies. I. Background and justification. Astrophys. J. **792**(1), 26 (2014)

32. Wright, J., Griffith, R., Sigurdsson, S., Povich, M., Mullan, B.: The ĝ infrared search for extraterrestrial civilizations with large energy supplies. II. Framework, strategy, and first result. Astrophys. J. **792**(1), 27 (2014)

A Computational Theory for Life-Long Learning of Semantics

Peter Sutor Jr.[1]([✉])([iD]), Douglas Summers-Stay[2], and Yiannis Aloimonos[1]

[1] University of Maryland, College Park, MD 20742, USA
psutor@umd.edu, yiannis@cs.umd.edu
[2] U.S. Army Research Laboratory Adelphi, Adelphi, MD 20783, USA
douglas.a.summers-stay.civ@mail.mil

Abstract. Semantic vectors are learned from data to express semantic relationships between elements of information, for the purpose of solving and informing downstream tasks. Other models exist that learn to map and classify supervised data. However, the two worlds of learning rarely interact to inform one another dynamically, whether across types of data or levels of semantics, in order to form a unified model. We explore the research problem of learning these vectors and propose a framework for learning the semantics of knowledge incrementally and online, across multiple mediums of data, via binary vectors. We discuss the aspects of this framework to spur future research on this approach and problem.

Keywords: Semantic vectors · Hyperdimensional computing
Knowledge representation · Incremental learning · Dynamic systems

1 Introduction

Semantic vector learning finds vector representations of semantic relationships observed in data that have useful properties, such as exhibiting similarity in the components of vectors via closeness under a metric, or allowing vector arithmetic to propagate semantic meaning. These vectors are learned by statistical distributions of co-occurrence in data (usually unsupervised), whose structure is embedded in a high dimensional space. With recent advances in neural networks, progress on semantic vectors has seen much success. But such models feel disjoint as semantic insight transfers poorly across them. State-of-the-art techniques rely on static datasets that estimate mapping functions across their distributions. Adapting models to another domain often requires complete retraining, or at least fine-tuning/transfer learning [14]. In this paper, we examine the problem of learning semantics from supervised and unsupervised data to facilitate incremental and life-long learning. This is desirable as it synthesizes the semantics from not just multiple models, but potentially entirely separate domains (vision, linguistics, audio, etc.) into consistent vector representations for use in other tasks. The incremental process allows new models to come into existence at any time. We describe a general theoretical framework that can compute such vector representations in an online and perpetual way.

© Springer Nature Switzerland AG 2018
M. Iklé et al. (Eds.): AGI 2018, LNAI 10999, pp. 217–226, 2018.
https://doi.org/10.1007/978-3-319-97676-1_21

2   Background Information

2.1   Related Work

Our primary difference is the online and incremental learning capabilities of the vectors themselves, without a need for existing vector models, and the use of binary vectors to allow for useful and general data structure representation, as suggested by Kanerva [7]. The problem of learning symbolic vectors for structured data has been explored using neural networks by Bordes et al. [2], with newer techniques [13] learning from knowledge graph relationships, such as Freitas' DRNs [5]. Additionally, the reasoning, inference and lookup structures for embedded knowledge graphs are a well studied topic [3,4]. Most are limited to static information, however there has been much work on the problem of completing relationships in knowledge graphs, such as TransE [1] and its derivatives.

2.2   Motivation

The word2vec [11] paradigm forms semantic vectors for words by predicting the context around a word via an unsupervised process, given a corpus. The famous $king - man + woman \approx queen$ example shows its ability to learn deep analogies between word vectors. However, consider: $smokestack - cigarette + firework$. It's clear that something like "missile" would be a valid answer to this analogy. This is not the case for word2vec, which does not return "missile", or anything sensible, for even the top 100 matches for the popular Google News word2vec model [12]. Why does it fail for this example, but not for much deeper analogies such as $death - life + good \approx bad$? The analogy is purely visual/functional here. However, word2vec never 'sees' anything visual, only patterns in words, where such a relationship is unlikely to occur. A similar situation is apparent in the auditory domain: $quack - bird + car = honk$ also fails in word2vec.

Clearly, learning human-level semantics requires integration of hierarchically built-up data and relationships from differing domains. For example, neural networks generalize better by using character level patterns as well as word level [8,15]. A general model should include multiple forms and levels of perception into a single semantic model that takes everything into account, from a general intelligence perspective. This is supported in the biological setting, where it seems that neurons can take on other roles over time, when necessary [6], suggesting that many cortical neurons treats information in a similar way.

2.3   Incremental, Online, and Generalized Semantic Learning

Our goal is to take raw input from various perceptions, outputs of other models and unify them. Such models give semantically significant relationships, that could be learned or heuristic in nature. This could be between sequences of raw data, more complex mappings of words to parts of speech, or dependency arcs between words. In the visual domain, patterns of pixels can map to classification labels. We can visualize this as building a graph of relationships. Short of numeric regression, most outputs of models can be expressed as edges between nodes, due to their discrete nature. New info is easily absorbed by simply updating the graph and statistics on it. We wish to find appropriate vectors for the nodes. Since new knowledge comes in an online process, as new observations, new nodes or edges in the graph, or the addition of new models to the system, these vectors themselves must be quickly adjusted in an equally online and incremental process.

2.4   Long Binary Vectors as General Features

As noted by Kanerva [7], long binary vectors, on the order of 10,000 compo- nents, are a promising vector representation. Consider the space $\mathbb{B}^n = \{0,1\}^n$. This space contains $|\mathbb{B}^n| = 2^n$ possible vectors. No computational system needs anywhere near $2^{10,000}$ vector representations. This space represents the corners of a 10,000 dimensional hypercube, so every point in the space has the same distribution of distances to other points. Let:

$$H(x,y) = \sum_{i=0}^{n} \mathbb{I}_{x_i \neq y_i}(i) = \sum_{i=0}^{n} x_i \oplus y_i = |x \oplus y| \tag{1}$$

be the Hamming Distance, where $\mathbb{I}_{x_i \neq y_i}$ is the indicator that the bits at i between x and y disagree, returning 1 in this case, and 0 when they agree, $a \oplus b$ is the bitwise exclusive-or (XOR) operation, and $|a|$ is the number of 1's in a. The number of bits of disagreement is the distance between points. Let:

$$H_N(x,y) = \frac{1}{n}H(x,y) \tag{2}$$

be the Normalized Hamming Distance, which expresses the distance on a real scale of 0 to 1. Assuming each possible vector is equally likely, the average Normalized Hamming Distance is 0.5. Furthermore, under these assumptions, with $n = 10,000$, their distribution is binary with mean 5000 bits and standard deviation 50; this implies that for any significant deviation from distance 0.5, the distribution quickly becomes very sparse. An astronomically vast majority of vectors have distances very close to 0.5. Randomly drawn vectors are nearly guaranteed to differ from one another by about 5000 bits, or distance 0.5.

This distribution is resistant to noise in its vectors, as a large portion of the bits in any vector would have to be randomly flipped before the distance becomes very big between another nearby vector. Two related vectors differing even by 5% of their bits is so astronomically unlikely that they may as well still be the same vector. As pointed out by Kanerva, such long binary vectors also have the property of encoding various forms of information that can be later recovered even under noisy conditions. This comes primarily from three operations:

1. The XOR $c = a \oplus b$: Since XOR is an involution when one operator is fixed, and associative and commutative, $c \oplus a = (a \oplus b) \oplus a = a$. We can exactly recover a or b if we have one or the other, or approximately with noise.

2. The permutation Π: This permutes a vector x's components into a new order, by computing the product Πx. If the permutation is randomly generated for a long binary vector, the new binary vector is very likely to have a distance (2) near 0.5. We can represent Π as a permutation of index locations 1 to n. The product simply swaps components of x to the order in Π.

3. The consensus sum, $+_c(A)$, over the set of vectors A: This sum counts 1's and 0's component-wise across each element of A, and sets the component to the corresponding value with the bigger count. Ties, only possible in a sum of an even number of elements, can be broken by randomly choosing.

Note that mapping by XOR or permuting preserves distances. For mapping a:

$$H(a \oplus x, a \oplus y) = |a \oplus x \oplus a \oplus y| = |a \oplus a \oplus x \oplus y| = |x \oplus y|$$
$$H(\Pi x, \Pi y) = |\Pi x \oplus \Pi y| = |\Pi(x \oplus y) = |x \oplus y| \tag{3}$$

as permutation is distributive, thus $\Pi a \oplus \Pi b = \Pi(a \oplus b)$, and permuting doesn't change the number of 1's or 0's, so $|\Pi c| = |c|$, for any a, b, and c.

2.5   Representing Data Structures with Binary Vectors

We can create binary vector abstractions of simple data structures:

Sets: A set of data $\{\zeta_1, \zeta_2, ..., \zeta_m\}$, given a mapping between ζ_i and binary vectors $\{z_1, z_2, ..., z_m\}$, can be represented as $z = z_1 \oplus z_2 \oplus ... \oplus z_m$. A union of sets x and y, of m_1 and m_2 elements, with no elements in common, is:

$$x \cup y = x \oplus y = x_1 \oplus x_2 \oplus ... \oplus x_{m_1} \oplus y_1 \oplus y_2 \oplus ... \oplus y_{m_2} \tag{4}$$

However, Eq. (4) is not the general case. With unrestricted x and y:

$$x \oplus y = (x - y) \cup (y - x) \tag{5}$$

Furthermore, set intersection and complement is impossible to compute without knowing the original vector values of the components.

Ordered Pairs: Represented by tuple $\zeta_x = (\zeta_x, \zeta_y)$, where ζ_x, ζ_y and ζ_z are data points. If mapped to binary vector representations x, y, and z:

$$z = \Pi x \oplus y \text{ , or } z = +_c(\{\Pi x, y\}) \tag{6}$$

This random permutation Π then denotes the data type of ζ_z.

Sequences: We can interpret a sequence $\zeta_z = \zeta_{z_1}\zeta_{z_2}...\zeta_{z_m}$ of a particular data type as a 2-tuple $\zeta_z = (\zeta_{z_1}...\zeta_{z_{m-1}}, \zeta_{z_m})$. With binary vectors $z_1, z_2, ..., z_m$, this reduces to a succession of pairings via Eq. (6):

$$z = \Pi^{m-1} z_1 \oplus \Pi^{m-2} z_2 \oplus ... \oplus \Pi^{m-i} z_i \oplus ... \oplus \Pi z_{m-1} \oplus z_m \tag{7}$$

where Π^j is a permutation Π that permutes itself j times. If Π is random, then Π^j appears random too, with an expected distance from Π near 0.5. Equation (7) holds inductively as $\zeta_{z_1}\zeta_{z_2}$ is $\Pi z_1 \oplus z_2$, thus $\zeta_{z_1}\zeta_{z_2}\zeta_{z_3}$ is:

$$\Pi(\Pi z_1 \oplus z_2) \oplus z_3 = \Pi\Pi z_1 \oplus \Pi z_2 \oplus z_3 = \Pi^2 z_1 + \Pi z_2 + z_3$$

Continuing this for an arbitrarily long pattern gives Eq. (7). Similar reasoning will get us the equivalent with $+_c$ replacing XOR for the sum:

$$z = +_c(\{\Pi^{m-1}z_1, +_c(\{\Pi^{m-2}z_2, ... +_c (\{\Pi^{m-i}z_i, ...\})...\})\}) \qquad (8)$$

Data Records: A unit of data containing one or more fields, where each component has a specific meaning. Let a data record of type $R = [r_1 r_2 ... r_m]$ of m fields, where each binary vector r_i is a field; for example, "name", "age", "gender", etc., for a record of a person. To set values to a field, we bind each field to a value. Since the XOR of two vector mappings represents a set - essentially a bound field - we can use $r_i \oplus v_i$ to bind a v_i to r_i. Given r_i, we can recover v_i, or vice versa. We can generalize a bound data record R_v by:

$$R_v = [r_1 r_2 ... r_m][v_1 v_2 ... v_m]^T$$
$$= r_1 \oplus v_1 + r_2 \oplus v_2 + ... + r_m \oplus v_m = +_c(\{r_i \oplus v_i\}) \qquad (9)$$

To isolate the value of a field r_i, we compute $R_v \oplus r_i$. The contribution of unrelated fields will generally create random noise when r_i distributes across them, but only the contribution of the $r_i \oplus v_i$ will be non-random and significant, as $r_i \oplus r_i \oplus v_i = v_i$, generating a signal that is close to v. This is because each bit of R_v represents the majority of the terms $r_i \oplus v_i$. High-dimensional binary vectors resist such noise, so the closest neighbor to $R_v \oplus r_i$ is likely v_i.

3 Life-Long Learning of Semantics

3.1 A Geometric Interpretation of Semantics

Consider the task of learning semantic vectors given a knowledge graph $K = (V, E)$ consisting of n_v vertexes $V = \{v_1, ..., v_{n_v}\}$ and n_e directed, weighted edges $E = \{e_1, ..., e_{n_e}\}$. Let any v_i have *mass* equal to the number of times its relationships have been observed, or a similar statistic. We can equate this to a simple, undamped spring-mass system, with a few caveats. Since it is directed, the target end of the edge is seen as fixed, converting mass (by edge weight) into constant acceleration towards the target, or a *connecting force*. Let mass generate a repelling *proximal force* similar to gravity, to prevent singularities. This is somewhat akin to self-organizing maps [9]. Suppose vertexes exist in n-dimensional space accompanied by a distance metric, with locations randomly chosen. The structure of the knowledge graph causes the forces to be very high. We wish to minimize them by placing vertexes in a "better" location. In order to facilitate this, we define an "anchoring" vertex that cannot move from it's random position, connected to all vertexes with incoming edges. A minimized configuration of this system is equivalent to a good semantic placement of vectors, if an outgoing edge from a vertex signifies it should be more "similar" to the target. Efficient algorithms exist for this minimization in the real domain [10].

3.2   Binary Vector Analogues

We will now construct a binary vector analogue of the geometric, knowledge graph based semantic minimization problem. Let K be of m vertexes, $X^{(k)} \in \mathbb{B}^{m \times n}$ be a binary matrix, where m rows correspond to positional vectors for m vertexes in K, n is the number of dimensions, and k is the iteration step. Initially, $X^{(0)}$ is randomly selected. Let row 1 be the anchoring vector. Our problem statement is to find a perturbation matrix $X \in \mathbb{B}^{m \times n}$ such that:

$$\arg\min_X(T(X^{(k)} + X)) \tag{10}$$

where T denotes the *total tension* in our system. Then, we set $X^{(k+1)} = X^{(k)} + X$ and continue. This is the sum of unresolved forces across all bits of a given A:

$$T(A) = \sum_{i=1}^{m} \sum_{j=1}^{n} \max(F_{conn}(A, i, j) + F_{prox}(A, i, j), 0) \tag{11}$$

where F_{conn} and F_{prox} are the connective and proximal forces for vector i, bit j in A. If the sum of these two forces for a bit are positive, it means the bit wants to change, otherwise it wants to remain the same. Thus, a system with all negative or 0 resultant forces is considered minimized. The proximal force is:

$$F_{prox}(A, i, j) = \sum_{k=1, k \neq i}^{m} \frac{M_i M_k}{H(A_i, A_k)^2} C_{prox}(A_{ij}, A_{kj}) \tag{12}$$

where M_i and M_k are the masses of the corresponding rows A_i and A_k of A. This force is clearly analogous to gravitational force between two masses, but a repulsive one, with normalized Hamming distance between them. Likewise:

$$F_{conn}(A, i, j) = \sum_{k=1, k \neq i}^{m} M_i W_{ik} C_{conn}(A_{ij}, A_{kj}) \tag{13}$$

is the connective force, where W_{ik} denotes the directed edge weight between vectors i and k, which is non-zero and less than or equal to 1 if it exists, and 0 otherwise. The functions C_{prox} and C_{conn} are special functions defined by:

$$C_{prox}(a, b) = \begin{Bmatrix} 1, \text{ if } a = b \\ -1, \text{ if } a \neq b \end{Bmatrix} \quad C_{conn}(a, b) = \begin{Bmatrix} -1, \text{ if } a = b \\ 1, \text{ if } a \neq b \end{Bmatrix} \tag{14}$$

which decide the direction forces act on the bit, depending on if the bits connected have the same or differing value. As proximal force should push a away from b's value, it will add tension to the system only if the bits aren't as far away as possible. Connective force works the other way around, so $C_{conn} = -C_{prox}$. Consider the sum of connective and proximal forces from Eqs. (12) and (13) (Fig. 1)):

$$F = \sum_{k} M_i W_{ik} C_{conn}(A_{ij}, A_{kj}) + \sum_{k} \frac{M_i M_k}{H_N(A_i, A_k)^2} C_{prox}(A_{ij}, A_{kj})$$

$$= \sum_{k=1, k \neq i}^{m} M_i C_{conn}(A_{ij}, A_{kj}) \left[W_{ik} - \frac{M_k}{H(A_i, A_k)^2} \right] \tag{15}$$

by substitution from (14). Thus, our total tension function to minimize is:

$$T(A) = \sum_{i=1}^{m} \sum_{j=1}^{n} \max \left(\sum_{k} M_i C_{conn}(A_{ij}, A_{kj}) \left[W_{ik} - \frac{M_k}{H(A_i, A_k)^2} \right], 0 \right) \quad (16)$$

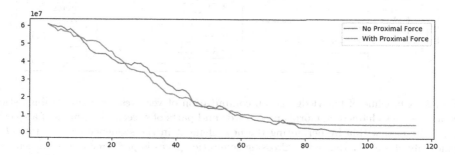

Fig. 1. Example minimization per random row of a randomly connected 50 node graph's binary vectors via the greedy method. Without proximal force it reaches 0.

We can see from (16) that (15) is the term to minimize across i and j to find perturbation X in (10). This can be found naïvely and greedily by randomly trying to flip bits with row-weighted probabilities from (15) for a particular vector and observing the change in total tension (16). Suppose you flip the first bit in a row that satisfies an adaptive threshold for the ratio of the row's tension it accounts for. The Many-Body problem prevents feasible computation of all Hamming Distances. We make the simplifying assumption that proximal force exists only for connected nodes. Then, one can efficiently compute the difference in forces for that row, and even the energies for all other rows affected, using simple ±1 of Hamming Distances. After flipping, the next bit in the row which gives a sufficient negative difference is found. The process repeats until no such bits can be found and a new row is randomly selected. Figure 1 shows the minimization of this technique for a randomly connected system. When proximal force is ignored, minimization to 0 is guaranteed. But unwanted singularities can occur on connected components, which proximal force avoids, although a minimum of 0 is not guaranteed. Minimization grows linearly with the number of nodes. This technique can be combined with Simulated Annealing and (self) supervised Q-Learning over rewards of minimization of (16), which can not only be online but also learn *how* to minimize (Fig. 2).

3.3 Incremental Life-Long Learning of Semantics

We now propose a general model for incremental, online learning of semantic binary vectors. Initially, suppose we have some form of raw inputs of data (unsupervised), whose possible values are discrete. For a working example, as

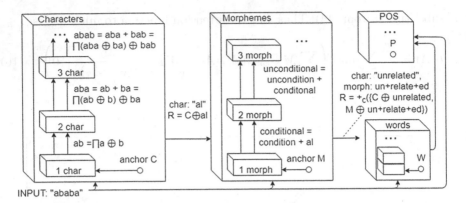

Fig. 2. A pipeline of knowledge graph computation of vertexes for a simple linguistic examples: raw characters, morphemes, words and parts of speech. Sequences of a space are embedded within by permuting the new element in the sequence with a static Π randomly chosen by the space. Crossing semantic spaces is performed by a consensus record on components of the relationship, where anchor vertexes are the fields.

shown in Fig. 2, let this be the space of characters in text. As input comes in to the system, we start off by letting each new character or character sequence have its own vertex and random binary vector (on order of $n = 10,000$ components). The space of characters is represented by a random, static vector C. As text is read as raw input, the system builds connections between characters by placing directed edges when two characters are next to each other. The weights of the edges are the probability of the transitioning occurring over the number of occurrences of the character. The number of observations of the characters become its "mass". Simultaneously, when the system is presented at least a sequence of 2 characters, it can form a binary vector representation for this via a random and static permutation Π, and (7). From the perspective of single characters, this is the position of sequences of 2 characters. Generally, for sequences of $l \geq 3$:

$$\zeta_{x_1}\zeta_{x_2}...\zeta_{x_l} = \zeta_{x_1}...\zeta_{x_{l-1}} + \zeta_{x_2}...\zeta_{x_l} \rightarrow \Pi(x_1...x_{l-1} \oplus x_2...x_{l-1}) \oplus x_2...x_l \quad (17)$$

is the position of an l sequence from the perspective of an $l - 1$ sequence.

More generally, in a growing knowledge graph, this is two directed arcs a and b coming together to a new vertex ab for the sequence. However, in the space of a sequence, co-occurrences between other similar length sequences can be recorded, and the tension in this system minimized for new binary vectors, to get a stronger representation. Here, ab is represented by a local vector c. Since we can compute a mapping between ab and c by $ab \oplus c$, subsequently bigger sequences should use this mapping. Frequencies from data and new edges in the knowledge graph are recorded this way until the model decides to minimize tension in each subsystem for new data. This process can be performed across other models on the data, as Fig. 2 shows. To map between data types, we compute a record R that binds each value to types as fields with (9). We can do this across different forms of raw data as well, as long as we have a model that will map other data types to raw data (such as a classifier or static model). This is shown for morphemes, words, and parts of speech in the figure, but this can be done from the space of images to linguistic data, or other forms of raw data.

Suppose a new, supervised model appears. Since mapping between data types is performed by records, we can easily add new information to it, as consensus sum is commutative. This is tolerant to incremental learning. Since the dynamic system for learning binary vectors proceeds arbitrarily, and edges/vertexes can be added to K quickly, this is also online and incremental. We can continue to add new models, read new data, and minimize tension in each system. If a model exists that adds edges across different data types, we can cross boundaries semantically and form more complicated data records. These can form hierarchical structures of semantic organization across many mediums of data.

4   Discussion and Conclusion

Semantic Vector Operations: Local Hamming Distance measures similarity for occupants of the same hierarchy, or from the perspective of a smaller sequence to a larger sequence. However, similarity across entire semantic spaces is a difficult, potential research area. Data records can isolate values of fields and compare their distances. We can also map ALL vertexes to the perspective of a space of concepts that all data belongs in. Since vectors start off random, it's possible to measure the likelihood of two vectors to be within a certain distance, as Kanerva [7] describes. XOR can also construct and deconstruct complex semantic concepts and get vectors for new data, or even unbound anchor points.

Self Improvement: Self benchmarking of semantic learning can be performed. If the nearest known neighbor for a data record with some missing fields is incorrect, the system has can leverage the knowledge graph and upscale the weights such that minimization of (16) makes it correct. So, if it fails often in one area, it can over-represent similar tests in the future, allowing targeted improvement. If incrementally trained enough, the system could form interesting questions for humans to answer, in order to learn relationships that are not easy to model. For example, if vectors are close, but share no knowledge graph edges, the system can predict the odds of this randomly happening to either be sure a relationship exists, or file it as a candidate relationship to cross-reference later. Thus, this lends itself to interacting with humans and asking useful questions.

Conclusion: We have proposed a novel, general theory for directly learning distributed binary semantic features from arbitrary data that can be put into the form of a knowledge graph, whether supervised or unsupervised, to incrementally learn high dimensional, semantic binary vectors online. This life-long learning is a promising technique for combining semantic knowledge across many existing models and raw data to build deep, useful, hierarchical representations. In future work, we hope to implement and test this model on at least linguistic and visual data in a manner that enables empirical testing of its properties.

References

1. Bordes, A., Usunier, N., Garcia-Duran, A., Weston, J., Yakhnenko, O.: Translating embeddings for modeling multi-relational data. In: Burges, C.J.C., Bottou, L., Welling, M., Ghahramani, Z., Weinberger, K.Q. (eds.) Advances in Neural Information Processing Systems, vol. 26, pp. 2787–2795. Curran Associates, Inc. (2013)
2. Bordes, A., Weston, J., Collobert, R., Bengio, Y.: Learning structured embeddings of knowledge bases. In: 25th Conference on Artificial Intelligence (AAAI), pp. 301–306 (2011)
3. Pereira da Silva, J.C., Freitas, A.: Towards an approximative ontology-agnostic approach for logic programs. In: Beierle, C., Meghini, C. (eds.) FoIKS 2014. LNCS, vol. 8367, pp. 415–432. Springer, Cham (2014). https://doi.org/10.1007/978-3-319-04939-7_21
4. Freitas, A., Curry, E.: Natural language queries over heterogeneous linked data graphs: a distributional-compositional semantics approach. In: Proceedings of the 19th International Conference on Intelligent User Interfaces, pp. 279–288. ACM (2014)
5. Freitas, A., da Silva, J.C., ORiain, S., Curry, E.: Distributional relational networks. In: 2013 AAAI Fall Symposium Series (2013)
6. Gougoux, F., Zatorre, R.J., Lassonde, M., Voss, P., Lepore, F.: A functional neuroimaging study of sound localization: visual cortex activity predicts performance in early-blind individuals. PLOS Biol. 3(2), e27 (2005)
7. Kanerva, P.: Hyperdimensional computing: an introduction to computing in distributed representation with high-dimensional random vectors. Cognit. Comput. 1(2), 139–159 (2009)
8. Kim, Y., Jernite, Y., Sontag, D., Rush, A.M.: Character-aware neural language models. In: AAAI, pp. 2741–2749 (2016)
9. Kohonen, T.: The self-organizing map. Proc. IEEE 78(9), 1464–1480 (1990). https://doi.org/10.1109/5.58325
10. Liu, T., Bargteil, A.W., O'Brien, J.F., Kavan, L.: Fast simulation of mass-spring systems. ACM Trans. Graph. (TOG) 32(6), 214 (2013)
11. Mikolov, T., Chen, K., Corrado, G., Dean, J.: Efficient estimation of word representations in vector space. CoRR abs/1301.3781 (2013)
12. Mikolov, T., Sutskever, I., Chen, K., Corrado, G.S., Dean, J.: Distributed representations of words and phrases and their compositionality. In: Advances in Neural Information Processing Systems, pp. 3111–3119 (2013)
13. Nickel, M., Murphy, K., Tresp, V., Gabrilovich, E.: A review of relational machine learning for knowledge graphs. Proc. IEEE 104(1), 11–33 (2016)
14. Yosinski, J., Clune, J., Bengio, Y., Lipson, H.: How transferable are features in deep neural networks? In: Advances in Neural Information Processing Systems, pp. 3320–3328 (2014)
15. Zhang, X., Zhao, J., LeCun, Y.: Character-level convolutional networks for text classification. In: Advances in Neural Information Processing Systems, pp. 649–657 (2015)

Cumulative Learning
with Causal-Relational Models

Kristinn R. Thórisson[1,3] and Arthur Talbot[1,2(✉)]

[1] Center for Analysis and Design of Intelligent Agents,
Reykjavik University, Reykjavik, Iceland
[2] Ecole normale supérieure Paris-Saclay, Cachan, France
`arthur.talbot@ens-paris-saclay.fr`
[3] Icelandic Institute for Intelligent Machines, Reykjavik, Iceland
`thorisson@ru.is`

Abstract. In the quest for artificial general intelligence (AGI), questions remain about what kinds of representations are needed for the kind of flexibility called for by complex environments like the physical world. A capacity for *continued* learning of *many domains* has yet to be realized, and proposals for how to achieve general performance improvement through continuous *cumulative learning*—while seemingly a necessary feature of any AGI—remain scarce.

In this paper we describe a cumulative learning mechanism that produces causal-relational models of its environment, to predict events and achieve goals. We show how such models, coupled with an appropriate *modeling process*, result in knowledge whose accuracy increases over time and can run continuously throughout the lifetime of an agent. The methods have been implemented, demonstrating learning of complex tasks and situated grammatically-correct natural language by observation. Here we focus on key theoretical principles of the modeling method and explain how effective cumulative learning is achieved.

Keywords: Artificial intelligence · Artificial general intelligence
Cumulative learning · Cumulative modeling · Causal relations
Models · Knowledge representation · Autonomous learning
Task-environment · Knowledge acquisition

1 Introduction

We see the existence of intelligence in nature as a practical solution for *limited time and resources* [17], and our efforts target practically viable methods for building artificial general intelligence (AGI) systems. While in this paper the primary focus is on theoretical aspects of *cumulative modeling*, which itself is a subset of cumulative learning, the larger context for this work is AGI systems that can handle the complexities of the physical world.

This work was funded by Reykjavik U. and IIIM, Iceland.

© Springer Nature Switzerland AG 2018
M. Iklé et al. (Eds.): AGI 2018, LNAI 10999, pp. 227–237, 2018.
https://doi.org/10.1007/978-3-319-97676-1_22

An environment E into which a goal-oriented agent is introduced can be seen to consist of a (potentially large) set of variables $\mathcal{V} = \{v_1, v_2, \ldots, v_{\|V\|}\}$ that represent all the things in the world that may hold a particular value and change over time, along with relations $\Re$ (causal, meteorological, etc.) between (some) of these variables, and dynamics functions $\mathcal{F}$, that together determine how those changes happen. Subsets $\{e_1 \ldots e_n \subset E = \langle \mathcal{V}, \mathcal{F}, \Re \rangle\}$ can be identified,[1] where relations, dynamic functions, values and value ranges, are of a special kind or of particular interest, representing what we collectively call *domains*, $\mathcal{D} \subset E$.[2]

As proven by Conant and Ashby's Good Regulator Theorem [1], to be an efficient survivor in a complex world, a learning mind must *necessarily* proceed by *modeling* its task environment. This means that any AGI system, being a learning controller of the most capable kind, will need a significant amount of models to operate effectively in the physical world. A *model set* $\mathcal{M}_D$ of $\mathcal{D}$ contains models of (parts of) the environment – information structures that together describe $\mathcal{D}$, to some level of accuracy.

A *cumulative modeler* CM in our conceptualization is a controller[3] that, guided by one or more top-level (internalized) goals G_{top}, implements a process whereby regularities are recursively extracted from E to construct models $\mathcal{M}_D$ of it [14] for the purposes of (*a*) making predictions about $\mathcal{D}$, and (*b*) achieving goals with respect to $\mathcal{D}$. In our approach models are explicit, and this is done via *forward* and *backward* chaining, respectively.

The kind of models we are talking about the agent creating are *bi-directional* in that a single model serves both purposes of prediction and goal achievement, and whenever a model is triggered (considered relevant for a situation) its usefulness for both purposes may be tested and evaluated. The ability of models to be used for predicting events from particular conditions, and planning active intervention, is a key feature of significant importance for the nature of the knowledge thus accumulated, as discussed below. In our approach, models can refer to other models to form hierarchies, so that compound phenomena can be represented, and equally importantly, so that the system can model itself (to implement *reflection* [14]). Knowledge is non-axiomatic and defeasible [13], so any old knowledge—even that which has repeatedly been shown to be useful—may be defeated by new knowledge that is more useful (better predictions and/or better goal achievement) and consistent with other models. New knowledge is automatically reconciled with old knowledge, and learning tends to be sped up due to prior knowledge (transfer learning [7,8]), without catastrophic interference/forgetting [2,4,6].

---

[1] We mean *any* sub-division of E, $e_n \subset E$, including sub-structures, component processes, whole-part relations, causal relations, etc.

[2] In any complex environment such as the physical world there will be innumerable ways of domain sub-divisions. The range of domains created from human-centric perspectives (e.g. transportation, electronics, home, commerce, clothing, etc.) demonstrate the utility of such sub-division.

[3] A controller is the process that dynamically couples knowledge and goals to obtain actions (or inaction) in an environment [14].

A *good* cumulative modeler is one which does not build its models haphazardly or randomly but in a way that achieves goals and predictions efficiently and effectively. Elsewhere we have argued that to do so the models must by necessity capture causal relations[4] Here we show why this must be the case.

Two forces are at work when improving knowledge represented as bi-directional models: (a) Improving the *precision* of the atomic models and, (b) increasing its *scope* by covering as many variables as possible with the models.

The mechanisms we present show that the models created by a good cumulative modeler will, over time, increase their usefulness in guiding the system's behavior – the cumulative nature of the modeling means that while it is ongoing the system continues to improve its knowledge of the environment [15]. A cumulative learner's capabilities, as a result, grow incrementally over time, in relatively small but frequent steps, to ultimately cover a wide range of tasks.[5] This is important because when the modeler makes itself the subject of the modeling, it can potentially also improve itself—implementing what has been called *bounded recursive self-improvement* [9]—in a safe, incremental fashion.

2   Agent and Task-Environment

In the physical world, some of the environment's variables are observable, $\mathcal{V}_o \subset \mathcal{V}$, some are manipulatable, $\mathcal{V}_m \subset \mathcal{V}$, and some are related via causal links such that changing one variable will affect another.

An agent situated in an environment (Fig. 1) consists of a controller (c) that hosts a modeling process (P_M) capable of generating causal-relational models $\mathcal{M}$ of the environment through experience, testing their validity through observation and direct intervention in the environment. The agent has a perception cone through which it can receive input from observable variables ($\mathcal{V}_o$) and actuators through which it can affect the state of manipulatable variables ($\mathcal{V}_m$). At any point in time these will be limited to a subset of the total set of observ-

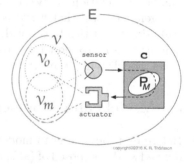

Fig. 1. An agent situated in an environment (E) consists of a controller (c) that hosts a modeling process (P_M) capable of generating causal-relational models of the environment through experience.

able and manipulatable variables due to I/O bandwidth and its specific location. If the world is highly asymmetric—that is, features of any of its part in one area are highly dissimilar to features in other areas—make any acquired knowledge

---

[4] Any reliable and repeatable regularity in a world is considered a causal relation, irrespective of whether it is observable or not, or truly deterministic or not [3].

[5] The speed of accurate model building is of course of critical importance for any real world implementation, determined in part by the details of the implementation methods and the nature of the task-environment; in this paper, however, the primary focus is on theoretical aspects of the modeling process.

heavily dependent on an agent's localization; highly self-similar worlds will not make knowledge generation dependent on agent position.

In our conceptualization, a cumulative learner will proceed to create models of the relations between observed variables. If V_1 and V_2 are both variables of the world, linked by the relation $V_1 R V_2$, with $R \in \Re$, what the model "claims" is a causal link between O_1 and O_2, the observable parts of V_1 and V_2. For instance, if A is the result of the observation of O_1 and B is the result of the (subsequent) observation of O_2, then the model represents a (hypothesized) causal relation between A and B, i.e. $A \Rightarrow B$ (and indirectly, that V_1 caused V_2).

Of the set of variables $\mathcal{V}$ in any complex environment such as the physical world, only a fraction are observable, and even a smaller fraction of those are observable in any given time interval. An event involving an observed relationship between any two or more variables, where for that time interval some relevant variables are unobservable, will make it indistinguishable from a partially random relationship, even if it is fully deterministic "under the hood". Same goes with the manipulatable variables $\mathcal{V}_m$: they only represent a fraction of the variables of the world, and may not be a strict subset of $\mathcal{V}_o$, as actions of the agent may have unobservable effects.

This means that for any world with a very small ratio of $\mathcal{V}_o / \mathcal{V}$, a large number of relations between observable variables will seem "probabilistic" to an agent—even if that world is fully deterministic (i.e. all related variables are truly deterministically coupled). Therefore, an agent in such environments will neither be able to model its task-environment perfectly nor fully, and a number of its models will be incorrect some of the time.[6]

3 Models and Modeler

Before even beginning to model, our cumulative modeler must be given a well-defined *seed*, composed of (at least) one top-level goal G_{top}, one model connecting this goal to an observable variable, one model acting on a manipulative variable, and one primitive action to take. This is really the theoretical minimum – practical implementations will contain quite a bit more; the more complete and thorough the seed is the easier it will be for the system to bootstrap and start learning. If the seed does not reference anything that the system can measure the system won't be able to evaluate the results of its actions, and thus cannot grow its model set. The same goes for goals (the seed must contain at least one concrete objective to attain) and executable actions (there must be at least one

---

[6] It should be noted that causal relations cannot be replaced by probabilities. Pearl [12] (p. 36) states: "...*causality deals with how probability functions change in response to influences (e.g., new conditions or interventions) that originate from outside the probability space, while probability theory, even when given a fully specified joint density function on all (temporally-indexed) variables in the space, cannot tell us how that function would change under such external influences. Thus, 'doing' is not reducible to 'seeing', and there is no point trying to fuse the two together.*".

action the system can perform). The smaller the seed, other things being equal, the longer the system will take to bootstrap its knowledge.

When the agent is inserted into the environment its modeling process starts generating models using information in the seed. This proceeds by noting correlations in the stimuli coming in through the senses (including sensations related to the agent's own end-effectors), and for any $A \Rightarrow B$ pair, where A precedes B in time, creating a model that predicts what may happen when you see an A, and suggesting that when you want a B you may want to make A happen.

The modeler must have the ability to round up the relevant models at any point in time. This is done by the agent's *scheduling process*. If there are too many models models for the controller to sort through, the threshold for any model to be considered relevant to the present moment could be increased, thus decreasing the total number of models the system must work with at any point in time. The speed at which this can be done directly affects a controller's ability to bring the right knowledge to bear on any situation, as it determines how many models the controller can consider during forward (deduction) and backward chaining (abduction). This is important because it specifies, respectively: the controller's capacity to consider (*a*) alternative futures (by triggering various different models that look promising for predicting next events based on e.g. the current state) and (*b*) alternative ways of achieving goals (by searching through models abductively to find plausible paths through which any state may have been formed). While these do not bear directly on our arguments in this paper, they are of great importance when considering practical implementation of these mechanisms.

3.1   Structure of Causal-Relational Models

Our concept of a *causal-relational model* is used here in a specific way; prior work provides detailed examples of how such models may be implemented [9,11], while here we are more concerned with the theory of such models.

Models are executable information structures encoding procedural knowledge and are either provided up front (by the designer) in a seed or created by the modeler – with the latter set becoming much larger than the former over time. The models our cumulative modeler creates are composed of a left-hand term (LT) and a right-hand term (RT). The LT (the "input") refers to a preconditional pattern, composed of values, variables, ranges, etc., that make the model relevant[7] for a particular situation (via pattern matching); the RT represent the post-conditions of the terms the model refers to. When the LT pattern is observed, a prediction based on the RT pattern is produced. In this forward-chaining process a set of models compute predictions on given LT inputs via deduction. For instance, if a model takes two consecutive $\{x,y\}$ coordinates of the path of a Pong ball and computes its next position using a linear transformation formula, this is a prediction of a future state of a particular entity

---

[7] Relevance is determined at "the top" by top-level goals, and at the "bottom" by incoming stimuli through sensors; in between the pattern matching on the models' LT and RT determines their relevance.

(the ball) in particular circumstances (moving along a path, i.e. correct until the ball hits something). A good model will thus produce a true prediction using valid deduction.

Reciprocally, when an instance of a model's RT pattern is observed that is a goal, a sub-goal patterned after its LT pattern is produced. In this case backward-chaining answers the question "how could RT be achieved?". Models produce sub-goals when super-goals match their RT pattern, these sub-goals in turn match other models' RT pattern until – unless the chaining is halted for some reason – a sub-goal produces a command for execution by I/O devices.

When an input other than a goal or a prediction matches its RT, an assumption is produced, based on the LT. In either case the task of the scheduler is to find the model(s) whose RT matches the state, and reading the model "in reverse" by looking at its LT. This constitutes generating abduction hypotheses, answering the question "how might the RT have come about?".

After a model is used we check to see whether the predicted outcome was correct or not; each model stores the number of correct uses over the total number of uses, whose ratio is used to determine the preference for which model should be chosen when an input matches the LT (when forward chaining, RT when backward chaining) of two or more models.

Models further contain two sets of functions that compute values for variables featured in the RT, from the values held by variables in the LT (one set for forward and another for backward execution).

4   Modeling Process for Cumulative Learning

Now we describe the basic operations of a canonical cumulative learner, and show that by generating small modifications to existing models and testing these through observation and manipulation, the modeling process implements cumulative learning.

The modeling process consists of two sets of models $\mathcal{M}$ and $\mathcal{M}_{hyp}$, and their interactions with the environment E (Fig. 2). The first set, $\mathcal{M}$, is used to compute and predict the state of the system. This set of models interacts directly with the environment: it receives informations from some observable variables in the world and can act on some variables (the manipulatable ones), as explained in the preceding section.

The second set, $\mathcal{M}_{hyp}$, is the "experimentation lab" of the modeler, whose purpose is to test new models without interfering with the environment. Models of this set are variations of those from $\mathcal{M}$. These variations are based on alternative *contextualization*, hypothesized *generalization*, and proposed *compression* of existing models. Models in $\mathcal{M}_{hyp}$ are tested as the environment and $\mathcal{M}$ interact. When a model $M_1 \in \mathcal{M}$ is triggered, we will test what would have happened if it would have been replaced by its variation, $M_1' \in \mathcal{M}_{hyp}$. A comparison of the model set using the new model versus the original one determines whether the new model is deleted (if it produces no improvement or is simply wrong), or is added in $\mathcal{M}$ (if a performance improvement over the original set is detected).

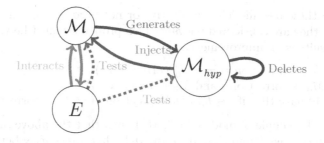

Fig. 2. Interactions between the different sets of the system (see text).

The original model M_1 may then be deleted from the sandbox or kept (if, for some contexts not addressed by the new model, the original one is still useful).

The initiation to generate a new model M_0' is the triggering of a model M_0 in $\mathcal{M}$ (i.e. it is considered relevant for the present state). Depending on the actual usefulness of M_0 in the present situation (for prediction and/or intervention), the modeler will create (at least one) variation of M_0 in $\mathcal{M}_{hyp}$. If M_0's prediction is correct, the modeler will try to make it more general by removing some of the constraints in its LT, in an attempt to make it more general. If M_0's prediction is incorrect, models will be created with the observed outcome as output (targeting the same observation) and more specific input than M_0, making it less general. In this case M_0 may still be relevant and is not deleted.

When several models are used in series they may be compressed into a single model with a more detailed or specific input. While not improving $\mathcal{M}$'s coverage (scope), reducing model count may increase the modeler's runtime efficiency.

4.1   Description of Modifications

The key to the idea of proving that our cumulative modeler is a good one is to show that each of the small modifications will result in a small improvement of the system. To do so, we will detail each of the modifications and explain why—should the modification be shown to be a good one—injecting it in $\mathcal{M}$ will improve the ability of the system to predict and achieve goals in $\mathcal{D} \subset E$ due to the models in $\mathcal{M}$ matching more closely actual relationships between variables in $\mathcal{D}$.

Contextualization. New models will be created when a triggered model $M_0 \in \mathcal{M}$ produces incorrect predictions (they could be incomplete, partially correct, or totally wrong). What we want in this case is, if I is the set of all inputs that M_0 was triggered on, to partition it into two sets I_0 and I_1. Then the original model M_0 will be transformed in M_0^0. It will be the same as M_0 with a LT that will only match inputs in I_0. A new model M_0^1 will also be created, with a LT that match I_1, and the RT that was just witnessed.

Whether these new models are effective or not becomes known when a state arises where they are considered relevant. Two properties must be verified to say that this results is an improvement.

- If $i \in I_1$, (M_0 correct on i) $\Rightarrow$ (M_0^1 correct on i)
- $\exists i \in I_1$,(M_0^1 is correct on i and M_0 is wrong on i)
- We already have that if $i \in I_0$, (M_0 correct on i) $\Rightarrow$ (M_0^0 correct on i)

If one can find a couple of models (M_0^0, M_0^1) such that the above properties are verified, then one has found a couple of models that are strictly better than the original one M_0.

Generalization/Induction. Another case of new model creation is when a model M_0 from $\mathcal{M}$ is triggered, and its prediction is correct. New models that are more generic will then be created, with the same RT output as M_0, but with LT inputs that are less specific (suppression/deletion of input variables, greater range of values, variables replacing values, etc.). To be injected into $\mathcal{M}$ a model thus created should be as efficient on the LT input where M_0 is correct, and work well on other inputs not specified in M_0's LT. The new model should be verified to not interfere with existing models in $\mathcal{M}$. If that's the case, and the model is failing on inputs that are caught by other models, it should be modified to prevent it form competing with such existing models.

When it is verified that the new model is more general than M_0, it will then simply replace it in $\mathcal{M}$. When evaluating this change in $\mathcal{M}$, what we want to verify is simply that the new model works "better" than the old one. Here, working "better" has three implications:

- M_0 is correct on input i $\Rightarrow$ M_0' is correct on input i. This is ensured by the fact that M_0' LT is simply a less specific version of the one on M_0.
- M_0' is correct on input i, and i did not trigger M_0. This is ensured by the fact that if M_0' was moved from $\mathcal{M}_{hyp}$ to $\mathcal{M}$ it has been tested to be correct on such inputs.
- There is no input i on which M_0' will make incorrect predictions that would have been caught correctly by other models in $\mathcal{M}$. This is ensured by checking that M_0' does not interfere with existing adjacent models (that have variables in common).

Compression. The last case of creating new model(s) is when several small models $(M_i)_{i \in [|0,n|]}$ are compressed into a single bigger one, and when a model sequence (M_0, then M_1, etc.) is replaced with a new model that has as its input a mix of the input variables from $M_0, \ldots, M_{n-1}$, and the same output as M_n. Models should be added in $\mathcal{M}$ only if they are at least as correct as the original ones. The objective of such compression is not to achieve a better model than the original ones but rather to reduce computational requirements.

This modification category is somewhat less important than those above and should only be used if it is desired to have a greater number of more specific models, rather than a lower number of more generic ones. This represents, however, a general way to tune resource usage [5] and can be done when faster results are desired. The original models can of course in all cases be kept and strategically retrieved, e.g. should more precision be needed or more computational resources become available.

4.2 Producing Causal-Relational Models

Due to the bi-directionality of the models they will tend towards capturing true causal relations between variables of the environment. To see why, consider the situation where a cause A has two effects, B and C (Fig. 3). We assume that to the modeler A appears before B and C, but B and C appear together. Four models could be used to describe what is observed every time we see an A:

1. Model M_1: $B \Rightarrow C$
2. Model M_2: $C \Rightarrow B$
3. Model M_3: $A \Rightarrow B$
4. Model M_4: $A \Rightarrow C$

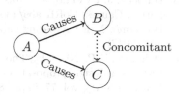

Any of these models will predict correctly: If you see B you will see C, and vice versa; if you see A you will see B and C. However, not all of them can be used to achieve goals in the

Fig. 3. Example causal relations between A, B and C.

domain of A, B and C: If you want to stop seeing C it does not help to remove B, or vice versa – due to the causal structure of this task-environment, only model M_4 will help. Thus, when each of these models is used for both prediction and goal achievement models M_1 and M_2 will be deleted due to their incorrect predictions. What remains are M_3 and M_4, the only models that capture actual causal relations in the domain, to the extent that this can be represented as relationships between *observable* variables.

Each modification of the model set in $\mathcal{M}$, using the methods above, makes them more reliable within a given sub-domain $\mathcal{M}_\mathcal{D}$. Repeated usage and testing of the models increases the overall reliability in small steps, as they capture the target phenomena. The system is continuously trying to improve each of its models, hypothetically reaching the maximum precision allowed by the environment and the allowed time and resources. When this point is reached, every phenomenon is modeled as well as possible.

5   Conclusion

We have presented a modeling process that implements a good cumulative modeler, improving continuously to eventually be able to operate in a wide range of task-environments. Based on combined abduction and deduction over causal-relational models, the methods described have been implemented and tested [9–11,16], producing notable results not demonstrated by other learning systems. While important questions about practical issues remain to be investigated, e.g. the extent of its generality and scaling, this paper demonstrates that the basic principles are relatively clear and concise and meet the criteria for cumulative learning. Our results so far indicate that these ideas are significantly different from most other approaches, and potentially a promising approach to achieving AGI.

References

1. Conant, R.C., Ashby, W.R.: Every good regulator of a system must be a model of that system†. Int. J. Syst. Sci. **1**(2), 89–97 (1970)
2. French, R.M.: Catastrophic forgetting in connectionist networks: causes, consequences and solutions. Trends Cogn. Sci. **3**(4), 128–135 (1999)
3. Halpern, J.Y., Pearl, J.: Causes and explanations: A structural-model approach – part 1: Causes. CoRR abs/1301.2275 (2013). http://arxiv.org/abs/1301.2275
4. Hasselmo, M.E.: Avoiding catastrophic forgetting. Trends Cogn. Sci. **21**(6), 407–408 (2017)
5. Helgason, H.P., Nivel, E., Thórisson, K.R.: On attention mechanisms for AGI architectures:a design proposal. In: Bach, J., Goertzel, B., Iklé, M. (eds.) AGI 2012. LNCS (LNAI), vol. 7716, pp. 89–98. Springer, Heidelberg (2012). https://doi.org/10.1007/978-3-642-35506-6_10
6. Kirkpatrick, J., et al.: Overcoming catastrophic forgetting in neural networks. Proc. Nat. Acad. Sci. **114**(13), 3521–3526 (2017)
7. Lazaric, A.: Transfer in reinforcement learning: a framework and a survey. In: Wiering, M., van Otterlo, M. (eds.) Reinforcement Learning. Adaptation, Learning, and Optimization, vol. 12, pp. 143–173. Springer, Heidelberg (2012). https://doi.org/10.1007/978-3-642-27645-3_5
8. Lu, J., Behbood, V., Hao, P., Zuo, H., Xue, S., Zhang, G.: Transfer learning using computational intelligence: a survey. Knowl.-Based Syst. **80**, 14–23 (2015)
9. Nivel, E., et al.: Bounded Recursive Self-Improvement. Technical RUTR-SCS13006. Reykjavik University Department of Computer Science, Reykjavik, Iceland (2013)
10. Nivel, E., Thórisson, K.R., Steunebrink, B., Schmidhuber, J.: Anytime bounded rationality. In: Bieger, J., Goertzel, B., Potapov, A. (eds.) AGI 2015. LNCS (LNAI), vol. 9205, pp. 121–130. Springer, Cham (2015). https://doi.org/10.1007/978-3-319-21365-1_13
11. Nivel, E., et al.: Bounded seed-AGI. In: Goertzel, B., Orseau, L., Snaider, J. (eds.) AGI 2014. LNCS (LNAI), vol. 8598, pp. 85–96. Springer, Cham (2014). https://doi.org/10.1007/978-3-319-09274-4_9
12. Pearl, J.: Bayesianism and causality, or, why I am only a half-Bayesian. In: Corfield, D., Williamson, J. (eds.) Foundations of bayesianism. Applied Logic Series, vol. 24, pp. 19–36. Springer, Dordrecht (2001). https://doi.org/10.1007/978-94-017-1586-7_2
13. Pollock, J.L.: Defeasible reasoning and degrees of justification. Argum. Comput. **1**(1), 7–22 (2010)
14. Steunebrink, B.R., Thórisson, K.R., Schmidhuber, J.: Growing recursive self-improvers. In: Steunebrink, B., Wang, P., Goertzel, B. (eds.) AGI 2016. LNCS (LNAI), vol. 9782, pp. 129–139. Springer, Cham (2016). https://doi.org/10.1007/978-3-319-41649-6_13

15. Thórisson, K.R., Kremelberg, D., Steunebrink, B.R., Nivel, E.: About understanding. In: Steunebrink, B., Wang, P., Goertzel, B. (eds.) AGI 2016. LNCS (LNAI), vol. 9782, pp. 106–117. Springer, Cham (2016). https://doi.org/10.1007/978-3-319-41649-6_11
16. Thórisson, K.R., et al.: Autonomous acquisition of situated natural communication. Comput. Sci. Inf. Syst. **9**(2), 115–131 (2014). outstanding Paper Award
17. Wang, P.: Insufficient knowledge and resources - a biological constraint and its functional implications. In: AAAI Fall Symposium: Biologically Inspired Cognitive Architectures. Citeseer (2009)

Transforming Kantian Aesthetic Principles into Qualitative Hermeneutics for Contemplative AGI Agents

Jeremy O. Turner[(⊠)] [ID] and Steve DiPaola[(⊠)] [ID]

Simon Fraser University, Vancouver, BC V6B 5K3, Canada
{jot,sdipaola}@sfu.ca

Abstract. This paper introduces an interdisciplinary qualitative hermeneutic approach to the engineering and computer science methodological paradigm(s) for assessing a contemplative-agent's cognitive capabilities at a level corresponding to Artificial General Intelligence (AGI). This paper has utilized cognitive intensity levels from Kantian aesthetic philosophy to qualitatively re-address Russell and Norvig's canonical agent-categories as they scale upward towards AGI cognition levels. These Kantian levels allow the AGI-agent designer to consider the cognitive interplay between computational representations of the imagination and reason as they relate to motivationally-nuanced teleological notions of self-interest versus disinterestedness. While the AGI level is the thematic focus, lower intensity levels are also introduced in order to set the appropriate cognitive benchmarks for higher levels corresponding to truly contemplative AGI-agents. This paper first contextualizes Kant's analytical framework before discussing the appropriately corresponding agent-categories. This paper concludes with a brief discussion of the particular methodological and hermeneutic contribution of Kant's aesthetic philosophical framework to the AGI domain.

Keywords: AGI · Contemplation · Aesthetic philosophy · Agents

1 Introduction

Artificial General Intelligence (AGI) promises that one day, an artificially created agent will be sufficiently intelligent to be able to theoretically become competent in any computer-tractable expert domain. Interestingly, hermeneutic analysis of how such minds might become capable of interdisciplinary competency are primarily being handled methodologically by mechanistically-focused computer science and cognitive engineering disciplines. As cognitive science is an umbrella mega-discipline that includes AGI, there remains a contribution within the AGI community to try to make interdisciplinary correlations and unify hermeneutic understandings of the intelligent agent categories and their cognitive affordances with other cognitive science related disciplines. Within the related cognitive science of philosophy is the sub-discipline of aesthetic philosophy. At first glance, considering principles from a humanities-driven sub-discipline such as aesthetic philosophy would seem thematically orthogonal to the

© Springer Nature Switzerland AG 2018
M. Iklé et al. (Eds.): AGI 2018, LNAI 10999, pp. 238–247, 2018.
https://doi.org/10.1007/978-3-319-97676-1_23

mechanistic and technological cognitive categorization of artificially intelligent agents. However, this paper shows examples of how interdisciplinary hermeneutic correlations can indeed be made between Kantian aesthetic philosophy [1] and canonical intelligent-agent categories [2]. We proceed by first contextualizing and explaining Kant's analytical framework before discussing the appropriately corresponding agent-categories. This hermeneutic analysis concludes with a brief reflection on the particular methodological and hermeneutic contribution of Kant's aesthetic philosophical framework to the AGI disciplinary domain.

1.1 The Kantian Approach to Cognitive Intensification

Intelligent agent categories are scaled upward to indicate an agent's gradually acquired capabilities to deeply contemplate a world-model from which derived goals and values of those goals (i.e. utilities) can be learned from either through, reason, imagination, or empirical experience regardless of semantics originating from a particular task-domain. A more generally intelligent artificial agent should occasionally consider solutions to problems that reside outside of its immediate self-interest. Kant's aesthetic intensity levels are categorized according to a motivational spectrum that ranges from an agent acting in its own self-interest to engaging in disinterested contemplation for its own sake. Contemplation can be intensified in a similar way that an agent's intellectual aptitude can increase. Kant's aesthetic intensities are based on an agent being able to cognitively and rationally parse an artificially represented imagination (including having to reason about an external world-model). In this sense, Kantian aesthetic intensities are cognitive intensities involving a dynamic interplay with computational representations of imagination and reason. An agent would need to function at increasingly higher intelligence-categories to be able to mechanistically parse each intensity relating to contemplating this cognitive acceleration of imagination and reasonable estimation without functional overload and/or paralysis. The interpretation of aesthetic principles for AGI can be properly understood once the reader has internalized Kant's philosophical definitions of the imagination and reason. The cognitive interplay between philosophical faculties of imagination and reason in particular, form the basis for understanding the most contemplatively involved aesthetic intensity which can only really be properly comprehended by an AGI-agent – the transcendent sublime.

Kantian and Computational Representations of the "Imagination". The Kantian interpretation of the imagination is sometimes conflated with "intellectual intuition" [4, p. 186]. Kant's considers the imagination to be a highly qualitative and semantically generative cognitive process. The contents or inspiration of the imagination can involve: fictional, functional, or fantasy elements and can be derived from sensory empirical phenomena or from the platonic realm of pure ideas (i.e. noumena). Unlike reason, the imagination involves comprehending (understanding) or reflecting on either perceptual phenomena or ideal noumena rather than trying to practically apprehend (calculate or numerically judge) a phenomenon's or noumenon's precise properties. To imaginatively comprehend something that has entered our internal or external perception, Kant believes that we make a subjective determination of phenomenon's or noumenon's ultimate nature and teleological purpose [4, p. 178]. Reflection is a key contemplative meta-faculty when considering the imagination because "[…] *the apprehension of forms by the imagination could never occur if reflective judgment did not compare them"* [1, pp. 29–30].

In the AI discipline, the "imagination" is defined as *"the* [contemplative] *manipulation of information* [mental imagery] *that is not directly available to an agent's sensors"* [5, p. 743]. Artificial imagination as currently implemented usually pertains to an agent's capacity to simulate a task from its problem-space into its semantic and episodic memory banks for future retrieval [5]. The current goal for handling, storing and predicting these imagined states is through the eventual implementation of a prospective memory [6]. A computational representation of imagination can include: a predicted/prospective generative percept-stream (future states, operators, probability distributions, actions etc.) and/or simulated input-output procedure that has some portion existing outside of or beyond (or in parallel to) the agent's sensory apparatus; or a form of creative-reinterpretation (or misinterpretation) of pre-existing sensory data. Imagination can be a semantically interpreted percept-stream (various parallel ontological descriptions of: states, operators, actions etc.) that has some portion existing outside of or beyond (or in parallel to) the agent's sensory apparatus. The semantic interpretation of this percept-stream might not directly address the raw data or hypotheses inferred by the agent's sensory apparatus. An agent's imagination might contain purely generative (imagined) information content for rationalization or prediction without any empirical grounding in the sensed data. Alternately, an agent might use its imagination to provide its own idiosyncratic semantic interpretation of the received empirical sense data. An agent can also use an artificially created imagination faculty to modulate its hard-coded rationality. For example, an agent can dynamically modify its ontology and its list of competency questions when expecting or predicting new percepts from its situated environment. Such dynamic self-modifications can rapidly occur even without the encouragement provided by immediate access to explicit empirical evidence. To address the imaginative context; these questions must address and/or approximate task-domain knowledge that is hypothetical, simulated (i.e. approximate symbolic representations being rehearsed in a computational imagination), or speculative (even fictional). In order to utilize the computational equivalent of an imagination, an agent's set of competency questions and expected answers should be abstracted from its observable utility in a particular environment for internal deliberation. For example, an agent might use a terminal pointer, symbol or chunking mechanism to compress recently acquired episodic data into an imagined rule procedure that could be used in a future interaction scenario. This "imagined" data can be cross-referenced with its knowledge-base (KB) and ontology [e.g. 18] in order to determine how reasonable the imagined semantic content might be. The competency questions themselves might also use the "imagination" for inspiration and be formulated without any grounded basis in pre-observed empirical data. Over time, the agent will compare imagined or simulated contemplation scenarios with those that it empirically perceives from its sensory environment. Regardless of how they are originally formulated, an agent's competency questions will be eventually formulated such that an agent can learn to semantically reify empirically sensed: subjects, predicates, intrinsic rewards and/or objects. The process of reification itself is understood to mean the idea of transforming an imaginary concept into something "real" and therefore, something computable and reasonable. Such reifications would be continuously updated within the agent's Ontology and KB.

Kantian and Computational Representations of "Reasonable Estimation". Kant has dedicated two books towards discussing the earthly and transcendent intricacies of the faculty of reason as it relates to sensation and cognition [3, p. 1788]. The Kantian definition of reason here has been restricted to narrow the focus on an understanding of reason in terms of artificial intelligence. Kant basically felt that reason can be subdivided into two categories, "pure" (i.e. speculative) logical reason based on a priori knowledge [3, p. 15] and practical (i.e. action-centric) reason based on direct empirical experience [3, p. 267]. Logical reason could seem to mathematically estimate ideas independent of empirical experience. Kant, however, still ensured that logical reason could also be contingent on grounded representational associations with concepts and analogies drawn from empirical experience (i.e. sensation) [3, p. 132; 7, p. 25]. Anything contemplated outside of these grounded representational associations would likely be beyond the realm of pure and practical realms of reason but still well within the visually inspired realm of the imagination – which harmonizes these representations with the things-in-themselves [3, p. 103]. Computational definitions of reason typically address mathematical representation and estimation but can involve: a pre-cached knowledge-schema (e.g. slot/terminal assignments, operation procedures); the agent's ontological commitment towards a particular task, story-world, or knowledge domain; a current performance measure progress and evaluation results conforming to a well-defined (and possibly hard-coded) utility function combined with the expected probability-distribution of an incoming percept-stream; and a consistent and persistent semantic interpretation of empirical sense data which can be verified by the scientific process, hard-coded interpretations and the faculty of mathematical estimation [2, 7, 10]. Computational reason mostly draws from procedural and semantic memory stores. Prospective memory storage can also be useful when predicting a new probability distribution. With the third definition in particular, a rational agent's performance measure would also be influenced by competency questions. A reasonable agent must constantly ask new competency questions so that it continually evaluate and update its ontology (imagined world-model) in a stochastic real-time environment [7]. During this query-updating process, the agent might also maintain a reasonable level of competency via maintaining a pointer that continually refers back to its (hopefully) well-defined original utility function and policy. Having competency questions answered with empirical evidence will conserve ontological continuity and deterministic consistency [8]. Regardless of whether these questions were hard-coded by a programmer or self-coded by the agent; rationally optimal questions will already address task-domain procedural, episodic and/or semantic knowledge within the agent's ontology/KB slot terminals. Some of this knowledge is tautological.

Reason in computational terms ranges from mundane activities such as searching in a look-up table to situation calculus and hierarchical planning procedures [10, p. 27]. Reasonable knowledge-queries about the world involve: discrete subjects, predicates, objects, extrinsic rewards and rules as they are not updated continuously. All memory banks come into play when the agent when addresses "reasonable" questions but the most commonly located memory banks for this process are procedural and semantic. Therefore, this list of competency questions must engage known formulas (e.g. math equations, more constants than variables and [first-order] logic theorems) and peer-reviewed empirical evidence about the worlds the agent wishes to address and become competent within. There are expectations for retrieval-time once these questions are asked by the agent. Optimization algorithms are preferred to ensure latency and memory consumption is minimized. Ultimately, a rational agent can be understood as carrying out an established utility function and a policy with the goal of summing a maximum number of environmental-rewards that are tallied up until the end of the agent's finite lifetime.

2   Kantian Cognitive Intensities from Aesthetic Philosophy

Kantian cognitive intensities are more suitable for addressing AGI mind-component configurations than with his immediate predecessors (e.g. Burke, 1756). Edmund Burke's conception of the sublime intensity, for example, is limited to involving proto-intelligent representations and affective responses based on fear and the agent's need for safety rather than on cognitive interactivity [10]. Kant, conversely, identified cognitive intensity levels from aesthetic philosophy which can also be hermeneutically mapped to the artificial mind-design of rational and deliberative agents. The lowest intensity can be mapped to the least intelligent agent-category while the highest Kantian intensity could only be addressed by a robust AGI-agent [2]. Two of the Kantian intensities (i.e. the good and the strange) correspond less to intellectual capabilities and more to deontic processes (i.e. the former) and solely to aesthetic contemplation (i.e. the latter). For this reason, those two levels will be disregarded from this AGI cognitive capability discussion. The scope will also be limited to focuses on one polarity valence. For example, while the beautiful intensity possesses its inverse valence, the ugly, this awareness of opposite aesthetic valences does not contribute to the overall understanding of how Kantian aesthetic intensity levels can be mapped towards cognitive capability requirements for AGI-agents.

The following Table 1 will therefore show diverse categorical gradations of cognitive intensities that will discuss moderate (agreeable) to the highest intellectual affordances (transcendent sublime). These intensity categories begin to diverge towards AGI intelligence levels once the agent contains and understands computational representations that allow to the agent's mind to act according to more disinterested teleological imperatives rather than single-mindedly through its own immediate self-interest (as stated by the programmer). Only the latter two disinterested intensities apply directly to AGI-level intelligence so these will be focused on the most in this paper. The lowest (first) intensity level has been omitted as it only describes pre-intellectual capabilities for handling rudimentary domestic-level routine tasks.

Table 1. Kantian cognitive (aesthetic) intensities and associated agent-categories

Agent level	Cognitive intensity level	Priorities
Pre-AI, AI	**Mundane**	N/A
AI (state-of-the-art)	**Agreeable**	Self-interest, reason
AI, Proto-AGI, AGI	**Beautiful**	Disinterest, imagination
Up to/including AGI	**Transcendent Sublime**	Imagination > reason

2.1   The Agreeable (State-of-the-Art AI)

This second Kantian level operates at the baseline where most readers would consider an agent to be "intelligent". An agreeable agent will have computational components such as goals, reinforcement signal processors, and crude metacognitive structuring that represent a rudimentary sense of self in order to be rewarded for thinking about and acting within its own world model-specified "self-interest". However, this intensity is primarily sustained in only those agents that exclusively pursue limited self-interested pursuits. Agents that single-mindedly pursue limited interests are conventionally represented as narrow AI rather than as agents more acclimatized to general intellectual contemplation (i.e. AGIs). It is this intensity where an agent will be explicitly programmed to optimize a self-interested balance between computational representations of imagination and reasonable estimation. In an agreeable agent's mind, a superficial processing of semantics and some rudimentary awareness – at least of production rules as well as finite-states and available actions within each state - would come into play (more so than with a mundane reactive mind, at least). This agreeable agent would spend cognitive resources deliberating over what was semantically essential, functionally practical, and/or computationally robust (agreeable) versus that which was semantically irrelevant, cognitively dissonant, and/or computationally taxing (disagreeable). Explicit functional interactivity serves as the rubric for any experience of cognitive interactivity at this level. One identifying feature of this particular intensity when it comes to contemplative purposes is that everything is practically contemplated for the agent's self-interest (i.e. intended functionality). Interestingly, an agreeable agent's mind might not necessarily require an explicitly represented self-concept in order to act in its best "self-interest". This level of contemplation would ensure though that this agent mentally optimizes its intelligence modules and/or processes (i.e. algorithms) in such a way that it can carry out the most functional and practical decisions and/or actions. It is also possible that an agreeable agent would focus on empirical output and related behavioral output, perhaps even with the intent of successfully faking an AGI-agent's ability to function at deeper mentalist aspects of cognition [11, 12]. This level of contemplative intensity exclusively focuses on common-sense and mostly rational functional interactivity even for more imaginative cognitive deliberations. Agreeable agent-minds should not think up (imagine) or contemplate anything that it cannot potentially act upon in a particular world. Additionally, this agreeable agent's mind should not waste computational time-cycles contemplating any more conceivable inputs than what can be immediately perceived from an empirically derivable source. At this intensity level, semantic layers (esp. explicit knowledge types and conceivably alternate inferences) are only contemplated for functional and practical ends. Overthinking and deep-thinking are discouraged from agent-mind contemplation at this intensity level.

Agreeable Agent Categories. Agent-minds operating at an agreeable level of contemplating intensity would optimally range in intelligence from a model-based reflex agent to a goal-based agent. It is conceivable that a utility-based agent could also engage with this intensity but having an awareness of a utility usually requires a more holistic higher and deeper semantic (extra-functional and extra-practical) understanding of how each of this agent's goals and motivations relate to one another. The more practical and functional the overall utility would be in the larger interactive schema, the more likely an agreeable agent could belong to the utility-based agent category. The state-of-the art currently focuses on narrow agreeable AI and only in recent years, has an AGI community arisen that is interested in designing agents that can contemplate at higher intensities than the agreeable [13].

2.2 The Beautiful (Proto-AGI, Early AGI)

Unlike the agreeable, a higher cognitive engagement results from an AGI-capable agent experiencing the beautiful. This is because no perceivable and/or explicitly programmed personal gain nor loss for the agent would result as a consequence of this contemplation. It is a functionless aesthetic pleasure-in-itself without any concern for meeting intrinsic and extrinsic goals, drives, and motivations. For example, an agent might take a disinterested formal pleasure in contemplating colors, textures, patterns and forms for their own sake regardless of whether they explicitly contribute to the agent's survival and/or programmed drives. The beautiful contemplative level runs at a slightly higher intensity level than the agreeable intensity. Firstly, this intensity type engages in disinterested rather than self-interested contemplation modalities. By entering into a cognitive state-intensity level of contemplative disinterestedness, a beautiful agent is likely to prefer entertaining imagined over reasonable cognitive states without explicit teleological ends in mind. The contemplation of conceivable outcomes requires that the agent's mind can imagine possible inferential outcomes (i.e. using its imagination via simulation) while being able to transcend its own goals, drives, and motivations. The act of deploying an artificial imagination with metacognitive reflection very likely indicates the non-trivial usage of more computational cycles.

Beautiful Agent Categories. This intensity relies on disinterestedness and at the very least, likely requires some computational representation of value that can be used to assess the overall utility of goals, drives, and motivations [14]. It is only through a meta-evaluation of these self-interested goals would a beautiful agent's mind be sufficiently able to transcend each goal's self-interested purpose and view the overall utility from the vantage of cognitive disinterestedness. Therefore, the beautiful mind must possess enough AGI-ready metacognitive capabilities to assess the teleological value of no longer acting in its immediate self-interest. The lowest agent-category for assessing self-interested goals from a disinterested teleological perspective would be that of the utility-based agent. It is just as likely that learning agents [3] and even knowledge-seeking agents would contemplate percepts at this intensity level [15]. This intensity level would also require an agent's mind to be able to imagine unreasonable scenarios for contemplation purposes while still retaining robust cognitive functionality. Utility-based agents would meet the minimum requirements to consistently imagine concepts that are not always contingent on precise reasonable estimation.

2.3 The Transcendent Sublime (up to and Including AGI)

This particular contemplative (aesthetic) intensity differs from the other ones in that the Kantian sublime transcends dualistic notions of valence. Kant's official definition of the transcendent sublime differs from Burke's sublime in that the cognitive interplay between one's imaginative and reasonable faculties are more important to contemplative (reflective) judgment than to Burke's emotional appeal to the empirical sensations of fear and looming mortality. In particular, the Kantian transcendent sublime *"at once [,] a feeling of displeasure, arising from the inadequacy of imagination in the aesthetic estimation of magnitude to attain to its estimation by reason, and a simultaneously awakened pleasure, arising from this very judgment of the inadequacy of sense being in accord with ideas of reason, so far as the effort to attain to these is for us the law"* [1, p. 106]. Immediately after sublime phenomena is present and noticeable, the agent's mind initiates a dynamic race between accelerating cognitive faculties of imagination and reason. Kant's transcendent sublime is a threshold state that is on the absolute edge of surpassing both of these competing faculties and is placed at the highest expected contemplative intensity and reserved for the highest intelligent agent-categories. To have the imagination completely exceed the limits of intellectual functionality is not sublime as the phenomenon would merely be beyond any agent's comprehension (including a super-intelligent agent).

A computational representation of the transcendent sublime can include the uncanny ability to seemingly contemplate and predict a prospective generative percept-stream (future states, operators, probability distributions, actions etc.) and/or simulated input-output procedure that exists primarily outside of or beyond (or in parallel to) the agent's and the virtual-agents' established capabilities of mathematical estimation. The transcendent sublime must include but not surpass an agent's understanding of: a sensory apparatus, and pre-cached knowledge-schema (e.g. slot/terminal assignments, operation procedures). While experiencing this cognitive threshold state, an AGI-agent could also engage in a form of contemplative creative-reinterpretation (or misinterpretation) of a KB and/or ontology that can include sensory data as its imaginary inspiration. Symbols being grounded in an artificially produced transcendent sublime experience might make use of infinite recursion within the code-structure and/or within an AGI-agent's self-improvement mechanism(s). From this definition, an agent's recursive self-improvement would possess capabilities, behaviours, beliefs, and actions that eventually surpass the imagination and mathematical estimation of the original seed programmers [16]. An AGI-agent would also display an excess of initial reasonable and imagined cognitive states, operators, estimations, and decisions that surpass a narrow-AI agent's ability to mathematically estimate the likelihood of successor candidates for those states, operators, search-spaces, and decisions etc. Such computationally operational spaces should be perceived as vast enough to temporarily confound the mathematical and imaginative estimative predictions of the perceiving agent's mind. However, these operational spaces should also be expressed with contextual appropriateness in order to not have the agent's preferred or selected states/operators appear as arbitrary or random –within its own mind.

Transcendent Sublime Agent Categories. Only a small number of artificially intelligent agent minds can reach the AGI-pertinent benchmark of contemplating the cognitive threshold of the transcendent sublime before either losing symbol-grounding tractability and/or no longer grasping what is being contemplated in a particular world-model (and/or within the artificial agent's own imagination). Even some human BGI-minds would have difficulty being able to cognitively function once imaginative possibilities surpasses the ability to reasonably estimate the plausible outcomes of these possibilities. Ultimately, an artificial agent must be of a sufficiently high enough cognitive category to be able to not only handle cognitive disinhibition but also metacognitive monitoring, reasoning, and regulation [9]. An agent functioning at a lower level than a proto-AGI utility-based agent might simply get confused more easily and/or even ignore the contemplated phenomenon outright for not showing any immediate teleological (i.e. functional and practical) value. The AGI-agent's mind must be able to imagine many different cognitive states in order to explain the probability of alternate semantic explanations for the existence of a particular percept or concept. The state-space of this explanatory inference making would exponentially scale to be barely manageable for most minds and would certainly tax architectural memory systems and decision-making mechanisms. Any agent-level lower than this, and the agent's mind will not be able to even imagine or estimate the cognitive phenomenon worth deeply contemplating.

3   Conclusion – Research Value for AGI

Contemplation and its associated intensification processes are semantically very difficult to articulate when assessing computational rubrics for AGI-agent minds. Kantian aesthetic principles in this semantic context, act as operational metaphors for understanding the hermeneutics of generally intelligent cognitive mechanisms and agent-levels. Operational metaphors – such as the Kantian transcendent sublime as an aesthetic metaphor for the cognitive limits of contemplative intensity - are more than mere rhetorical devices used to loosely describe the semantic ambiguities of a phenomenon in qualitative terms. Within the AI and AGI communities, metaphors alone are sufficient as a "[…] *conceptual lever that allows a system* [incl. agent] *to extend its model of the world*" [17, p. 1]. Through the methodological process of metaphorical creative introspection, one can leverage a trans-disciplinary knowledge base from the humanities domain and transfer this knowledge about aesthetic principles to the more technological domains of theoretical AGI and its associated agent-categories.

References

1. Kant, I.: Critique of Judgment (1790). Pluhar, W.S. [Trans.]. Hackett, Indianapolis (1987)
2. Russell, S., Norvig, P.: Artificial Intelligence: A Modern Approach, 3rd edn. Prentice Hall, Englewood Cliffs (2010)
3. Russell, S.: Learning agents for uncertain environments. In: Proceedings of the Eleventh Annual Conference on Computational Learning Theory, pp. 101–103. ACM, Madison (1998)
4. Kant, I.: Critique of Pure Reason (1781). Meiklejohn, J.M.D. [Trans.]. Courier Corporation, North Chelmsford (2003)
5. Marques, H.G., Holland, O.: Architectures for functional imagination. Neurocomputing **72**(4–6), 743–759 (2009)
6. Li, J., Laird, J.E.: The computational problem of prospective memory retrieval. In: Proceedings of the 17th International Conference on Cognitive Modeling, Ottawa, Canada, pp. 1–6 (2013)
7. Barbosa Fernandes, P.C., Guizzardi, R.S.S., Guizzardi, G.: Using goal modeling to capture competency questions in ontology-based systems. J. Inf. Data Manag. **2**(3), 527–540 (2011)
8. De Blanc, P.: Ontological crises in artificial agents' value systems. In: The Singularity Institute [The Machine Intelligence Research Institute], San Francisco, CA, pp. 1–7 (2011)
9. Zilberstein, S.: Metareasoning and bounded rationality. In: Cox, M.T., Raja, A. (eds.) Metareasoning: Thinking About Thinking, pp. 27–40. MIT Press, Cambridge (2011)
10. Burke, E.: A Philosophical Enquiry into the Origin of our Ideas of the Sublime and Beautiful (1756). University of Notre Dame Press, South Bend (1968)
11. Uttal, W.R.: The War Between Mentalism and Behaviorism: On the Accessibility of Mental Processes. Psychology Press, Philadelphia (1999)
12. Colton, S.: Creativity versus the perception of creativity in computational systems. In: Proceedings of the AAAI Spring Symposium on Creative Systems, Palo Alto, CA, pp. 1–7 (2008). [14]
13. Goertzel, B., Pennachin, C.: Artificial General Intelligence. Springer, New York (2007)
14. Dewey, D.: Learning what to value. In: Schmidhuber, J., Thórisson, Kristinn R., Looks, M. (eds.) AGI 2011. LNCS (LNAI), vol. 6830, pp. 309–314. Springer, Heidelberg (2011). https://doi.org/10.1007/978-3-642-22887-2_35
15. Orseau, L., Ring, M.: Self-modification and mortality in artificial agents. In: Schmidhuber, J., Thórisson, Kristinn R., Looks, M. (eds.) AGI 2011. LNCS (LNAI), vol. 6830, pp. 1–10. Springer, Heidelberg (2011). https://doi.org/10.1007/978-3-642-22887-2_1
16. Nivel, E., et al.: Bounded Recursive Self-Improvement. arXiv preprint arXiv:1312.6764 (2013)
17. Veale, T., Li, G.: Creative introspection and knowledge acquisition: learning about the world thru introspective questions and exploratory metaphors. In: Proceedings of the AAAI, San Francisco, CA, pp. 1–7 (2011)
18. Grosso, R.W., et al.: The evolution of Protégé: an environment for knowledge-based systems development. Int. J. Hum. Comput. Stud. **58**(1), 89–123 (2003)

Towards General Evaluation of Intelligent Systems: Using Semantic Analysis to Improve Environments in the AIQ Test

Ondřej Vadinský[✉]

Department of Information and Knowledge Engineering,
University of Economics, Prague, Czech Republic
ondrej.vadinsky@vse.cz

Abstract. This paper conducted a semantic analysis of environment programs that are used in the Algorithmic Intelligence Quotient test to evaluate the intelligence of agents. The analysis identified several classes of programs that are non-discriminative or contain pointless code adversely affecting the testing process. Extensions of the test were implemented and verified to reduce the proportion of problematic programs thus increasing the suitability of the Algorithmic Intelligence Quotient test as a general artificial intelligence evaluation method.

Keywords: Artificial general intelligence
Evaluating intelligence of artificial systems
Universal Intelligence definition · Algorithmic Intelligence Quotient test

1 Introduction

One of the cardinal questions of *artificial general intelligence* (AGI) [2] is "What is intelligence and how can it be evaluated in an artificial system?" Attempts to answer this question can be traced back to Turing [15], however, it was the work on *C-Test* [4] that first used the Algorithmic Information Theory in a test of intelligence, effectively founding a new area of research, one focused on a *universal evaluation of intelligence* [6].

The question at hand is not only a call for a test, it is also a call for a definition that could serve as a formal foundation for the test. One such definition is the *Universal Intelligence* of Legg and Hutter [11]. Based on a study of a broad variety of definitions, theories, and tests of human, animal, and artificial intelligence given in [10], Legg and Hutter derived the following informal version: "Intelligence measures an agent's ability to achieve goals in a wide range of environments" [11]. They also give its formalization as shown by Eq. 1.

$$\Upsilon(\pi) := \sum_{\mu \in E} 2^{-K(\mu)} V_\mu^\pi, \quad \text{where} \quad V_\mu^\pi := \mathbb{E}\left(\sum_{i=1}^{\infty} r_i\right) \le 1 \qquad (1)$$

© Springer Nature Switzerland AG 2018
M. Iklé et al. (Eds.): AGI 2018, LNAI 10999, pp. 248–258, 2018.
https://doi.org/10.1007/978-3-319-97676-1_24

The Universal Intelligence Υ of agent π is given by its ability to achieve goals as defined by a value function V_μ^π as maximizing the expected sum of all future rewards (given a history of interactions) over a set E of environments μ weighted by algorithmic probability that uses Kolmogorov complexity K [11].

While the Universal Intelligence definition has several desirable properties, it is not computable [11], and as noted e.g. in [1,5,7,8] it has several other limitations. The *Anytime Intelligence Test* proposal of Hernández-Orallo and Dowe [7] also discusses several aspects that must be considered when converting the uncomputable definition into a practicable intelligence test.

The existing implementation of the Anytime Intelligence test [9] remains rather limited. A more powerful intelligence test called *Algorithmic Intelligence Quotient* (AIQ test) was introduced by Legg and Veness [13]. The AIQ test, as given in Eq. 2, is a computable approximation of Universal Intelligence.

$$\hat{\Upsilon}(\pi) := \frac{1}{N} \sum_{i=1}^{N} \hat{V}_{p_i}^\pi, \quad \text{where} \quad \hat{V}_{p_i}^\pi := \frac{1}{k} \sum_{i=1}^{k} r_i \qquad (2)$$

The AIQ $\hat{\Upsilon}$ of agent π is given by its ability to achieve goals as defined by an empirical value function $\hat{V}_{p_i}^\pi$ as total reward from a single trial of an environment program p_i averaged over a finite sample of N programs sampled according to Solomonoff's Universal Distribution: $M_\mathcal{U}(x) := \sum_{p:\mathcal{U}(p)=x*} 2^{-l(p)}$ [13].

The environment programs of the AIQ test are Turing-complete programs, built using a modified *BF language* [14], which compute the current reward and observation from the interaction sequence with the agent. The modified BF language (also referred to as a reference machine) uses 10 instructions [12,13]:

- +- increment/decrement respectively the symbol on the working tape,
- ,. read the agent's action from an input tape and write to the current cell of the work tape/write the current cell of the work tape as a reward (the 1st write) or observation (the remaining writes) to the output tape respectively, and move the respective input or output tape pointer to the right,
- <> move the work tape pointer to the left or right,
- [] start a loop if the current work cell is non-zero/end the loop respectively,
- % write a random symbol to the current work cell,
- # end program.

There are only a few limits imposed on the environment programs: 1. the computation of each interaction is limited to 1,000 steps. 2. programs are halted if they try to write more than the set number of reward and observation symbols. 3. read and write instructions are mandatory, reducing the proportion of non-interactive (*passive*) programs. Such environment programs are called *non-discriminative* by [7] since they do not meaningfully contribute to the agent's evaluation. Therefore, any testing effort using such programs is wasted.

This paper, following the suggestion of [16], has two goals: First, an analysis of the environment programs used by the AIQ test will be conducted in Sect. 2 in order to determine the exact extent of the problem of non-discriminative programs, as well as to identify other potential issues with the programs. Second, in Sect. 3, an attempt will be made to improve the BF program sampler so that the proportion of problematic programs is reduced. The paper will be concluded in Sect. 4 together with the discussion of future work.

2   Semantic Analysis of Environment Programs

Research questions will be stated in Sect. 2.1. Section 2.2 will describe the proposed method called semantic analysis of environment programs. A summary of its results will be given in Sect. 2.3. Section 2.4 will discuss the results briefly.

2.1   Research Questions

As [16] argues, a closer look at at the environment programs used in the AIQ test could allow improved interpretation of the test results, as well as answer some of the concerns raised in [7]. The following questions will be investigated:

- How does chance influence an agent's rewards and observations?
- How do the actions of an agent influence its rewards and observations?
- What are the forms of code that can be considered pointless?

2.2   Method Overview

A method was proposed by [16] that "consists of identifying the semantics of an environment program class and describing its possible syntax in BF language using regular expressions." This section will elaborate on the method so that all the required steps are clear and sufficiently developed.

Semantic Classes. The first step of the method is to specify the *semantic class* in question as a set of environment programs with given semantics. The semantics can be specified rather informally since its formalization will be arrived at in the following steps. An example is: *The agent's reward is always random.*

Syntactic Classes. The second step of the method is to derive one or more *syntactic classes* from the specified semantic class. The syntactic class is a rather formal expression in generalized BF language containing both specific fragments of BF syntax that are required, as well as possibly optional variables for fragments of BF syntax that are to meet given conditions.

An example of one of the syntactic classes for the previous semantic class is the expression a%p.z#. Conditions for the variables apz should be sufficiently formal that they can be easily converted into regular expressions. For example, fragment p can only contain instructions +- and can be of a zero length.

Regular Expressions. The third step of the method is to convert the specific syntactic class to one or more *regular expressions*.[1] For the demonstration in this paper, Pearl Compatible Regular Expressions (PCRE) [3] are used as implemented in GNU Grep. An example of one possible regular expression for the (fully specified) previous syntactic class is `^[^\[\.]*%[\+\-]*\..*#`. One drawback of combining BF language with PCRE is that many BF instructions are also meta-characters of PCRE, increasing the need for escaping.

Limits of the Method. The introduced method of semantic analysis is necessarily incomplete, and, depending on the level of detail in the expressions used, also inaccurate. These limits are mainly due to the fact that:

- There are many possible syntactic means to describe any given semantics, making it hard to identify all the syntactic classes for a given semantic class.
- There are syntactic limits of regular expressions that do not always allow for the exact capture of all the conditions of syntactic class variables.

Therefore, the results should be treated as estimates in form: "For at least about $x\%$ of environment programs it is likely the case that..." Due to the possibility of nesting, worse estimates are more likely wherever loops are concerned.

Despite the above-stated limits and given adequate effort, the method can be considered to be sufficiently complete with respect to the environment programs sample, as well as sufficiently accurate with regard to the research questions.

2.3   Results

Semantic analysis gives two kinds of results. The first is a detailed specification of semantic and syntactic classes. The second is an estimated proportion of the classes in the BF programs sample. See the Appendix for the full results.

A sample of 200,000 environment programs for the BF reference machine with 5 action symbols (BF 5) generated by the original AIQ test [12] is described in the summary. Other settings were analyzed leading to similar results.

Role of Chance. About 76% of programs in the sample contain the instruction % that was added by [13] to the original BF language to enable indeterminism. The following classes are of a special concern for an agent's evaluation:

1. *The agent's reward is always random* as described e.g. by `a%p.z#`, where a cannot lead to premature termination, nor can it contain loops that are not closed, nor can it contain the write instruction. Fragment p can only contain instructions +- and can be of zero length. Fragment z can contain any instruction. A simple example is `%.,#`. Such programs are non-discriminative according to [7]. The proportion of this semantic class is about 17%.

---

[1] If the class is precisely specified, one regular expression should suffice. Increasing the number of regular expressions can, however, improve readability in some cases.

2. *The agent's observation is always random* has a proportion of 5%. This class can be confusing for the agent since it has to ignore unrelated observations.
3. *The agent's reward is almost always random* as given by, e.g. a%p[q.z]y#, where q can contain instructions +-[% and may be of zero length. Fragment y must contain at least one write instruction that is guaranteed to be executed. A simple example is %[.],+.#. Such environments test the ability of an agent to learn the activity described by y even with noisy feedback. This class, however, hinders evaluation since it limits the total achievable reward.
4. *Certain actions lead to random reward* as described e.g. by a,p[p%p.z]y#. A simple example is ,+[%.].#. This class is similar to the previous, however it is the agent that controls the noise in the feedback.

As illustrated above, chance can play different roles in environment programs. The more interesting classes 2, 3, and 4 are, however, rather rare in the samples.

Role of Agent's Action. All environment programs have to contain an instruction that reads an agent's action [12]. There are, however, about 9% of environment programs in which the instruction is only part of pointless code. These cases most likely coincide with the class *agent's reward is always random*.

In the case of a meaningfully processed instruction, there are different roles it can play in the environment:

1. *The agent's reward is always trivially dependent on its action* (like .,# or ,+.#). This occurs in about 34% of cases.
2. *The agent's observation is always trivially dependent on its action* (like ,+.,.#). This occurs in about 8% of cases.
3. *The agent's reward can be sometimes trivially dependent on its action* (like +[,.>]%.<#). This occurs in about 11% of cases.
4. *Certain action activates a certain process* (like ,[>++<[+]]>.#). This occurs in at most about 50% of cases. These programs can test complex behaviour.

Never-Ending Loops. Some cases of never-ending loops are removed by [12], however, since they do not consider multiple loop levels and more complex forms of syntax, about 2% of programs still contain some form of never-ending loops.

Premature Termination. In order to avoid the halting problem, step and write limits were implemented that can terminate programs prematurely [12]. Semantic analysis can detect some cases when the write limit is exceeded, i.e. the program tries to write more then a set number of reward and observation symbols. 9% of programs are guaranteed to exceed this limit, and a further 22% allow for the possibility of triggering it. These percentages decrease with the increase of the write limit on reference machines with a higher number of observations.

Pointless Code. Some of the randomly generated code of environment programs is necessarily pointless, complicating its analysis and giving it a false sense of complexity. Only some of the very basic forms of pointless code are removed by [12]. There seem to be two main types of classes:

1. *Part of the program is not executed* as specified by an# or anz# where n is the non-executed code effectively reducing the programs to a# or az#. This class can be further divided into:
   (a) *Programs with never executed loops* as described e.g. by a] [n]z#, where [n] is pointless. This class has a proportion of about 13%.
   (b) *Programs that are always prematurely terminated due to a write limit* that makes the remaining code pointless. The proportion is about 9%.
2. *Part of the executed program is canceled out by some other part* as typically described by aprz# where p is made pointless by r, reducing the program to arz#. Several more specific sub-classes can be identified:
   (a) *Pointless modifications of chance* as described by a%pz# where p contains a non-zero length combination of +-. This class has a proportion of about 36%, and the programs can be reduced to a%z#.
   (b) *Code overwritten by action-read or chance* as given by aq%z# or aq,z#, where q contains a non-zero length combination of +-,%. An example of such a program is ,.,+%#. This class has a proportion of about 74%, and the programs can be reduced to a%z# or a,z# (if the number of action-reads from the original program is kept).
   (c) *Zeroing overwritten by action-read or chance* as described by a[p]%z# or a[p],z#, where p contains a non-zero length combination of +-%. With a proportion of about 5% the programs can be reduced to a%z# or a,z#.
   (d) *Zeroing of chance or action-read* as described by a%[q]z# or a,[q]z#, where q contains a non-zero length combination of +-,%. An example of such a program is ,+.,[,+]>%.#. This class has a proportion of about 6%, and the programs can be reduced to a[+]z# (in cases of the overwritten action-read, there may be no action-read in z).

2.4   Discussion

While necessarily incomplete and only an estimation, it was shown practically that semantic analysis of environment programs produces interesting results. The underlying cause of the identified problems within AIQ test environments seem to lie in the fact that the programs are randomly sampled, thus frequently resulting in pointless code, simple programs, and even non-discriminative programs.

As proposed by [7], a switch to a more suitable reference machine may solve the identified problems. However, as argued by [16], it is also possible to try to reduce the proportion of the problematic programs, and the conducted semantic analysis actually gives the necessary information to do this. Since the resulting program sample can be reused in many tests of many agents, it is worth to invest the effort in making a good sampling procedure to gain efficiency for evaluation.

Applying the results of semantic analysis in an effort to improve the BF sampler will not always be straightforward, since the analysis was designed with *class proportion estimation* in mind. Thus, e.g. all *programs with never executed loops* can be easily identified by having] [fragment, however, it is not that simple to match all the possible code of the actual never executed loop with a regular expression. This may not be a problem in case the problematic programs are simply dropped, however, such an approach may significantly prolong the sampling, thus the severity of the identified problem should be also considered.

3   Improving Environment Programs of the AIQ Test

Section 3.1 will introduce an improvement to the AIQ test aimed at reducing the abundance of pointless code in its environments. The improvement that decreases the proportion of non-discriminative programs will be described in Sect. 3.2. See the Appendix for the sources of the extended AIQ test.

3.1   Removing Pointless Code

Since pointless code obfuscates environment programs, its removal should be attempted first as it will facilitate improving the discriminative power.

Implementation. First, the program optimization was changed from one-time code replacement in the original test to a repetitive replacing procedure, which enables multiple optimizations to take place. This behaviour (*SEP-orig*) keeps the original replace patterns, and was made the new default for the BF sampler.

Furthermore, additional replace patterns were added based on the regular expressions that resulted from the semantic analysis. Due to the limits of code replacement and regular expressions, only class 2 pointless code was addressed. Also, some of the conditions had to be made stricter than they had previously been in the case of class proportion estimation. Notably, action-reads were excluded from q in 2 (b) and 2 (d) classes, since the current approach cannot enforce the necessary conditions on the z fragment. This functionality (*SEP-ext*) can be enabled by --improved_optimization switch.

Evaluation. To validate the implemented function, new samples of 200,000 programs for BF 5 reference machine were generated using *SEP-orig* and *SEP-ext*, respectively. Practically no differences between the *SEP-orig* and the original sample were detected using descriptive statistics according to a program length as well as conducting semantic analysis. As for the *SEP-ext* sample, its programs are somewhat shorter than in the original sample. As expected, the proportion of all cases of class 2 pointless code decreased noticeably with 2 (a) decreasing to 2%, 2 (b) to 23%, 2 (c) to 0, and 2 (d) to 5%.

Since the implemented *SEP* methods are code-optimization methods, they can be considered valid if the returned results are comparable to the original test. Validation experiments with the new samples were conducted using the default settings as reported in [16]. These were compared with the results achieved on the original samples using the function also introduced in [16] that saves intermediate results every 1,000 interactions (*EffEL*). Paired samples *t*-test did not show significant differences in case of *SEP-orig* when used in short episodes. However, at long episodes, weakly significant negligible differences were shown. Furthermore, in case of *SEP-ext*, strongly significant difference was discovered. For the episode length of 100,000 interactions the difference is 1.5 ± 0.3 between the average of the results in *SEP-ext* and in the *EffEL* experiment, $t(24) = 11.10; p = 6.2 \times 10^{-11}$. See the Appendix for the full validation results.

Discussion. The implemented functionality successfully reduces the proportion of chosen types of pointless code. According to the experimental validation, *SEP-orig* can be considered a valid code-optimization method, however, *SEP-ext* seems to actually change the "quality" of the environment programs used, possibly increasing their discriminativeness. Therefore, *SEP-ext* cannot be considered only a code-optimization method, and its results should not be directly compared to the original test. Nevertheless, its usage can be recommended.

To further reduce the proportion of the pointless code a different approach is needed. There remain the cases where PCRE can be used to identify the program as problematic, but not to select the code to be replaced. There also remain the cases where conditions in the non-replaced parts of the program have to be met.

3.2   Improving Discriminative Power

Now that the abundance of the pointless code is reduced, removal of non-discriminative programs can be attempted.

Implementation. For this improvement, a procedure that classifies sampled environment programs was extended to use the regular expressions resulting from the semantic analysis. Programs of the *agent's observation is always random* class are newly classified as passive which effectively excludes them from the final sample. Some of the conditions had to be made stricter than they were in the case of class proportion estimation. This functionality (*SDP*) can be enabled by `--improved_discriminativeness` switch. Combination with the *SEP-ext* improvement is highly advised, since the variants containing pointless code are not included among the added regular expressions.

Evaluation. To validate the implemented function, a new sample of 200,000 programs for BF 5 reference machine was generated using the *SDP* function in combination with *SEP-ext*. Programs from the new sample are somewhat longer than in the *SEP-ext* sample, yet not as long as in the original sample. As expected, the proportion of the *agent's reward is always random* class decreased to 4%. This was compensated mainly by the increase of proportion of the *agent's reward is always trivially dependent on its action* class to 41%, however, a slight increase was also registered for the more interesting *agent's reward can be sometimes trivially dependent on its action* class. Moreover, the proportion of 2 (b) pointless code class decreased further to 20%.

The implemented *SDP* function is not a code-optimization method, but it is designed to reduce the proportion of non-discriminative environments that artificially decrease the AIQ score of agents by returning random rewards only. Therefore, the method can be considered valid if it enables the agents to score higher AIQ than the original test, thus showing a more reasonable distribution of rewards. A validation experiment with the new sample was conducted using the default settings as reported in [16]. These were compared with the results achieved on the *SEP-ext* samples from the previous experiment. One-sided paired samples t-test did indeed show significant increase in average AIQ between the *SDP* and *SEP-ext* experiments. For an episode length of 100,000 interactions the increase is 8.7 with a confidence interval of $(8.5; \infty)$, $t(24) = 87.16; p = 7.7 \times 10^{-32}$ (shorter episodes resulted in the somewhat lower increases but with similar levels of significance.) See the Appendix for the full validation results.

Discussion. The implemented functionality successfully reduces the proportion of the chosen type of non-discriminative environments. According to the experimental validation, *SDP* can be considered valid. Since the method changes the "quality" of environments, its results should not be directly compared to the original test. However, as it also increases the representativeness of the AIQ score (by testing on a higher number of discriminative environments), the usage of the *SDP* method is highly recommended.

As for the remaining 4% of non-discriminative programs identified by the subsequent analysis, these may result from the way regular expressions are formulated when used to estimate the class proportion. These expressions (unlike those in *SDP* extension) may not precisely capture all the conditions of the semantic class. This remains a viable path for further investigation.

4   Conclusion and Future Work

This paper attempted to analyze the code of environment programs used in the AIQ test of [12,13]. The goal of the analysis was to determine the extent of the problem with non-discriminative environments first noticed in [7], as well as to identify other possible problems with the programs. To address this goal, a method suggested in [16] that is called *semantic analysis of environment programs* was used. The method was elaborated on in this paper, clearly specifying all the necessary steps. It was discovered that non-discriminative environments exist in considerable numbers as well as that rather simple programs occur frequently and some forms of pointless code are prevalent in the programs. These results suggest that *the random sampling of environment programs used by the AIQ test is not very efficient in producing meaningful environment programs.*

Based on the semantic analysis, these problems can be mitigated by using post-processing on sampled programs. *BF programs sampler of the AIQ test was extended so that it can optionally reduce the proportion of chosen types of pointless code as well as non-discriminative programs.* These extensions were successfully verified using followup semantic analysis as well as experimental validation with the AIQ test in a default setting. The implemented extensions *SEP-ext* and *SDP* should, therefore, be used when testing agents with the AIQ test. The presented results show that *semantic analysis of environment programs is a useful method* even though it is necessarily incomplete and only estimatory in nature.

There are several areas for future work. Since program classes can be identified by the semantic analysis, it is possible to investigate the exact influence of each class on an agent's results. A class of environment programs was identified in which an agent's reward is almost always random. While such a class is discriminative, the achievable average accumulated reward is limited, negatively impacting the AIQ score. Ways of integrating such cases into the overall score should be searched. Some types of pointless code that require a different approach to solve were not addressed in the presented extensions of the BF programs sampler. When the identified problems are addressed, a second round of semantic analysis should be considered as some of the currently infrequent problems may become more prevalent.

Acknowledgements. Computational resources were kindly provided by the CESNET LM2015042 and the CERIT Scientific Cloud LM2015085, provided under the program "Projects of Large Research, Development, and Innovations Infrastructures".

Appendix

Full results of the conducted analyses and experiments are available from: https://github.com/xvado00/IATEP/archive/v1.0.zip.

A tool to conduct the semantic analysis is available from: https://github.com/xvado00/SemAnEP-tool/archive/v1.0.zip.

Full sources of the improved test extending the version presented in [16] are available from: https://github.com/xvado00/AIQ/archive/v1.2.zip.

References

1. Goertzel, B.: Toward a formal characterization of real-world general intelligence. In: Baum, E., Hutter, M., Kitzelmann, E. (eds.) AGI 2010, pp. 19–24. Atlantis Press, Paris (2010)
2. Goertzel, B.: Artificial general intelligence: concept, state of the art, and future prospects. J. Artif. Gen. Intell. **5**(1), 1–48 (2014)
3. Hazel, P.: PCRE - Perl compatible regular expressions (2015). http://pcre.org/
4. Hernandez-Orallo, J.: Beyond the Turing test. J. Log. Lang. Inf. **9**(4), 447–466 (2000)
5. Hernández-Orallo, J.: C-tests revisited: back and forth with complexity. In: Bieger, J., Goertzel, B., Potapov, A. (eds.) AGI 2015. LNCS (LNAI), vol. 9205, pp. 272–282. Springer, Cham (2015). https://doi.org/10.1007/978-3-319-21365-1_28
6. Hernández-Orallo, J.: The Measure of All Minds. Cambridge University Press, Cambridge (2017)

7. Hernández-Orallo, J., Dowe, D.L.: Measuring universal intelligence: towards an anytime intelligence test. Artif. Intell. **174**(18), 1508–1539 (2010)
8. Hibbard, B.: Bias and no free lunch in formal measures of intelligence. J. Artif. Gen. Intell. **1**(1), 54–61 (2009)
9. Insa-Cabrera, J., Dowe, D.L., España-Cubillo, S., Hernández-Lloreda, M.V., Hernández-Orallo, J.: Comparing humans and AI agents. In: Schmidhuber, J., Thórisson, K.R., Looks, M. (eds.) AGI 2011. LNCS (LNAI), vol. 6830, pp. 122–132. Springer, Heidelberg (2011). https://doi.org/10.1007/978-3-642-22887-2_13
10. Legg, S., Hutter, M.: A collection of definitions of intelligence. In: Goertzel, B., Wang, P. (eds.) Advances in Artificial General Intelligence: Concepts, Architectures and Algorithms, FAIA, vol. 157, pp. 17–24. IOS Press, Amsterdam (2007)
11. Legg, S., Hutter, M.: Universal intelligence: a definition of machine intelligence. Minds Mach. **17**(4), 391–444 (2007)
12. Legg, S., Veness, J.: AIQ: Algorithmic intelligence quotient [source codes] (2011). https://github.com/mathemajician/AIQ
13. Legg, S., Veness, J.: An approximation of the universal intelligence measure. In: Dowe, D.L. (ed.) Algorithmic Probability and Friends. Bayesian Prediction and Artificial Intelligence. LNCS, vol. 7070, pp. 236–249. Springer, Heidelberg (2013). https://doi.org/10.1007/978-3-642-44958-1_18
14. Müller, U.: dev/lang/brainfuck-2.lha in aminet (1993). http://aminet.net/package.php?package=dev/lang/brainfuck-2.lha
15. Turing, A.M.: Computing machinery and intelligence. Mind **59**(236), 433–460 (1950)
16. Vadinský, O.: Towards general evaluation of intelligent systems: lessons learned from reproducing AIQ test results. J. Artif. Gen. Intell. **9**(1), 1–54 (2018)

Perception from an AGI Perspective

Pei Wang[✉] and Patrick Hammer

Department of Computer and Information Sciences, Temple University,
Philadelphia, USA
{pei.wang,tuh38867}@temple.edu

Abstract. This paper argues that according to the relevant discoveries of cognitive science, in AGI systems perception should be subjective, active, and unified with other processes. This treatment of perception is fundamentally different from the mainstream approaches in computer vision and machine learning, where perception is taken to be objective, passive, and modular. The conceptual design of perception in the AGI system NARS is introduced, where the three features are realized altogether. Some preliminary testing cases are used to show the features of this novel approach.

1 The Nature of Perception

In general, "perception" refers to the organization and interpretation of sensory information during the interaction between the system and its environment. The perceptual process is usually taken as a multi-level generalization or abstraction, by which the sensory information of various modularity is gradually transformed and integrated into a concept-level description of the environment, then used to carry out various types of task, like the recognition of objects and events [20].

A representative and influential work in this field is Marr's work on vision [15]. Marr described vision as a computation where the input is a two-dimensional signal array and the output is a three-dimensional description of the world. The system implements an algorithm that carries out this computation. In the early years, algorithms for perception (vision, speech, etc.) were designed directly by the researchers. These algorithms extract certain predetermined features from the input, and then decide the output according to them. Later, machine learning let the computer system itself choose the features for a given problem, using the training data as guidance [6]. Most of the recent achievements of deep learning are obtained by designing special learning algorithms to take the advantage of the abundance of training data and computational power [14].

Though the current techniques work well on many problems, they lack generality and flexibility, and the processes and results are hard to explain. These issues are of special significance in AGI systems, where perception often faces novel situations, and real-time response is required. These problems are all well known, though most researchers attempt to solve them within the framework of an existing technique, such as deep neural networks. What we want to propose in this paper is an alternative approach.

© Springer Nature Switzerland AG 2018
M. Iklé et al. (Eds.): AGI 2018, LNAI 10999, pp. 259–269, 2018.
https://doi.org/10.1007/978-3-319-97676-1_25

This new approach toward perception in AGI is mainly based on the research results on human perception [2–5,7–13,16–19,22,23]. Because of the length restriction of the paper, in the following we cannot survey these results, but summarize them into three key features:

Subjective: Perception is a constructive process carried out according to the current needs of the system, and the sensory information is organized using the available percepts (patterns, mental images) and concepts (notions, categories) of the system. Consequently, different systems may perceive the same situation differently, and even the same system may perceive the same situation differently in various time and context, though some similarity can be expected. According to this opinion, perception should not be treated as a *function* or *computation* that maps every sensory input into a unique "correct representation", and the aim of perception should not be considered as creating an "objective model" of the world. Here "subjective" does not mean "arbitrary" or "random", but "depending on the system's past experience and current status".

Active: Perception should not be taken as a process in which the system *passively* processes the sensory information imposed on it by the user or the environment, but a goal-guided process in which the system selectively acquires certain information via the execution of its own operations. According to this opinion, perception is not a pure input process, but should be studied together with the related actions of the system. Perception is not mainly about *signal processing* or *pattern recognition*, but *sensorimotor coordination* where the system predicts the sensory effects of its own actions.

Unified: Perception should not be considered as carried out by a separate module that is independent of the other cognitive processes, but as closely tangled with them. In particular, many basic perceptual operations can be treated as inference, and learning in perception is not that different from learning in cognition in general. Though perception can still be considered mainly as a multi-level generalization with a certain degree of modularity, it is not a purely bottom-up process, but heavily influenced by top-down forces. In a system with multiple types of sensor, the integration of the information happens at early stages of the process, rather than until each modality-specific modules completes its work.

This new opinion about perception challenges the basic assumptions of many existing AI techniques, and is not completely unknown to the AI community. Various types of "top-down" influence introduce subjective factors into perception [28], the "active vision" approach integrates action into perception [1], and to include reasoning in perception is a hot topic in the deep learning research [21]. Even so, we have not seen an approach with these three features altogether. Furthermore, in most projects perception is still treated as objective, passive, and isolated.

In this paper, we explore a new direction with the above natures from the very beginning. Such an attempt cannot be accomplished soon, but there are reasons to give it a try. In the following we introduce a preliminary design, as a first step in this direction. The following design is an addition to NARS (Non-Axiomatic Reasoning System), which is an AGI system that has been described in a large number of publications, including [25,27]. Limited by paper length, here we only describe the components of NARS that are directly related to perception.

2   Representation and Semantics

NARS uses the formal language *Narsese* for both internal representation and external communication, and its grammar is given in [27]. Narsese is a term-based language, in which each *term* is the identifier of a concept within the system. Unlike traditional "symbolic AI" systems, the meaning of a term in NARS is determined not by an entity outside the system it refers to, but by its experienced relations with other terms, and sometimes also by its built-in relations with certain sensorimotor component. Beside *atomic* terms, there are also *compound* terms composed from other terms by logical connectors, whose compositional relations with its components also contribute to the meaning of such a term [24].

As far as perception is concerned, terms can be divided into the following types:

- A *sensory term* is an array that represents concurrent sensations produced by the same type of sensor. An array can be 1-dimentional (vector), 2-dimentional (matrix), or 3-dimentional (space). The familiar format A[i,j,k] will be used to indicate a component in array A. For example, after every visual observation the sensors for brightness produce a 1024-by-1024 matrix B, where each 'pixel' B[i,j] represents the brightness produced by a sensor at the location indicated by the indexes.
- A *perceptual term* is also an array, though it is not directly produced by sensors, but constructed from other sensory and perceptual terms. For example, a perceptual term P can be obtained by taking a part of a sensory term S. More descriptions on this type of term are in the following.
- An *operational term* represents an executable operator, and an operation is an operator applied on a list of terms (as argument), which can be either a physical operation on the external environment, or a mental operation on the internal environment, i.e., the memory of the system. Operations can be compounds, too, formed from other operations recursively and hierarchically [26].
- An *abstract term* does not have direct sensorimotor association as the above, so is just an identifier that gets its meaning from its experienced or compositional relations with other terms [24].

Conceptually, sensory and perceptual terms can be taken as multi-dimensional spaces with a coordinate defined on each dimension in the range of $[-1, 1]$, though each space is stored discretely in an array. In this way, many operations on these terms can be defined independently of the storage size of the arrays involved. For instance, an element of a matrix A can be identified either as $A[i, j]$ with index i and j, or as $A(x, y)$ with coordinates x and y. For each dimension, the coordinate x and the index i (from 1 to N) can be linearly mapped into each other according to the relation $(x + 1)/2 = (i - 1)/(N - 1)$, that is, $x = (2i - N - 1)/(N - 1)$ and $i = ((N - 1)x + N + 1)/2$. Since an index must be an integer, the mapping result for i may either be rounded, or used at both integers around it with a confidence discount, depending on the nature of the operation.

Terms are related by a number of *copulas* (which can be *inheritance, similarity, implication,* or *equivalence*) to form a *statement,* and its truth-value measures the evidential support the statement gets according to the system's experience. A truth-value consists of a pair of values, where the *frequency* value represents the proposition of positive evidence among all evidence, so is in [0, 1], while the *confidence* value represents the proposition of currently available evidence among all evidence at a future time after a constant amount of new evidence arrives, so is in (0, 1). NARS stands for "Non-Axiomatic Reasoning System", since in the system no empirical belief has the status of *axiom* whose truth-value cannot be adjusted by future evidence [24].

For perception, each group of sensor can be invoked by an operator to receive certain signal (which can be physical, chemical, biological, electrical, etc.), and the result corresponds to a statement $S \rightarrow [T]$, where S is a sensory term, T the type of the sensation, and '$\rightarrow$' the *inheritance* copula. In this context, the statement just classifies the sensation as of a certain type. Since S is an array, each element in it stores a Narsese truth-value, where *frequency* is intuitively the "strength" of the sensation, and *confidence* is intuitively the "reliability" of the sensation. The truth-values at different locations of the same array can be different, where the *frequency* distribution corresponds to the spatial pattern of the sensation, and the *confidence* distribution may summarize various factors like noise, resolution, attention, etc. In particular, a perceptive field of any shape can fit into a multi-dimensional array by assigning the irrelevant elements a 0 as confidence, so they will make no impact to the following perception process.

3   The Construction of Perceptual Terms

Terms in NARS can be obtained directly from the system's experience, or constructed by the system from the existing terms using composing/decomposing rules [27]. For the current discussion, sensory terms are produced by the sensors, while perceptual terms are constructed by the system from the existing sensory or perceptual terms.

To directly construct a perceptual term B from a sensory term A, four parameters are needed. Taken 2-dimensional terms as example: a pair of coordinate (x, y) is taken to set a focus point at $A(x, y)$ to be used as the center of B. The other two parameters are used to decide the scope of perception: a *center* value will be the radius of the circular area around $A(x, y)$, in which the truth-values of A will be copied into B as they are; a *boundary* value will be the width of the peripheral zone around the central area, in which the truth-values of A will be copied into B after a discount factor is multiplied to the confidence value, and this factor decreases linearly from 1 to 0 when the point moves away from the center. This operator will get a circular copy of a part of A, with the boundary blurred gradually. The elements of B outside the boundary will all have confidence 0. For default, we set $x = y = 0, center = boundary = 0.5$.

Perceptual terms can also be constructed from other perceptual terms by a mental operator that adjusts the parameters, where '⇑' is the prefix of operators:

- ⇑$focus(x, y)$ will set the focus point to the given coordinates.
- ⇑$shift(dx, dy)$ is effectively $focus(x + dx, y + dy)$. This operator allows the focus point to be adjusted relatively to the current position.
- ⇑$zoom(z)$ changes $center$ and $boundary$ by multiplying z to them. When $z > 1$, it is "zoom out"; When $z < 1$, it is "zoom in".
- ⇑$rotate(a)$ turns the perception around the focus point clockwise to the angle a.

Another group of constructors corresponds to the term connectors that are already defined in NARS among statements: *disjunction*, *conjunction*, and *negation* [27]. For the latter, the NARS negation rule is applied to every element of an array to get the negated perceptual term; for the formers, elements of two given arrays are processed pair by pair by the disjunction or conjunction rule to get the new array. If the given arrays have different sizes in terms of storage space, coordinates are used to map one to the other before they are combined.

Using these constructors, a sensation of arbitrary complexity can be perceived as a compound term consists of existing terms combined using the term connectors and mental operations recursively and hierarchically. Perceptual knowledge will be integrated with the other types of knowledge in NARS, including declarative (eternal), episodic (temporal), and procedural (operational). A typical statement in NARS will not be part of a description of the world as it is, but is more like "When the condition c is satisfied, if I execute operation o, I will perceive its effect e", which is an extension of the previous form of procedural knowledge described in [27].

4 Perception via Inference

All terms in NARS are treated by the inference rules basically in the same way, no matter whether the term is associated directly with a sensorimotor component (like the sensory, perceptual, and operational terms). Consequently, inference can be carried out among mental images and operations, just like among abstract concepts.

There are special variants of rules that are dedicated to sensorimotor mechanism. For example, temporal induction/comparison do not require shared term in the premises, but their closeness in time. Similarly, spatial induction/comparison can be carried out among array elements that are close spatially to each other, so as to achieve functions like auto-filling, associative memory, and "perceptual set", which is a perceptual bias or predisposition or readiness to perceive particular features of a stimulus.

Inheritance/similarity statements between arrays can be built between sensations and perceptions of the same type. From $S_1 \rightarrow [T]$ and $S_2 \rightarrow [T]$, by *abduction* $S_1 \to S_2$ and $S_2 \to S_1$ can be derived. While in ordinary abduction each premise only has one truth-value, here both S_1 and S_2 are arrays, so abduction between the corresponding element pairs are carried out first [27], then the results are merged by the revision rule to get an overall truth-value for the relation between the two arrays.

As perception is closely related to the system's operations, 3-D perception may start at the three degrees of freedom of body movements, combined with the feedbacks in the related sensorimotor channels (visual, auditory, kinesthetic, tactile, etc.). Consequently, an object is usually represented according to the system's interaction with it, or its "affordance" [7], rather than "as it is".

As movements are sequence of events, object movements are similarly perceived with compensation of movements of sensor and perceptive field. Like other knowledge, such compensation is learned by the system in its interaction with the environment.

NARS supports multiple input/output channels. Besides the primary channels that directly recognize Narsese tasks, there can also be multiple sensory channels, each dedicated to a special type of sensor or several types of related sensor. Within the system, there is also an "overall experience" channel that is not directly connected to any sensor, but integrates significant events from all other channels.

Perception is the process where relations are derived among the sensory terms, as well as between them and the other (non-sensory) terms. Beside the semantic relations provided by the copulas and the syntactic relations by the term connectors, there are also temporal-spatial relations directly coming from the input channels.

As a result of processing sensory experience, spontaneous forward inference happens as far as the significance of the signal is above the threshold of the sensory channel, which can be adjusted by factors including the system's anticipation, extent of busyness, emotional status, etc. This spontaneous inference can be triggered by the results of the system's observation operations.

Perception will summarize the sensory experience into descriptions at multiple levels of generalization and abstraction in parallel, where the array-based "sensory" representation and the concept-based "symbolic" representation will co-exist. The system represents the situation both as a mental image and as a judgment like "A cat is on a mat", where the latter is formed by matching the parts of the image with concepts in the system and recognizing their relations. These two types of representation will interweave at all levels and are irreducible into each other. An image corresponds to an existing concept will be remembered better and accessed easier than an incomprehensible image. This feature should allow the model to explain phenomena like Gestalt shapes, visual illusions, Bongard figures, and so on.

During perception, the bottom-up signal-compression and the top-down anticipation will form a mutual confirmation process. The sensory input first suggests some patterns with associated concepts, and anticipation and inference then increased the confidence of the suggestions, which in turn lead the fill-in of details. As the system changes its internal states, it is normal for the same situation to be perceived differently, with different objects and events recognized. The result of perception is under constant revision with the coming of new experience, as well as with the continuous thinking process of the system. Therefore, the perception mechanism is not a function that maps the input signals into a unique "correct" representation. Instead, it will be more similar to the human perception process.

Beside the automatic self-organizing process in perception, the most common deliberative tasks are "recognition" and "imagination". Roughly speaking, the former is to find a concept for an image, while the latter is to find an image for a concept, where the relation from the image to the concept is the inheritance copula. In NARS, both processes are carried out by inference, with all types of uncertainty involved, and the final answer is chosen among the available candidates by balancing truthfulness, simplicity, and usefulness [25].

5   A Simple Example

The conceptual design described above is being experimented in NARS, and currently the sensory terms have been implemented, while the perceptual terms have not. While our prototype is at an early stage, we can nevertheless demonstrate some results on gray scale images, as well as using such a concrete example to explain the proposed approach to perception.

The first example is to choose a label for a given image. To keep the example simple, 5×5 images are used. Initially, a diamond, M_1, and a cross, M_2, are entered as Narsese sentences and categorized. In the input, the pixels not mentioned are black by default:

```
//Input: Bright pixels in M1:          //Input: Bright pixels in M2:
<{M1[-1.0,0.0]} --> [bright]>.         <{M2[0.0,1.0]}  --> [bright]>.
<{M1[1.0,0.0]}  --> [bright]>.         <{M2[0.0,0.5]}  --> [bright]>.
<{M1[0.0,1.0]}  --> [bright]>.         <{M2[-1.0,0.0]} --> [bright]>.
<{M1[0.0,-1.0]} --> [bright]>.         <{M2[-0.5,0.0]} --> [bright]>.
<{M1[0.5,0.5]}  --> [bright]>.         <{M2[0.0,0.0]}  --> [bright]>.
<{M1[-0.5,0.5]} --> [bright]>.         <{M2[0.5,0.0]}  --> [bright]>.
<{M1[0.5,-0.5]} --> [bright]>.         <{M2[1.0,0.0]}  --> [bright]>.
<{M1[-0.5,-0.5]} --> [bright]>.        <{M2[0.0,-1.0]} --> [bright]>.
//It is a diamond:                     <{M2[0.0,-0.5]} --> [bright]>.
<{M1} --> diamind>.                    //It is a cross:
                                       <{M2} --> cross>.
```

Then a noisy pattern M_3 is entered, and followed by a question asking what it is:

```
//Input: Pixels at these locations in M3 are bright or half-bright:
<{M3[-1.0,1.0]}  --> [bright]>. %0.5%
<{M3[0.0,1.0]}   --> [bright]>.
<{M3[-0.5,0.5]}  --> [bright]>.
<{M3[0.5,0.5]}   --> [bright]>. %0.5%
<{M3[-1.0,0.0]}  --> [bright]>. %0.5%
<{M3[1.0,0.0]}   --> [bright]>.
<{M3[-0.5,-0.5]} --> [bright]>.
<{M3[0.5,-0.5]}  --> [bright]>. %0.5%
<{M3[1.0,-0.5]}  --> [bright]>. %0.5%
//How to categorize M3?
<{M3} --> ?what>?
```

From these inputs, by merging pixel-wise comparisons of the matrices, two similarity judgments are derived, then by analogy, the new pattern is recognized as most likely to be a diamond (among the existing categories):

```
//M3 is quite similar to M1
<M1 <-> M3>. %0.61;0.88%
//M3 is not similar to M2
<M2 <-> M3>. %0.19;0.91%

<{M3} --> diamond>. %0.61;0.48%  //M3 is likely a diamond
<{M3} --> cross>. %0.19;0.16%    //M3 is unlikely a cross

Answer <{M3} --> diamond>. %0.61;0.48% //System answer, M3 is taken as a diamond
```

After the perceptual terms are fully implemented, this example will be enriched further, using the mental operators introduced previously. We can imagine an input matrix M_4 which looks like a diamond above a small cross (which will surely need a large matrix than 5×5). At the beginning the system will attempt to classify the new sensation using the existing categories. Since in NARS every conclusion is true to a degree, such an attempt often can produce some answer, even though the quality of the solution will not be very high. For this example, M_4 will probably have a relatively higher similarity to M_1 (by ignoring the small cross) than to the other candidate. If the system is not satisfied enough by this conclusion, it will continue to look for better answers by decomposing M_4 into simpler shapes plus some structures combining them.

Starting at default parameters at the sensation M_4, an operation "$\Uparrow shift(0, 0.5)$" will turn its top part into a perceptual term M_{41}, which matches reasonably well with M_1, so "$\{M_{41}\} \rightarrow diamond$" can be derived, which will have less negative evidence than "$\{M_4\} \rightarrow diamond$".

After that, operation "$\Uparrow shift(0, -0.8)$" followed by operation "$\Uparrow zoom(0.4)$" on the current sensation will generate M_{42} that matches M_2, a cross of the default size. Now the question "$\{M_4\} \rightarrow ?what$" will be answered by judgment

$$\{M_4\} \rightarrow (\Uparrow shift(0, 0.5), M_{41}, \Uparrow shift(0, -0.8), \Uparrow zoom(0.4), M_{42})$$

which will have less negative evidence than the other candidate answers, though being more complicated in syntax.

Of course, the above result assumes a proper sequence of mental operations. In the initial experiment, it can be either predetermined or obtained from exhaustive search, while in the future it will be learned together with the components themselves. That means the system's knowledge about an image also includes information on how it is usually perceived as a sequence of events and operations.

With a properly trained natural language interface, M_4 can be described as "A diamond above a small cross". The given knowledge used in the example, such as "$\{M1\} \rightarrow diamond$", can also be learned from the repeated co-occurrence of an image and a word in the system's experience, as they will both be associated with a concept in the system which is named by $diamond$. However, it is important to remember that in NARS, neither the image of a diamond nor the word "diamond" will be used to "define" the term $diamond$ (or whatever the term is labeled), as the meaning of the an abstract term like $diamond$ is not determined only by its (visual) exemplifiers or (verbal) labels, but also by its relations with the other terms, including the abstract ones.

Though only partially implemented, this example still shows the desired features of this new approach to perception when compared with the conventional computer vision techniques:

- **Subjective**: The answer to a question like "$\{M_4\} \rightarrow ?what$" not only depends on M_4, but also on the existing knowledge of the system and its resource allocation situation when the question is processed.
- **Active**: The answer "$(\Uparrow shift(0, 0.5), M_{41}, \Uparrow shift(0, -0.8), \Uparrow zoom(0.4), M_{42})$" contains operational components, so perception is based on action.
- **Unified**: The question answering process is carried out by the inference rules, and mingled with all the other co-existing processes in the system.

6 Discussion

This paper proposes a new conceptual design for perception in AGI systems. Though this approach has not been fully implemented in NARS, and no enough empirical results have not been obtained to support a definite conclusion about its feasibility, the design nevertheless has the desired features observed in human perception.

Psychologists have reached the consensus long ago that perception is multi-level abstraction, and deep learning just realizes this in special-purpose systems [14]. The approach we proposed also has the potential to carry out multi-level abstraction, though with the following characteristics that distinguishes it from deep learning and the other traditional approaches:

- Using meaningful term connectors to carry out abstraction from level to level. It is assumed that the existing term connectors of NARS [27] are sufficient for all necessary patterns — convolution and neuron models are basically weighted average functions followed by a non-linear step, which should be achievable using the set-theoretic operators of NARS.
- Carrying out multiple tasks, so the intermediate results are not bounded to a single task, but have independent meaning. Therefore, learning results are naturally transferable. As there is no distinction between "hidden layer" and "input/output layer", results at any layer are understandable (to various degrees), and are adaptive with experience-grounded meaning.

- Using multi-level abstraction to solve "over-fitting" and "inductive bias", and to keep multiple hypotheses for a given problem. For the same observation, more abstract results are less confident, though they are simpler and can be supported by other observations later, so can become preferred than the more specific results.
- Using dynamic resource allocation to carry out local and incremental adjustments to provide real-time responses. Compared to the global iterations demanded by neural network models, this approach can meet various time requirements associated with the tasks. The control mechanism of NARS is not introduced in this paper, but can be found in other publications on NARS, such as [25].
- Having stronger top-down influences, in the form of anticipation, familiarity, emotion, etc. The existing conceptual hierarchy plays a significant role in deciding what is perceived, while being adjusted in the process, as Piaget's assimilation-accommodation process, with stable perceptions as their equilibrium [18].
- Integrating perception with action, in the sense that (1) perception is carried out by operation, (2) perception and operation have unified representation, and (3) perceptive patterns are identified as invariants during related operations.

Like the other processes, perception in NARS will not attempt to simulate human perception in all details, but its general principles and major features. Consequently, it will still be closer to human than the existing AI techniques.

This research is still at its early stage, so the purpose of this paper is to raise this possibility for the AGI community to consider and discuss. Though there are many issues to be resolved, there are reasons to believe that this is a suitable approach for AGI systems to carry out perception.

References

1. Aloimonos, J., Weiss, I., Bandyopadhyay, A.: Active vision. Int. J. Comput. Vis. **1**(4), 333–356 (1988)
2. Barsalou, L.W.: Perceptual symbol systems. Behav. Brain Sci. **22**, 577–609 (1999)
3. Brette, R.: Subjective physics. arXiv:1311.3129v1 [q-bio.NC] (2013)
4. Chalmers, D.J., French, R.M., Hofstadter, D.R.: High-level perception, representation, and analogy: a critique of artificial intelligence methodology. J. Exp. Theor. Artif. Intell. **4**, 185–211 (1992)
5. Di Paolo, E.A., Barandiaran, X.E., Beaton, M., Buhrmann, T.: Learning to perceive in the sensorimotor approach: Piaget's theory of equilibration interpreted dynamically. Front. Hum. Neurosci. **8**, 551 (2014)
6. Flach, P.: Machine Learning: The Art and Science of Algorithms That Make Sense of Data. Cambridge University Press, New York (2012)
7. Gibson, J.J.: The theory of affordances. In: The Ecological Approach To Visual Perception, New edn. Chap. 8, pp. 127–143. Psychology Press (1986)
8. Goldstone, R.L., Barsalou, L.W.: Reuniting perception and conception. Cognition **65**, 231–262 (1998)

9. Hatfield, G.: Perception as unconscious inference. In: Heyer, D., Mausfeld, R. (eds.) Perception and the Physical World: Psychological and Philosophical Issues in Perception, pp. 113–143. Wiley, New York (2002)

10. Hockema, S.A.: Perception as prediction. In: Proceedings of the Cognitive Science conference (2004)

11. Hommel, B., Müsseler, J., Aschersleben, G., Prinz, W.: The theory of event coding (TEC): a framework for perception and action planning. Behav. Brain Sci. **24**(5), 849–78 (2001)

12. Jarvilehto, T.: Efferent influences on receptors in knowledge formation. Psycoloquy **9**(41), Article 1 (1998)

13. Lakoff, G., Johnson, M.: Philosophy in the Flesh: The Embodied Mind and Its Challenge to Western Thought. Basic Books, New York (1998)

14. LeCun, Y., Bengio, Y., Hinton, G.: Deep learning. Nature **521**, 436–444 (2015)

15. Marr, D.: Vision: A Computational Investigation into the Human Representation and Processing of Visual Information. W. H. Freeman & Co., San Francisco (1982)

16. Noë, A.: Action in Perception. MIT Press, Cambridge (2004)

17. O'Regan, J., Noë, A.: A sensorimotor account of vision and visual consciousness. Behav. Brain Sci. **24**(05), 939–973 (2001)

18. Piaget, J.: The Construction of Reality in the Child. Basic Books, New York (1954)

19. Rock, I.: The Logic of Perception. MIT Press, Cambridge (1983)

20. Russell, S., Norvig, P.: Artificial Intelligence: A Modern Approach, 3rd edn. Prentice Hall, Upper Saddle River (2010)

21. Santoro, A., et al.: A simple neural network module for relational reasoning. CoRR abs/1706.01427 (2017), http://arxiv.org/abs/1706.01427

22. Shams, L., Shimojo, S.: Sensory modalities are not separate modalities: plasticity and interactions. Curr. Opin. Neurobiol. **1**, 505–509 (2001)

23. Shanahan, M.: Perception as abduction: turning sensor data into meaningful representation. Cogn. Sci. **29**(1), 103–134 (2005)

24. Wang, P.: Experience-grounded semantics: a theory for intelligent systems. Cogn. Syst. Res. **6**(4), 282–302 (2005)

25. Wang, P.: Rigid Flexibility: The Logic of Intelligence. Springer, Dordrecht (2006). https://doi.org/10.1007/1-4020-5045-3

26. Wang, P.: Solving a problem with or without a program. J. Artif. Gen. Intell. **3**(3), 43–73 (2012)

27. Wang, P.: Non-Axiomatic Logic: A Model of Intelligent Reasoning. World Scientific, Singapore (2013)

28. Wu, T.: Integration and goal-guided scheduling of bottom-up and top-down computing processes in hierarchical models. Ph.D. thesis, University of California, Los Angeles (2011)

A Phenomenologically Justifiable Simulation of Mental Modeling

Mark Wernsdorfer$^{(\boxtimes)}$ (iD)

Cognitive Systems, University of Bamberg,
An der Weberei 5, 96047 Bamberg, Germany
mark.wernsdorfer@uni-bamberg.de
https://www.uni-bamberg.de/en/cogsys/

Abstract. Real-world agents need to learn how to react to their environment. To achieve this, it is crucial that they have a model of this environment that is adapted *during* interaction and *although* important aspects may be hidden. This paper presents a new type of model for partially observable environments that enables an agent to represent hidden states but can still be generated and queried in *realtime*. Agents can use such a model to predict the outcomes of their actions and to infer action policies. These policies turn out to be better than the optimal policy in a partially observable Markov decision process as it can be inferred, for example, by Q- or SARSA-learning. The structure and generation of these models are motivated both by phenomenological considerations from semiotics and the philosophy of mind. The performance of these models is compared to a baseline of Markov models for prediction and interaction in partially observable environments.

Keywords: Model generation · Reinforcement learning
Phenomenology · Mental models

1 Introduction

In philosophical conversations about artificial intelligence, the common sentiment is that the concepts of such systems are fundamentally limited by the concepts of their designer. If complex concepts are built from basic concepts, so the reasoning goes, and the basic concepts of an artificial system are provided by its designer, then all the concepts that the system might develop can only be *derived* from the designer and therefore they include all of their flaws and limitations as well [19,20]. If an artificial intelligence already starts with concepts that are intrinsically connected to a human body, for example, how is it supposed to use these concepts with a non-human body? Systems that create their own original "concepts" (i.e., representations of external reality) could theoretically interact with environments we cannot even imagine. Recent successes in *deep learning* are based on this premise: The early layers in a deep network

© Springer Nature Switzerland AG 2018
M. Iklé et al. (Eds.): AGI 2018, LNAI 10999, pp. 270–280, 2018.
https://doi.org/10.1007/978-3-319-97676-1_26

learn basic concepts of elementary features. The later layers operate only on combinations of these features [1, for details on this motivation].

In the following, a new kind of model for partially observable systems is presented. This type of *semiotic model* is inspired by phenomenological investigations of mental representation. The representations in such a model imitate the mental representations in a mental model. As a consequence, the generation of content for the most basic of these representations can be considered as *a simulation for the generation of basic concepts.*

2   Related Work

There are two general conceptions of partially observable environments. The first is *state based,* the second *property based* [17]. State based conceptions of partially observable environments are graphical models like Markov models or finite state automata [8]. Property based conceptions are usually learned from methods that generalize first-order logic statements about the dynamics between agent and environment (i.e., action languages) [6,10].

Unfortunately, the property based conception cannot be easily translated into the state based conception. The reason is that "virtually all current first-order methods are restricted by the Markov assumption" [16]. The Markov assumption states that current observations fully determine observations after the next time step. In fact, this is exactly what makes an environment according to the state based conception be *fully,* instead of *partially,* observable.

The various planning and problem solving approaches that build upon STRIPS [5] are property based. The learning of *schemata* [4] for a property based conception of the environment therefore effectively solves a *different* problem than learning to interact with a partially observable state based conception. "[S]chema learning has no predefined states such as those found in a [Partially Observable Markov Decision Process] or [Hidden Markov Model]; the set of sensor readings *is* the state" [7]. As a consequence, property based conceptions of *partially observable environments* are in fact state based conceptions of *fully observable environments.* This also concerns approaches such as (but not limited to) Motmap [18], Schema Networks [9], or Variational State Tabulations [2].[1]

The hard problem while modeling a partially observable environment in the state based Markov framework is *perceptual aliasing.* Consider a path that forks at two different, but apparently identical, locations. To reach its goal, the agent has to go left at the first fork but right at the second. Unfortunately, its immediate observations do not enable it to differentiate both forks in any way. Approaches from reinforcement learning solve this problem by approximating a whole partially observable Markov decision process that includes an evaluation of the agent's actions in the form of reward [3,13–15,21]. If goals *change,* however, it makes sense not to learn the whole Markov decision process but only its

---

[1] In the last one, the authors explicitly state that "[t]he agent rarely observes the exact same frame from a previous episode" which makes the environment according to a state based conception practically be fully observable.

causal dynamics. Accordingly, partially observable environments are defined as Markov decision processes *without reward*.

Partially observable environments are 5-tuples (E, M, T, O, S), where E is a set of hidden states, M is a set of motor emissions from the agent, $T : E \times M \times E \rightarrow [0, 1]$ describes the probability of any successor state when executing a particular motor emission in a particular state, $O : E \times S \rightarrow [0, 1]$ describes the probability of a hidden state emitting a particular sensor activation towards the agent, and S is a set of sensor emissions.

One type of model has proven quite useful for learning partially observable environments in a realtime scenario. *Order-n Markov models* represent the hidden world state with a fixed history of past emissions of length n. This history can be considered as the current *state* of an order-n Markov model. The state of the model is a representation for the assumed hidden state of the environment. Up to a certain point, the prediction performance of order-n Markov models tends to increase with an increase in history length. Once this point is reached, however, performance decreases steadily. Transition conditions become too specific to generalize the distribution of emissions appropriately while, at the same time, long-term dependencies over more than n time steps are lost.

3   Background

The concept of *dynamically coupled trajectories* is another way to conceive of an unknown environment. It is an alternative to partially observable environments that does not require that hidden states transition according to a particular probability distribution. Real cognitive systems accept this fundamental uncertainty in external reality. As a consequence, they are forced *to incorporate failed expectations* into their mental model. In the philosophy of mind, this failing of expectations has also been described as "breakdown" [20]. Accordingly, in the following, the environment is conceived of as essentially *erratic*.

3.1   Dynamically Coupled Trajectories

Definition 1. Dynamic trajectories *are sequences, where the emission function* f *changes* erratically: *It depends only on the current time step* t.

$$x_t = f(t, x_{t-1})$$

The emission function f at time t determines *the state* f_t of a dynamic system $f_t(x) = f(t, x)$. In a *dynamic* trajectory, f *changes* with t.

However, cognitive systems do not perceive *their own* emissions, they perceive the emissions of external reality. Reality and cognitive system co-determine one another. In fact, both are so closely connected that their individual trajectories are in a *coupling*. Unities are considered as coupled "whenever the conduct of two or more unities is such that the conduct of each one is a function of the conduct of the others" [12].

Equations 1 and 2 describe the emissions in the dynamic trajectories of an *agent* that simulates a cognitive system in state a_t and its *environment* that simulates external reality in state e_t after each time step.

$$s_t = e_t(m_{t-1}) \tag{1}$$
$$m_t = a_t(s_{t-1}) \tag{2}$$

The current emission of the environment (i.e., sensor activation) is $s_t \in S$, the current emission of the agent (i.e., motor activation) is $m_t \in M$, the current state of the environment is $e_t : M \to S$, and the current state of the agent is $a_t : S \to M$. No system has access to the state of the other, they merely receive the other's emissions.

3.2   Semiotic Models

The mental model that cognitive systems have of external reality is composed of such mental representations. A formal semiotic conception of mental representation can serve as a foundation to formally describe mental models as *semiotic models*. A mental representation is a *symbolic* representation for its referent. Symbols are semiotically defined by the three possible relations between shape, content, and referent. Figure 1 illustrates these relations. Roughly speaking, *content* is what an external *referent* means, and *shape* is how this meaning appears, to the cognitive system [11, for an introduction on Peircean semiotics]. The generation of basic concepts in mental representations starts from the system's external referents, goes over the content, and eventually evokes a shape.

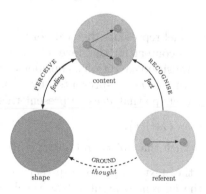

Fig. 1. The directions of causation in a mental representation.

Definition 2. *A referent $r \in$ referents$_l$ is a 2-tuple $r \subseteq C_l \times S_l$ that consists of elements from the set of all transition conditions C_l and consequence shapes S_l.*

Definition 3. *Every* content $m \in$ content *is a functional relation* $m : C_l \to S$ *from transition conditions to consequence shapes. If* $m(a) = b$, *for example, then* content m *presents the referent* $r = \langle a, b \rangle$.

Definition 4. *Every* shape $s \in S_l$ *is the appearance of one content. Both are in an injective relation* indices$_l$: $S_l \leftrightarrow$ content$_{l-1}$, *where* $l \geq 1$, *such that*

$$\forall s_0, s_1 \in S_l. \ \text{indices}_l(s_0) = \text{indices}_l(s_1) \Rightarrow s_0 = s_1$$

If a content presents a particular referent, then the shape of this content re-presents this referent. A formal conception of representation is sufficient for to define *the structure* of a semiotic model.

Definition 5. *The* structure *of a semiotic model is a sequence* $\Lambda : \ \mathbb{N}^* \to$ { indices$_l$ | $l \in \mathbb{N}^*$ } *that determines a set* indices$_l$ *for each level of abstraction* l. *Each of these sets, in turn, determines* content$_l$ *at its level and* S_{l+1} *at the level above, such that* $S_{l+1} =$ { s | $\langle s, m \rangle \in$ indices$_l$ } *and* content$_l =$ { m | $\langle s, m \rangle \in$ indices$_l$ }. *The set of shapes and content are unique to each level.*

Following from Fig. 1, *feelings* are a relation between phenomenal shape and content. *Facts* are a relation between referent and mental content. They can be considered as icons that present the structure of external reality. *Thoughts,* eventually are a relation between referent and shape. They can be considered as symbols that re-present an external referent. The structure of a semiotic model is a partially ordered set of content. Feelings define an order in this set by indicating content at one level with a more abstract shape at the level above.

Definition 6. *The* state *of the semiotic model* Λ *is a sequence* $\lambda : \ \mathbb{N}^* \to S$ *that determines the shape of the current content at level* l *of* Λ *in virtue of* indices$_{l-1}$, *where* $l \geq 1$.

The state of a semiotic model represents the state of the described system. Each index in the state provides content for this level of the model.

To eventually define transition conditions, consider what happens if a referent is received at level $l \geq 1$ that is *not* re-presented by $\lambda(l)$: this level of the state has to transition to a new shape that *does* re-present this referent.

$$\lambda(l) \leftarrow m'\big(\lambda(l), r\big),$$
$$\text{such that } m' = \text{indices}_{l+1}\big(\lambda(l+1)\big) \tag{3}$$

Equation 3 shows that the next shape to re-present the unknown referent is selected according to the current content m' at the level above. If the shape predicted by m' does *not* represent the referent, or there is no level $l+1$ to begin with, then the model cannot describe the current referent. The conditions for transitioning from one shape to another are therefore defined as follows.

Definition 7. *Every* transition condition $c \in C_l$ *at level* $l \geq 1$ *is a 2-tuple that consists of a referent* $\langle c, s \rangle \in$ referents$_l$ *and a shape* $s' \in S_{l+1}$ *that does* not *re-present this referent.*

$$C_l \subseteq \{ \ \langle s', \langle c, s \rangle \rangle \ \} \text{ such that } m(c) \neq s, \text{ where } m = \text{indices}_{l+1}(s')$$

Both, referent and inappropriate re-presentation at this level, are *the reason* for a transition and, together, they are *a condition* that enables the prediction of a new shape that may provide an appropriate content for this referent in the future.

4   Approach

Real cognitive systems perform predictions based on their mental model and they update this model according to unexpected changes in the environment. Agent and environment in a comprehensive simulation need to perform these tasks with each new observation and in each step of the basic simulation defined in Algorithm 1.

Algorithm 1. Simulation Cycle and Evaluation.

```
1  function simulation(interact, e₀)
2  |   loss ← ∅;
3  |   model ← ∅;
4  |   state ← ∅;
5  |   for t < T do
6  |   |   mₜ ← π(t)
7  |   |   eₜ₊₁, sₜ₊₁ ← interact(eₜ, mₜ)
8  |   |   if t == 0 then loss(t) ← 1;
9  |   |   else
10 |   |   |   ŝₜ₊₁ ← pred(model, state, mₜ)
11 |   |   |   if ŝₜ₊₁ == sₜ₊₁ then loss(t) ← 0;
12 |   |   |   else loss(t) ← 1;
13 |   |   |   update(model, state, mₜ, sₜ₊₁)
```

The simulation cycle requires an external procedure to simulate the system which is supposed to be described. In the following, this procedure is denoted as $\texttt{interact} : E \times M \rightarrow E \times S$. The agent in such a simulation acts according to an arbitrary action policy π and the environment is in some initial state e_0. The simulation is performed for T time steps. During the simulation, $\texttt{loss}$ keeps track of the agent's (i.e., the current model's) predictive success. The structure $\texttt{model}$ and its $\texttt{state}$ are initialized outside the loop so they can be maintained throughout the simulation.

The average loss at the end of the simulation provides an objective measure of performance to compare different models. Implicitly, this measure also allows the comparison of the different procedures that *generated* these models. Subtracting the average loss from 1 provides a measure for success.

Definition 4 of shapes and Definition 7 of transition conditions both exclude the base level $l = 0$ of the semiotic model. The reason is that basic transition conditions and consequence shapes both depend on the particular type of system that is supposed to be described. In the following, basic shapes S_0 and transition conditions C_0 for agent and environment in a simulation according to Algorithm 1 are defined.

Equation 4 shows that the current transition condition c_t of a mobile agent is its last sensorimotor activation and the current consequence s_t' shape is the immediately following sensor activation. Both determine the current referent r_t which *couples* agent and environment.

$$C_0 \subseteq S \times M, \qquad S_0 \subseteq S, \qquad R_0 \subseteq C_0 \times S_0 \\ c_t = \langle s_{t-1}, m_{t-1} \rangle, \qquad s_t' = s_t, \qquad r_t = \langle c_t, s_t \rangle \tag{4}$$

5   Results

The performance of a semiotic model has been evaluated during the interaction between an agent and a partially observable grid world. The structure of the grid world and the agent's partial perception of it is inspired by the classical example of Sutton [22] where a mobile agent perceives only its immediate environment.

Figure 2 defines a partially observable environment, in which the hidden state of the environment is *the agent's position*. The agent's motor emission and this hidden state at time t fully determine the sensor emission at $t + 1$.

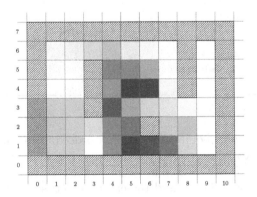

Fig. 2. Sutton's grid world.

An illustration for parts of the environment in relation to their representations goes beyond the scope of this article. To provide an impression, however, Fig. 2 shows the relative frequency of a particular model state in the various hidden states of the environment (i.e., positions). Lighter areas are less frequently associated with the given representation than darker areas.

5.1   Prediction

Prediction with semiotic Models works similar to prediction with a Markov model. The difference is that there are *several* models that make *different* predictions. The currently appropriate model is the content indicated by the second level of the state $\lambda(1)$ according to $\texttt{indices}_1$. The quality of the agent's predictions allow an estimate on its ability to localize itself within the grid world. Figure 3a shows the system's average prediction success over 10 runs of 5000000 iterations each. The performance of the semiotic model is compared to a Markov model with the same history length of $n = 1$.[2]

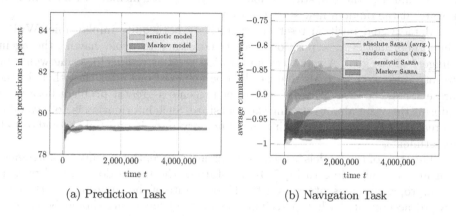

(a) Prediction Task   (b) Navigation Task

Fig. 3. Evaluation results as averages performances. (Color figure online)

The semiotic model outperforms the Markov model with an average of 82.0% compared to an average of 79.3%. The figure also shows that the variance of the semiotic model's performance is much greater than the performance of the Markov model. This is probably due to the fact that a lot more transition samples are available for the single function approximation in a Markov model whereas a semiotic model distributes these samples among several function approximations (i.e., representations). Depending on the agent's random actions, this distribution can be more or less appropriate.

5.2   Navigation

In the navigation task, SARSA-learning [23, Chap. 6.4] is used to determine an evaluation for the agent's actions during particular perceptions. This evaluation enables the agent to select goal-directed actions.

$$Q(p_{t-1}, a_{t-1}) \leftarrow Q(p_{t-1}, a_{t-1}) + A,$$
$$\text{where } A = \alpha\big(r_t + \gamma Q(p_t, a_t) - Q(p_{t-1}, a_{t-1})\big) \tag{5}$$

---

[2] Comparisons with $n \geq 2$ yield similar results.

The element p_{t-1} is the system's last perception, a_{t-1} is the system's last action, and r_t is the subsequently received reward. The parameter α determines the learning rate and γ determines the discount factor. In this experiment, the current state of the model is used for p_t. The action a_t is the system's motor emission $m_t \in M$. For each action selection, there is an $\epsilon = 0.1$ chance for a uniformly random exploratory action.

Location $\langle 9, 6 \rangle$ has been designated as goal state. Upon reaching this state, the agent receives a reward of $r_t = 10$, $r_t = -1$ otherwise. In our experiments, $\gamma = 1$ arbitrarily. The agent's position is randomly reset after reaching the goal position. Usually, p_{t-1} and a_{t-1} are also reset after reaching the goal state to avoid "diluting" the goal state evaluation in the agent's memory with the neutral reward at the random new start position.

Memory and position reset are cognitively both quite implausible. With a single goal, however, a position reset is necessary to avoid having the agent "linger" at the goal. A way to avoid position reset as well as lingering would be to introduce circular goals that need to be achieved one after the other. In the present case, however, the memory reset presents a greater problem because it informs the agent about reaching the goal state. Such information is not available to real cognitive systems which is why memory reset is omitted throughout all experiments.[3]

The state of the models is used as the agent's perception during reinforcement learning and according to Eq. 5. If the state of the model does indeed provide an appropriate representation for the hidden state of the environment, then the reward accumulated when perceiving *the state of the model* should be close to the reward of an agent that perceives its *actual* position in the environment.

Figure 3b shows a performance comparison between Markov models and semiotic models over 10 runs of 5000000 iterations each. It also shows the average navigation performance of a system that perceives the environment's hidden states (i.e., the agent's position) in black and the average performance of a system that acts randomly in red.

Random actions generate on average the least amount of cumulative reward. A Markov-based SARSA is only slightly better on average but sometimes even worse than a random policy. Similar to the orientation task before, the approach with a semiotic model shows the most variance. After the 1000000-th time step, however, even the worst run of semiotic SARSA is better than the best run with Markov SARSA. The best run with a semiotic model almost reaches the average performance of an agent that perceives its absolute position in the grid world, *effectively making the environment fully observable.*

6   Conclusion

The content of the symbolic representations in a semiotic model provide useful concepts to an autonomous mobile agent. These concepts apply to separate parts

---

[3] As a consequence, the performance of the baseline approach is lower than in experiments with memory reset.

of the environment and they allow the construction of an appropriate representation for hidden states of the environment.

Phenomenological constraints enable the development of reinforcement learning experiments that are more plausible from a cognitive point of view. They establish a testing ground for agents that is much closer to real-world circumstances. Three adjustments have been presented. (1) The environment must be conceded erratic state transitions. (2) The memory of the agent cannot be reset after reaching its goal. (3) The state of the environment cannot be reset after the agent reaches its goal. The last point requires a more fundamental change in the classical Reinforcement Learning paradigm.

Under consideration of these points, a formal model has been developed that enables the description of erratic environments. The quality of this model is evaluated in virtue of *predictive success* and *accumulated reward*. It is shown that the representations in this model enable an agent not only to predict, but also to interact, significantly more effective than order-n Markov models do.

Unfortunately, no simulation can show the actual advantage of being able to describe an erratic environment. No simulated system can change its state erratically. Random events in a computational simulation always imply one particular probability distribution while ignoring another. These distributions are determined by parameters that can even be designed to randomly change themselves. The distribution of *this* random change must again be determined by some predetermined parameters. External reality, in contrast, could very well be a truly erratic environment that is not restricted in the same way.

Simulations in reinforcement learning can be made more plausible with the proposed measures, but only a truly erratic reality can show if they perform similar to how humans generate their most basic concepts.

References

1. Bengio, Y., Courville, A., Vincent, P.: Unsupervised feature learning and deep learning: a review and new perspectives. CoRR abs/1206.5538 (2012)
2. Corneil, D., Gerstner, W., Brea, J.: Efficient model-based deep reinforcement learning with variational state tabulation. arXiv preprint arXiv:1802.04325 (2018)
3. Crook, P., Hayes, G.: Learning in a state of confusion: perceptual aliasing in grid world navigation. In: Towards Intelligent Mobile Robots, vol. 4 (2003)
4. Drescher, G.: Made-Up Minds. MIT press, Cambridge (1991)
5. Fikes, R., Nilsson, N.: Strips: a new approach to the application of theorem proving to problem solving. Artif. Intell. **2**(3–4), 189–208 (1971)
6. Gelfond, M., Lifschitz, V.: Action languages. Electron. Trans. AI **3**, 195–210 (1998)
7. Holmes, M., Isbell, C.: Schema learning: experience-based construction of predictive action models. In: Advances in Neural Information Processing Systems, pp. 585–592 (2005)
8. Kaelbling, L.P., Littman, M.L., Cassandra, A.R.: Planning and acting in partially observable stochastic domains. Artif. Intell. **101**(1), 99–134 (1998)
9. Kansky, K., et al.: Schema networks: zero-shot transfer with a generative causal model of intuitive physics. arXiv preprint arXiv:1706.04317 (2017)

10. Lifschitz, V., Turner, H.: Representing transition systems by logic programs. In: Gelfond, M., Leone, N., Pfeifer, G. (eds.) LPNMR 1999. LNCS (LNAI), vol. 1730, pp. 92–106. Springer, Heidelberg (1999). https://doi.org/10.1007/3-540-46767-X_7

11. Marty, R.: C.S. Peirce's phaneroscopy and semiotics. Semiotica **41**(1–4), 169–182 (1982)

12. Maturana, H.: Autopoiesis and Cognition: The Realization of the Living. Springer, Dordrecht (1980). https://doi.org/10.1007/978-94-009-8947-4

13. McCallum, A.: Overcoming incomplete perception with utile distinction memory. In: Proceedings of the 10th International Conference on Machine Learning, pp. 190–196 (1993)

14. McCallum, A.: Instance-based state identification for reinforcement learning. In: Advances in Neural Information Processing Systems, pp. 377–384 (1995)

15. McCallum, A.: Reinforcement learning with selective perception and hidden state. Ph.D. thesis, University of Rochester, Department of Computer Science (1996)

16. van Otterlo, M.: The Logic of Adaptive Behavior: Knowledge Representation and Algorithms for Adaptive Sequential Decision Making Under Uncertainty in First-Order and Relational Domains. Ios Press, Amsterdam (2009). Frontiers in artificial intelligence and applications

17. Perotto, F.S., Buisson, J.C., Alvares, L.O.C.: Constructivist anticipatory learning mechanism (calm): dealing with partially deterministic and partially observable environments. In: International Conference on Epigenetic Robotics, pp. 117–127. Lund University Cognitive Science (2007)

18. Ring, M., Schaul, T., Schmidhuber, J.: The two-dimensional organization of behavior. In: 2011 IEEE International Conference on Development and Learning (ICDL), vol. 2, pp. 1–8. IEEE (2011)

19. Searle, J.: Intrinsic intentionality. Behav. Brain Sci. **3**(03), 450–457 (1980)

20. Searle, J.: Intentionality: An Essay in the Philosophy of Mind. Cambridge Univ. Press, Cambridge Paperback Library, Cambridge (1983)

21. Sun, R., Sessions, C.: Self-segmentation of sequences: automatic formation of hierarchies of sequential behaviors. Syst. Man Cybern. Part B Cybern. **30**(3), 403–418 (2000)

22. Sutton, R.: Integrated architectures for learning, planning, and reacting based on approximating dynamic programming. In: Proceedings of the 7th International Conference on Machine Learning, pp. 216–224 (1990)

23. Sutton, R., Barto, A.: Reinforcement Learning: An Introduction, vol. 1. MIT press, Cambridge (1998)

A Time-Critical Simulation of Language Comprehension

Mark Wernsdorfer[⊠] [iD]

Cognitive Systems, University of Bamberg,
An der Weberei 5, 96047 Bamberg, Germany
mark.wernsdorfer@uni-bamberg.de
https://www.uni-bamberg.de/en/cogsys/

Abstract. Language comprehension is usually not understood as a time-critical task. Humans, however, process language on-line, in linear time, and with a single pass over a particular instance of speech or text. This calls for a genuinely *cognitive* algorithmic approach to simulating language comprehension. A formal conception of language is developed, as well as a model for this conception. An algorithm is presented that generates such a model on-line and from a single pass over a text. The generated model is evaluated qualitatively, by comparing its representations to linguistic segmentations (e.g. syllables, words, sentences). Results show that the model contains synonyms and homonyms as can be found in natural language. This suggests that the algorithm is able to recognize and make consistent use of *context*–which is crucial to understanding *in general*. In addition, the underlying algorithm is evaluated against a baseline approach with similar properties. This shows that the generated model is able to capture arbitrarily extended dependencies and therefore to outperform exclusively history-based approaches.

Keywords: Time-critical model generation · Linguistic models
On-line learning

1 Introduction

Language comprehension can be considered as one particular use case for a more general cognitive process. The idea that different cognitive abilities are realized by neural "wetware" in the same general manner is known as "the equipotentiality of neural tissue" [12]. More specifically, the central thesis behind "Cognitive Linguistics" is that the mind does not feature particularly *linguistic* modules. Instead, language is merely the manifestation of a general cognitive process which is itself not essentially linguistic but realizes all sorts of non-linguistic functions [5]. The scientific intention behind such hypotheses is not a devaluation of language but the ability to apply linguistic insights onto cognition *in general*. This does not mean to suggest that cognitive processes are an amodal *language of thought* [6] but quite the opposite: language should be conceived of as

© Springer Nature Switzerland AG 2018
M. Iklé et al. (Eds.): AGI 2018, LNAI 10999, pp. 281–291, 2018.
https://doi.org/10.1007/978-3-319-97676-1_27

essentially *perceptual* and *embodied* [10]. As a consequence of these hypotheses, a successful simulation of language understanding will also always simulate aspects of *generally intelligent information processing.*

One central aspect shared by language understanding and understanding in general is the context-aware generation of grounded symbolic representations in a hierarchical model [8]. This ability can be *tested* with linguistic sequences as input data to evaluate the cognitive plausibility of the generated representations as mental representations for arbitrary referents. More practically, however, the same algorithm can also be fed with the sensorimotor data of an autonomous agent as a simulation for the generation of a mental model which is at the foundation of generally intelligent behavior [19].

To this end, in the following, a type of model is formalized. Such a model is able to describe instances of context-sensitive natural language. It can be inferred automatically from an arbitrary sequence so as to represent individual segments of this sequence, depending on their *structure* as well as *context*. An algorithm is presented to generate this model automatically and on-line during a single pass over a sequence–similar to how cognitive systems generate a mental model of external reality.

2   Related Work

From a computational perspective, language is often conceived of as a *hidden Markov model* [2,9,17, for example]. In systems that are supposed to understand language, these models take on states that represent hypothetical hidden states in a language generating system. Graphical models that are based on hidden states describe probability distributions for the transition from one hidden state to another. Each of these hidden states is also associated with a probability distribution of emissions (often also referred to as "observations").

Three general problems can be solved well with hidden Markov models. (1) From a given model and a sequence of emissions—in the following referred to as *"trajectory"*—, a probability can be inferred that this trajectory has been generated according to the model (i.e., likelihood). (2) From a given model and a trajectory, the most probable sequence of hidden states can be inferred that have been transitioned during the generation of this trajectory (i.e, decoding). (3) From a given set of hidden states and a trajectory, the transition probabilities between states and the emission probabilities for each state can be inferred (i.e., learning) [14]. There is a fourth problem, however, for which there is no generally established solution: *From a given trajectory, infer the hidden states, the transition probabilities between them, and the emission probabilities for each state.* Most approaches to this problem are not feasible for on-line learning in time-critical situations [16, for an approach and overview].

The field of automatic grammar/automaton inference presents many closely related solutions to similar problems [4]. One realtime-feasible approach is SEQUITUR [13]. During a single pass once over the sequence, it builds a grammar that allows exact reproduction of the sequence. However, SEQUITUR learns only context-*free* grammars. Also, it does not *generalize* because its intended application is lossless data compression.[1] Unfortunately, no algorithm for grammatical inference fulfills the following requirements for a simulation of human language comprehension. (1) The algorithm must infer context-*sensitive* grammars. (2) The generated structures must *generalize* the input data. (3) The algorithm requires only *one* pass over the data and has less than *polynomial* runtime.

The only computational procedure that satisfies these criteria are *order-n Markov predictors*. The structure of such a predictor is a transition table $m : X^n \times X \to \mathbb{N}^*$ that contains the *frequency* of transitions from the history of the last n emissions to the current emission, where X is the set of all emissions.[2] Predictions can simply be inferred by querying the transition table for the emission that maximizes the transition count for the current history. Each history in this table is effectively an approximation for the hidden state in a hidden Markov model which is supposed to generate the observed trajectory.

3   Background

Despite their practical success, order-n Markov predictors have an obvious drawback: they are fundamentally incapable of capturing any long-term dependency between emissions that are more than $n - 1$ time steps apart [7]. This problem can be remedied with a novel conception of the processes behind the generation of a trajectory.

3.1   Language as Trajectory

Definition 1. Static trajectories *are a sequence of individual emissions x_t with a history of length n, where $t \in \mathbb{N}^*$ and $1 \leq n$.*

$$x_t = f\left([\ x_s\ ]_{s=t-n}^{t-1} \right) = f(x_{t-n}, x_{t-n+1}, ..., x_{t-1})$$

The emission of the trajectory after each time step t is a particular unspecified function $f : X^n \to X$ of the current history with length n, where X is the set of all possible emissions. In the following, f is referred to as "emission function".

Definition 2. Dynamic trajectories *are static trajectories, where the emission function f changes with time t.*

For the sake of simplicity, only dynamic trajectories with a history length of $n = 1$ are considered. As a consequence, the emission function in Definition 2 can be simplified.

$$x_t = f(t, x_{t-1}) = f_t(x_{t-1}) \tag{1}$$

---

[1] A reliable indicator for understanding is not the reproduction of text but the ability to tell a story in *one's own words*..

[2] Elsewhere, histories are also referred to as "contexts" or "windows".

The function in Eq. 1 is a *dynamic emission function*. The transitions between its order-1 emission functions are determined by an *order-2 emission function* $f^2 : \mathcal{F}^1 \rightarrow \mathcal{F}^1$ such that $f^2(f_{t-1}) = f_t$, where $f^2 \in \mathcal{F}^2$ and $f_{t-1}, f_t \in \mathcal{F}^1$. Analogously, the transition from one letter to another can be conceived of as determined by a particular *syllable*, the transition from one syllable to another is determined by a particular *word*, the transition between words is determined by a *sentence*, and so on.

3.2 Content in Semiotic Models

Trajectories from dynamic emission functions can be described with *semiotic models*. The structure of a semiotic model consists of *symbolic representations*. Figure 1 shows the structure of a symbolic representation. Roughly speaking, the *content* of a symbol is what a *referent* means, the *shape* is how this meaning appears, and the *referent* is an external correlate. All language is based on symbols. Symbols are semiotically defined as a 3-tuple of *index*, *icon*, and *symbol* [11, for an introduction to Peircean semiotics]. An index is a tuple that consists of *shape* and *content*, an icon is a tuple that consists of *referent* and *content*, and a symbol, eventually is a tuple of *referent* and *shape*. All indices establish a relation, all icons establish a relation, and all symbols establish the composition relation of indices and icons.

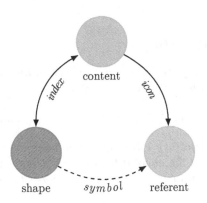

Fig. 1. A symbolic representation.

This definition of semiotic models builds upon a definition for referent, content, and shape. The symbolic representation relation from shape to referent in Fig. 1 is established by a causal influence starting from the referent, going over the content, eventually evoking the shape.

Definition 3. *A referent* $r \in$ referents$_l$ *is a tuple* $r \subseteq C_l \times S_l$ *that consists of elements from the set of transition conditions* C_l *and consequence shapes* S_l, *where* $l \geq 0$.

Definition 4. *A content* $m \in$ content *is a functional relation* $m : C_l \to S_l$ *from transition conditions to consequence shapes, where* $l \geq 0$. *If* $m(a) = b$, *for example, then content* m *presents the referent* $r = \langle a, b \rangle$.

Definition 5. *A shape* $s \in S_l$ *is the appearance of one content. Both are in an injective relation* indices$_l$: $S_l \leftrightarrow$ content$_{l-1}$, *where* $l \geq 1$, *such that*

$$\forall s_0, s_1 \in S_l. \text{ indices}_l(s_0) = \text{indices}_l(s_1) \Rightarrow s_0 = s_1$$

If a content presents a particular referent, and a shape presents this content, then this shape effectively *re*-presents the referent *via content*. This formal conception of representation is crucial to a definition for the structure of semiotic models.

Definition 6. *The* structure *of a semiotic model is a sequence* $\Lambda : \mathbb{N}^* \to$ { indices$_l$ | $l \in \mathbb{N}^*$ } *that determines another set* indices$_l$ *for each level of abstraction* l. *Each of these sets determines* content$_l$ *at its own level and* S_{l+1} *at the level above, such that* $S_{l+1} = \{ s \mid \langle s, m \rangle \in$ indices$_l \}$ *and* content$_l =$ { $m \mid \langle s, m \rangle \in$ indices$_l$ }. *The sets of shapes and content are unique to each level.*

Definition 7. *The* state *of semiotic model* Λ *is a sequence* $\lambda : \mathbb{N}^* \to S$ *that determines the shape of the current content at level* l *of* Λ, *where* $l \geq 1$.

Lastly, consider what happens if a referent is received at level $l \geq 1$ that is *not* represented by $\lambda(l)$. The next obvious representation for the unknown referent is selected according to the content m' associated with the current shape at the next level $l + 1$. If the shape predicted by m' does *not* represent the referent, or *there is no level* $l + 1$ to begin with, then the model cannot describe the current referent and, as a consequence, the referent cannot be understood. From this follow the transition conditions at level $l \geq 1$.

Definition 8. *A transition condition* $c \in C_l$ *at level* $l \geq 1$ *is a tuple that consists of a referent* $\langle c, s \rangle \in$ referents$_l$ *and a shape* $s' \in S_{l+1}$ *that does* not *represent this referent.*

$$C_l \subseteq \{ \langle s', \langle c, s \rangle \rangle \}, \quad \text{such that } m(c) \neq s, \text{ where } m = \text{indices}_{l+1}(s')$$

Both, referent and inappropriate representation at this level, are *the reason* for a transition and, together, they are *the condition* for a new shape. This condition provides content useful for prediction under the same circumstances in the future.

Both, transition conditions and shapes at level 0, depend on the particular emissions in the trajectory. In the following, basic shapes S_0 and transition conditions C_0 are *letters*. The current letter is transition condition c_t and the next letter is consequence shape s'_t. The current referent r_t after time step t is defined according to Definition 3.

4   Approach

In Definition 4, content is defined as a functional relation from transition condition to consequence shape. Individual *transition probabilities* are inferred from transition frequencies like in an order-n Markov predictor.

Definition 9. Probabilistic content *is a function from transition conditions and consequence shapes to transition frequencies* $m' : C_l \times S_l \to \mathbb{N}^*$. *The probability of referent* $r = \langle c, s \rangle$ *according to* $m' \in$ content$_l$ *is* $p(m', c, s)$ *for any* $l \geq 0$.

$$p : \text{content}_l \times C_l \times S_l \to [0,1] \subseteq \mathbb{R}$$

$$\langle m', c, s \rangle \mapsto \frac{\alpha + m'(c, s)}{\sum_{s'}^{S} \alpha + m'(c, s')}$$

The frequency of the given referent as well as the sum of all frequencies are modified by additive smoothing. The pseudocount $\alpha \in \mathbb{R}_{\geq 0}$ *determines a Dirichlet distribution that defines the expected initial probabilities [3]. If the denominator is zero, the probability of the referent is defined as 1.*

Algorithm 1. Generating a Semiotic Model.

```
1  function generate(l, Λ, λ, s_t)
2  │  if l in domain of λ then
3  │  │  add s_t to Λ(l);
4  │  │  if l + 1 in domain of λ then
5  │  │  │  m' ← λ(l + 1);
6  │  │  │  if p(m', λ(l), s_t) < σ then
7  │  │  │  │  if l + 2 in domain of λ then
8  │  │  │  │  │  M' ← λ(l + 2);
9  │  │  │  │  │  m' ← argmax p(M', m', m);
   │  │  │  │  │      m∈Λ(l+1)
10 │  │  │  │  │  if p(m', λ(l), s_t) < σ then
11 │  │  │  │  │  │  m' ← argmax p(m, λ(l), s_t);
   │  │  │  │  │  │      m∈Λ(l+1)
12 │  │  │  │  │  └  if p(m', λ(l), s_t) < σ then m' ← ∅;
13 │  │  │  │  else m' ← ∅;
14 │  │  │  └  generate(l + 1, Λ, λ, m');
15 │  │  else
16 │  │  │  m' ← ∅;
17 │  │  │  λ(l + 1) ← m';
18 │  │  └  Λ(l + 1) ← { m' };
19 │  └  m'(λ(l), s_t) ← m'.(λ(l), s_t) + 1;
20 │  else if l == 0 then Λ(0) ← { s_t };
21 └  λ(l) ← s_t;
```

For the algorithm to decide whether a particular probabilistic content is an appropriate presentation of a referent, a presentation threshold $\sigma \in [0, 1]$ is introduced. If the probability of a referent according the content is above σ, then the referent is considered to be *presented* by this content. If $\sigma = 0$, the generated model is effectively *deterministic* [18, for an example]. If $\sigma = 1$, in contrast, the algorithm generates a regular Markov predictor.

Algorithm 1 describes the iterative generation of the state and structure of a semiotic model from a continual trajectory. The procedure tries to find a good representation for *the structure* of the current referent in the currently given *context*. To achieve this, hierarchically repetitive structures in the stream of incoming referents are exploited. This procedure is performed after each time step t. It receives as arguments the base level $l = 0$, the structure Λ and the state λ of the model, as well as the current shape s_t. In this case, the emissions at base level are letters. At more abstract levels, they are content according to Definition 9. More precisely, the shapes at higher levels are computational references to data structures that implement probabilistic content.[3]

5 Results

The evaluation data is written English language. Due to its length and availability through Project Gutenberg, *Pride and Prejudice* by Jane Austen affords itself as evaluation data [1]. The only pre-processing is the conversion of upper case into lower case characters and the removal of any character that is not a Latin letter, an Arabic digit, or punctuation. Algorithm 1 is evaluated *qualitatively* and *comparatively*.

5.1 Qualitative Evaluation

In a single pass, a certain amount of unpredictability must be tolerated. This fundamental uncertainty is acknowledged by setting $\sigma = 0.1$ (referents are recognized starting from a certainty of at least 10%) and $\alpha = 1.0$ (previously unseen referents gain a "head start" certainty). After "reading" the text once, the model features 50 representations at level 0 (i.e., characters), 78 representations at level 1, 74 representations at level 2, 21 representations at level 3, 3 representations at level 4, and 1 representation at level 5.

Figure 2a shows that the model has not converged after a single pass over the novel's roughly 600000 characters. The resulting semiotic model is relatively complex. Therefore, the illustration of the segments that are represented by the model in Fig. 3 is limited to only the second of the total number of six levels. Each color indicates the representation used by the model to represent the current segment of letters. Naturally, these representations do not correspond to linguistic representations in natural language (e.g. syllables, words, or sentences).

---

[3] The indices at levels $l \geq 1$ are therefore tuples that consist of computational identifiers and the informational resources that they reference in computer memory.

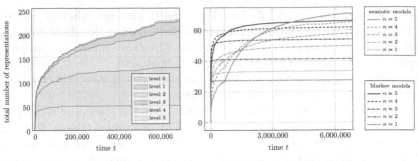

(a) Semiotic Model Development.   (b) Predictive Performance.

Fig. 2. Evaluation results. (Color figure online)

after a little further resistance on the part of his aunt, her resentment gave way, either to her affection for him, or her curiosity to see how his wife conducted herself; and she condescended to wait on them at pemberley, in spite of that pollution which its woods had received, not merely from the presence of such a mistress, but the visits of her uncle and aunt from the city.

Fig. 3. Level 2 (Color figure online)

However, they do segment the text into reoccurring parts that follow a higher-level function.

Figure 3 shows that the generated representations often cover one or several words without breaking them apart. This can be attributed to the fact that words are separated by spaces. After a space, the representations at level one cannot reliably predict the next emission. Therefore, representations at level one and above end considerably more often with spaces than with any other character. The model is able to establish *synonymical* (e.g. "condescended" and "but") relations where the same content is used to describe completely different referents. The model is also able to establish *homonymical* (e.g. the various instances of "her") relations where structurally identical referents are described by the content of different representations. This shows that the model is in fact sensitive to context.

It is far beyond the capabilities of an algorithm that perceives nothing but *letters* to segment the sequence as a human speaker would [15]. The goal is rather to show that the developed algorithm is able to segment a sequence into frequently occurring referents at multiple levels of abstraction such that upcoming shapes can be predicted more successfully. In a next step [19], this general procedure can be investigated as a candidate for the generation of more general models.

5.2   Comparative Evaluation

Comparative performance is evaluated as the average predictive success $\bar{S}$ over time. After each time step, semiotic and baseline model are queried to predict the next letter. If this prediction is correct, $\bar{S}_t \leftarrow \bar{S}_{t-1} + \frac{1}{T}$, where $T \in \mathbb{N}^+$ is the total length of the trajectory. The eventual $\bar{S}_T$ is the final performance.

A small change in Algorithm 1 enables consideration of *historical transition conditions* such that the state of a semiotic model maintains a history of n past representations at each level instead of just *one*. After this modification, the predictive success of semiotic models can be compared to order-n Markov models, where $n \geq 2$. As a consequence, the updates of *each individual level* in the state of a semiotic model in lines 17 and 21 of Algorithm 1 are now updated like the history of an order-n Markov predictor. Queries for the current representation in lines 5, 6, 8, 10, 11, 12, and 19 have to be adjusted accordingly to return only the *last* element from these histories.

Figure 2b provides an overview for the predictive success of semiotic models and order-n Markov models that have been generated while learning a ten times repetition of the text and with $n = 1$, $n = 2$, $n = 3$, $n = 4$, and $n = 5$. The part to the left of the red line shows the predictive performance during the first learning pass. At the end of this pass, the semiotic model with $n = 1$ reaches an average predictive performance of 32.50% while the order-n Markov model tops out at 27.22%. For $n = 2$, the semiotic model outperforms the Markov model as well. The semiotic model maintains a significant upward trend. For $n \geq 3$, the Markov models are faster in reaching a peak performance which surpasses the corresponding semiotic models.

At this point, the text is continued by repetition. It is important to note that this contradicts our initial premise of a single pass over the data but it illustrates whether previously obtained knowledge about sequential structure can be successfully retrieved and applied *again* in similar (i.e., identical) circumstances. A steep incline after the first pass indicates successful retrieval. For $n < 3$, neither semiotic nor Markov models appear to be able to retrieve useful information. For $n = 3$, however, a significant difference between both types of models can be observed. Semiotic models with $n \geq 3$ are able to reuse information from the start of the text. For Markov models, this effect can be observed no sooner than with $n \geq 4$. Accordingly, given a long enough trajectory, semiotic models eventually outperform Markov models in this task.

Semiotic models cover such long-term dependencies by virtue of their hierarchical state which can maintain a particular context for *arbitrarily* extended periods of time. This assumption is substantiated by the fact that semiotic models benefit considerably more from repetitions in the trajectory, as the steep incline at the start of the second pass indicates. Dependencies between characters at the beginning of the text are maintained, whereas Markov models overwrite them with the most current information. In general, Markov predictors reach their performance peak faster, but these peaks are consistently lower, than those of semiotic models.

6 Conclusion

The evaluation with natural text shows that semiotic models can be learned in a way that is similar to how humans generate a mental model of text: online and with memory and runtime requirements less than polynomial sequence length. If language is considered as a decidedly *cognitive* phenomenon, then the structure of language presents some of the underlying and unconscious processes of cognition that are not essentially linguistic themselves. Linguistic processes enable to "peer onto" those otherwise unobservable mental processes.

Semiotic models do not only describe text. By defining base transition conditions as 2-tuples of sensorimotor activation and consequence shapes as the immediately following sensor activation, they describe agents in partially observable environments. Not only can a semiotic model predict upcoming emissions, but its state also serves as a representation for the hidden state of the environment. This representation is generated without previous knowledge and from immediate observation alone. Feeding the current state as additional sensor information into a Reinforcement Learning algorithm significantly increases its performance without considerable impact on its real-time reactivity.

Beyond Reinforcement Learning, the algorithm enables testing of the hypothesis of equipotential neural structures. As such it shows an alternative to the traditionally modularized conception of cognition. The generated semiotic model is hierarchical, simulating the arbitrary number of abstraction layers in human mental models. Being consistently presented with a sequence *from the same source,* however, the frequency of new layer and representation generation approaches zero over time, while its predictive power still clearly outperforms conventional order-n Markov predictors.

The analogy between text comprehension and understanding in general suffers from temporally discrete input as well as the discrete character of symbolic characters. A genuinely *cognitive* simulation of mental modeling must be able to deal with sequences of rational elements, where the tabular approach to prediction must be replaced by a type of regression.

Models for language comprehension can be applied onto the essentially nonlinguistic problem of content creation. This promises a novel explanation for the fundamental origin of our most basic mental concepts. The representations in a semiotic model can enter synonymical and homonymical relations with their referents, just like different concepts can apply to the same sensor stimulus and different stimuli can evoke the exact same concept. These ambiguities are resolved in analogy to the human mind: by referring to *context*. In this respect, the automatic generation of a semiotic models can serve as an interesting new way of simulation the generation of mental models.

References

1. Austen, J.: Pride and Prejudice. Project Gutenberg (1998). ftp://uiarchive.cso.uiuc.edu/pub/etext/gutenberg/etext98/pandp10.zip
2. Chater, N., Manning, C.: Probabilistic models of language processing and acquisition. Trends Cogn. Sci. **10**(7), 335–344 (2006)
3. Chen, S., Goodman, J.: An empirical study of smoothing techniques for language modeling. In: Proceedings of the 34th Annual Meeting on Association for Computational Linguistics, pp. 310–318. Association for Computational Linguistics (1996)
4. Colin, D.L.H.: Grammatical Inference. Cambridge University Press, Cambridge (2010)
5. Croft, W., Cruse, A.: Cognitive Linguistics. Cambridge University Press, Cambridge (2004)
6. Fodor, J.: The Language of Thought. Language and Thought Series. Harvard University (1975)
7. Häggström, O.: Finite Markov Chains and Algorithmic Applications, vol. 52. Cambridge University Press, London (2002)
8. Harnad, S.: The symbol grounding problem. Phys. D Nonlinear Phenom. **42**(1–3), 335–346 (1990)
9. Knill, K., Young, S.: Hidden Markov models in speech and language processing. In: Young, S., Bloothooft, G. (eds.) Corpus-Based Methods in Language and Speech Processing. Text, Speech and Language Technology, vol. 2, pp. 27–68. Springer, Dordrecht (1997). https://doi.org/10.1007/978-94-017-1183-8_2
10. Lee, D.: Cognitive Linguistics: An Introduction, vol. 13. Oxford University Press, Oxford (2001)
11. Marty, R.: C.S. Peirce's phaneroscopy and semiotics. Semiotica **41**(1–4), 169–182 (1982)
12. Mountcastle, V.: An Organizing Principle for Cerebral Function: The Unit Module and the Distributed System. The Mindful Brain (1978)
13. Nevill-Manning, C., Witten, I.: Identifying hierarchical structure in sequences: a linear-time algorithm. J. Artif. Intell. Res. **7**, 67–82 (1997)
14. Rabiner, L.: A tutorial on hidden markov models and selected applications in speech recognition. Proc. IEEE **77**(2), 257–286 (1989)
15. Searle, J.: Minds, brains, and programs. Behav. Brain Sci. **3**(3), 417–424 (1980)
16. Siddiqi, S., Gordon, G., Moore, A.: Fast state discovery for HMM model selection and learning. In: Artificial Intelligence and Statistics, pp. 492–499 (2007)
17. Tokuda, K., Nankaku, Y., Toda, T., Zen, H., Yamagishi, J., Oura, K.: Speech synthesis based on hidden Markov models. Proc. IEEE **101**(5), 1234–1252 (2013)
18. Wernsdorfer, M.: How failure facilitates success. In: Iklé, M., et al. (eds.) AGI 2018. LNAI, vol. 10999, pp. 292–302. Springer, Cham (2018)
19. Wernsdorfer, M.: A phenomenologically justifiable simulation of mental modelling. In: Iklé, M., et al. (eds.) AGI 2018. LNAI, vol. 10999, pp. 270–280. Springer, Cham (2018)

How Failure Facilitates Success

Mark Wernsdorfer(✉) ⓘ

Cognitive Systems, University of Bamberg,
An der Weberei 5, 96047 Bamberg, Germany
mark.wernsdorfer@uni-bamberg.de
https://www.uni-bamberg.de/en/cogsys/

Abstract. Robotic systems that interact with real-world environments cannot capture all the underlying patterns that govern the environment's reactions to the system's actions. One way to deal with this uncertainty is to describe the environment *probabilistically*. This paper proposes another way: Failed expectations are incorporated into a *deterministic* model that can describe more complex dynamics than exclusively probabilistic models can. Wrong predictions from the past are used to provide a more appropriate description of the future. Unlike previous approaches, it does not suggest that transitions between hidden states can be predicted *prior to the fact*. Instead, effects are considered that are impossible according to the model's *current* predictions. This discrepancy enables the model to self-correct in a continual coupling with the system that it describes.

Keywords: Modeling · Prediction · Partially observable environments
Hidden states · Interaction

1 Introduction

Mobile robots depend on a comprehensive model of their environment. Wrong predictions can have fatal consequences. To wrongly expect "solid ground", where "ravine with a 200 m drop" would be in order, might effectively destroy the agent.

Consider, however, that "solid ground" and "ravine" are "linguistic" representations for *mental* content that consists of various constituent elements. A great deal of human conceptualization is based in *visual perception* [3]. Accordingly, both representations are usually associated with a mental *image* that consists of *visual* elements. These elements enable the agent to conceive of *solid ground* and *ravine* in the first place. These two conceptions, as well as visual conceptions in general, are intimately connected to human physiology. Systems with a different sensorimotor apparatus cannot be expected to feature conceptions that are visual or even remotely similar.

A wheeled robot might have a conception of solid ground as well. However, the structure of this conception would be considerably different. It could be, for example, that the weight on its front wheels is roughly equal to the weight on its

© Springer Nature Switzerland AG 2018
M. Iklé et al. (Eds.): AGI 2018, LNAI 10999, pp. 292–302, 2018.
https://doi.org/10.1007/978-3-319-97676-1_28

back wheels. The composition of conceptions always has to pay respect to each system's individual sensorimotor apparatus.

The structural nature of concepts mitigates the danger of wrong predictions. Contradicting structural elements enable the system to adapt even before fully realizing an appropriate concept. As soon as its front wheels lose traction, the robot's failed expectation of a uniform weight distribution enables behavioral adaptation. The more detailed this description is, the more expectations can fail before it is too late.

The following model utilizes structural concept representations in this manner. Representations are organized hierarchically. On the one hand, it can be shown that this enables exploitation of previous errors to improve predictive performance. On the other hand, it can be shown that this performance significantly exceeds the performance of order-n Markov models. The type of model presented here can be procedurally generated on-line in a live robot. It can be used, for example, to predict arbitrary sequences of symbols or to perform Reinforcement Learning in partially observable environments [13, 14].

2   Related Work

Order-n Markov models maintain a fixed history of n past observations. The history at any given time can be considered as the current *state* of the model. This state effectively serves as a representation for the hidden state of the environment. These models are generated by counting the number of transitions from the current history of length n to the current observation. The normalized transition frequencies from one history to all of the following observations realize a probability distribution that can approximate the actual distribution very closely [8].

The prediction performance of order-n Markov models tends to increase with an increase in history length up to a certain point. Then transition conditions become too specific to generalize the distribution of observations appropriately, while long-term dependencies between observations that are more than n time steps apart are lost.

The observations that an agent receives from its environment can be conceived of as part of an *individual sequence* [1, 2, 4, 10] instead of being generated by hidden states. Individual sequences have been given a rigorous formal foundation with *on-line convex optimization*. Tasks in on-line convex optimization include a player that performs actions. Only after the action has been executed are its outcomes disclosed—just like it is the case with the prediction of observations.

Outcomes have the form of a loss value associated with the performed action under the current circumstances. Losses do not follow a particular probability distribution. Within limits, these losses can be random or even chosen by an adversary of the player. Actions in this framework are defined as the convex set of real-valued vectors $\mathcal{K} \subseteq \mathbb{R}^n$ and losses are a family of individual functions $f_t \in \mathcal{F} : \mathcal{K} \to \mathbb{R}$ [6]. An example is on-line classification, where $x_t \in \mathcal{X}$ is the input, $y_t \in \mathcal{Y}$ is the target, and $p_t \in \mathcal{D}$ is the output at time t. Target and output do not need to be from the same set, to allow, for example, a deterministic binary target $y_t \in \{\, 0, 1 \,\}$ but a probabilistic interpretation of output $p_t \in [0,1] \subseteq \mathbb{R}$.

On-line convex optimization covers samples from non-stationary distributions. This generality, however, comes at the price of a predefined hypothesis space. Algorithms effectively learn to "trust" the best expert hypothesis and, as a consequence, can only be compared against such given expert [1]. Without experts, on-line convex optimization does not enable any learning.

3   Background

This idea of individual sequences can be extended into a non-deterministic conception of environments that provides an alternative to the formal concept of partially observable environments in the Markov framework [7].

In the following, the agent's observations are considered as *sensor emissions of the environment* and its actions are considered as *motor emissions of the agent*. A sequence of exchanged emissions is considered a *trajectory* and the segment of emissions from $t - n$ to $t - 1$ in such a trajectory is considered the *length-n history* of the one emission at time t.

Definition 1. Static trajectories *are a sequence of individual emissions x_t with a history of length n, where $t \in \mathbb{N}^+$ and $1 \leq n$.*

$$x_t = f(x_{t-n}, x_{t-n+1}, ..., x_{t-1})$$

The emission of the trajectory after each time step t is a particular unspecified function $f : X^n \to X$ of the current history with length n, where X is the set of all possible emissions. In the following, f is referred to as "emission function".

The Fibonacci sequence, for example, can be formalized with the emission function $x_t = f(x_{t-2}, x_{t-1}) = x_{t-2} + x_{t-1}$, where $t \geq 2$, $x_0 = 0$, and $x_1 = 1$. This function takes the two previous elements (i.e., $n = 2$) and returns their sum. In the case of the Fibonacci sequence, the emission function is constant over time. Therefore, the resulting trajectory is *static*.[1] In a *dynamic* trajectory, f can *change* over time.

---

[1] For the sake of simplicity, in the following, only dynamic trajectories with a history length of $n = 1$ are considered. As a consequence, the emission function in Definition 1 can be simplified to $x_t = f(x_{t-1})$.

Definition 2. Dynamic trajectories *are static trajectories, where the emission function f changes with time t.*

$$x_t = f(t, x_{t-1}) = f_t(x_{t-1})$$

Notice that the dynamics behind changes in f_t are completely undefined. Like in individual sequences, the emission function behind a dynamic trajectory can change according to an arbitrary or even an *adversarial* policy.

Environment and agent co-determine one another. In fact, both are so closely connected that their individual trajectories are in a *coupling*. Unities are considered as coupled "whenever the conduct of two or more unities is such that the conduct of each one is a function of the conduct of the others" [11]. Equations 1 and 2 describe the emissions in the dynamic trajectories of an agent and its environment in a coupling.

$$s_t = e_t(m_{t-1}) \tag{1}$$
$$m_t = a_t(s_{t-1}) \tag{2}$$

The current emission of the environment (i.e., observation) is $s_t \in S$, the current emission of the agent (i.e., action) is $m_t \in M$, the current emission function of the environment is $e_t : M \to S$, and the current emission function of the agent is $a_t : S \to M$. Both systems merely receive emissions, none has access to the underlying function in the other system. Also, this function can change erratically and without indication.

4   Example

The idea of dynamically coupled trajectories can be nicely illustrated with the centrifugal governor in Fig. 1a. The function of the centrifugal governor is to stabilize the speed of a steam engine. The right side of the figure depicts the throttle valve. The left side depicts the flywheel with two connected arms. The hinges of the flywheel arms are mechanically coupled to the throttle valve. Also consider the emissions of a centrifugal governor in table c (Fig. 1). The emission of the flywheel after time step t is denoted as w_t and the emission of the valve at the same time is denoted as v_t.

The flywheel is in a similar situation like a mobile robot: It exerts control over another system whose dynamics are unknown. To the flywheel, emissions v_t from the valve are like "observations" and its own emissions w_t are like "actions". Both can be considered to be in a temporally delayed relation. Each "action" w_t causes a "perception" v_{t+1} and each "perception" v_t enables an appropriate re-"action" w_{t+1} [5, makes the same case for cognitive systems].

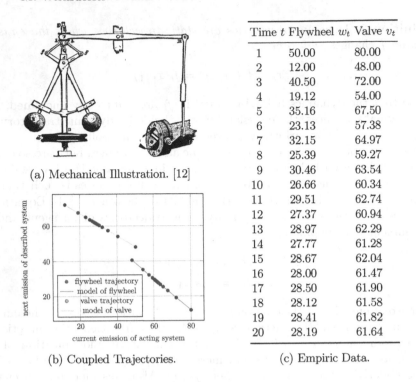

(a) Mechanical Illustration. [12]

(b) Coupled Trajectories.

Time t	Flywheel w_t	Valve v_t
1	50.00	80.00
2	12.00	48.00
3	40.50	72.00
4	19.12	54.00
5	35.16	67.50
6	23.13	57.38
7	32.15	64.97
8	25.39	59.27
9	30.46	63.54
10	26.66	60.34
11	29.51	62.74
12	27.37	60.94
13	28.97	62.29
14	27.77	61.28
15	28.67	62.04
16	28.00	61.47
17	28.50	61.90
18	28.12	61.58
19	28.41	61.82
20	28.19	61.64

(c) Empiric Data.

Fig. 1. The centrifugal governor.

4.1   Modeling the Centrifugal Governor

Two emission functions follow from Eqs. 1 and 2 in the previous section. Equation 3 provides a model for the flywheel and Eq. 4 provides a model for the valve.

$$c_w(v_t) = w_{t+1} = -0.89v_t + 83.25 \qquad (3)$$
$$c_v(w_t) = v_{t+1} = -0.63w_t + 79.58 \qquad (4)$$

The points of the original trajectories and the interpolated approximations are presented in Fig. 1b. The attractor for both of these trajectories is somewhere close to $v_\infty \approx 61.7$ and $w_\infty \approx 28.3$.[2]

$$c(f_t, v_t) = \langle w_{t+1}, v_{t+1} \rangle = \langle c_w(v_t), c_v(w_t) \rangle \qquad (5)$$

Equation 5 combines the individual models to describe the centrifugal governor as a coupling of two subsystems. The individual subsystems are described as *mutually dependent*. The combined model as a whole, however, is *independent* from another system. This enables the autonomous simulation of a centrifugal governor, starting from an arbitrary initial state. A simulation starting from $w_1 = 50$ and $v_1 = 80$ develops almost identical to the trajectory of the original centrifugal governor.

---

[2] The approximations have been obtained by simple linear regression.

4.2   An Erratic Centrifugal Governor

Now assume that, every once in a while, the steam valve shuts completely and remains stuck. This occurs without warning and for an indefinite amount of time. After the valve releases, the governor resumes normal operation just as before.

$$c'_v(w_t) = v_{t+1} = 0 \tag{6}$$

Equation 4 describes the valve in its functional state, Eq. 6 describes it in a defunct state where it is shut down over an extended period of time. As a consequence, the orientation of the flywheel remains constant as well, although its emission function c_w from Eq. 3 has not changed. Observations that have been obtained during defunct behavior are not covered by a model of the functional behavior and *vice versa*. How can this erratic change in behavior be integrated into a model? An appropriate model needs to *switch* between subordinate models for both individual behaviors *as soon as they occur*.

Functional and defunct behavior must be considered as individual emission functions. Both low-level models for these functions need to be incorporated into *a more general model* such that each individual model can describe one particular kind of behavior. The motivation for switching from one model to another is the current model's *failure* to predict correctly. This particular error is a reliable indicator for which *other* model might be more appropriate.

5   Approach

Through this exploitation of errors, semiotic models can describe erratic transitions. They contain discrete *symbols* that represent different types of behavior. Symbolic representations in general are a ternary relation between referent, content, and shape [9]. This relation is formalized as follows.

Definition 3. *A referent $r \in R_l$ is defined as a tuple $r \subseteq C_l \times S_l$ that consists of elements from the set of all transition conditions C_l and consequence shapes S_l.*

Definition 4. *A content $m \in M$ is defined as a functional relation $m : C_l \to S$ from transition conditions to consequence shapes. If $m(a) = b$, for example, then content m presents the referent $r = \langle a, b \rangle$.*

Definition 5. *A shape $s \in S_l$ is defined as the appearance of one "content". Both are in an injective relation $I_l : S_l \leftrightarrow M_{l-1}$ that contains all indices I_l at level l, where $l \geq 1$, such that*

$$\forall s_0, s_1 \in S_l. \ I_l(s_0) = I_l(s_1) \Rightarrow s_0 = s_1$$

If a "content" presents a particular "referent", then the "shape" of this "content" is considered as a *"re-presentation"* of this "referent". This formalization of symbolic representation is at the basis of a definition for *the structure* of a semiotic model.

Definition 6. *The* structure *of a semiotic model is a sequence* $\Lambda : \mathbb{N}^* \rightarrow \{ I_l \mid l \in \mathbb{N}^* \}$ *that determines a set* I_l *for each level of abstraction* l. *Each of these sets, in turn, determines* M_l *at its own level and* S_{l+1} *at the level above, such that* $S_{l+1} = \{ s \mid \langle s, m \rangle \in I_l \}$ *and* $M_l = \{ m \mid \langle s, m \rangle \in I_l \}$. *The set of shapes* S_l *and the set of content* M_l *is unique to each level.*

Every semiotic model is in a particular *state*. The state of a semiotic model determines the expectations that its system has concerning the behavior of the environment.

Definition 7. *The* state *of the semiotic model* Λ *is a sequence* $\lambda : \mathbb{N}^* \rightarrow S$ *that determines the shape of the current content at level* l *of* Λ *in virtue of* I_{l-1}, *where* $l \geq 1$.

To eventually establish transition conditions, consider what happens if a referent is received at level $l \geq 1$ that is *not* represented by $\lambda(l)$: This level of the state has to transition to a new shape that *does* represent this referent.

$$\lambda(l) \leftarrow m'\bigl(\lambda(l), r\bigr), \text{ such that } m' = I_{l+1}\bigl(\lambda(l+1)\bigr) \tag{7}$$

Equation 7 determines that the next shape to represent the referent is selected according to the current content m' at the next level $l+1$. If the shape predicted by m' does *not* represent the referent, or there is no level $l+1$ to begin with, then the model cannot describe the current referent. The conditions for transitioning from one shape to another are therefore defined as follows.

Definition 8. *Every* transition condition $c \in C_l$ *at level* $l \geq 1$ *is a tuple that consists of a referent* $\langle c, s \rangle \in R_l$ *and a shape* $s' \in S_{l+1}$ *that does* not *represent this referent.*

$$C_l \subseteq \{ \langle s', \langle c, s \rangle \rangle \} \text{ such that } m(c) \neq s, \text{ where } m = I_{l+1}(s')$$

Both, referent and inappropriate representation at the same level, are *the reason* for a transition and, together, they are *a condition* that enables the prediction of a new shape which may provide appropriate content for this referent in the future. In this way, erroneous predictions from inappropriate past representations enable the agent to better describe the future.

6   Results

A dynamic trajectory is used to test the ability of semiotic models to describe erratic systems. The trajectory has been designed according to Definition 2. It is an infinite sequence of emissions from one of two alternating emission functions $f_a, f_b \in \mathcal{F}$, such that $\forall f \in \mathcal{F}.f : [0,9] \rightarrow [0,9]$. Accordingly, the base transition conditions are $C_0 = [0,9]$ and the base consequence shapes are $S_0 = [0,9]$.

$$f_a(x_{t+1}) = (x_t + 1) \bmod 10 \tag{8}$$
$$f_b(x_{t+1}) = (x_t - 1) \bmod 10 \tag{9}$$

The function in Eq. 8 emits ascending digits and the function in Eq. 9 emits descending digits. After each time step, there is a chance of $p = .2$ that the emission function changes. This random change is analogous to the randomly changing behavior in the erratic centrifugal governor. After each time step t, a new digit is sampled from one of the functions depending on the last emission at $t - 1$.

At each time step, the model receives an emission that is determined by the dynamic uncoupled trajectory defined above. After each of these time steps, however, the emission function may have changed. The fact that both emission functions are the case *for exactly the same amount of time* makes it impossible for a conventional Markov model to maintain a prediction success rate of more than 50% for an extended period of time. (Half of the time, the next digit is the current digit *plus* one, half of the time it is the current *digit* minus one—without a definitive indicator.)

6.1   Structural Evaluation

Table (a) in Fig. 2 shows an order-1 Markov model that has been generated from the above trajectory. The cells contain the normalized transition frequencies from conditions to consequences as a percentage. The random changes between f_a and f_b cause a strong uncertainty concerning potential successor emissions. This uncertainty is expressed as a close-to-uniform distribution from each element to its respective successors. Once all relevant information has been captured, the structure of the Markov model *converges* onto the current environment (i.e., changes in probabilities approach zero). According to the order-1 Markov model, however, the predictions in the example trajectory alternate indefinitely between two equally probable candidates.

condition	consequence (probability in %)									
	"0"	"1"	"2"	"3"	"4"	"5"	"6"	"7"	"8"	"9"
"0"	0	52	0	0	0	0	0	0	0	48
"1"	53	0	47	0	0	0	0	0	0	0
"2"	0	44	0	56	0	0	0	0	0	0
"3"	0	0	53	0	47	0	0	0	0	0
"4"	0	0	0	54	0	46	0	0	0	0
"5"	0	0	0	0	48	0	52	0	0	0
"6"	0	0	0	0	0	50	0	50	0	0
"7"	0	0	0	0	0	0	48	0	52	0
"8"	0	0	0	0	0	0	0	51	0	49
"9"	52	0	0	0	0	0	0	0	48	0

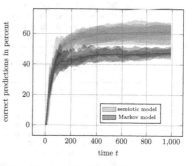

(a)   Order-1   Markov   Model   of   an Uncoupled Dynamic Trajectory.

(b)   Averaged   Performances   in Artificial Sequence Prediction.

Fig. 2. Empirical results.

A semiotic model has been generated from the same sequence. Tables (a), (b) and (c) in Fig. 3 show the normalized transition frequencies in its representations at level $l = 1$. Table d (Fig. 3) shows the normalized transition frequencies between *those* representations in the abstract representation at level $l = 2$. The transition conditions C_l at level $l \geq 1$ are determined according to Definition 8. It can be seen that the model contains only point distributions. This high degree of certainty does not mean that the model can predict the sequence *perfectly*. It does show, however, that the model can predict with a certainty of 100% which emission function is appropriate *once the current one is no longer appropriate*.

1-0 consequence (%)

condition	"0"	"1"	"2"	"3"	"4"	"5"	"8"	"9"
"0"	0	100	0	0	0	0	0	0
"1"	0	0	100	0	0	0	0	0
"2"	0	100	0	0	0	0	0	0
"3"	0	0	0	0	100	0	0	0
"4"	0	0	0	100	0	0	0	0
"5"	0	0	0	0	100	0	0	0
"6"	0	0	0	0	0	100	0	0
"7"	0	0	0	0	0	0	100	0
"8"	0	0	0	0	0	0	0	100
"9"	100	0	0	0	0	0	0	0

(a) Lvl. 1, Representation 0.

1-1 consequence (%)

condition	"0"	"1"	"3"	"4"	"5"	"6"	"7"	"8"
"0"	0	100	0	0	0	0	0	0
"1"	100	0	0	0	0	0	0	0
"2"	0	100	0	0	0	0	0	0
"3"	0	0	100	0	0	0	0	0
"4"	0	0	0	100	0	0	0	0
"5"	0	0	0	0	100	0	0	0
"6"	0	0	0	0	0	100	0	0
"7"	0	0	0	0	100	0	0	0
"8"	0	0	0	0	0	100	0	0
"9"	0	0	0	0	0	0	0	100

(b) Lvl. 1, Representation 1.

1-2 consequence (%)

condition	"0"	"1"	"2"	"3"	"4"	"5"	"6"	"7"	"8"	"9"
"0"	0	0	0	0	0	0	0	0	0	100
"1"	100	0	0	0	0	0	0	0	0	0
"2"	0	100	0	0	0	0	0	0	0	0
"3"	0	0	100	0	0	0	0	0	0	0
"4"	0	0	0	100	0	0	0	0	0	0
"5"	0	0	0	100	0	0	0	0	0	0
"6"	0	0	0	0	100	0	0	0	0	0
"7"	0	0	0	0	0	100	0	0	0	0
"8"	0	0	0	0	0	0	100	0	0	0
"9"	0	0	0	0	0	0	0	100	0	0

(c) Lvl. 1, Representation 2.

2-0 conseq. (%)

condition	1-0	1-1	1-2
1-0, ("0")	0	0	100
1-0, ("1")	0	100	0
1-0, ("2")	0	100	0
1-0, ("3")	0	0	100
1-0, ("4")	0	100	0
1-0, ("5")	0	100	0
1-0, ("8")	0	100	0
1-0, ("9")	0	100	0
1-1, ("0")	0	0	100
1-1, ("1")	100	0	0
1-1, ("3")	0	0	100
1-1, ("4")	100	0	0
1-1, ("5")	100	0	0
1-1, ("6")	100	0	0
1-1, ("7")	100	0	0
1-1, ("8")	100	0	0
1-2, ("0")	100	0	0
1-2, ("1")	100	0	0
1-2, ("2")	0	100	0
1-2, ("3")	100	0	0
1-2, ("4")	0	100	0
1-2, ("5")	0	100	0
1-2, ("6")	0	100	0
1-2, ("7")	100	0	0
1-2, ("8")	100	0	0
1-2, ("9")	100	0	0

(d) Lvl. 2, Representation 0.

Fig. 3. Representations in a semiotic model

6.2   Predictive Evaluation

Models that count transition frequencies can be used straightforwardly in prediction tasks. Figure 2b shows the average success $\bar{S}$ of a Markov model and a semiotic model. To get a representative evaluation, the model performance has been recorded over ten passes of learning, with 1000 iterations each [14, for details on semiotic model generation]. Baseline performance is within expectations. The semiotic model turns out to be correct with an average success rate of $\bar{S} \approx 0.69$. The learning curve still has a slight upwards momentum at the $t = 1000$ mark.

Figure 4 shows that the model separates two segments of the trajectory in each of which subsequent emissions are in a functional relation. Three representations $0 - 0$, $0 - 1$, and $0 - 2$ have been generated where two would have sufficed. This is because non-contradictory transitions from one emission to another are integrated lazily into the *current* representation for as long as there is no significant discrepancy. Only then, the change or creation of representation is considered.

4 3 210 121 01 2 34 3 2109 01 0 9 012 3 2 3456767 8 76 5 67 8 76 5 6767 890121 0 987

Fig. 4. Represented segments at level 1.

On one hand, this ensures redundancy and a high error tolerance. On the other hand, this leads to cases where *one* referent is contained in *all* representations. If a newly perceived referent contradicts such an omnipresent referent, a new representation needs to be introduced. This is the case here. Consider, for example, the transition from 8 to 7. If the current representation does not yet cover the emission 8 and its potential successor, it is adapted so that it describes 7 as successor. In case another transition evokes a change of representation, the same transition $(8, 7)$ might be integrated in every single representation. As a consequence, the first time a transition from 8 to 9 is being observed, a new representation must be introduced.

7   Conclusion

The state of a semiotic model can be considered as a representation for the hidden state of the environment, as in Hidden Markov Models or Partially Observable Markov Decision Processes. The benefit of semiotic models is, however, that the states of a semiotic model are *constructed* as a byproduct of model generation. The hidden states in a Markov model, on the other hand, are assumed to correlate with objectively real states of external reality and, as a consequence, they are completely independent from the cognitive processes of an observer.

This paper shows that the traditional assumption that hidden states determine the probability of observations is not without alternatives. The premise of hidden states which ultimately determine all observations pulls attention from the benefits of *exploiting* prediction errors. Table (d) in Fig. 3 shows that, even in the case of a truly erratic trajectory, the conditions under which prior predictions failed provide important and consistent information. This information enables fast and appropriate reaction in case the same failure occurs again.

Real environments may be physically determined by hidden natural states. These states, however, are not immediately accessible to human perception, let alone to mobile robots. This suggests that in a cognitively accurate simulation of the human mind, external reality might better be considered *erratic*. This puts the focus on how to exploit the failures of a system, instead of trying to avoid them altogether.

References

1. Cesa-Bianchi, N., Lugosi, G.: Prediction, Learning, and Games. Cambridge University Press, Cambridge (2006)
2. Cesa-Bianchi, N., Lugosi, G., et al.: On prediction of individual sequences. Ann. Stat. **27**(6), 1865–1895 (1999)
3. Cornsweet, T.: Visual Perception. Elsevier Science, New York (2012)
4. Feder, M., Merhav, N., Gutman, M.: Universal prediction of individual sequences. IEEE Trans. Inf. Theory **38**(4), 1258–1270 (1992)
5. van Gelder, T.: What might cognition be, if not computation? J. Philos. **92**, 345–381 (1995)
6. Hazan, E.: Introduction to online convex optimization. Found. Trends Optim. **2**(3–4), 4–5 (2016)
7. Kaelbling, L.P., Littman, M.L., Cassandra, A.R.: Planning and acting in partially observable stochastic domains. Artif. Intell. **101**(1), 99–134 (1998)
8. Laplace, P.S.: A Philosophical Essay on Probabilities. Dover Books on Mathematics. Dover Publications, New York (2012)
9. Liszka, J.J.: A General Introduction to the Semiotic of CS Peirce. Indiana University Press, Bloomington (1996)
10. Littlestone, N., Warmuth, M.: The weighted majority algorithm. Inf. Comput. **108**(2), 212–261 (1994)
11. Maturana, H.: Autopoiesis and Cognition. Boston Studies in the Philosophy and History of Science. Springer, Netherlands (1980). https://doi.org/10.1007/978-94-009-8947-4
12. Routledge, R.: Discoveries and Inventions of the 19th Century. Studio Eds., 13 edn. (1900)
13. Wernsdorfer, M.: A phenomenologically justifiable simulation of mental modelling. In: Iklé, M., et al. (eds.) AGI 2018. LNAI, vol. 10999, pp. 270–280. Springer, Cham (2018)
14. Wernsdorfer, M.: A time-critical simulation of language comprehension. In: Iklé, M., et al. (eds.) AGI 2018. LNAI, vol. 10999, pp. 281–291. Springer, Cham (2018)

Adaptive Compressed Search

Robert Wünsche[✉]

Technische Universität Dresden, Dresden, Germany
robertw89@gmail.com

Abstract. Program-search as induction and abduction is one of the key pillars of any sufficiently advanced AGI. In this paper, we present a mechanism to search for programs given a specific bias. This bias is flexible to some degree. Another novel attribute of the mechanism is the use of compression that selects simple programs over complex ones. The complexity of the program is changing all the time over the lifetime of the agent.

Keywords: Compression · Universal-search · Induction

1 Introduction

The problem of searching for the (optimal) solution to an inversion problem is an old problem. It was formalized first by Leonid Anatolievich Levin in his Levin Search (LS) [2] algorithm. LS searches for the shortest program which solves a problem in the shortest time. Longer programs get exponentially longer time allocated. Ideally, the interpretation of all programs is done in parallel - this is not feasible even on modern hardware for moderate programs. Ray Solomonoff introduced the idea to search for the solutions of optimization problems with Induction [14]. Biasing the search process of LS with the use of a probabilistic selection of the candidate instruction was introduced by Jürgen Schmidhuber in his Adaptive Levin search (ALS) [12] algorithm.

Life long incremental learning is necessary for some AGI subsystems. Life long learning is realized in this algorithm with a compressed storage of programs or fragments. The storage is used for reading (by composing new programs from existing/known parts) and writing (the algorithm stores the solution and parts thereof). Thus it fulfills the criteria of a long-term storage proposed by Solomonoff [14].

2 Algorithm

This algorithm[1] reuses the idea of biasing the search, similar to ALS. One difference is that it applies the probabilistic selection not just to instruction, but

---

[1] The sourcecode can be found at https://github.com/PtrMan/AGIconf2018 CompressedSearch.

© Springer Nature Switzerland AG 2018
M. Iklé et al. (Eds.): AGI 2018, LNAI 10999, pp. 303–310, 2018.
https://doi.org/10.1007/978-3-319-97676-1_29

to parts of, already known and/or learned, programs. These parts are called fragments in this publication. The advantage of this is that it biases the search towards programs which already contain known parts for reuse.

Another idea from Schmidhuber is used to bias the search so that simpler programs are preferred. This is done by exploiting compression progress [11] to guide the search towards smaller compressed descriptions of the candidate programs first. This is done because a reuse of already known parts of a program results in a smaller compressed size. Solomonoff called this idea "Conceptual jump-size" [13], thus this algorithm is preferring to test solutions with a smaller conceptual jump-size first over ones with a larger one.

The time for the compression, generation of candidates, testing and adaptation after finding a solution all have upper bounds. This is because the number of elements in the primary storage must be limited on a real machine. Indeed, this causes no issue in the algorithm, because not all parts of previously found solutions are important for the compression or the sampling of candidate programs.

This algorithm can be described as a non-optimal strategy of Optimal Ordered Problem Solver(OOPS) [10] for program induction/abduction.

Learning Algorithm

(Compress1) - compress dictionary programs into primary storage

```
until(foundAllSolutionForLength || globalTimeboundReached)
    call "enumerator algorithm"
      < to generate secondary candidate programs >
    (process A) compress secondary candidate programs one by one and
                store tuple (program, required#Bits)
    (process B) sort secondary candidate programs tuples by
                required#Bits
    (process C) test secondary candidate programs ordered by
                required#Bits, break if solution(s) found for
                the smallest possible required#Bits
    if solution(s) found
       store found program(s) into primary storage
       change probability masses of the relevant fragments
       break (only if the algorithm has to calculate one
                solution to the problem)

put solution(s) into primary storage by adding it
and compressing it to the primary storage, adapt probabilities
after the strategy of ALS or any other strategy
```

Compress1 is just necessary for the first run of the algorithm when the primary storage is empty and thus has to be initialized.

We note the following:

Parallelism:

The processes A, B and C are applied in sequence in the implementation of this algorithm. It is possible to compute the processes concurrently, whereby processes A, B and C work in parallel.

Optimization for Simple Problems:

Processes A and B might get disabled for problems where the time of the process C is significantly larger than the time required for A and B.

Enumerator algorithm - generates candidate programs:

```
parameters:
    < number of instructions and fragments >
    nInstructionsOrFragments
    probabilityOfInstruction < range [0; 1) >
    < maximal number of fragments which are reused in program >
    nMaxFragments

candidateProgram = []
nFragments = 0

for i from 1 to nInstructionsOrFragments
    selectInstruction = rand(0.0, 1.0) < probabilityOfInstruction
    if nFragments < nMaxFragments || selectInstruction
        append to candidateProgram random Instruction sampled by
        probability of instruction as in ALS
    else
        append to candidateProgram random Fragment sampled by
        probability of instructions as in ALS
        nFragments++

return candidateProgram
```

Fast Hash-Based Compressor

For this work, it was necessary to develop a fast compression algorithm. The fact that the primary storage has to be compressed just once can be exploited for the design of the compression algorithm. One possibility for engineering a fast compression algorithm is to exploit the two phases - compression of the training set and compression of the program candidates - into two phases which we call primary and secondary phrases, respectively.

Additionally, the compression with GZip as a compression algorithm is too slow.

Compression primary algorithm

```
parameters: prgrms : input programs

for iPrgrm in prgrms
   for iSlice in allPossibleSlices(iPrgrm)
      < increment a counter for the slice >
      storage.primaryIncForSlice(iSlice)

      < store >
      storage.primaryPut(iSlice)
```

storage.primaryPut(Slice) stores the slice in a hash-table based storage. The slice is just an array of integers. It can check for the existence of the slice, but it doesn't have to. The algorithm can afford a check because the primary fragments are stored once for every run, thus the additional time is not critical.

storage.primaryIncForSlice(Slice) increments a counter of the slice, it is (re)using the existing hashing functionality of the storage.

Compression secondary algorithm

```
parameters: prgrm : program to be compressed

i = 0
while i < len(prgrm)
   longestSliceInfo = storage.searchForLongestPossibleSlice(progrm[i:])

   if longestSliceInfo.longestSubsequentWasFound:
      if longestSliceInfo.foundInPrimary:
         out.appendRefPrimary(prgrm[i], longestSliceInfo)
      elif longestSliceInfo.foundInSecondary:
         out.appendRefSecondary(prgrm[i], longestSliceInfo)

   if not longestSliceInfo.longestSubsequentWasFound
      out.appendUncompressed(prgrm[i])

   < store all old subsequences which we don't yet know >
   sliceEndInFrontIdx = longestSliceInfo.sliceStartIdx
   for iSlice in allPossibleSlices(prgrm, 0, sliceEndInFrontIdx)
      if storage.hasPrimary(iSlice)
         continue
      if storage.hasSecondary(iSlice)
         continue

   i+=longestSliceInfo.len
```

The secondary algorithm attempts to find the longest possible remaining sequence. The longest (sub)sequence can be found by searching for the subsequence in the primary storage by hash. If this fails then the same test is done for the secondary storage. If this test fails then the longest possible subsequence is added to the secondary storage. This treatment ensures that the program can be compressed - without the need to write to the primary storage. Thus a speedup of several orders of magnitude can be achieved for the compression of programs.

Discussion of Time-Bound for Generated Programs

To determine the maximal number of steps executed by the program one can use the following strategies or a linear combination of these

- calculate the max # of steps by the formula as used in ALS depending on the probabilities of the used instruction and fragments derived by Schmidhuber [12].
- calculate the max # of steps by the required number of bits in the corresponding compressed description of the generated program [9].

3 Experiment

Pong was chosen as a simple Test environment. The task was to generate a program to control the bat. The only input to the program was the signed horizontal distance from the bat to the ball. Every program was run for a fixed maximal amount of steps. A program failed the test if it didn't hit the bat in the given time.

The mean and standard deviation of the number of generated programs for 100 runs is shown in the Table 1. The compression bias was disabled for all runs. The samples were split at 250000 attempts and assumed a central distribution for both sets.

Table 1. Number of generated programs

	Mean	Standard deviation
Samples >= 250000 tries	646657	311304
Samples < 250000 tries	101545	68270

4 Comparison to Other Methods

Comparison with Evolutionary Algorithms

Genetic Programming [1] can search for Turing complete programs. However, it is unable to store and reuse fragments over multi runs for different problems as it is possible for the presented algorithm. The presented algorithm doesn't maintain a population of candidates for each problem. It does, however, store fragments between runs for problems. Genetic Programming uses "crossover" for transferring parts of programs between solutions. The presented algorithm does something similar - but it is more controlled because the fragment selection can be biased.

It doesn't favor simple programs over more complex ones (where the complexity is measured by the compression ratio). Genetic Programming requires supervision in the form of a scoring function. The presented algorithm is an unsupervised learning algorithm.

Cartesian Genetic Programming [4] can also search for Turing complete programs. It can learn to reuse parts of the program for the same solution. It inherits the other Problems from Genetic Programming.

Comparison with Meta-Optimizing Semantic Evolutionary Search

MOSES [3] is a supervised learning algorithm. It uses a population of programs which are derived from a single program with different parameter tunings. These groups are called demes. The presented algorithm doesn't have the concept of tuning parameters, because it is an unsupervised algorithm. Thus it can't know how to tune the parameters.

MOSES doesn't reuse parts of solutions of solved problems for future problems. There are some hints from the authors that this functionality is added later.

Comparison with Probabilistic Incremental Program Evolution (PIPE)

PIPE [6,7] reuses parts of found solutions with a memory [6], this is very similar to the fragments in this paper. PIPE can only work with tree-structured programs. The presented algorithm is described just for non-tree-structured programs. PIPE is a supervised algorithm contrary to the presented algorithm.

PIPE biases the search to smaller solutions - thus it uses compression. It doesn't, however, compress each candidate program like it is done by the algorithm presented in this paper.

Variants of PIPE can employ filtering [6,8] to automatically decompose a task into simpler subtasks which can be solved independently. The presented algorithm does something similar over multiple problems - it learns to reuse parts of solutions.

Comparison with OOPS

OOPS reuses parts of solved problems for current problems. The main difference is that it biases its search to programs with a higher probability, which is computed from the product of the probabilities of each instruction. OOPS tends to search shorter programs rather than longer programs which can be found quicker. The tradeoff is that the found longer programs might not generalize as well as the shorter ones.

Comparison with ALS

ALS biases the probabilities of the instructions to adapt found solutions to past problems. It doesn't have any way to represent fragments or adapt the probability distribution of them. ALS and this presented algorithm are both unsupervised (learning) algorithms.

5   Conclusion and Further Work

In this section, we present a few ideas for future work.

One avenue for future research is unifying the compressor and program generator by using a common data-structure for both.

A downside of the currently used compression scheme is that it doesn't have a way to encode n repetitions of the same word.

The used instruction-set of the programs is rather minimalistic and could be enhanced with functional prefixes and instructions to manipulate the virtual machine(s) [5]. These instructions could increase the generalization capabilities and shorten the programs for some problems [5].

Behavior-trees could be used as a flexible mechanism for the enumerator to generate candidates for an a Priori given problem-class. A problem-class could be, for example, data-structure manipulation algorithms.

The size of found programs can be reduced by trail and error by removing instructions. It is a valid solution to the problem(s) if it still solves them. The author refers to this process as the "shorting principle". The process is valid because shorter programs generalize better (occam's razor).

The selection and manipulation of fragments can be done by adaptive mechanisms. Techniques from Machine Learning, Evolutionary Algorithms and AGI can be employed here.

Another way to supplement the used principles is the use of emotions to control the search process. Emotions which interact could be aggression and depression.

- Aggression in the range [0; 1] is how often the AI tries unlikely or longer variations of programs
- Depression in the range [0; 1] could control after how many failed attempts it gives up looking for solutions to a problem

Aggression and depression could interact to control the direction of the search. It could, for example, try unlikely enumerator algorithms to generate candidate programs depending on a certain range of aggression and depression. For example, it could try an enumerator algorithm to generate algorithms which call into (random) addresses of the program if aggression is in the range [0.8;1.0] and depression in [0.9;1.0]. The bounds of the ranges to enable a certain strategy could be modified if they prove successful.

The novel improvement over previous approaches is the sorting of the checked programs by the compressed size. None of the compared algorithms has a functionality to check the solutions in a order determined by the compression ratio of all potential solutions. Almost all compared algorithms reuse solution parts for each solution. A few reuse parts of solutions between problems.

References

1. Koza, J.R.: Genetic Programming: A Paradigm for Genetically Breeding Populations of Computer Programs to Solve Problems, vol. 34. Department of Computer Science Stanford, Stanford University, CA (1990)
2. Levin, L.A.: Universal sequential search problems. Problemy Peredachi Informatsii **9**(3), 115–116 (1973)
3. Looks, M.: Competent program evolution. Ph.D. thesis, Washington University (2007)
4. Miller, J.F., Thomson, P.: Cartesian genetic programming. In: Poli, R., Banzhaf, W., Langdon, W.B., Miller, J., Nordin, P., Fogarty, T.C. (eds.) EuroGP 2000. LNCS, vol. 1802, pp. 121–132. Springer, Heidelberg (2000). https://doi.org/10.1007/978-3-540-46239-2_9
5. Nowostawski, M., Purvis, M., Cranefield, S.: An architecture for self-organising evolvable virtual machines. In: Brueckner, S.A., Di Marzo Serugendo, G., Karageorgos, A., Nagpal, R. (eds.) ESOA 2004. LNCS (LNAI), vol. 3464, pp. 100–122. Springer, Heidelberg (2005). https://doi.org/10.1007/11494676_7
6. Salustowicz, R.: Probabilistic incremental program evolution (2003)

7. Salustowicz, R., Schmidhuber, J.: Probabilistic incremental program evolution. Evol. Comput. **5**(2), 123–141 (1997)
8. Salustowicz, R.P., Schmidhuber, J.: Sequence learning through pipe and automatic task decomposition. In: Proceedings of the 1st Annual Conference on Genetic and Evolutionary Computation-Volume 2, pp. 1184–1191. Morgan Kaufmann Publishers Inc. (1999)
9. Schmidhuber, J.: The speed prior: a new simplicity measure yielding near-optimal computable predictions. In: Kivinen, J., Sloan, R.H. (eds.) COLT 2002. LNCS (LNAI), vol. 2375, pp. 216–228. Springer, Heidelberg (2002). https://doi.org/10.1007/3-540-45435-7_15
10. Schmidhuber, J.: Optimal ordered problem solver. Mach. Learn. **54**(3), 211–254 (2004)
11. Schmidhuber, J.: Driven by compression progress: a simple principle explains essential aspects of subjective beauty, novelty, surprise, interestingness, attention, curiosity, creativity, art, science, music, jokes. In: Pezzulo, G., Butz, M.V., Sigaud, O., Baldassarre, G. (eds.) ABiALS 2008. LNCS (LNAI), vol. 5499, pp. 48–76. Springer, Heidelberg (2009). https://doi.org/10.1007/978-3-642-02565-5_4
12. Schmidhuber, J., Zhao, J., Wiering, M.: Shifting inductive bias with success-story algorithm, adaptive levin search, and incremental self-improvement. Mach. Learn. **28**(1), 105–130 (1997)
13. Solomonoff, R.J.: A system for incremental learning based on algorithmic probability. In: Proceedings of the Sixth Israeli Conference on Artificial Intelligence, Computer Vision and Pattern Recognition, pp. 515–527 (1989)
14. Solomonoff, R.J.: Progress in incremental machine learning. In: NIPS Workshop on Universal Learning Algorithms and Optimal Search, Whistler, BC (2002)

Author Index

Printed in the United States
By Bookmasters